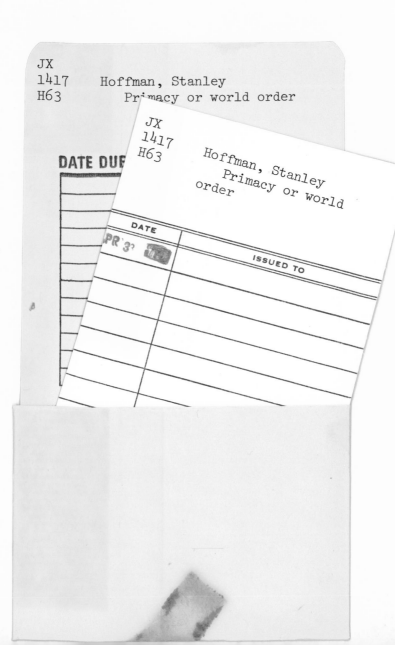

PRIMACY
OR WORLD ORDER

AMERICAN FOREIGN POLICY
SINCE THE COLD WAR

PRIMACY
OR
WORLD
ORDER

American Foreign Policy
since the Cold War

STANLEY HOFFMANN

McGRAW-HILL BOOK COMPANY

New York   St. Louis   San Francisco
Auckland   Bogotá   Düsseldorf   Johannesburg   London   Madrid
Mexico   Montreal   New Delhi   Panama   Paris   São Paulo
Singapore   Sydney   Tokyo   Toronto

The editors of this book were Thomas Quinn, Michael Hennelly, and Karen Seriguchi. Christopher Simon was the designer. Teresa Leaden supervised the production. This book was set in Times Roman by University Graphics, Inc.; it was printed and bound by R. R. Donnelley & Sons.

Library of Congress Cataloging in Publication Data

Hoffmann, Stanley.
  Primacy or world order.

  Includes bibliographical references and indexes.
    1. United States—Foreign relations—1977–
2. United States—Foreign relations—1945–
I. Title.
JX1417.H63   327.73   77-19216
ISBN 0-07-029205-1

1 2 3 4 5 6 7 8 9 RRDRRD 7 8 3 2 1 0 9 8

To four friends without whom this book
would not have been written:

RUPERT EMERSON,
teacher, colleague, and inspiration,

JOSEPH NYE,
colleague and example,

MARIE-FRANCE and OLIVIER CHEVRILLON,
who are French and (yet) who like the United States.

Contents

Preface

Thirty years ago the United States emerged from the Second World War as the most powerful nation on earth. Its leaders had postponed the solution of the troublesome issues of world politics until after victory was achieved. The disintegration of the wartime alliance compelled the United States to play a major, steady, and absorbing role on a world stage which it had, in the past, either shunned or merely visited. For thirty years, America's involvement in world affairs has been profound and passionate, a source both of pride and of controversy at home, of relief and of revulsion abroad.

Just as the scarred and sobered America of the Bicentennial year was not the somewhat shrill and naïve America of 1946, the world outside is no more the simple world in which, it seemed, only two great antagonistic powers mattered. The purpose of this essay is to ask a series of questions: What have we learned, or rather what should we have learned from our experience? What kind of world are we facing today? What policy does it make sense for the United States to follow, and what are our assets and handicaps? In other words, where are we, and where should we go from here?

This is an essay, not a thorough analysis of the many complex issues our leaders must confront. It is the work of a citizen rather than of a scholar— or rather, it is the effort of a professional student of international affairs to try to draw some general lessons and to paint a broad picture for his fellow citizens, instead of addressing himself primarily to his colleagues, his students, and public officials or experts. One of my central convictions is the growing, indeed the decisive, importance of world affairs for the life of each of us; and yet, a recent poll shows that only five percent of the American public listed foreign policy problems as the "most important . . . facing this nation today."[1] One of my chief concerns is the gap between this brooding or booming omnipresence of world affairs and the limited understanding most persons, even in democracies, have of foreign policy— between the technical complexity, political implications, ideological overtones, and moral ambiguity of a bewildering array of discrete issues, and the mix of ignorance, prejudice, and atavistic reflexes with which people, common or uncommon, react to the outside world. If I can contribute, however marginally, to narrowing that gap, I will have done part of my job as a teacher. The range and the nature of today's problems seem to make of foreign policy a fragmented preserve of disparate experts; but in a democratic country, the policy will be effective only if the citizens support it— which means that they have to understand it, not just to submit to exhortation or manipulation.

The reader will find here neither detailed policy prescriptions nor grand designs. Neither suits academic writers. Their proper role is not to serve as mere lights of the advancing official car (or as flashlights when it gets stuck). In the realm of tactics, the advantages lie with the policy makers. Many of the foreign policy errors of the sixties can be traced to academics determined, once in power, to prove their short-range sophistication and "pragmatic" bureaucratic skills. Nor should scholars peddle grand designs if the price paid for the sweep of vision is terrible oversimplification. And anyhow, the world has become too complicated for such schemes. The proper role of scholars—one which is both faithful to the values that ought to inspire academic research and potentially useful to policy makers—is to examine critically the premises of official policy, to compare intentions and results. In other words, a scholar is to judge the performance of the official vehicle and of its drivers, and also to provide as searching a survey as possible of the terrain ahead in order to bring to light alternative itineraries, their costs, and their benefits.

This essay constitutes a kind of a sequel to an earlier work on United States foreign policy,[2] but tries, however unsuccessfully, to avoid repeating its long analyses, and to correct its errors or omissions. It incorporates ideas and arguments presented, sometimes in greater detail, by the author in a series of essays published during the past six years.[3] It owes a great

deal to the papers prepared by a real army of talented scholars for the
Council on Foreign Relations' current 1980's Project (of which this book
constitutes an illegitimate offspring). It also owes much to the discussions
held by this project's ancestor, a working group on International Order
which met between 1971 and 1973 under the auspices of the Council and the
chairmanship of Miriam Camps. One member of that group whose ideas I
have found particularly stimulating, and from whose works (often co-
authored by Robert Keohane) I have massively borrowed, was my Harvard
colleague and friend, Joseph S. Nye, Jr. He is not responsible for what I
may have done to his insights, but they have been invaluable. The fact that
we have been teaching together may help explain mutual loans. But it also
points to another sort of "debt"—the one I owe to my Harvard students,
whose eagerness, wit, critical sense, good spirits, and refusal to take
anything on faith have been, over the years, the best goad to protracted
reflection, and the surest path to premature exhaustion.

1. William Watts and Lloyd A. Free, "Nationalism, Not Isolationism," *Foreign Policy,* no.
    24, Fall 1976, p. 10.
2. *Gulliver's Troubles, or the Setting of American Foreign Policy,* McGraw-Hill, New
    York, 1968.
3. "Will the Balance Balance at Home," *Foreign Policy,* no. 7, Summer 1972; "Weighing
    the Balance of Power," *Foreign Affairs,* vol. 50, no. 4, July 1972; "Choices," *Foreign
    Policy,* no. 12, Fall 1973; "Flaws and Omissions in the New Foreign Policy," in *Pacem
    in Terris III,* vol. 1, Center for the Study of Democratic Institutions, Santa Barbara,
    Calif., 1974; "The International System and United States Policy toward Latin Amer-
    ica," in *The Americas in a Changing World,* Quadrangle, New York, 1975; "Notes on
    the Elusiveness of Modern Power," *International Journal,* vol. 30, no. 2, Spring 1975;
    "The Sulking Giant," *The New Republic,* May 3, 1975; "Toward a New World Order,"
    New York Times, Section 4, Jan. 11, 1976.
       An abbreviated version of Chapter Five of this volume has been published under the
    title, "No Choice, No Illusions," in *Foreign Policy,* no. 25, Winter 1976–77. And a part
    of Chapter Six has been published under the title, "The Uses of American Power," in
    Foreign Affairs, vol. 56, no. 1, October 1977.

THIRTY YEARS OF FOREIGN POLICY

What have we done, what have we learned?

1

Let us leave aside the noisy debate on the origins of the cold war and the brief period of transition between the end of the Second World War and the beginning of the cold war (1945–1947).[1] American foreign policy since then can be divided into two cycles of uneven length. The first lasted from 1946 to 1968; it was the cold war cycle, or the cycle of containment. The second one, which I shall call the Kissinger cycle, lasted from 1969 to 1976. Despite its spectacular early initiatives, which often seemed to be pointed rebukes of Kissinger's style and acts, the Carter administration may continue or revert to many of his policies—in which case the assertion that the cycle has ended would be premature. And yet, by contrast with the previous era, what provided the unity of that cycle was the personality of one man, rather than a central concept. Thus, even apart from the substantive difficulties he encountered, I believe that the second cycle ended with his departure and that a new period has begun, however considerable the continuity of policy might turn out to be.

The ends of the two cycles show interesting similarities. In 1976, as in 1968, there was an internal frustration with foreign policy, a divorce between the public and its leaders. It was far more emotional in 1968 because of Vietnam, but such frustration is no less real when it is expressed in acts of congressional revolt or in applause for critics of Dr. Kissinger (whether from the left or from the right) rather than in marches and sit-ins. In both years, there was a sense of unfulfilled promises, a resentment of

3

policies deemed overambitious and damaging. Moreover, the outside world exhibited much hostility to or unhappiness with American behavior. Allies were wondering about United States drift, and asked themselves whether the internal debate was not weakening American power and positions abroad. Other nations and vast segments of opinion in allied countries criticized American stands as reactionary or cynical, oppressive or destructive. But the two cycles must be dealt with separately.

I shall briefly review the first cycle as it has been analyzed and assessed often. I shall look at the second cycle, at greater length since only now can one evaluate it in its entirety. Earlier, partial studies always risked being overtaken both by events and by Dr. Kissinger's agile way of never standing still where he could, so to speak, be shot at. Between those two sections, I shall insert some reflections on an episode that remains the most tragic and traumatic of postwar American foreign policy: Vietnam. The purpose of these investigations is double. First, how successful has American foreign policy been? A policy can be called successful either when it reaches its objectives in ways that entail a lasting assent (enthusiastic, resigned, or constrained) of its foes, rivals, and clients abroad, and of the public and its representatives at home, or else when it shows itself capable of coping with failure abroad and with crises within in a way that minimizes losses and preserves opportunities for recovery and future action. Secondly, insofar as American foreign policy has not been successful, what lessons can be drawn from its fiascoes, both about America's role in and understanding of the world, and about the domestic handicaps to its participation in world affairs?

The Burdens of Containment

SECTION ONE: THE COLD CRUSADE

To draw a balance sheet of the first cycle, I shall try to answer four questions. Two refer to America's position in the world. First, what have been Washington's role, achievements, and losses in the world contest? That contest, or "state of war," even in peacetime, describes the nature of so much of international politics—all that which is either sheer conflict or the cooperation of those who share a hostility against others—and characterizes especially the competition among the chief rivals. Second, any lasting international system requires that this competition be compatible with a minimum of order, i.e., formal or informal rules that allow for the moderation of disputes and for a measure of security and stability. Moreover, for a great power, success, as defined above, is inseparable from the creation and maintenance of such rules—rules that will of course serve its interests and be backed by its power, yet will also provide others with enough safety of life and possessions to ensure the great power against hostile coalitions and decisive challenges. One must therefore ask whether the United States succeeded in establishing or in contributing to the establishment of such an order and what its character was.

The two other questions refer to the domestic aspects of foreign policy. First, was the foreign policy based on a national consensus, and, if so, how was it achieved, at what price, by what means, with what effects, and for how long? Second, what was the policy's relation to the two great faults (I use this word in its geological meaning) characteristic of the American style in foreign affairs (which I have analyzed at some length elsewhere)?[1] One fault is the existential tension between an instinct toward violence to eliminate obstacles and the aspiration for harmony; it is America's dualism. The other is a historical tension between the two *tempi* of America's foreign policy, the two poles of the Wilsonian syndrome: America's oscillation between quietism and activism, withdrawal and intervention.

Isolationism and intervention can be the opposite poles of a perfectly banal nationalism that tries to protect the nation's interests from the maneuvers of other, more powerful or deceitful players (Hamilton's concern) and that seeks to promote these interests abroad by direct (usually violent) action (as in Theodore Roosevelt's rhetoric of toughness). But there is another, quite extraordinary kind of American nationalism (one that Americans usually refuse to acknowledge as such). More often than not, it is this nationalism that the two poles of isolation and intervention, as well as the two sides of America's dualism, seem to illustrate. I refer to what has often been called America's exceptionalism:[2] the deep and lasting faith in the singular, unique, "unprecedented" and "unrepeatable"[3] character of the United States in its mission as a model democracy that is, at times, the lone and shining guardian of certain values and institutions, at times their missionary. Uniqueness was seen as emanating from the domestic harmony of ends; force was seen as the legitimate and only way of dealing with conflicts of ends and with those who would not compromise. Uniqueness was to manifest itself in the rejection of the cynical balance of power games characteristic of traditional European diplomacy—a rejection that could take either the form of idealistic seclusion or the expansive form of, say, the ideology of the Fourteen Points. How would America, now a major actor on the world stage, relate to its own traditions and to those foreign practices that had dominated the stage during the centuries of America's absence?

To be sure, the long cold war was not a single period. One ought to distinguish three phases: the era of President Truman, during which the policy of containment was initiated, a heated debate between Democrats and Republicans broke out over Asia, and McCarthyism spread; the Eisenhower phase, which lowered voices, dampened conflicts, and turned containment into routine; and a new Democratic period, which began as a revival of activism, fervor, and "vigor," and ended in the Vietnam quagmire. But, throughout those three phases, there was an overwhelming continuity, not only of policies, but of central concept. Let us return to our four questions.

THE STATE OF WAR

Throughout this cycle, America's concern for the great powers' contest prevailed over its concern for world order, or rather, the world order that American leaders were eager to establish was considered mainly a dam against communism. The great moves of 1947 were symbolic of this concern. First came the Truman Doctrine, which went far beyond the issue of aid to Greece and Turkey and declared universal war on communist expansion. Then came the Marshall Plan; its author had been keen on presenting it as a world order measure, but Soviet rejection turned it into a central piece of containment. The militarization of containment, so deeply deplored by its spiritual father, George Kennan, testifies to the priority that the competitive aspects of world affairs received throughout this period.

What did Washington achieve in this "state of war"? We must distinguish between objective results and perceptions. Throughout this period, Americans perceived the contest in a contradictory, almost schizophrenic way. On the one hand, we felt besieged. Whereas the monstrous cruelties of Stalinism in the Soviet Union and in the East European countries subjugated by the Soviets can be partly explained by Stalin's internal insecurity, heightened by the turmoil of the war so well described by Solzhenitzyn, in Washington *external* insecurity explains much of what happened between 1947 and 1950. The official tendency was to interpret every move on the other side as part of a coherent, unfolding plan (the Korean war was seen as a prelude to an attack on Western Europe just as, twelve years later, the Cuban missile crisis was suspected of being a prelude to a power squeeze in Berlin). And a hyperbolic conflict broke out between the policy makers and those who accused them of lacking vigilance at home and toughness abroad. Both sides reflected the psychological stress of a nation that had found at the end of a titanic war, not the delights of harmony, but the labors of leadership in an unsettled world. How, indeed, could a nation suddenly promoted to the rank of superpower, suddenly burdened with the responsibility of nuclear weapons and the guilt of having been the first to use them, suddenly entrusted with global tasks without adequate preparation, be anything but insecure about its performance? True, this feeling began to fade, insofar as Russia was concerned, after the missile crisis of October 1962; not only were the post-Sputnik terrors and the nightmare of the missile gap dispelled, but the intensity of the struggle decreased. However, the same sense of insecurity, the same "paranoid style," to use Richard Hofstadter's happy phrase, the same turning of foe into daemon, reemerged with respect to China, which Lyndon Johnson's team considered far more potent and dangerous than it was, the scheming and perhaps irrational instrument of "Asian communism."

On the other hand, while fearing the worst—the foes' cunning, their lack of scruples, their totalitarian discipline and efficiency, their often hidden accomplices, and so forth—we Americans did not really question our moral and material superiority. To be sure, the speed with which the Soviets, and later the Chinese, broke the United States' nuclear monopoly caught us by surprise. But the protracted debates on strategic doctrine that filled the fifties and the sixties all dealt with the best way of preserving America's nuclear superiority and of exploiting it so as to neutralize the adversaries' assumed quantitative advantage in conventional forces. And the sense of the overwhelming preponderance of America's economy over Russia's was always strong. What some Republicans blamed Truman for in 1948–1950, what many Democrats blamed Eisenhower for during his second term, was the President's alleged incapacity to use this superiority to stop communist progress in Asia or to slow down Russia's imagined advance in missile launching power after Sputnik.

Indeed, the objective balance sheet was impressive. True, there *was* a debit side quite apart from Vietnam. China's civil war had been won by Mao; North Vietnam had become a communist state when the French decided to cut their losses; Castro had moved into the camp of America's foes. But most Americans did not feel responsible for those setbacks. How could the United States alone have saved Chiang Kai-shek from collapse?[4] Short of carrying out against an ally the anti-French inclinations of F.D.R., and of forcibly preventing de Gaulle from restoring French presence in Indochina, how could the United States have stopped the French from losing politically their Indochina war? And how could it have stopped them from losing their will to fight, short of taking over the war *in extremis* militarily and in disastrous circumstances politically? How could the United States have predicted that the Cuban Robin Hood would convert to Marxism-Leninism? And even if Dulles could have been less brutally clumsy in refusing American aid for the construction of the Aswan Dam in Egypt, could Washington have prevented Nasser from seeking Soviet-bloc arms against Israel? Those communist successes were, thus, due either to the windfalls of local revolutions or to the artful exploitation of a Western political weakness, as in the Middle East.

Moreover,the debit side consisted largely, not of communist successes, which were few, but of mere manifestations of America's incapacity to roll communism back: in North Korea, in Eastern Europe, at the Bay of Pigs. Anyhow, the break between Moscow and Peking, fifteen years after the split between Stalin and Tito, revealed the fragility of the other camp. Of course, there were tensions in our camp also; but Gaullism did not spread outside France, and after the May 1968 upheaval in France and the August 1968 invasion of Czechoslovakia by the Soviets, Gaullist "dissidence" lost its edges, and in the last months of 1968 the General and the Americans got closer.

The credit side was much the longer one. Here, one finds the nuclear arsenal, built up and diversified by Robert McNamara. One finds the collecting of allies and the military presence of the United States in more than seventy countries—a worldwide network of bases, the military structure of the North Atlantic Treaty Organization (NATO) (despite de Gaulle's semisecession) and the Japanese aircraft-carrier at America's disposal. In other words, the United States had succeeded in integrating into the American world system the two main defeated powers of World War II. America's resistance to Stalin's blockade of Berlin and its opposition to North Korea's invasion of South Korea had made this integration easier. On the credit side, we also find Israel's might (for Israel is a subjective if not formal ally of the United States), in the midst of an Arab world where America's interests and positions remained strong—in Saudi Arabia and in Jordan—even after the six-day war. Here we find three Soviet fiascoes, the failure of Khrushchev's gambles: in Berlin, in Cuba, in the Congo.

This brings us to another line on the credit side—a line many Americans no longer associate with success: decolonization. In those days, we saluted it as a vindication of our principles of self-government and self-determination. Our support earned us more sympathy among the new regimes than hostility among the colonial powers. For the latter depended too much on Washington for security and economic help to afford a schism: when Britain and France tried to defy and outsmart the United States during the Suez crisis, their impotence quickly brought them to heel. Of course, there had been tense moments when Mossadegh ruled in Iran, or Lumumba in the Congo, or in the last years of Sukarno's stormy reign in Indonesia. But directly, indirectly, or through sheer luck, Washington always came out on top.

Why then did so many Americans feel a sense of failure around 1968, even though the six-day war was a humiliating defeat for the Arab clients of the Soviet Union, various foreign commentators and even some Americans were describing the United States as the only superpower, and negotiations with Moscow over the limitation of strategic forces seemed on the verge of beginning? Partly, because Strategic Arms Limitation Talks (SALT) not-withstanding, the future seemed to provide for nothing more exalting than the pursuit of containment. The authors of the policy had talked about negotiating from strength and hinted at a possible Soviet thaw, if contain-ment worked well. But far more building of strength had taken place than negotiation. From the conclusion of a handful of European peace treaties until 1968, for all the summitry, only three meaningful agreements had been made with the U.S.S.R.: the agreement over Laos in 1962, the ban on atmospheric nuclear tests in 1963, and the nonproliferation treaty of 1968.

This sterility (which approximated Acheson's private skepticism about Soviet-American relations, rather than Kennan's desire for mutual disen-gagement or Dulles's hope for the contagion of freedom) had many causes: the fundamental incompatibility of positions (over Germany or disarma-ment), a heavy layer of mutual mistrust (hence the question, so tantalizing to the roaming imaginations of historians, of missed opportunities), a series of restraints that weighed heavily on Washington, such as the fear of being duped (a residue of wartime diplomacy), the fear of unraveling alliances, and the fear of actually consolidating the enemy by negotiating with him (coupled with an overconfidence in one's capacity to outstare him)— another reaction to the 1930s. And there was no thaw. A Soviet Union that cut off the ''Prague spring,'' a Red China in the throes of the cultural revolution, did not promise any horizons beyond containment.

The main reason for frustration, however, was Vietnam. The misapplica-tion of containment to that country seemed to have petrified and paralyzed American policy throughout the world. It now appeared as the extreme but logical, absurd but unavoidable end of the policy of confrontation. Thus it put into question the policy itself. America's inability to force Hanoi and the Viet Cong to give up, the impotence of the American Goliath stuck between the fear of escalation and the refusal to withdraw, meant local defeat. It would not have seemed to spell defeat for the whole strategy of containment, had the means involved not been so huge, and had the inflation of these means not led officials to inflate the stakes as well (as had happened in the First World War). For in politics, perceptions dictate behavior, and realities sometimes weigh less than beliefs, myths, and obsessions.

PATTERNS OF ORDER

And yet, behind the dikes—or the quicksands—of containment, the United States had succeeded in putting into place, if not a scheme of world order—this would have required communist participation—at least functional and regional elements of order. Regionalism fell short of various hopes but played a modest part. The Organization of American States (OAS) remained dominated by Washington, which always succeeded in getting its interventions endorsed by its associates and in getting them to share its harsh views on Cuba. European integration was constantly encouraged by American leaders, as long as it followed the supranational process of Jean Monnet, Washington's favorite European, and not the intergovernmental method of de Gaulle; as long as its policies conformed to Atlantic orthodoxy; and as long as its scope did not extend to what had become, in 1955, NATO's exclusive domain: defense. The Organization of African Unity (OAU) owed much less to United States initiative, but Washington thought it most useful, insofar as it might be able to keep Black Africa outside the great powers' competition. This would serve the American interest, because Washington had good relations with most of the new African states.

On the global level, three structures of order had been established. First, by trial and error, rules of the game had gradually been developed by the two superpowers, eager to prevent their contest from degenerating into a world holocaust. One such informal rule was the nonresort to atomic weapons by one against the other, or the other's allies (although the threat of resorting to them was not excluded and served as a stabilizing device). A second rule was the avoidance of direct military clashes between their armed forces. This meant that their games of chicken had to end with the retreat of one of the players rather than with a fight: crises could lead to defeats but not to wars. And the Russians had had to give in. They had done so several times in Berlin, where the very weakness of America's defensive military position and the strength of its political position placed on Moscow the dangerous burden of having to take a potentially fatal initiative; and it happened once in Cuba, where the Americans turned the tables on Khrushchev and, having enforced a blockade, obliged him once again to choose between reckless escalation and defeat. A third element was the slow and (for America) painful learning of limited wars, not between the main foes, but between one of them and the allies or clients of the other, wars whose goals, means, and scope had to be calculated so as to limit the risks of escalation, even if these constraints made a clear-cut victory or a rapid settlement impossible. Later came the beginnings of nuclear arms control between Washington and Moscow.

Dare one include among those informal rules of order the right of each superpower, acknowledged by the other, to police its own zone of control: Guatemala and Hungary in the fifties, Santo Domingo and Prague in the sixties? Alas, it is of the essence of international relations that order and justice are not synonymous. Nevertheless, thanks to all these arrangements and to the replacement of direct armed fights with tests of will or limited or indirect tests of force, the confrontation of the two camps did not end up as the rivalry of Athens and Sparta did, and bipolarity, for once, was not the synonym of catastrophe. This muting of the bipolar contest was partly responsible for the crack-up of one camp and the loosening of the other, i.e., for the creation of conditions that made the old version of containment obsolete, even though these informal rules were themselves an expression of the policy of containment. For the latter meant resistance without annihilation, and indeed promised to avoid both the kind of war that follows Munichs and a crusading war. As Raymond Aron once put it,[5] survival itself meant victory, for it entailed both a victory over the risk of total nuclear war and a failure of the foe to prevail.

A second element of order was the United Nations. The world organization, darling of American wartime planners, never fulfilled their hopes. The system conceived at Dumbarton Oaks and San Francisco never worked, because it rested on the assumption of a five-power concert in charge of collective security. But a substitute system was quickly established. The Security Council might have been paralyzed, but at the time of the Korean war, the United States got the members of the United Nations to turn the General Assembly into the principal organ in fact if not in law. Even after the massive entry of new states into the Organization in the second half of this period, the United States succeeded in getting its preferences endorsed by the necessary majorities. There may have been tense moments between American officials and Dag Hammarskjöld, and in his last year in office the Secretary General chose to present himself as the protector of small states against the schemes of the big ones. But this conception did not displease Washington, which feared above all the machinations of Moscow and Peking amidst the small nations. Moreover, the improvisation of United Nations emergency forces for the Middle East, Congo, or Cyprus, the sending of observers to Kashmir or to Indonesia—unmuscular secular arms of the United Nations financed by the United States—allowed Washington to get the Organization to play a soothing role that served American interests, either by moderating clashes that involved allies or friends of the United States (for instance over decolonization) or by preventing direct Soviet interventions.

A third structure was the economic order of the noncommunist world. Its components are well known: the specialized agencies of the United Nations system in which weighted voting provides the United States with a preponderant role (such as the World Bank and the International Monetary Fund), the monetary regime of Bretton Woods, the General Agreement on Tariffs and Trade (GATT), the Organization for European Economic Cooperation (OEEC) later the Organization for Economic Cooperation and Development (OECD), and the like. One must also list among them the network of multinational enterprises centered in the United States, whose expansion in Western Europe and Latin America was most impressive, and which, throughout this cycle, ensured the supply of Middle Eastern oil for America and its allies at very low prices.

Many theories try to account for this economic order, which faithfully reflected America's preferences for universal free trade and served American interests in monetary matters. These preferences included an exchange-rate stability so as to avoid competitive devaluations, convertibility to gold, the avoidance of direct controls on current transactions, and the dollar as the international reserve currency. One theory is the mistaken notion of a "depoliticized" world economy. There are various theories of imperialism, marxist or "structural"; and there is the theory of the two tracks: a high policy track dealing with matters of national security and survival, and a low policy track of economic issues kept "off the agenda of high diplomacy."[6] Finally, there is the concept of the more or less explicit deal between the United States and its allies in Western Europe and Japan.[7] The latter accept Washington's favorite rules of the game in exchange for military protection, but Washington accepts certain exceptions to these rules to safeguard some important allied interests, or to accelerate the economic recovery of the allies, or to help their political consolidation. For instance, Washington allowed the Common Market countries to create a regional trade bloc and a protectionist common agricultural policy, and permitted Japan to keep restrictions on American imports and to keep American multinational enterprises out, even though the huge American market was opened to Japanese exports.

This last theory is important, because it illuminates two essential features of the postwar economic order. It was not a bipolar, but a hegemonic order. Here (although not in the realm of diplomacy and strategy), the role of the United States can be compared to that of Great Britain in the nineteenth century. Moreover, for hegemony to lead to even partial world order, it must avoid being purely exploitative, it must provide other nations with reasons to take part in the management of that order, it must rest on more than the material preponderance of one country. The leading state must make its long-term, enlightened interest prevail over short-term, narrower, or more selfish definitions of its interest. It must, in defining its policy, take into account the interests of those it wants to tie to its own might; reciprocity, not force alone, must be the basis of the system. What is involved here is a choice between two ways—long-term versus short term—of calculating benefits, not a choice between more or fewer gains. The priority given to the enlightened interest allowed Washington to shape the economic order in accordance with American material and ideal wishes, and the recovery of its allies favored the expansion of American goods and investments.

Just as containment seemed stuck in dead-ends after 1965, these fragile structures of order started showing cracks. The six-day war weakened the United Nations' role in the Middle East. The succession of crises in the Dominican Republic, the Middle East, and Czechoslovakia, the wars in Vietnam and Yemen, the civil war in Biafra, proved that moderation was a highly relative notion. Above all, the world monetary order was being upset by the deficit of America's balance of payments. This deficit had been aggravated by Vietnam, but the privileged role of the dollar in the world economy and of America in world affairs allowed Washington to perpetuate it without external constraints obliging the United States to adopt internal remedies. Between the devaluation of the British pound in November 1967 and Nixon's Inauguration, two serious crises of "speculation" shook up the fixed-exchange rates system, and the convertibility of the dollar into gold had, in fact, to be suspended when the central banks, at America's request, decided no longer to sell or buy gold on the private market.

America's inflation, fed by Johnson's refusal to choose between his costly domestic programs and his war, began to get exported through the mechanism of the monetary system—the accumulation of dollars held by America's allies, who were financing Washington's deficits—and thus undermined the economic order. The complex bargain on which this system rested was becoming partly unsatisfactory to all parties. The United States, even though it wanted to preserve the dollar as the key currency, was prevented by the very rules of Bretton Woods from devaluating an overvalued dollar, and so stuck to a rate that harmed United States exports and encouraged investments abroad (thus contributing to the payments deficits). And its allies, even though the abundance of liquidity had helped the expansion of their economies and trade, were irritated by the special privilege of the preponderant power, which could perpetuate its deficits at their expense, so to speak.

THE AGE OF CONSENSUS

American foreign policy during this period had an exceptional internal consensus. It did not emerge at once. But if one remembers that the wartime leaders feared a return to isolationism comparable to the one that had followed the First World War, if one remembers the abrupt suspension of lend-lease and the swift demobilization as soon as fighting had ended, then the way in which, by 1946, the "soft" wing of the Democratic party, led by Henry Wallace, was rendered harmless, the relative ease with which, from 1947 on, the great programs of containment—Truman Doctrine, Marshall Plan, and North Atlantic Treaty—were endorsed by Congress, and the basic agreement of Truman and Dewey on foreign policy in 1948, show how wide the consensus was. It resulted both from the style of Stalin's postwar diplomacy and from the way in which Americans interpreted it—as a grand, global, offensive design to which the imperative, "no more Munichs," had to be applied.[8]

This consensus left room for broad differences and a stormy debate between, generally speaking, Republicans and Democrats in Congress. Who was responsible for the "loss" of China? Who was responsible for the North Korean aggression? Should the Executive alone have decided to send American troops to South Korea? Should he have hampered General MacArthur's strategy? Who was guilty for the apparent impossibility of bringing that war to a close? But the Republican opposition was split in two. Some, like Senator Taft, feared above all the risks and costs of a containment not limited to our naval power and were nostalgic for a "Fortress America" policy recommended by the old survivor, Herbert Hoover. Others blamed the Democrats for not waging the war on communism with the will to win. Indeed,the will to win the presidential election of 1952 was all that united the Republicans, stunned by their unexpected defeat in 1948. As for the attempts in Congress to clip the ever-growing wings of the Presidency in foreign affairs (for instance by curbing executive agreements, which, unlike formal treaties, escaped senatorial supervision), none of them succeeded. To be sure, the 1952 campaign witnessed a foamy and phony debate between the defenders of containment and the champions of rollback. But the election of Eisenhower ushered in the era of the unbroken consensus around a policy for Western Europe that had been bipartisan for a long time and a policy for Asia and Eastern Europe that was entirely in accordance with the one the Democrats had tried to wage. Left-wing critics of the cold war policy were hard to find, right-wing apostles of total victory against atheistic communism were hard to take seriously.

This is the time when Congress adopted without recrimination the military budgets prepared by the Executive and voted, at the request of the President, the resolutions—on Formosa, the Middle East, or the Tonkin gulf—that were meant to show the resolution of America to defend the free world. This is when, helped by favorable Supreme Court decisions, the Presidency became "imperial," wrapped in a network of bureaus, agencies, and departments, a hierarchy of councils, committees, and task forces in charge of waging the cold war and of protecting American interests across the world. The only new cracks in the consensus had limited significance. There was the debate over "massive retaliation," later the fight over the "missile gap," which allowed the Democrats to repay the Republicans in kind. But what was the Inaugural Address of President Kennedy if not the eloquent (or grandiloquent, depending on literary tastes) assertion that a new generation had picked up the torch of containment? In 1960, between Nixon and Kennedy, foreign policy differences belonged to the realm of public relations. If Senator Goldwater failed so lamentably in 1964, it was because his rhetoric, both vague and peremptory, made even Republicans uneasy.

In its first phase, the era of consensus brought with it a disquieting variety of witch hunts. They expressed not at all the seriousness of the division between anti-Communists and "Reds" or "Pinkoes," but on the contrary an American phenomenon already analyzed by a worried Tocqueville: the tyranny of the majority and its intolerance of small minorities suspected of nonconformity. The cold war was both an occasion for a good number of settlements of old accounts going back to the thirties—an occasion to try to roll back or to stop the New Deal—and a source of new anxiety: Was it not reassuring to be able to attribute to conspiracies and acts of treason the fact that the great winner of a total war had found itself doomed to the cold war and to limited hot wars, both equally frustrating? Since fighting it out with the external foe was too risky, one battled the enemy within on whom one could project fantasies that magnified him and justified exorcism. Here, as on the world scene, Eisenhower reassured and quieted things down, in his indirect and indolent way. Once McCarthy was eliminated—Eisenhower having let him have all the rope he needed to hang himself—there were no more dramas. In this period the Executive could count on the support of the media and on a vast foreign policy Establishment composed of former and future high officials, business leaders, lawyers, former military leaders now in business, public relations experts, scientists, and academics, many of whom worked for or gave advice to the government. This was the thick and rich turf in which foreign policy was rooted. Or, to change the metaphor, it was the transmission belt with which the Executive could mobilize the support of a nation that wanted both peace and primacy.

Paradoxically, it was the very strength—the brute strength—of this consensus that pushed Lyndon Johnson into the Vietnamese slaughter-house and kept him there. A more defeatist or more extreme policy would have destroyed the support he needed for his domestic plans and for his foreign programs. And yet the war in Vietnam would finally destroy both Johnson and the consensus.

Not only did the drafted or draftable young, many blacks, and hippie *provocateurs* rebel between 1965 and 1968, but the foreign policy Establishment split wide open. Retrospective revisionism and recrimina-tory radicalism prevailed, and opinion divided into three camps: defenders of the official line, supporters of unlimited force to win the war, partisans of a speedy negotiation to end it. During the Korean war, after the tempest provoked by MacArthur's demands and dismissal, a sullen consensus had allowed Truman to stick to his guns. The reason was simple: On the battlefield, the *status quo ante* had been restored; the desultory battles that were still fought did not imperil it. In Vietnam, abruptly following the hordes of happy statistics dressed up and displayed by officialdom, the shock produced by the Tet offensive convinced many Americans that only a change of policy could lead either to victory or a negotiated settlement. And even though Johnson embarked on a new course, his offer to the enemy was too hedged and ambiguous and his responsibility for the disas-ter was too obvious to save from defeat the man he had chosen as his successor, or to save from decay the consensus that had frozen around a few simple and clear notions: the threat of Moscow-led communism, the mobilization for the crusade of containment. These notions appeared inade-quate to the world of the late sixties and instrumental in setting up the bloody trap.

THE CONTAINED CRUSADE

For twenty years, official dogma and quasi-official authors had preached "realism." Niebuhr and Nitze, the Bundy brothers, the Rostow brothers, Schlesinger (Arthur), and Kissinger proclaimed that the impotent or impa-tient moralism characteristic of America as long as the United States had remained separated from the world was obsolete. Force and policy now had to be integrated (by contrast with what had happened from 1941 to 1944). One could no longer count on force's ability to put an end to the history of force and to bring forth the age of harmony. One could hope for distant accommodation, not real concord, among rival states and ideolo-gies. One could no longer vacillate from insulation to world utopias. One had to say good-bye to Briand-Kellogg pacts that excommunicate war, to policies of nonrecognition without sanctions, to bills and resolutions that try to build safe walls for isolation in the hope that evil would not seep through. One had to say good-bye to foolish illusions about the rule of trust among the great powers, or the rule of law among states through the ministry of a world organization; but one also had to give up the dream of the universal triumph of democratic ideals through an armed crusade, through "just war." In the atomic age, this would put an end to history itself. The old tensions and oscillations had to be put aside, and replaced, not by narrow nationalism, deemed inadequate to the task with which the United States was confronted, but by a new synthesis around a new guideline: the national interest. The national interest required a Clausewitzian policy: limited force for limited ends, unlimited (nuclear) force for deterrence only. The national interest required a policy both reasonable and enlightened: neither the triumph of utopia nor the rule of sacred egoism, neither appeasement nor impetuousness.

There is something touching in those adult education courses for simpleminded citizens, in the effort of leaders and intellectuals to convince Americans to overcome their past, to live in the present, and to learn classical European traditional practices—disdained for so long—so as to do better than the Europeans, who had mismanaged or forgotten them. "Realism" was better at stating what it was not or what it was against, than at clarifying what it stood for. Each realist had his preferred policy and cast doubts on the realism of others. But the consensus on containment seemed to provide the substance and, on the whole, the lessons seemed to have been well learned. Was it still the same nation that had put all its trust in unlimited war and demanded the unconditional surrender of evil as the necessary prelude to universal concord? Was it the same pendulum that had once swung from nonentanglement to imperial impulses, from the neutralist Wilson to the missionary Wilson, from the repudiation of the Versailles Treaty to the annihilation of Germany and Japan? The arrogance of "the best and the brightest," those men of unlimited self-confidence (derived from personal success) but limited social and international experience, whose earnest, cheerful, and self-assured memoranda can be found throughout the Pentagon papers, those who told their President that we were on the right tracks, and did not notice until too late that they had been derailed, was the arrogance of quick thinkers who thought they had found the golden mean and of skilled operators who believed they had concocted the necessary and sufficient recipes. They were earnest; they were agile; they were superficial.

And yet, one does not rid oneself of atavism so easily. The old "exceptionalism" had been reconverted but not discarded. In order to "sell" containment, one had had to present it in moral terms; this was the condition for massive and fervent support. The cold war was a contained crusade, but it was still a crusade. The world was divided into us and them, the good guys and the bad guys, the free world and the oppressors. Among the good guys, only the Americans had worldwide responsibilities. Containment was doubly moral because it would save the world from the inevitable catastrophe that would occur if the communists faced only cowards or firebrands and because it would gradually provoke the transformation, the moderation if not the conversion, of the enemy. The dream of final harmony was postponed, not put aside. Even Morgenthau asserted that the policy of the national interest was ethical. What I have elsewhere called the Myth of the Magic Flute—Zarastro's victory over the Queen of the Night, Tamino's reunion with Pamina after the long ordeal—thus transfigured realism and made it more attractive to Americans, as determined as ever to do better than the amoral great powers of the past. Conversely, the elements of world order I have listed were presented as contributions to the moral success of containment: Aid to underdeveloped nations (from Truman's Point Four to the Alliance for Progress), support for the United Nations. European integration were stations on the way to a world whose features would be more like America's.

Moreover, the methods that were made to serve realism were perfectly characteristic of America's exceptionalism, of its existential tension, and of its historical pendulum. The instinct for violence in the face of conflicts of ends may have been curbed by an even more powerful instinct—survival. But it still expressed itself in two ways. We built up nuclear forces far beyond the requirements either of minimal deterrence or deterrence that would also cover one's chief allies. For reasons that cannot be ascribed only to what has become the most facile explanation of every policy— bureaucratic politics, the demands of each and every service (for one still has to explain why the demands were set so high and usually accepted)— we went for "overkill." Even if, as Albert Wohlstetter has argued,[9] we sometimes underestimated Soviet capabilities, we launched in the 1960s a program of land-based missiles and nuclear submarines and proceeded to tactical nuclear deployments that provoked, in response, the huge Soviet program whose results have unfolded in the 1970s. And we initiated a program of Multiple Independently Targeted Reentry Vehicle (MIRV) testing and deployment based on exaggerated estimates of Soviet antimissile defenses. The militarization of containment deplored by Kennan—the tendency to define security in military terms, the weight of the Pentagon in the definition and enforcement of American policy abroad, indeed the frequent identification of foreign policy and "national security"—point to the continuing privilege enjoyed by one particular instrument of policy, the one most usually and expertly employed (embraced might be a better word) by Americans faced with discord at home or abroad.

Realism also became hard to distinguish from a traditional activism aimed at spreading American features across the world. Anti-Communism appealed both to the nationalism of toughness and to the idealism that needs a moral goal higher than national triumph in order to legitimize power and manipulation. It also allowed for a huge expansion of American business, the practical servant of American ideals and the companion of America's might. A major concern, a priority goal for the world, was economic efficiency and high productivity—not, of course, an absurd objective, given the conditions after the end of the world war, yet one that almost always seemed to come ahead of social reform, an abstractly desirable yet unfamiliar objective with which the American experience was ill at ease. As a result, and because of the similarity of views on the external threat, the United States has tended to support political forces that were above all conservative, or whose liberalism, being quantitative (progress through material enrichment, not social overhaul), stayed well on this side of radicalism.

This is how the United States shaped or influenced the political profile of Western Europe and Japan and obtained abroad the support it needed for its foreign policy. Far more than the American public realized, with its rather naïve belief in the spontaneous convergence of autonomous forces, we recruited and shored up political clienteles of "like-minded" people. Our favorite means were military and economic assistance, the most readily available and successfully tested American devices. Our emphasis on the similarity of values, visions, and techniques, our quest for a kind of universal pragmatism, to use Walt Rostow's favorite word, all show that the "American empire," far more than the British, expressed a certain expansive notion of the ideal social order, not merely a mix of external realism and will to preserve hard-won advantages.

But this is precisely where some trouble and contradiction broke in. Niebuhr and his disciples had taught that in public life, group selfishness being what it is, whoever plays the angel ends up the beast. Moralism would be debased into serving the will to dominate, even as it tried to tame that will. Furthermore, impenitent idealists had warned that the new compass, the national interest, would destroy America's old and noble ideals, not just by converting them into sly rationalizations, but by pushing them aside or by raping them, by bringing about the triumph of naked force. In other words, both groups warned against teaming up power politics and ethics, because the latter would be the victim. But one group, afraid above all of hypocrisy and eager to abandon the illusions of the past, concluded that undisguised power politics had to be practiced and would be ethical in proportion to its realism and moderation, while the other group, fearful above all of brutalization and clinging to old ideals, concluded that moralism had to be given free rein, as long as the United States was its secular arm. The abandonment of East Europeans, Chinese, or North Koreans to evil and the sermons of John Foster Dulles about the immorality of neutralism seemed to spring from the second approach—and vindicated thereby Niebuhr's own, for nothing was more hypocritical, or more inspired by electoral calculations, than the call for rollback, and nothing was more in contradiction with the preachings of Eisenhower's Secretary of State than his behavior during the Suez crisis. Finally, there remained a small reservoir of aggressive, repressed nationalism, impatient both with the universalist ideals of the "realists," and with the restraints prudently imposed on anti-Communism. To the Americanists, the contained crusade, however militarized in its instruments, was a doubly frustrating approach. They found a spokesman, if not a leader, in Barry Goldwater.[10]

The Vietnam war was to inflame the other kind of frustration: that of Americans who were coming to believe that the warnings of Niebuhr and of the idealists had been correct. They observed that in many parts of the world, quite apart from South Vietnam, the United States had shored up corrupt or tyrannical regimes while posing as the champion of freedom. Anti-Communist moralism resulted in calling whoever said he was against the Reds a "free world ally" and in justifying any means, any dirty trick, in the name of the good end.

However, these Americans did not decide, *à la* Niebuhr, that it was therefore better to give up ethical pretenses and to admit that one cannot have clean hands in politics. Nor did they opt for reinjecting morality into foreign affairs to clean up both the United States and the world. They proclaimed instead that America, having dirtied its hands, had to abandon its perverted dream of saving the world from evil and to purify itself above all. If there was so much evil in the world, it was in good measure because America had projected abroad the evil that was brewing inside. Radicals and revisionists played out the Wilsonian syndrome. Their denunciation of the horrors inflicted by the United States upon the world was the emotional twin of the previous good conscience. The teacher-judges had bred judge-penitents. There was the same naïve conviction that America by itself can shape the world: yesterday, by global intervention on behalf of its principles, now by leaving it (and especially the Third World), to its beneficial revolutions. In both cases, we find the same belief that conflict could have been avoided if it had not been for one devil on the road to harmony: the Soviet Union in the old view, the United States in the new one. The fear of a Stalinist masterplan for world domination was replaced by the denunciation of an American masterplan for world empire.

The clash over Vietnam ended up as the cacophony of three opposed moralisms. The captives of the middle of the road were trying, with decreasing self-confidence, to prove that their policy was morally superior to abandoning one's allies or to escalating ruin. The Hawks were convinced that America was fighting for a nation's freedom and for freedom everywhere (shades of the Truman Doctrine . . .) and should stop doing so half-heartedly (had Goldwater not explained that extremism on behalf of liberty is no vice?). The Doves, whose moral indignation sometimes drowned out their political arguments, wished, as McGovern would put it later, that America would come home to take better care of its virtue. The pendulum seemed to have reverted to its Wilsonian vacillation.

SECTION TWO: THE ORDEAL OF VIETNAM

Vietnam dominated the end of the first cycle of postwar America and played an important role during most of the second. Much has already been written about the "lessons" of Vietnam.[11] One of them is precisely the uniqueness of Vietnam or, rather, the need to refrain from mechanically applying disembodied principles, whatever their moral worth or their political success elsewhere—the need to take into full account the specific features of each country and issue. This makes any generalization of the lessons of Vietnam somewhat paradoxical and self-defeating. To some extent, Vietnam was one more application of the imperative, "no more Munichs" (as Munich itself was the result of the imperative that dictated French and British behavior in the thirties—"no more summers of 1914"). A blanket rule of "no more Vietnams" could easily be as calamitous as previous retrospective analogies.

However, just as there was something to be learned from the summer of 1914, and something to be avoided after Munich, much ought to be remembered from Vietnam. For if we do not remember, we shall reproduce. We were determined not to "lose" Vietnam the way we had "lost" China, because we deemed the internal and external costs too high. And yet, we had not learned the really significant lessons from our China experience and repeated the same mistakes in Vietnam. We could encapsulate them in one phrase: the neglect of local circumstances.

In postwar China we had already set ourselves an impossible goal (a coalition under Chiang's leadership—something both he and the Communists rejected) and a contradictory goal (a unified and democratic China under Chiang—but under Chiang it would be neither united nor democratic, and it could not be unified and democratic under any existing *and* significant force). We had already been trapped in a dilemma of ends and means. What means did we have to force Chiang to adopt our policy, except aid that would only encourage him to persevere or a denial of assistance that would undermine him? We had already engaged in wishful thinking (both about Chiang *and* about the Communists). We had already settled for a "middle course" that produced turmoil at home without staving off defeat on the ground. Yet all we learned was not to incur again domestic division and a victory for Communism. The first renewal of wishful thinking was our belief that small Vietnam was manageable by us, whereas huge China had been beyond our control.

IMPOSSIBILITIES AND MISBELIEFS

One must go back to the roots of our mistake. The first was the belief that in a battle between an opponent with a formidable will, the advantage of geography, patience, and available supplies, and a "friend" who, for all his dislike of communism and of Hanoi's rule, showed neither the ability nor the determination to mold his country into a national community, American power could redress the balance. America's will and cause could be injected into the patient as if they were a blood transfusion. But Washington could only delay the outcome and shape the specific form the inevitable end would take. The equation never changed in more than fifteen years. The goal, a "free" South Vietnam, could only be reached, if at all, through means that were either repugnant or unlikely to work. For a successful outcome would have required either the physical annihilation of North Vietnam, obliterated from the air or occupied on the ground, or else the establishment of a genuine South Vietnamese nation.

But we never wanted to incur the costs and risks of a major onslaught on North Vietnam. We feared turning a limited or proxy war into a direct clash with Moscow or Peking, and we feared the casualties that would accompany such a war even if it remained limited to Vietnam. In other words, however much our leaders proclaimed the importance of our stand and stakes, there was always a contradiction between the *real* importance of South Vietnam to our world position and the nature of our involvement there. A limited involvement was incapable of bringing victory (even modestly defined as a North Vietnamese decision to leave its neighbor alone); a massive involvement was deemed unacceptable. But if we recognized this, then we would have to start reflecting on two points. One was disturbing enough: if our real interests there were limited, if what made victory impossible at a reasonable price was specific to Vietnam, was there not something absurd and self-defeating about grand displays of force and tenacity justified, not by the intrinsic importance of the stakes in Vietnam, but by the notion that in an age of deterrence (which is a gamble on credibility) and of contests of will, each confrontation becomes a test of our global credibility, of our resolve everywhere? If one pushed this bizarre argument to its logical extreme, one had no other alternatives than either limited victories (unlimited ones being too dangerous) or being stuck without being able to cut one's losses when limited victory was impossible. And by definition limited victory was ruled out in Vietnam: either *we* won, which supposed the destruction of North Vietnam—not an unlimited achievement—or sooner or later *they* won, unless we remained impaled forever on the stupid-heroic horn of our own dilemma.

A second reflection was even more gloomy. If we gave up the absurd belief that even tests for limited stakes had unlimited importance because of credibility (and if we thus followed the example of the Soviets, who obviously did not believe that setbacks in Berlin or Cuba undermined their manhood, power, or prospects), if we thus confessed the meagerness of our interests in Vietnam, then we were doomed to lose, for our adversary's interests were literally unlimited and far more vital than ours. Our limited war was their struggle for liberation and unity.

We avoided facing these questions by clinging to the hope that "nation building" could save South Vietnam. But the very forces on which we relied and which we maintained in power were the least capable of such a feat. We had, of course, ruled out communists as genuine nationalists; we did not encourage the hapless groups that hoped to be a "third force," insofar as they might have accommodated the communists. And so, our proclamation of support to "a nation fighting for its freedom" became an exercise in self-deception and ventriloquy. We kept projecting on South Vietnam a pattern that had been genuine in Europe and in Korea. Even in South Vietnam, there were groups and people fighting for freedom from communism, but there never was a general will or a national regime. At worst, we had clients; at best, a South Vietnamese army living off, rather than for, its people. Having, in effect, given up the attempt to create such a will or regime, yet not the hope to "hold" South Vietnam militarily, we merely held back the flood at a terrifying human cost. We combined the ineffective and the destructive, the futile and the corrupt. As Elliot Richardson suggested in an interview shortly after the fall of Saigon, surely the same result could have been achieved sooner at less cost.

Vietnam shows how a moral disaster can result from radically flawed political premises. The point needs to be hammered in. For some still think our effort was somehow justified by the immorality of our opponents (and they mention the bloodbath in Cambodia). But the communists' cruelties do not vindicate our own acts; the peoples of Indochina have had to suffer from the combination of our war and of the communists' methods. And we should be the last to speak of a bloodbath. Would Cambodia today be in the hands of a small, insulated clique of Khmers Rouges, had we not come to the help of Lon Nol, ravaged the country, destroyed its traditional social bases and elites, rejected all suggestions to turn back to Sihanouk once Lon Nol's defeat seemed certain, and thus prepared the ground for the nightmarish, surgical radicalism we now deplore? Others still believe that whatever else may be said, our effort was not immoral because our intentions were good. But the ethics of political action is not an ethics of motives, it is an ethics of consequences. Ends that cannot be reached at a price commensurate with the importance of the stakes, and means disproportionate to the stakes yet ineffective and destructive of the very values one pretends to save, are components of an ethical catastrophe. The impulse to help others is indeed a mark of American generosity in world affairs, and the defense of freedom is a worthy cause. But there is nothing moral *or* politically sensible about the hubris that makes us substitute "our" dream for "their" realities, and (when the latter do not fit the dream) either pretend that they are what we want them to be or use vile and violent means to try to reach the dream that conflicting realities have made unrealizable.

These are lessons that remain valid from the whole experience. Other lessons can be derived from each of the two phases of the war: before and after the Democratic debacle of 1968. The main lesson of the Kennedy-Johnson phase is about the error of simple, universal slogans, the danger of turning containment into a panacea, the excessive momentum of unexamined consensus. Those who tell us that the cold war villains are the momentum of the national security bureaucracy, or the dynamics of American capitalism, must still explain how the few succeeded so easily in carrying with them the many for so long.

Once these errors were made, we managed to make matters worse. We did so, first, by throwing more men and money into the inferno to vindicate our assertion of the importance of the stakes, and because everything else—even more massive escalation, or extrication—seemed worse. Thus we ensured that the end would be dreadful for us, and even more so for those with whom we shared the illusion of ultimate salvation. Indeed, the more we supported them (or substituted ourselves for them), the more we undercut them and undermined their pretension to genuine nationalism. We made things worse, secondly, by trying to get from our allies as much support as we could, telling them in the process that our stand was a test of our reliability anywhere. Thus we strained the very bonds whose solidity we claimed to defend, and we raised universal doubts about our wisdom by inventing, in effect, what could be called a self-domino theory. We weakened our own credibility by asserting that our failure to do the impossible in Vietnam affected our capabilities to do the possible and necessary elsewhere. Third, the Vietnam quagmire paralyzed us in our relations with our main adversaries. We failed to exploit the Sino-Soviet split and persisted in treating Peking as our most implacable foe. And "peaceful engagement" in Eastern Europe was one of the war's casualties.

Fourth, we made matters worse by misreading the stakes in another way. If our global credibility was involved, it was not only because discrete crises test a single will, it was also because we insisted on seeing in Hanoi an arm of international communism, one head of a single, multiheaded hydra. We had to prove that the free world would not yield, and we believed that the only way to cope with the hydra was to do battle; for all the heads sprung from a single body, and any communist victory would bring forth more heads. This was the domino theory, another way of ignoring the specifics of each country and of ascribing to one's adversaries diabolic capabilities. That a communist victory in Saigon would affect Laos and Cambodia was never much in doubt; Laos was part of the battlefield, Cambodia openly became one as of 1970. That a communist Indochina might bring about some changes in Thai or Filipino policy was likely; but that this would be tantamount to "falling dominoes" was a masochistic myth.

Fifth, we made matters worse by never resolving what I have called, above, America's existential tension. I refer to Johnson's way with the drama of ends and means. We offered concord to Hanoi, but on our terms, and these terms made little political sense. We demanded that Hanoi leave its neighbor alone—literally an impossible goal given Hanoi, given Saigon, and given our own limits. The ironical truth of the matter is that in the Johnson years the military were strictly submitted to civilian power, but civilian power and politically sensible ends were two totally different things. The use of force to oblige Hanoi to accept our olive branch resulted in more violence in the South than in the North, for understandable reasons—the fear of escalation by Hanoi's patrons. But while it did not break Hanoi's will, it destroyed in South Vietnam much of what we were pretending to save, and by turning the war into an American crusade against the Vietnamese, it fed Hanoi's propaganda and threatened to turn an alleged war of self-defense against communist aggression into a war of national liberation against imperialism. A final irony lies in the fact that the use of ineffective and counterproductive means toward an unreachable goal led, not to a reassessment of the goal, but merely to an exhausting contest between military leaders eager for more bombs and a Secretary of Defense caught between belated lucidity and stolid loyalty to the President. The mere acceptance of fewer new targets than were demanded by the Joint Chiefs thus became a form of damage limitation—until the Tet offensive tore up the heavy veil of illusions.

THE "SETTLEMENT"

The Kissinger era radically changed the picture on most of these aggravating points. We stopped pressing our allies. We began to turn, so to speak, the domino theory against Hanoi, by getting Moscow and Peking to coax or coerce North Vietnam into an agreement. We reshaped our means: We pulled out troops, we "Vietnamized" the war, we curbed search and destroy operations in the South; but we did not hesitate to resort to massive attacks on the North in 1972 when the danger of escalation had receded.

And yet, nothing had changed in the original equation. To be sure, the goal of the Nixon administration sketched out by Henry Kissinger in 1968[12]—a political settlement accompanying the withdrawal of outside forces, leaving the ultimate fate of South Vietnam open and giving each side a chance for the future—*seemed* sensible. Actually, we had not changed our original objective. As Kissinger put it, "the United States cannot accept . . . a change in the political structure of South Vietnam brought about by external military force." This meant, clearly, more than giving Saigon the benefit of a "decent interval." He explicitly rejected a United States–North Vietnamese agreement on a coalition government for the South, and while he wrote that "once North Vietnamese forces and pressures are removed, the United States has no obligation to maintain a government in Saigon by force," this was a meaningless statement. For what, once we were out, could keep away North Vietnamese pressures?

And if they resumed, how could we prevent the "change in the political structure of South Vietnam brought about by external military force," if not through continuing military help?

The only difference in goals, between the Johnson and the Nixon periods, was that Johnson had never clarified his view of how he would get Hanoi to cease and desist, whereas his successors opted for a negotiated settlement. But this "settlement," while leaving the future open, could not change the realities; and because our goal had not changed either, all the innovations introduced by Nixon and Kissinger ultimately did not matter or (as in Cambodia) only made things worse. It is therefore not surprising, first, that in order to reach a settlement, we had to enlarge the war (first in Cambodia, later in response to Hanoi's 1972 offensive, finally after the breakdown of negotiations at the end of 1972)—thus living one more paradox: a bigger war for extrication. Second, the bargaining remained sterile for years. One side aimed at a deal that would clearly put it in control of Indochina, while the other wanted one that would give Saigon the best chance for survival. Third, finally reaching the kind of deal we had sought settled nothing; such an agreement could be no more than a smokescreen— a screen behind which we got out, inevitably leaving Hanoi in place. We and they had had a common interest: the extrication of America's residual forces. All we got in exchange was a purely temporary concession by Hanoi to let Thieu remain—and to obtain this concession, we had had to agree to let the North Vietnamese stay in the parts of the South they had occupied, that is, we had to accept a de facto second partition. *This* in turn ensured that the agreement would not even bring a truce, because each side would be eager to grab as much territory from the other as possible. And it ensured more refugees, more uprootings, more destruction, and as little "nation-building" as before, in the unfortunate South.

Once we were out, the outcome was, as it had been ever since the beginning, in the hands of an obstinate enemy and a shaky ally. There still remained only two theoretical possibilities. One was a protracted and uncertain war to preserve Indochina from communism, the other was Indochina under communist influence or control. The 1973 agreement that postponed the reckoning did not change the situation. What half a million American troops and our air power had only slowed down could not be contained forever by mere American military aid. If, or rather, when, Hanoi would resume its offensive, we would again be faced with the same old choice: reintervene, or let it fall. Kissinger has argued that reintervention, of the sort promised by Nixon to Thieu, would have occurred if

Watergate had not undermined the President's authority. But how many times would Congress and the public allow a replay of the useless tragedy? Each time American force was needed to delay the inexorable, even an administration that was trying to avoid the errors of its predecessors had to fall back on their kind of hyperbolic rhetoric to justify its moves: the United States could not let itself be treated as a helpless, pitiful giant, and so on. . . . The reintroduction of American troops was unthinkable, and airpower alone was unlikely to stop the flood forever. Moreover, even without Watergate, the return to massive air warfare after the disengagement of 1973 was politically and psychologically most unlikely.

In other words, there was nothing the Nixon-Kissinger team could do to reverse what could be called America's original sin in Vietnam. Its task was a thankless retreat in any case. But a choice of avenues still presented itself. The strategy of an apparently honorable retreat would leave Thieu in temporary control of his part of the South. The strategy recommended by George Ball—pure and simple extrication, leaving Thieu to himself— would in fact, although not explicitly, have abandoned the unreachable original goal.[13] And the strategy I recommended in 1970—the attempt to reach not merely a negotiated yet doomed truce, but actual accommodation based on the acceptance of major communist influence in Indochina— would have been achieved "by the United States and by a South Vietnamese government determined to seek a peace of reconciliation and to move toward free elections under conditions accepted by the other side," in a genuine international framework.[14] At the time, the latter suggestion seemed almost like a perverse quest for national humiliation, and it entailed risks and difficulties. But the alternative that was followed did not save us from humiliation, and—as so much else in the Kissinger era—consisted of what the French call *reculer pour mieux sauter,* a retreat that merely postponed the apocalypse. In effect, it combined the worst aspect of the Ball solution and the unrealism of the earlier Vietnam policy. We left the South Vietnamese to themselves, claiming to have remained loyal to our ally, yet in effect washing our hands of the country's fate, and ensured that the victory of Hanoi, being a military one, would wipe out not only Thieu but all the factions caught in the middle. Yet we still claimed that we wanted to ensure Saigon's survival. To stop all aid while Thieu kept fighting, as we did in the spring of 1975, may indeed have been callous. But to keep feeding the flames (while pretending, in the last days of Saigon, that our supplies might "stabilize" the situation long enough to provide for the negotiated political accommodation we never sought to achieve when

Thieu seemed in firm control) would have been equally callous. When we decided, as late as 1971, to maintain in power the cliques that relied on us, we made sure that we would have a choice only between ignominious endings.

In 1970, I had acknowledged that our Vietnamization policy might have one advantage: "if Saigon falls, it pins on South Vietnam, not on us, the loss of another country to Communism." (This advantage never materialized, partly because we kept propping up Thieu, partly because Ford and Kissinger themselves blamed Congress for his final collapse.) Indeed, "Vietnam has been a burning tunic against the United States skin too long for us to deny some part in the outcome." Therefore, "the last service we [could] perform for Indochina—and, concerning Indochina, for the conscience of our own nation—[was] putting our energies behind an effort to bring back peace" based on the realities of South Vietnam. But we preferred a truce that allowed *us* to leave, kept *them* fighting, and had us and our clients half-heartedly "stoking the fire of war" in order to suppress these realities a little longer.[15]

Nixon and Kissinger were shrewd enough to liquidate the Vietnamese disaster—and it took them so long that when the end came, the backlash they said they dreaded never occurred: the nation wanted oblivion, not revenge. But what, in the case of Algeria, Raymond Aron called "the style of giving up" affects the whole of domestic and foreign policy. The *way* in which they liquidated it deserves blame more than the *time* it took them (the length of time was largely a function of the method). It also shows two essential areas of continuity between the two cycles. One concerns the domestic aspects of foreign policy. Aiming at the impossible brought about a corruption of our institutions, from Johnson's politics of deceit,[16] and the demoralization of the United States army, to the secret war in Cambodia, the epidemic of wiretaps, the Ellsberg affair, and the Huston plan. The other aspect concerns our policy abroad. We clung to Thieu and to the flimsy hope of avoiding the minute of truth because of our quest for "stability," and our fear of what "instability," especially in the form of a Communist take-over, could do to our position in the world. But, as many critics have pointed out, there can be no stability where there is profound dissatisfaction with the political, economic, or social situation, and, to quote Hans Morgenthau, "a policy committed to stability and identifying instability with Communism is compelled by the logic of its interpretation of reality to suppress in the name of anti-Communism all manifestations of popular discontent and stifle the aspirations for reform. . . . Thus . . . tyranny becomes the last resort of a policy committed to stability as its ultimate standard."[17] At best, we persuade ourselves that those who cling to us because they see in us the guardians of their order are true reformers, as long as they tell us so.

Morgenthau may, in turn, be too optimistic when he contrasts "the short-run stability and long-run instability of tyrannical rule" with "the short-run instability and long-run stability of revolution and radical reform." Revolution and radical reform are often not stable in the long-run, and as we shall see later, it is not easy for America to associate itself with them—even when this would be in the national interest. But it surely is not in that interest to embrace the status quo, when it is so shaky as to be doomed, and surely it is right at least to ask whether it is in the national interest to embrace the status quo when it is maintained by sheer repression. For, as we shall argue again, whatever the limits and dangers of moral action in world politics may be, the definition of the national interest, especially in the United States, cannot leave out moral issues—if only because political choices are inherently moral choices, too.

NOTES

PART ONE

1. For my own sketchy evaluation see "Revisionism Revisited," in Lynn H. Miller and Ronald W. Pruessen, *Reflections on the Cold War,* Temple University Press, Philadelphia, 1974.

CHAPTER ONE

1. *Gulliver's Troubles, or the Setting of American Foreign Policy,* McGraw-Hill, New York, 1968, part 2.
2. See David Bell, "The End of American Exceptionalism," *The Public Interest,* Bicentennial Issue, no. 41, Spring 1975, pp. 193–223.
3. Daniel Boorstin, quoted in Bell, ibid., p. 197.
4. Anyhow, America's China policy was not, originally, a part of "containment." The application of United States military force to stopping the Communists was not suggested until the Wedemeyer mission, when Chiang's regime was already breaking down. The solution to the communist problem had been seen as political: America's policy was to make of China a great and friendly power, and the means, pursued throughout 1945 and 1946, was peaceful unification. When it proved unworkable, Washington's only alternatives, from the viewpoint of efficacy, were massive intervention to try to save Chiang—a choice that was both risky and unpalatable—or withdrawal into impartiality. For domestic reasons, the United States followed an intermediate policy, the worst possible mix: too limited to even begin to help Chiang, but sufficient to turn the Communists into bitter foes leaning toward Moscow, and yet incapable of protecting the administration from its domestic critics. For the parallels with Vietnam, see Section Two.

5. *Peace and War*, Doubleday, New York, 1966.
6. Richard N. Cooper, "Trade Policy Is Foreign Policy," in Cooper (ed.), *A Reordered World*, Potomac Associates, Washington, D.C., 1973, p. 47.
7. Robert Gilpin, "The Politics of Transnational Economic Relations," in Robert O. Keohane and Joseph S. Nye, Jr., *Transnational Relations and World Politics*, Harvard University Press, Cambridge, Mass., 1972.
8. See Ernest R. May, *Lessons of the Past*, Oxford University Press, New York, 1973, chaps. 2–4.
9. See his essay, "Is There a Strategic Arms Race?" *Foreign Policy*, nos. 15 and 16, Summer and Fall 1974; also, "How to Confuse Ourselves," *Foreign Policy*, no. 20, Fall 1975.
10. I do not find the distinctions made by Franz Schurmann (*The Logic of World Power*, Pantheon, New York, 1974) persuasive. He attributes postwar American imperialism to the New Deal ideologues and contrasts it with expansionism, endorsed by "interests." American "interests" have actually expressed a variety of beliefs, both over time and at any given moment. Schurmann recognizes that these "interests" became convinced that imperialism served them, and that the concept of national security provided a synthesis.
11. See in particular Richard M. Pfeffer (ed.), *No More Viet Nams?* Harper & Row, New York, 1968; and Anthony Lake (ed.), *The Legacy of Viet Nam*, New York University Press, New York, 1976.
12. "The Viet Nam Negotiations," *Foreign Affairs*, vol. 47, no. 2, January 1969, pp. 211–234; reprinted in his *American Foreign Policy*, Norton, New York, 1974.
13. *Diplomacy in a Crowded World*, Atlantic-Little, Brown, Boston, 1976, chap. 5.
14. "Viet Nam: An Algerian Solution?" *Foreign Policy*, no. 2, 1971, pp. 3–37, at p. 25.
15. Ibid., p. 37.
16. Cf. the National Security Action Memorandum of Apr. 6, 1965, quoted by Philippe Geyelin in Anthony Lake, op. cit., pp. 166–167.
17. "Three Paradoxes," *The New Republic*, Oct. 11, 1975, p. 17.

CHAPTER TWO

The Course
of Dr. Kissinger

It is not easy to analyze Dr. Kissinger's era. A first obstacle lies in the uncertainty that still exists about the respective roles of President Nixon and of his foreign policy adviser in the formulation of American policy and particularly of its more daring innovations. However, the shadow of Henry Kissinger on American diplomacy visibly grew. In the first phase, from early 1969 to the fall of 1971, his bailiwick was relatively well circumscribed: Vietnam and our relationship with the chief communist rivals, in other words, the universe of conflict. From the fall of 1971 to that of 1973, he was led, first by the consequences of the Nixon-Connally economic shocks, then by the very momentum of détente policies, to look also after America's relations with Western Europe and Japan. After he was appointed Secretary of State, while remaining National Security Adviser, the whole world became his domain, and economic issues played a major role in his policy. No one had previously succeeded in centralizing so thoroughly the main decisions on America's actions abroad, even if, on the technical aspects of defense and on key policy orientations in international economic affairs, he had to leave some leeway to the Pentagon and the Treasury.

A second obstacle is more serious. It lies in Kissinger's devilish nimbleness. It would be instructive to collect the main attacks launched against

him over the years to see which remained valid throughout, and which were
made obsolete by his agility, for he showed a remarkable talent for under-
cutting his adversaries by annexing their ideas and leaving them either
unaware of their sudden nakedness or furious about the delicacy with
which their clothes had been removed. During the campaign of 1976, many
of the charges brought either against his style, or against his alleged neglect
of America's allies, seemed antiquarian complaints or deliberate inaccura-
cies emanating from eager would-be successors who either had, in their
rage, failed to, or in their calculations, decided not to, notice that the
current Dr. Kissinger was making almost a speech a day—not bad for the
high priest of secrecy—and that relations with allies had become remarkably untroubled. It was fashionable, a few years ago, to draw attention to
Kissinger's indifference to the Third World. This could hardly be argued
seriously from the middle of 1975, whatever one's opinion of his proposals.
As for the critique of his amorality, it suddenly had to cope with lofty
statements about America's moral inspiration and the need to have allies
who are linked to us not merely by bonds of interests but by common
values.

This chameleon-like ability to embrace views that first seemed alien to
him testifies to his cleverness, resilience, talent for changing course when a
previously set direction seems wrong, and determination never to get stuck
or to compound error with obstinacy. But what may be high talent for a
diplomat causes great embarrassment to an analyst. For one can interpret
such behavior in at least two ways. One is to dismiss all Kissinger's
numerous conceptualizations as obfuscations, ex-post rationalizations, or
hypocritical tributes paid by the vicious statesman to the virtuous academic
he had once been. In this view, Kissinger was a deft opportunist, splendid
at exploiting opportunities but not at creating them, far better at short-term
shots than at long-range plans, concerned above all with the game of
nations for the game's sake, and confusing friends and foes with words
strewn to cover his traces (a similar critique had often been made of de
Gaulle's diplomacy).

But there is another way of looking at this dizzying course. It consists of
taking the intellectual side of Dr. Kissinger more seriously and of believing
that he came to power, if not with a full-fledged doctrine, at least with a
definite set of dogmas. The contradictions between his earlier beliefs and
his acts, the evolution of his stands, then become the normal consequence
of the gap between abstract notions or historically based "lessons," and
political realities. This second interpretation does not deny that Kissinger
was eager to deny such contradictions, to present his policy as the coherent

unfolding of a plan, and to describe abrupt changes of course as a natural succession of deliberate phases. But I have two reasons for arguing that he had definite ideas that often turned wrong and thus had to be adjusted (or replaced), rather than stating that it was all done with mirrors: it is far closer to the truth, and it is much more interesting.

I will not try to write a history of the Kissinger era. As in the previous chapter, I want to present a balance sheet, to study the degree of success or failure of American policy, to indicate what lessons can be learned for the future: what is the legacy, positive and negative, what backfired and must be avoided. I shall first analyze Dr. Kissinger's concepts, methods, and problems, and examine later the condition in which he left American foreign policy.

SECTION ONE: A DESIGN AND ITS FATE

KISSINGER'S EARLY IDEAS

We can distinguish between the ideas Dr. Kissinger brought to Washington from his years as a student of diplomacy and those that framed his actual policy. His pre-Washington ideas have been scrutinized at length in distinguished books and articles.[1] I shall select what seems most essential to an understanding of his policy. For all his criticisms of postwar American diplomacy, he was, so to speak, a member in good standing of the foreign policy Establishment (I am speaking of its intellectual content more than of its social role). He fully endorsed the two fundamental ideas of the containment era. One was the Clausewitzian notion of the need for integrating force and diplomacy, the imperative of "power politics." Kissinger's books belong to the same universe of discourse as Morgenthau's and Kennan's. As in their works, one finds a definite disdain for America's past behavior in world affairs. *A World Restored* gives a sense of multiple exposures, for it is at the same time a study of the Congress of Vienna, a critique of Versailles (and particularly of Wilsonian diplomacy), and a series of shots at American diplomacy in World War II (and at the diplomacy of the democracies in the thirties). A book that concludes that most great statesmen are either conservatives or revolutionaries obviously has little sympathy for statesmen who, when they cared for world affairs at all, were essentially liberal reformists—either impotent reformists, as in the thirties, or, *à la* Wilson, reformists more concerned with achieving utopias in the existing international structure than with either overhauling that structure or ensuring stability. As he put it in *Nuclear Weapons and*

Foreign Policy, the United States now had to learn "how to relate the desirable to the possible."[2] The desirable, peace, was not a useful goal (to aim at peace is to risk appeasement); it was a by-product of the possible: a policy conceived in terms of power but purged of absolutes.

As for the substance of such a policy, he accepted the second basic idea of the age: containment of the Soviet Union. It is interesting to recall, at a time when several critics accuse him of having been duped by détente, outsmarted by the Soviets, and of almost having made the world safe for communism, that Kissinger, in those years, was on the tough side of the consensus, eager to stress the differences between the U.S.S.R. and ordinary, nonrevolutionary powers, skeptical of negotiations (precisely because they were not means to a settlement but springboards for further advances of a revolutionary state), and concerned with finding an American military policy that could effectively thwart its advance—something which massive retaliation could not do. *The Necessity for Choice* dismissed summitry, blasted the theory of "convergence" between the communist and the liberal versions of industrial society, and constantly called for a strengthening of America's alliances and for a sense of purpose and self-confidence in the United States. Indeed, Kennedy's handling of alliance matters contributed to Kissinger's secession from the Kennedy administration in 1961. In the Berlin crisis of that year, he seems to have been closer to Adenauer's position than to that of the administration. On the importance of credibility in an age of alliances and deterrence, he was strictly orthodox. It was this conviction that made him adopt, for Vietnam, a policy that was in profound, if well-hidden, contradiction with his own acid assessment of South Vietnamese realities.

Where, then, did Kissinger's originality lie? On the one hand, in some variations on the common themes. In his books, the Clausewitzian tune was sung with an insistently European accent. The critique of American idealism went beyond the standard attacks on legalism and moralism; his was a quest for a *Realpolitik* devoid of moral homilies and of reminiscences of crusades (hence the paradox of an intense cold warrior without most of the cold war rhetoric). The model was provided by his analysis of nineteenth century, balance of power diplomacy—not a distinctive point if one compares him to Morgenthau, but an original one nevertheless if one compares him to the architects of postwar diplomacy. His enthusiasm for the balance heightened his anti-Wilsonianism, and it showed a preference for a multipolar diplomatic game at a time when Wilsonian ideals were being drafted against the communists and bipolarity seemed preferable to the uncertain ties of multipolar systems. The goals, moderation and restraining the forces of revolution, may have been the same; the preferred methods were not.

Insofar as the second common theme, containment, is concerned, his chief mark of distinctiveness could be called a certain degree of tactical flexibility, in two different directions. One was his critique of the paternalism of American policy in Western Europe, as well as of the McNamara doctrine and of the Multilateral Force (MLF). *The Troubled Partnership* was an attack on the Kennedy administration's policies toward Gaullist France (particularly toward the *force de frappe*), of its lack of adequate consultations, of its insensitivity to the specific, vital interests of key allies. It was, once again, the theme of the subordination of force (whether as strategic doctrine or as weapons) to policy; but the policy he advocated seemed to leave more of a say to the allies. However, those who later denounced the contradiction between his European policies and his writings failed to note the skepticism toward European integration that the book expressed, his emphasis on the need for "a political mechanism to plan long-term policy" for NATO—not at all what Gaullists had in mind in the sixties—and his assertion of the central importance of West Germany for United States policy.

The other distinctive point is more curious, has often been overlooked, and yet provides an important clue to his diplomacy. For all his warnings about the use of standard American bargaining techniques toward the Soviet Union, for all his skepticism about "peaceful coexistence," for all his stress on the importance of Soviet ideology and the suspiciousness and purposefulness of Soviet leaders, Kissinger blamed Dulles for his rigidity and advocated negotiations with the U.S.S.R.—particularly on arms control, seen as one of the ways to stability—as long as the United States knew exactly what it wanted and had no illusions about its adversary.

International Legitimacy   On the other hand, his real originality lay elsewhere: in a curious mix of neoclassicism and neoromanticism. For both, one must return to his most revealing book, *A World Restored.* Among his contemporaries, Kissinger was unique in attempting to use the past as a normative model of world politics instead of treating it merely as history or as a prelude to the present. The neoclassical political scientist, trying to analyze the conditions of a stable international order, turned to the Congress of Vienna and to the years that followed it. In this book we find his concept of international legitimacy. Such a lasting order, in his view, supposes a sense of legitimacy; such a sense has nothing to do with justice, but with "an international agreement about the nature of workable arrangements and about the permissible aims and methods of foreign policy."[3] This is vague enough, but there are a few precisions. Obviously, such an order must not seem oppressive and unacceptable to any major actor, for he would otherwise follow a revolutionary course. This tells us what the order must be like in order *not* to induce a power to become revolutionary. But it does not deal with another source of revolutionary behavior: not external frustrations, but domestic upheaval. Nor does it tell us how a revolutionary power is induced to accept a moderate world order. On this point, however, a second clue might help. The mix of relative security and insecurity for each power on which a stable order rests—for the quest of absolute security leads to absolute insecurity—and the possibilities of gradual evolution by common consent that it must entail, presuppose a balance of power, which induces self-restraint. To be sure, the existence of a balance makes aggression by a revolutionary power more difficult, but it does not rule it out. Kissinger himself, writing of revolutionary France and thinking of Hitler's Germany, showed how such states can succeed in destroying a preexisting order. So we have to fall back on a third clue: Legitimacy also requires the existence of a *principle* of legitimacy capable of justifying the adjustment of conflicting claims.

Actually, a reader of the book never quite finds out whether self-restraint results merely from the constraints of the balance, or also from the acceptance of a common principle. Kissinger is both vague and ambivalent about the latter. At one point he says that "the legitimizing principle . . . establishes the relative 'justice' of competing claims"; at another he states that to found an international order "entirely on submission to a legitimizing principle . . . is the quest of the prophet and dangerous because it presupposes the self-restraint of sanctity."[4] And yet there is no doubt that legitimacy, in his view, is more a matter of consensus, hence of beliefs and perceptions, than a matter of mechanics. If the order of the Congress of Vienna lasted, it was because "there was created a balance of forces which, because it conferred a relative security, came to be generally accepted."[5] Indeed, in his essay on Bismarck, Kissinger criticizes the "white revolutionary" for having reduced the European balance to a mere "statistical balance of forces in flux."[6] As a statesman, his own drama would be the attempt to recreate a legitimate order in a world of revolutionary players, a task that was not comparable to that of the Congress of Vienna, which met after Napoleon's fall, or even to that of Versailles, which dealt with Weimar but left Soviet Russia out. What would the legitimizing principle be now?

Can the mere establishment of a balance have "its legitimacy . . . be taken for granted" in such a world?

Of course, to a large extent, Kissinger was merely finding historical roots and letters of nobility for America's postwar quest of stability, which had also been plagued by the contrast between its goal and the realities of an unstable world agitated by a major revolutionary actor. But if one reads a bit more deeply in this rich and elusive volume, especially his analysis of the differences between Metternich and Castlereagh, of the nature of the post-Napoleonic peace, and of Metternich's futile efforts at shoring up Austria's rigid domestic structure, one reaches another point of interest in understanding Kissinger's political performance. The consensus legitimacy requires is not a consensus of statesmen on the principles of domestic government, on the internal social order. The Congress of Vienna had to accommodate both Alexander and Castlereagh, just as the moderate system of the nineteenth century consisted of authoritarian as well as of liberal states. The consensus has to deal only with what is tolerable, and what is not, in the states' external behavior. Thus, another condition for a legitimate world order—one that he does not draw out explicitly—is a willingness of the main actors to separate their internal convulsions and convictions from their external conduct. One may prefer any social and political regime, as long as one behaves moderately on the world stage. Thus, the coexistence of different ideologies in the same legitimate structure should be possible. To be sure, again, a balance of power is a potent factor in obliging states to curb the export of their beliefs. But this is not enough; the divorce must, at least in part, be willed.

This, in turn, raises some interesting questions. First, are all ideologies equally susceptible to such a divorce? Does it not depend on their content? Some, after all, expressly aim at reshaping world order. Second, doesn't the divorce between domestic credo and external conduct require—as Kissinger recognized in his assessment of Metternich[7]—that all the players be "products of essentially the same culture, professing the same ideals, sharing similar tastes, . . . conscious that the things they shared were much more fundamental than the issues separating them"? If this is so, can one expect the products of today's ideologies to be as ready for accommodation as in 1815? Third, insofar as the domestic scene is not insulated from the world stage—what people do at home will affect others, either by contagion or by deliberate export—are not some ideologies compelled to intervene abroad to protect their domestic base from external contamination? Was this not precisely what Metternich had done in his attempt at stopping liberal or national revolutions that could have been contagious and destructive of Austria? Neither conservative nor revolutionary powers can always practice the self-restraint that legitimacy demands.

Statecraft The discourse on legitimacy, the meditation on international stability, thus lead—despite, or rather just because of, the emphasis on the necessary separation of domestic from external behavior—to a reflection on the relation between domestic structure and the international order. A statesman who "too far outruns the experience of his people" will fail to achieve a domestic consensus, and this failure in turn will undermine his policy: witness Castlereagh. But a statesman who equates stability and status quo in a revolutionary period "will doom himself to sterility": witness Metternich, who "reinforced the tendency towards rigidity of Austria's domestic structure";[8] and out of its petrification came the shock that, in 1914, destroyed the stable order. What, then, is the proper relation, since the statesman needs both a domestic consensus and an internationally "legitimate" diplomacy?

Nowhere do we find Kissinger more obscure: he tells us—rightly, and ominously for himself—that diplomacy, Metternich's forte, was not "a substitute for conception: its achievements will ultimately depend on its objectives, which are defined outside the sphere of diplomacy."[9] What should Metternich's objectives have been? We do not know, and thus we never find out how to preserve stability from becoming hostage to the status quo, any more than we solved the riddles of legitimacy. Kissinger himself was singularly ambivalent about Metternich. While he deemed his domestic policy futile and smug, he admired his international *tours de force,* interventions included.

His most ambitious exploration of the past ultimately does not tell us enough about three problems its author was to face as a statesman: the relation between the weak and the strong (not a major concern in books that either dealt with the tests of the strong or else saw the weak, most traditionally, as stakes or pawns); how to establish international legitimacy in a world of revolutionary powers; and how to prevent the domestic structure from becoming the statesman's nemesis, since "even when there exists no fundamental ideological gulf, a nation's domestic experience will tend to inhibit its comprehension of foreign affairs."[10]

The neoromantic aspect tells us more about Kissinger's coming style and philosophy of action than the neoclassical concepts tell us about his future policy (although they help us understand some of its troubles). Here, we must go back to Kissinger's undergraduate thesis at Harvard, *The Meaning of History* (no less), which provides the intellectual foundation of much of *A World Restored*. We find another pair of opposites: not legitimacy and revolution, but creativity and bureaucracy. Creativity is necessarily individual, and while it can take many forms in foreign affairs—Kissinger distinguishes prophets and statesmen, conservatives and revolutionaries— it always entails elements of conjecture and persuasion, a gift of informed imagination and a skill that partakes of artistry. Bureaucracy is always described as the enemy of creation, as mediocrity and routine. "Profound policy thrives on continuous creation," but "the essence of bureaucracy is the quest for safety."[11] Bureaucracy is in permanent conflict with statecraft, because it negates imagination. (The other enemy is the statesman's national scene and the national experience, which is always in conflict with the nation's external experience; and if the statesman tries to fuse the two by claiming universal validity for its domestic principle of legitimacy, there shall be no legitimate world order).

Statecraft and bureaucracy seem to embody the two notions of Kissinger's thesis: freedom and necessity. His fascination with the former, particularly with the more mysterious and intuitive aspects of it—the art of combining for action the different aspects of reality revealed by intellectual analysis, a sense of timing, inspiration that "implies the identification of the self with the meaning of events" and is a "timeless call for greatness"[12]— remind one of the young de Gaulle's enthusiasm for the great leader, *le caractère,* in the *Edge of the Sword*. What is more Gaullian than this sentence: "For men become myths, not by what they know, not even by what they achieve, but by the tasks they set for themselves"?[13]

This aspiration also explains Kissinger's interest for statesmen who seemed to have the qualities he admired: Metternich (despite his rigidity), Bismarck (despite his early recklessness), Adenauer, and de Gaulle. History is not primarily the product of deep, irresistible forces; it is a clash of wills and a stage for leaders who are either the carriers of new principles or the creative defenders of past experience. This emphasis on leadership was just as unfashionable in political science as the return to history. It underlay Kissinger's critique of the American style and personnel in foreign affairs, for the latter are organization men, not inspired leaders, and what the former needs is a sense of purpose instead of its preoccupation with compromise and ad hoc solutions.

This original stance helps explain the style of his diplomacy, its quest for interpersonal bonds abroad, its concentration of power inside. Against the dead weight of bureaucracy, Kissinger knew how to defend himself. He was less successful in bridging the gap between the world stage and the domestic experience. In addition to stressing, as I mentioned above, the "incommensurability between a nation's domestic and its international experience,"[14] he also saw the enemy, bureaucracy, as the normal instrument of domestic policy, a rather simple view which shows conservative scorn for, or skepticism about, internal politics. But had he not foreseen that the statesman, like the hero of Greek tragedy, could not communicate his vision to his compatriots? His vision of "domestic structure" as bureaucracy (his writings contain few references to other domestic forces: parties, interests, intellectual currents, or media) could only strengthen his desire to separate domestic behavior and external conduct and heighten the contradiction between the felt need to reserve the world stage for creative, individual leadership, and the need for a domestic consensus lest the leader meet Castlereagh's fate.

The combination of a romantic view of statecraft, and of a pessimistic one of the split between the requirements of external success and those of domestic support, also helps explain two other weaknesses of his future diplomacy. The proper domain of imaginative statecraft is traditional diplomacy: the politics of territorial shifts and adjustments, the balancing of military might. To focus on it is to neglect the new diplomacy, which expresses the deep, anonymous forces of technology and economics and which seems to require more "organization" than "inspiration." It is called, nowadays, the diplomacy of interdependence—a severe cramp on the freedom of statecraft. If Kissinger's attitude toward Western Europe and Japan appeared, at times, so contemptuous, was it not in part because bureaucracy seemed to him to have taken over both domestic and foreign policy there, or to have gotten such a hold on domestic affairs that little room was left for any statecraft? Was it not also because the nations of Western Europe and Japan now seemed to be singularly devoid of creative leaders?

THE STATESMAN'S IDEAS

Let us turn to what could be called the statesman's doctrine, by contrast with the scholar's. It did not appear at once; it unfolded gradually, blending earlier insights with new opportunities. The old policy framework was no longer serviceable. The United States was stuck in Vietnam, and Kissinger was on record seeking disengagement without debacle. The communist world was no longer monolithic. Containment of the U.S.S.R. seemed doubly inadequate: in part because, as the invasion of Czechoslovakia had shown, it had led to no Soviet change of conduct, in part because, in the nuclear realm, both superpowers were ready to acknowledge mixed interests. The skill of the Nixon-Kissinger team consisted in seizing this moment to change, not America's objectives, but their presentation, their modalities, and the style of American action. It took as its point of departure two obvious but contradictory facts. One was the importance of the United States for military balance and political and economic order in the world, the other was the public's fatigue with the manning of all barricades, its desire to turn inward. Shrewdly, Nixon and Kissinger adopted a style and scheme that seemed to reconcile the need for active involvement and the desire for some shrinking of burdens. It promised both to lighten the load and to boost the benefits.

THE NEW "LEGITIMATE ORDER"

The objectives remained, on the one hand, the containment of the main adversaries, on the other, the preservation of American primacy. Both required the maintenance of America's principal alliances in Western Europe, the Far East, and Latin America. But their presentation was changed: In official statements, the idea of a "stable structure of peace" becomes the fuzzy guideline and the flickering lodestar. The idea was a modern version of the "legitimate order" Kissinger had analyzed; that structure had to be "built with the resources and concepts of many nations," so that they would "contribute to its vitality and accept its validity."[15] Thus, the new policy seemed to take care—verbally—of the flaws of containment. By reducing the latter to an instrumental role within a grand strategy of universal accommodation, it promised something more dynamic than the stoic or stolid immobility of containment—shades of the Republicans' criticisms of 1952—and it took into account the new possibilities of great-power cooperation: it stressed not only motion, but the positive rather than the negative.

As for the modalities, one has to distinguish between relations with adversaries and relations with friends or third parties. On the first front, containment by confrontation was to be replaced with containment through negotiation: a more "creative connection."[16] To be sure, continued tests and tensions were deemed likely. And each of the two great powers was expected to keep its imperial zone free from outside interference—Russia in Eastern Europe, the United States in Latin America. But the administration called for "a mutual search for a stable peace and security," for an "international structure based on self-restraint in the pursuit of national interests." This call raises three important questions.

First, why did the administration attach so much importance to a "breakthrough with our adversaries"? Three main reasons can be invoked. Nixon and Kissinger, rightly enough, saw in the points of crisis between the United States on one side, and Moscow and Peking on the other, the most dangerous issues for mankind. Other troubles might lead to local wars, to economic calamities, or to ecological disasters, but only these might incinerate the world. Even if they did not, the amount of time, money, and attention lavished on them seemed exorbitant. In other words, security relations were deemed fundamental even in the "age of interdependence," and they were commanded by that triangular relationship. It was therefore astute and sensible to try to moderate it by bringing to bear on each of the two communist powers the weight of an American rapprochement with the other—a classical game on behalf of a classical vision.

But the triangular relationship was seen as more than central to international politics; it was thought commanding. Undoubtedly the hope existed that since the great powers were—through alliances and clienteles—directly or—through the very dynamics of their competition—indirectly engaged in and tied to the whole world, a dampening of their rivalry and an incipient cooperation between them would affect third parties as well. Some conflicts involving these other parties could be settled or tamed through the advice, pressure, or even withdrawal of the great power that had kept feeding the flames—getting Moscow and Peking to moderate North Vietnam would complement the "Vietnamization" of the South and make an honorable American retreat possible. Other areas would stop being arenas of contest between the great powers once they had decided that, in the context of their triangular relationship, the peripheral stakes were not important enough: winning them would not fundamentally improve one's position but might destroy the new relationship. Finally, this approach would also have the advantage of restoring flexibility to United States diplomacy. For with the area of rivalry shrinking, with "proxy conflicts" either muted from above or disconnected from the great powers' confrontations, and with the latter giving way to joint projects, America could afford some disengagement in areas of overexposure. Washington could also exert firmer authority over allies whose every whim or fear it no longer felt compelled to heed. Undoubtedly, the new administration, like its predecessors, saw in the great-power relationship the masterkey to world order, but derived from this conviction the conclusion that it had to change the relationship to change the world.

Second, what made it possible for Kissinger now to believe that America's chief rivals were no longer revolutionary powers and might accept separating their ideology from their conduct abroad? The answer seems to be: a combination of their self-interest and of necessity. The primacy of security considerations over revolutionary aspirations was compelling in the case of China. Not only was the call for a worldwide crusade against imperialism already divorced from the concern for self-sufficiency and internal consolidation (even during the Cultural Revolution, China's message to outside clients or disciples was, "do it yourself"), but with the Soviet Union poised threateningly along China's long and controversial border, with the Ussuri River clashes coming on the heels of the Brezhnev doctrine, survival became the overriding priority, and ideology had to be strictly confined. Moreover, a "softer" attitude abroad might bring such rewards as participation in the United Nations and a rapprochement with the power that had deterred Moscow over much of the globe.

In the case of the Soviet Union, Khrushchev himself had widened the Sino-Soviet split by stating that in the nuclear age, "the fatal inevitability of war" could no longer be part of the dogma. Even a revolutionary state is forced to behave with prudence in a world in which any military clash between the two great powers could lead to universal destruction. The other side of that coin was the security afforded the U.S.S.R. by deterrence. If revolutionary states in the past became expansionist at least partly out of fear for their very base, threatened—in fact or in their imagination— by status quo states, there was no longer reason for such a fear.

Moreover, even at a lower level of peril, revolutionary opportunities were poor. The splits in the communist world, the barriers that the rise of national sovereignty throughout the world erected against overt aggression, the economic and political strength of many of America's allies, the autonomous intractability of many issues and regional conflicts that made their exploitation by the U.S.S.R. or their annexation by the cold war difficult, all this created a situation in which grand designs died of starvation (or, which amounts to the same thing, lived forever in the mind). Also, the U.S.S.R. had itself become, after fifty years, something of a status quo power, as its behavior in Eastern Europe showed, and even in those parts of the world where it was definitely not so, it increasingly chose to operate, not through local revolutionary forces, including communist parties (which it often seemed in no hurry to help to power), but through the established governments. It was a safer way, usually, to try to curry favors and to dislodge Western influence, but it put Soviet behavior much closer to the traditional manipulations of great powers. Thus, both nuclear bipolarity and what might be called the end of political bipolarity could be seen as opportunities for moderation.

Finally, there was "the desire of the Soviet people for the benefits which would be theirs if their government could reduce the vast investment of resources in international competition with us,"[17] and indeed for receiving some of the resources of the West. While the drive for economic development, as Professor Kissinger had written, does not, by itself, induce either liberalization or convergence—for it does not transform a regime—it may impose some restraints on its actions abroad, given the nature of economic interdependence.

Third, how did Nixon and Kissinger expect to drag a Soviet Union whose few contacts with the United States had been more contentious than friendly into the new order? Two notions were developed, with some complacency. The first was the notion of linkage. "Both sides had to understand that issues were interrelated," and agreements had to be reached on "a broad range of issues,"[18] lest an isolated deal fall victim to the other surrounding conflicts. Again, a sensible notion in the abstract, but it must have entailed a somewhat more chancy calculation. For in the realm of strategic forces, and of European security, each side needed something from the other, so that the balance of interests was about even. This being so, "linkage" had to mean that since the U.S.S.R. needed economic benefits from the West, which in turn needed very little that the Soviets could offer to sell, the West ought to demand political concessions in return. Indeed, in March 1969, Mr. Nixon mentioned Berlin, Vietnam, and the Middle East as areas for progress.

The second notion was that of the net. Linkage suggested a process. The net was to be the outcome. The Russian bear had to be caught in a dense web of agreements it would have neither the interest nor the possibility of breaking out of. Thus, containment in its new, more "creative" form, and a legitimate "structure of peace," would both be obtained. How should this be done? Literally, by applying behavioral psychology. The bear would be treated like one of B. F. Skinner's pigeons: There would be incentives for good behavior, rewards if such behavior occurred, and punishments if not. It may have been a bit pedantic, or a bit arrogant; it certainly was rather theoretical.

Primacy Redesigned   But it showed that primacy remained an American goal. American leaders were playing bear tamers and would provide the honey and the sticks that would maneuver the bear into the stable structure. Here too, however, was a change of modalities. Primacy in a game where priority is given to the restoration of horizontal relations between the major powers does not need to be assured by the same methods as primacy in a contest of camps *à la* Athens and Sparta, in which each leader must above all look after his vertical relationships: the care and feeding of his brood.

Hence a double transformation. On the one hand, primacy would be assured at less cost, in two ways. One was a modicum of disengagement from areas whose importance to the national interest could now be acknowledged as secondary. This was the meaning of the so-called Nixon doctrine, both a cover for "Vietnamization" and part of the incentives offered to China for Chinese-American détente. This was also why Africa slid even farther down the list of American priorities. The new policy offered the minimum reconversion of America's external commitments compatible with internal demands for change (and it was, therefore, more spectacular in Southeast Asia than in Western Europe), as well as the maximum reconversion compatible with the desire to preserve as much of America's predominance as possible (for the Nixon doctrine represented not a repudiation of commitments, but a redistribution of burdens).

A second way of reducing costs was a change in the instruments of primacy. There would be fewer overt military interventions, more covert action (as in Chile); less open advice to friends and allies as to preferred behavior (as in the days when European supranational integration was an American objective) and more "conditioning," i.e., moves aimed at placing others in situations in which they would act as one wished; fewer troops and bases, but more transfers of arms and investments (including in the white states of Southern Africa); less food aid and military assistance, more food and arms sales, to help America's balance of payments and to make buyers indebted to American banks.

On the other hand, a return to the primacy of horizontal relations also released the United States from some of the "servitudes" of camp leadership. Vertical relations provide the weak with fine opportunities for blackmail. Now the time had come for "a more balanced alliance with our friends," for "more equal partnerships based on a more balanced contribution of both resources and plans,"[19] i.e., for an economic offensive aimed at shoring up primacy by eliminating some of the advantages that the monetary system, or the concessions made by the United States to West European or Japanese commercial interests, had given to Washington's allies. Thus primacy was to be maintained by a combination of greater subtlety and greater toughness, two ways of restoring flexibility.

These changes of modalities had important effects for America's main alliances. On balance, America's grip was tightened, and the gains in flexibility the allies made were strictly subordinated to those of the United States. Insofar as the old goals of containment and primacy persisted, there could be no loosening of America's hold on its allies. Since the success of the new approach to the Soviet Union depended on Washington's ability to manipulate the incentives, Kissinger frowned upon Chancellor Brandt's *Ostpolitik*. He feared both that Bonn might make concessions to Moscow that could weaken the alliance and that Bonn might offer the Soviets economic rewards that would make Washington far less attractive to Moscow. The Japanese were kept in the dark about Washington's whisperings to Peking; the United States had to get there first. Since the success of the new approach also depended largely on America's might, there would be no question of allowing communism, however remote from Moscow, to progress in America's sphere of influence. In background briefings, Kissinger never concealed his hostility to Allende, who governed with communist support. In one's zone, one could not take the risk that there might come to power groups whose hostile beliefs might dictate their conduct. Here, indeed, Kissinger interpreted stability not as the separation between domestic policies and foreign behavior, but as Metternich had done: as requiring the domestic status quo. Moreover, since one knows the worth of what one has, but not the troubles something new might bring—for the best may be the foe of the good—there would be no tinkering with the shape of NATO, with the United States–Japanese treaty, or with the Organization of American States (OAS).

Insofar as there *was* a new policy on behalf of the old goals, it amounted to a multiple demotion of the Alliances, which resulted partly from the new ordering of priorities. The top of the agenda was now occupied by the search for the "stable structure" and the new triangular relationship. Yesterday, the Alliances were the stable structure, and, in the absence of an East-West dialogue, they had become almost a goal in themselves; now they were stepping stones to fruitful negotiations. Partly, the demotion was sharpened by the new nationalistic style: the return to an "American national interest" approach after years of an "interest of the free world." It was this style that pervaded the Nixon doctrine: a unilateral decision, not to reduce commitments, but to differentiate the way in which they would be carried out, according to a hierarchy of American interests. It was also this style that blossomed into an economic offensive on many fronts and at Western Europe's and Japan's expense. All these methods of demotion came together in Kissinger's famous "Year of Europe" speech of April 1973, in which—as had been implicit in his books—he sternly reasserted the priority of Atlantic concerns over a separate West European identity or over distinctive Japanese goals. There, he also made this subordination to common aims far more compelling, first by expanding the joint agenda (defined by the United States) to a whole new range of global issues, far beyond the original scope of the Alliances, secondly by demanding linkage from the allies and a quasi right of American participation in West European decision making.[20]

These changes in presentation, modalities, and style seemed to carry many promises in the world of the late 1960s. They seemed to draw shrewd consequences from the muting of the bipolar conflict by such factors as nuclear weapons, the quasi-universal legitimacy of independence, the heterogeneity of a world filled with stubborn local crises. The new diplomacy would allow the leading actors to return to relations of mixed interests. There would be flexible alignments again. Incompatible beliefs would not prevent temporary coalitions. Internal turbulence need not lead to international instability. Most importantly, an international hierarchy would reappear: diplomacy would again be the preserve of the major powers. Local shifts of power would matter less. The small nations would find security in the balance of power itself. Changes in the international system would again come from the diplomatic game, rather than from either the external fall-out of internal upheavals, or that nerve-racking *ersatz* of war in the nuclear age—crises in which the great play a risky game of chicken.

Whatever reservations Kissinger may have had about the post-1871 Bismarck, there was something neo-Bismarckian in this whole construction. To be sure, no power was comparable to the Soviet Union in Bismarck's constellation. But he had put Germany as the spider at the center of the web. France was to be both isolated and made incapable of seeking *revanche* by being carefully deprived of allies. Britain would not become France's ally, since Germany's self-restraint would avoid posing the kind of threat to Britain's security that might provoke such an alliance. An alliance between France and Russia, or France and Austria, or a conflict between Russia and Austria, were to be averted by having Germany allied both to Vienna and to St. Petersburg. In other words, even though Berlin's power was not overwhelmingly greater than that of its rivals, its position and the skill of its leader would allow it to play off the others.

In Dr. Kissinger's functional equivalent, the United States reserved to itself the management of the triangular relationship to turn it into a net of partly adversary, partly friendly relations, and he kept the allies from interfering by reminding them of the importance of the security function that tied them to the United States, i.e., of the residual hostility of the U.S.S.R. or Peking. The United States, on the other hand, could use the Alliances as stilts on which to tower over its communist rivals or over other blocs that might challenge the United States, such as the Organization of Petroleum Exporting Countries (OPEC), or the Group of 77 Third World nations. And the United States wanted to be the chief, indeed the sole, peacemaker in third-party disputes on its side of the great divide, while preserving its predominance in the world economy. Indeed, primacy presumed a reasonably passive, or docile, or dependent, or at least feeble Third World. The new triangular relationship, aimed at taming the rivals, also sought to diminish the attractiveness mischief making might have had for them in the Third World (a double calculation that helps explain why Nixon and Kissinger, by adopting, in 1969, "option two" of the National Security Study Memorandum number 39, chose to base their Southern African policy on the premise that "the whites are here to stay, and the only way that constructive change can come about is through them.")[21] It was breath-taking. And yet, one cannot forget Kissinger's two post-mortem remarks about Bismarck's cobweb: He made Germany so powerful as to provoke others into hostility, and his system was so complex as to be unworkable by his successors. "The very magnitude of Bismarck's achievement mortgaged the future."[22] The very magnitude of Kissinger's scheme defeated it in the present.

THE ART OF CREATIVE STATECRAFT

No evaluation of the Kissinger era can deal merely with the doctrine and leave out the methods. They, too, reflected his earlier ruminations and exploited the circumstances. As for his mode of operating, it reminds a student of French affairs of the style of General de Gaulle, another believer in statecraft as creative artistry. Abroad, as is well known, Kissinger—and Nixon—introduced on a grand scale maneuver, shock tactics, and surprise—the opposite from what one had come to expect from the highly predictable and heavy diplomacy of the sixties. Indeed, the issues Kissinger took into his domain, in the years before his appointment as Secretary of State, were those that lent themselves best to secret diplomacy: SALT, Vietnam, the opening to China. Even more important was Kissinger's preference for personal diplomacy, for dealing with statesmen whose trust he was eager to obtain, rather than with institutions. It was a choice that flowed from a quest for flexibility but also from his psychological gifts, his talent for patient persuasion, his art of making his interlocutor share his concerns and empathize with his plight. It was particularly suited to diplomacy with dictators, ruling monarchs, or presidents untroubled by checks and balances, i.e., the kinds of leaders one found among one's adversaries and in the Third World, although not among one's closest allies.

Another method of action abroad consisted in finding in each area a lever thanks to which he could try to move things. He used China as a lever for the transformation of the triangular relationship, he had hoped that Egypt could play the same role in the Arab world, he tried and often succeeded in getting Saudi Arabia to play a moderating role in OPEC, he chose Brazil as his point of anchorage in Latin America. And while his troubles with Europe in 1973 came partly from his failure to find a similar pivot among the Nine and his anger at being faced instead with the rigid and not very potent institutions of the EEC, in 1976 he found in Bonn, if not a lever, at least a brake capable of slowing down the European Community's inclination to accommodate, at least verbally, some of the more sweeping demands of the Third World countries.

Similar methods were applied inside. Here, Nixon's eagerness for control and Kissinger's fear of being controlled or tied down by the bureaucracy, converged. Nixon distrusted the State Department (and appointed a thoroughly unqualified friend to preside over it—which assured that it would do no harm yet provide no impetus). His Assistant for National Security Affairs was to be his own agent. And Kissinger's first concern was to neutralize the bureaucracy through a complex process of centralization that put him at the head of a series of high-level committees, which in turn either harnessed or pushed aside the regular bureaucracy. Whether at the White House or in the State Department, he surrounded himself with a small team of associates recruited largely from, and therefore familiar with the bureaucracy; and he saw to it that key positions in the latter be occupied by people close to him. A comparable attempt was made at captivating potential sources of domestic opposition or criticism and at gaining internal support, but once again it consisted of efforts at winning the minds of key influentials in the media or in Congress. It involved no major institutional effort; it concentrated on a few points in the vast system of relays or intermediaries that had formed the foreign policy Establishment and only on a few persons at each point.

To be sure, this method did not fit only the inclinations of a man who, by temper, because of the special character of his own history, and by deliberate choice, always preferred to be a lone actor moving above, and capable of darting in and out of, the heavy and intricate structure of American institutions—a gifted individual for whom it was always easier to serve other individuals through close ties of loyalty and service (for these ties, at least, left his creativity intact) than to serve bureaucratic or other establishments. It also corresponded to the circumstances: the splintering and demoralization, indeed the fading away, of the foreign policy elite, which no longer had to be nurtured, humored, and mobilized; and the new priorities of the public. The electorate was weary of the turmoils that had marked the whole postwar era, especially the sixties. The new policy, and the methods that made it shine, seemed to guarantee lower tensions, fewer commitments, better returns, without either humiliation or general retreat (except from Vietnam, but even there, without defeat). Both the promise of détente and the style of the new relations with the allies were popular, for they managed to convey both a prospect of peace and a pride of toughness—and the latter not with foes armed with nuclear weapons, but with friends engaged in economic competition and therefore more bothersome in daily life.

TROUBLES ABROAD

What were the problems that came to plague him? To begin with, the world scheme was too clever by half; by offering something to everyone, it contained contradictions that had to explode. There was progress on arms control, but also an expansion of arms sales abroad and of new weapon systems within; an offensive to free the United States from "unfair" burdens, but also tributes to (and stern reminders of the need for) allied solidarity; the negotiation of explicit codes of conduct with adversaries, but also the violation of at least tacit expectations about conduct among friends; a more aggressive pursuit of the national interest, but a search for stable structures. This could not go on forever.

Historically, one ought to separate three phases. During the first (1969–1970), things moved slowly. The United States had to resort to Vietnamization because the peace talks, public or secret, got nowhere. Relations with China were still frozen, despite United States hints for change, and relations with the Soviets were still tense, especially in the Middle East. A second, triumphant phase covered 1971, 1972, and the first half of 1973. There was the China "breakthrough." Linkages and nets appeared to succeed around the Soviet Union, which signed a new agreement on Berlin, accepted mutual balanced force reduction (MBFR) talks, held a summit in Moscow despite the blockade of Haiphong, and had to remove its advisers from Egypt because of Sadat's dissatisfaction with Russia's moderation. SALT I, the agreements of the second summit in 1973, and the Paris "peace" accords on Vietnam marked that period. A third phase began, ironically enough, as soon as Kissinger became Secretary of State, and it brought unending turbulence. The three problems that the new diplomacy had to face were: a recalcitrant world, a restive nation, and a flawed architect.

A Narrow Triangle Abroad, three kinds of difficulties must be noted. The new triangular relationship did not radically change the world. Its effects on the relation between Washington, Moscow, and Peking have been mixed. And primacy, however modernized, proved frustrating. First, Kissinger overestimated the impact of the triangular relationship on the rest of the world. The very reasons why the two main communist powers might have found the exercise of revolutionary policies abroad so difficult, also reduced the impact of improved relations between the great powers on the rest of the world. The great powers have found themselves caught in an iron dilemma. Tense confrontation projects their influence, and their instruments of intervention, all over the globe, but it also creates high risks and, as in any situation of incandescent bipolarity, it puts the mighty uncomfortably at the mercy of their clients. Yet better relations among the mighty, which reduce these risks and allow some "decoupling," also favor the emancipation of the others—those lesser powers that are always eager to justify their national ambitions with the argument that they are now being abandoned by their Protector, or else threatened with Condominium. Of course, Peking and Moscow could, if they wanted, "moderate" their most intimate or dependent clients. But like Egypt or Syria, some clients whose links with Moscow were bonds of interest rather than of ideological solidarity had their own games and causes. Insofar as the great-power confrontations were not ended by the détente, the old logic of "vertical" politics, i.e., the need for the major player to heed the vital interests of his allies, still applied. Moreover, the world was full of conflicts that were separate from the great powers' contest, even if their participants often took advantage of it. Soviet attempts to curb Sadat's impatience, in 1971 and 1972, did not make him change his mind; they merely cost Moscow much influence. If, by 1975, the Middle East appeared again more "moderate," it was not significantly due to the new triangular relationship. Nor did the latter have any noticeable impact on Cyprus, or any moderating one in the crisis over Bangladesh. And if the Soviets (and the Chinese) seemed to put pressure on North Vietnam in 1972, it was to get Hanoi to accept a tactical shift, yet toward the same objective as before. In Angola, the old logic of confrontation and commitment worked remarkably well to escalate a local conflict in

1974–1975. (The only innovation being that it was a triangular game this time, since the Soviets seemed to have reacted at first to China's involvement, and we later reacted to theirs.)

The whole realm of economic issues that also came to crowd the agenda was particularly independent from the triangular relationship, given Moscow's and Peking's absence from that particular scene. In the matter of nuclear proliferation, the improved relation between Moscow and Washington has not prevented several industrial nations from selling reactors or worse, as if these were mere commercial operations; it has indeed been used as a pretext by some for seeking independence in the realm of nuclear energy, peaceful or military. This relative, and troublesome, emancipation of much of the world, and of many of the issues, from the East-West drama does not mean that Kissinger was wrong in attaching great importance to changing its tone. As we shall see again, the difficulty and the originality of the international system lie in the fact that one can neglect neither that drama nor all the other aspects of world affairs; one can indeed argue that the multiplication of the latter is made possible by the very stability of the central balance. But if those who take this stability for granted are mistaken in believing that the world ought to be reformed as if the great-power contest did not exist, it is equally wrong to believe that the central balance shapes most of everything else.

The Misadventures of Détente: China   The second problem Kissinger faced in the world, the one that has produced the biggest flow of ink, was that of the misadventures of détente. Not only did the expectations about its impact on other relations and situations turn out wrong, but so did hopes about the transformation of the triangular contest itself. In my opinion, the charges about the vast price the United States has paid the Soviet Union in return for little or nothing are wildly exaggerated. SALT I "gave" the U.S.S.R. more land- and sea-based missiles, nuclear submarines, and throw-weight than to the United States, but Soviet programs were in full swing, the agreements left us with our advance in bombers and MIRV, and we obtained curbs in areas where they, not we, had on-going programs (ICBM's, submarines), while avoiding curbs in the areas where we wanted to stay ahead (such as MIRV, the Trident, and the future B-1). At Vladivostok, the cap put on the number of missiles and of MIRV-able missiles was the same for both sides. While this leaves the Soviets with their superiority in throw-weight, it leaves us with ours in warheads, with a huge payload from bombers, and with the possibility, should we decide to do so, to increase the throw-weight of our missiles rather than their range, as we had preferred to do before. Angola is not a matter of a deliberate American concession on the altar of détente, but of whether "sanctions" should have been used—a different subject, examined below.

It is hard to accept the view that détente, by providing a kind of Western endorsement for the Kremlin's leaders, discourages or weakens the forces of change in Russia; surely, they were not more potent in the days of the cold war. It is hard to see a sell-out in the Helsinki agreements (mostly attacked by those who have not read them). The West did not "recognize" the Soviet sphere of influence, it merely restated what was already in the United Nations charter and countless other documents—that force would not be used to change borders. The worst that can be said about these texts is that they are of little practical significance. But one should not neglect the symbolic meaning of some of the *verbal* concessions the Soviets made at Helsinki, with respect to military maneuvers or human contacts or exchanges of information; they can be sources of embarrassment for the Soviets and have been used by Soviet dissidents. Nor should one forget the interest of the East Europeans (including some of their own communists) in contacts and trade with the West, the only way in which the bars of their cage can be widened and some outside air let in. The scope of United States–Soviet economic exchanges is not yet such as to make one fear that our credits and technology actually play a major role in shoring up Russia's economy and in allowing Moscow to transfer more resources into the arms build-up. The wheat deal of 1972 is the one legitimate example of an outrageous agreement; but its rotten aspects are not the fruit of Dr. Kissinger's desire to appease Brezhnev; they are the result of a series of narrow concerns of Agriculture Secretary Butz. The problem is not what we have "given away"; it is rather, what have we, and the world, received?

In the case of China, the grand shift of 1971–1972 was a fine example of reciprocity. We did take advantage of all that had doused China's revolutionary fires: domestic priorities and the overwhelming fear of the Soviet Union. The rapprochement allowed China to replace Chiang's representatives at the United Nations, to obtain Washington's acknowledgment (if not outright recognition) of the "one China" principle with respect to Taiwan, and to gain a kind of diplomatic protection against Soviet pressures. The United States gained, in the short run, some cooling of relations between Peking and Hanoi, justification for a further enforcement of the Nixon doctrine, and, in the long run, both a valuable asset in its dealings with Moscow and a lever for consolidating the alliance with Japan, which Peking clearly wanted to remain in America's orbit. But there have obviously been obstacles to any deepening or strengthening of the relationship. One lies in the thorny problem of Taiwan. A closer tie with Peking depends on the jettisoning of America's diplomatic bond with Taipei, on the Japanese model. But, partly at least for electoral reasons, partly for more serious ones, the United States has been slow in moving. Japan does not have a defense treaty with Taiwan; we do. China cannot give up insisting that *we* give it up. Its leaders may be willing to keep their anti-imperialism war-cry from guiding their actual policy, but they cannot cease screaming it, and in this instance, concerning the integrity of China's territory, it is indeed more than a cry. We cannot drop the treaty without an explicit commitment by Peking to resolve the dispute with Chiang's heirs peacefully—a most unlikely prospect. We could, as some have suggested,[23] replace the treaty with a unilateral guarantee and continue to provide Taiwan with military supplies; but China is unlikely to deem this move satisfactory, unless Chinese-American relations have much improved generally.

But here we meet two other, and in my opinion more serious, obstacles. They too concern the relation between the domestic scene and foreign policy. One is the uncertainty of political succession in China. Kissinger had relied on Chou En-lai, and on Mao, with whom he had established a strong connection. After Chou's death, the brief demise of the man who had been Chou's heir, the death of Mao, and the purge of the radicals, the course of Chinese domestic politics is unclear. All factional battles in the past have had a foreign policy component. There are many objective reasons for continuing distrust between Russia and China. But China need not remain in a situation of quasi-total enmity with Moscow while the United States is the only one of the three players who can speak to the other two. This is a link with the last obstacle.

Something of a misunderstanding arose between Kissinger and his Chinese counterparts—or rather, the 1972 Shanghai communiqué concealed a deliberate ambiguity—that cannot persist forever. The United States was eager to establish a triangular balance; its relation with each of the communist giants would help improve the relation with the other. Still, its main target, or potential "partner," was the Soviet Union, given its might and the scope of its ambitions. China was used, so to speak, to "soften up" Moscow (which had proved to be rather obdurate in 1969–1970). The United States was, of course, aware of the usefulness of the Peking-Washington rapprochement for the containment of Soviet designs in Asia, or even in Africa, but it was not trying to enlist one more ally for a containment of Russia in the style of Acheson or of Dulles's pactomania. And yet, especially during Chou's illness, it appeared that the Chinese were interested in a kind of alliance against the U.S.S.R. Indeed the way in which they have encouraged the West Europeans to coalesce militarily and politically, their advice to the Japanese, their more discrete winks at Israel despite their ideological pro-Arab line, their ceremonial enthusiasm for hard-line politicians from the Western world, all showed that they favored a kind of world league against the social imperialist power—I would almost say a Holy Alliance, except that in this instance the domestic make-up of the allies seems to the Chinese a matter of sublime indifference (Pinochet's Chile could be included), as long as they all have the same foe. Mao's invitation to Nixon, so shortly after a rather bland visit by Ford, and not so long after a Soviet-American deal at Vladivostok, i.e., on China's border, made the point perfectly clear, and in a very Chinese way (for the hosts deliberately forgot that Nixon had launched détente with Moscow, just as the Chinese leaders, in their celebration of Stalin to annoy and oppose Khrushchev, had closed their eyes to Stalin's mistreatment of the Chinese Communists). It is difficult to see how this misunderstanding could have been avoided, except by a different Chinese policy, less expressive of China's own ideological stand on the matter of Soviet deviationism. But if the United States, saddled with the problem of Taiwan and eager to preserve a dialogue with Moscow, continues to be deaf to China's hints, a Chinese attempt, some day, to put some distance between beliefs and behavior by improving official relations with Moscow would not be surprising. Indeed, it would be in the best traditions of *Realpolitik:* if you cannot get an ironclad protection against your main foe—putting him, so to speak, in a straitjacket—try to increase security by decreasing tension.

The *Misadventures of Détente: The Soviet Union* The troubles of Soviet-American détente stem from a comparable ambiguity. The two sides have been making contradictory bets about the future, as well as acknowledging one obvious truth. The interest of both in regulating the strategic arms race is clear. An unregulated race spells, at worst, the risk of one side's breakthrough, at best, the spending (for more weapons than are needed for pure deterrence and even for fighting war, if one accepts the idea of a counterforce nuclear war) of ever-more huge sums of money to preserve the central balance. The contradictory wagers deal with everything else. The Soviets seem to have bet that détente will actually help them consolidate their camp—directly, through economic aid in the form of trade and credits, indirectly by allowing for some increase in resources available for consumer goods. They have bet that détente will "soften" their enemies by favoring forces for social and economic change inimical to the United States and by putting domestic rather than external priorities on top of their rivals' agenda. The leaders of the United States have placed their hope in the gradual breaching of Russia's autarky by the establishment of links that would amount to Soviet "dependencies" (Helmut Sonnenfeldt's expression), and in a Western ability to "impose a degree of discipline"[24] on the Soviet Union and to introduce the outside world into the Soviet policy process (his analysis of the more recent grain deal). Thus we would create a Soviet interest in moderate behavior in exchange for the benefits such dependencies would bring.

Now, in the first place, this analysis suggests something that thwarts the original Kissinger doctrine. If one area is of overriding mutual interest, it is unlikely that progress in it will be subordinated to progress elsewhere, or that setbacks elsewhere will be deterred by or punished with a threat to stop progress here. To be sure, the United States has the theoretical capacity to outspend Russia in the arms race, but before an unlimited race brings the U.S.S.R. to its knees—a doubtful proposition—the United States would suffer at least as serious domestic turbulence from such a shift in resources as the U.S.S.R. (One would soon hear modern versions of the old Republican warning that the arms race was a devilish *Soviet* way of bleeding the United States white!) In other words, as an instrument of political blackmail, as well as a set of military means, nuclear weapons simply are not very usable. This already dents the linkage theory and weakens the notion of the net (for the Soviets know that they can, at least in some ways, try to limit the size of the net or even to break out of it without risking a collapse of arms control).

In the second place, insofar as the strategic arms race is concerned, progress has been slowed by two factors that are more durable than the effect, in 1976, of Mr. Reagan's rhetoric on Mr. Ford's determination to persist. One is the tendency for technology to run ahead of diplomacy. No sooner has a weapons system been finally regulated than a new one emerges that requires further, and often drastic, reconsideration of everything. The other is the asymmetry of the two nuclear forces. This makes it more difficult to reach an agreement (each side has a different reason for fearing an enemy first-strike aimed at its land-based missiles: the United States, because of superior Soviet throw-weight, the U.S.S.R., because a far larger fraction of their force than of ours consists in such missiles, and our weapons have greater accuracy). It also makes the acceptability of an agreement by the United States more difficult, since each asymmetry incites the kind of "worst case analysis" that starts with a demand for "essential equivalence" (a fuzzy concept), continues with a request for fearful symmetry and in fact ends as a drive for "high-grade deterrence," a catchword for superiority.[25]

In the third place, the Soviet bet appears today to have been more vindicated than America's. Critics of détente point, of course, to the tightening of repression at home that has followed the Helsinki finale—an argument often made by Solzhenitzyn. Clearly, it has not turned out perfectly: in basket three (human rights) of the Helsinki Agreements, the Soviets had to pay at least a symbolic price for increased economic and scientific cooperation with the West, and both this price and the exchanges, however limited, have created some turbulence at home and in Eastern Europe. For the world outside the Soviet zone, they show, on the one hand, that *after* the second Nixon-Brezhnev summit (June 1973) it becomes pretty hard to find any evidence of Soviet moderation of conflicts in which Russia was directly or indirectly involved. There is evidence of moderation in the earlier phase, *before* the agreements that the Soviets needed were signed—SALT I, with its recognition of parity; the trade and credit deals; Helsinki, with its acceptance of the division of Europe. In order to get there, Brezhnev had offered to hold MBFR [or at least Mutual Force Reduction (MFR)] talks, he had concluded the Berlin negotiations, limited arms sales to Egypt even as Washington was selling phantoms to Israel, displeased and pressured Hanoi. But later, the Soviets certainly neither stopped Egypt and Syria from attacking on October 6, 1973, nor warned the United States as the letter of the June 1973 agreement on the prevention of nuclear war suggested, nor failed to resupply their clients. The North Vietnamese offensive of March 1975 rolled on with Soviet equipment. Initially at least, Soviet aid and advice to Cunhal's Communists in Portugal were loud and open. And Soviet support for the Popular Movement For the Liberation of Angola (MPLA) and transportation of Cuban troops there demonstrated both the fact that its considerable effort at conventional rearmament now allowed the U.S.S.R. to project its power abroad in a way that once was an American monopoly (one thinks of Russia's meager attempt to help Lumumba in 1960) and the assurance with which the Soviets now dared escalate a local conflict in order to have their side prevail. This was something only the United States had done successfully when it treated the Berlin crises as direct United States–Soviet tests, not as an intra-German or a Soviet–East German matter, for example, or when Kennedy treated the Cuban missile crisis as a Soviet-American duel and not as an issue involving Cuba at all.

To be sure, none of these cases is clear-cut. Could Moscow have stopped Damascus and Cairo without ruining its influence there? Was it conceivable that it would, so to speak, squeal on its clients to Israel's advantage? Was the resupplying effort all that massive (once the war started, could one expect Moscow to wait passively until the Israelis had turned the tables once more?). Had we not, in 1973, provided Thieu with far more equipment than Hanoi received from its big brothers? Didn't our own mismaneuvers in Angola provide the Russians with a spectacular opportunity they would have had to be saintly to resist (just as we did not resist ours in the Middle Eastern diplomacy after October 1973)? The trouble is that the defenders of détente certainly cannot prove that there was Soviet restraint. To point out that neither in the Middle East after October 1973, nor during the Cyprus crisis did the Soviets try to disrupt American diplomacy is unhelpful, for it did a fine job of disrupting itself in the latter case, and in the Middle East one can argue both that Soviet opportunities were poor and that Soviet strategy consisted in waiting for an American fiasco, or for the moment when Soviet participation could no longer be avoided.

In other words, plausibility seemed to be on the side of the critics; the burden of proof weighed on the defenders, and they were embarrassed. As Theodore Draper has remarked,[26] to reply, as Kissinger and Sonnenfeldt have often done, that détente could in no way stop the Soviets from increasing their might, which is true, provokes one into asking what détente is for. And to suggest that its purpose is precisely to help us cope with Russia's new global policy induces one to ask either what the difference from the old containment is, or, if there is one, how one can prove its effectiveness. At a minimum, one must note the discrepancy between our original doctrine of détente, and the Soviets' notion, expounded by Georgy Arbatov, which distinguishes between the sphere of intergovernmental agreements (the proper domain of détente) and the sphere in which "social forces" compete—a highly elastic division, which has the double quality of being most un-Marxist (aren't governments the expression of dominant social forces?) and most artificial in a world in which struggling social forces receive hefty support from foreign governments.

The American wager was in trouble becase of the flaws of the linkage and net theory. To state that "for us détente is indivisible"[27] is doubly dangerous. One, if linkage does not succeed in making it so, if our rival seeks cooperation selectively, we are then faced with a difficult choice: either we accept limited détente (and aim for mutual concessions within each area), or we refuse and thus return to the minefield notion of world politics. It is a choice between fragmented progression, and regression.[28] Throughout the cold war, we had in fact learned to make peace, or war, divisible. A crisis in one spot may have been resolved through the fear of nuclear escalation, yet it did not *ipso facto* provoke geographical escalation, or, if you prefer, it did not automatically spread to other spots. Was it not a bit absurd to expect détente to be more contagious? Second, the chances of making detente indivisible through linkage are slim. It is easier to impose linkage on an ally than on a foe. Allies huddled together against a peril can be asked by their protector to sacrifice some economic gain to the maintenance of their protection; it is much more difficult to get a comparable handle on an antagonist, and indeed all Western attempts to use Russia's need for grain, or Russia's and Eastern Europe's greed for technology, as a way to get concessions in the realm of European security, for instance, have been half-hearted or futile.

There can be voluntary linkage by the other side when it is eager to get something in exchange: hence Soviet moderation on Berlin, for instance, in 1971, or the acceptance of MBFR leading to a Western endorsement of the Conference on Security and Cooperation in Europe (CSCE), or the delicate balance of Helsinki's three "baskets." But a rule of the game among equals is that such linkage must not seem imposed: witness the effects of the Jackson amendment tying economic benefits to Jewish emigration from the U.S.S.R. Moreover, it is difficult to play linkage with totalitarian powers, for it is an essential part of their strategy to separate the benefits they need to buy from the penetration the benefactor wants. The benefactor is therefore faced with a choice: either try to impose linkage and be rebuffed, as happened to Senator Jackson, or else retreat, either by explaining—in contradiction with one's own dogma—that the counterpart of the service one was rendering (such as increased Jewish emigration) would come later, if all went well and quiet diplomacy prevailed, or by resigning oneself to the absence of linkage, thus making each deal strictly on its merits (in economic matters, project by project); which singularly restricts one's leverage. Finally, linkage is made more difficult by the fact that on each issue, a separate domestic constituency develops, which objects to being treated as a pawn in a global log-rolling game.

Just as serious is the problem of incentives and sanctions to obtain good behavior. Political incentives are limited. Once the United States and its European allies acceded to the Soviet wish for a CSCE, that particular goad was used up. Swaps are not conceivable, precisely because the contest continues, and neither side really wants to obtain the other's moderation in one area by making concessions in another. It did not occur to us to "grant" the Soviets a decisive role in Angola in exchange for their quasi exclusion from Dr. Kissinger's Middle Eastern peace process. The most effective incentive is economic. The granting of the most-favored-nation clause and of credits, the sale of grain, or of plants and equipment, even the stationing of engineers—all things badly needed by the U.S.S.R.—have undoubtedly created a minimum of Soviet "dependency," in the sense that a Soviet decision to return to autarky (as had happened twice before) would be much more costly. Economic cooperation with capitalist countries has led to some strains between the U.S.S.R. and its East European allies, insofar as Western trade with them reduces their dependence on Moscow. Soviet oil exports outside the Soviet bloc, essential for obtaining the hard currency needed to pay for imports, have had the same result. Soviet "dependency" has allowed the United States, after the bad experience of the 1972 grain deal, to demand and obtain terms that introduce some order in the grain market and entail the spending of Soviet hard currency (as in the grain deal of 1975). But there are strict limits to this "dependency" and to Western penetration. We have nibbled at our own carrot with the Stevenson amendment on credits and the Jackson amendment on most-favored-nation status, and Moscow's predictable reaction to it. Soviet exports remain limited both by their nature ("Soviet sales are usually spot deals"[29] or parts of barter deals, like the accord with India in December 1976) and by the lack of hard currency, which leads to an increasing trade deficit and to a Western dilemma: Either limit trade with the U.S.S.R. (thus slowing the recovery from the recession as well as weaving a looser web), or finance one's own exports with credits. Moreover, the eagerness of some of our allies to grant credits, sometimes at low rates of interest, and to increase sales to the U.S.S.R., seems more likely to profit the Soviet economy than to make it dependent, precisely because the Russians can then choose and spread their deals among their clients.

Since there has been rather little "good" Soviet behavior, and since we do not reward but rather exploit the little that exists (as in the Middle East), we are therefore left with the punishments. But we have found no more sticks than carrots, and our sticks have turned into boomerangs. We could threaten to suspend the MBFR talks, but this would not hurt the Soviets and might actually create some trouble for us, since one of our hopeless objectives in that charade is to obtain a "balanced," i.e., more than proportional, reduction of Soviet conventional forces. A unilateral suspension by us might provoke a rash of proposals, here or in European countries, for unilateral reductions. We were in no position to threaten military retaliation in a situation such as Angola's final ordeal, given the mood of Congress and the memory of Vietnam. Indeed our last-minute attempt at raising the ante only exposed our bankruptcy. Again, we are left with economic sanctions. But American industrial trade and credits are just not big enough to be decisive, and the Soviets could always turn to other clients. We have asked our OECD allies to coordinate their East-West trade with ours,[30] but their own need for exports, often much bigger than ours, and their growing dependency on imports of Soviet raw materials (such as natural gas), promise to make this exercise in American leadership as painful as some others. As for the one item the Soviets have indeed desperately needed, to the extent of preferring massive imports to domestic restrictions—grain—the very determination of American farmers to sell it and thus to increase their profits has deterred our leaders from using this particular threat.

The grain deals teach us some lessons about the notion of a net. We have to be satisfied when we reach an agreement in which the Soviets merely agree to buy our wheat in such a way as not to disrupt the market (note that the oil deal we sought was discussed independently). This may "discipline" them, but it scarcely changes their economy. To be sure, growing economic ties would increase Soviet concern for a measure of stability in world affairs: foreign trade is part of Soviet planning. This is far from negligible. But there always was some naïveté in the belief that trade would be the royal way to changing Soviet conduct—and we are back once more at the connection between domestic structure and foreign policy. Trade and credits that do not force modernization and decentralization of the Soviet economy run the risk of helping it and are not likely to be large enough to create a real dependency (although they may help introduce some greater predictability in international economic relations, not an insignificant objective). Trade and credits that would oblige the Soviets to give far greater importance to consumer demands, and to reform their whole system, would raise two contradictory problems. First, why would a hideously centralized state, in full control of its faucets, let itself be forced to keep open the one spigot that might flood everything it has been trying to achieve? When we deal with economic structures, we deal with the very core of the system of power. The U.S.S.R., after all, is not comparable to the countries of Western Europe. It has no commitment to an open economy, and the level of its transactions with the market economies remains low. Second, even if we should succeed in forcing some changes, can we be sure to gain sufficient "control over the direction of Soviet economic development,"[31] so that the main beneficiary of improved productivity would not be the Soviet Union? Will trade with capitalist countries lead consumers to demand freedoms along with goods, or will it only make it easier for the regime to gain public support and to train efficient technicians? A risky gamble, to say the least, for who can say that an "interdependent" but efficient Soviet Union would not be a more formidable, albeit more moderate, competitor?

The greatest irony has been our creation of a web in which *we,* not they, are entangled. The trainer of the bear has been caught in the net he has woven. Our businesses rush to Moscow and offer terms that sometimes amount to a subsidy by the American taxpayer. Our eagerness to sell, and thus to help employment and growth at home, makes us grant credits to cover the Soviet and East European trade deficit with us. Our farmers look at the Soviet market with greed. To some extent, even our leaders could not acknowledge much disappointment, since they had made the triangular relationship the heart of their policy. Even though punishment for bad behavior is an integral part of the concept, it becomes, in a democracy, embarrassing to administer, since the punishment would be seen as evidence of the policy's failure to induce good behavior! The Soviets can conceal fiascoes or concessions and boost their own "sanctions." America's position is exactly the reverse.

Détente undoubtedly has advantages for the United States. Not only does it allay the psychological obsession with the East-West conflict that immobilized containment diplomacy, but it also makes needed cooperation possible within East-West relations, for instance, on the control of the strategic arms race and nuclear proliferation. And while economic cooperation has both limited prospects and some real dangers, mutual advantages can be expected: some help to Western economies and a raising of the cost of autarky for the Soviet economy in exchange for the help it receives.

But the U.S. has made two serious errors. Détente was oversold, especially by Mr. Nixon. Nothing could have been more misleading than the fatuous agreement of June 1972, by which the two parties proclaimed that they were giving up claims of special influence in the world and attempts to exploit tensions to gain unilateral advantages. Even life-long drinkers occasionally try to stay on the wagon, but great powers rarely give up playing international relations. After all, what has the United States been doing in the Middle East since October 1973? And the theory of linkages, incentives, and rewards was flawed. Therefore, in the final months of the Kissinger era, official rhetoric staged an elastic retreat.

There was no longer any talk of linkage. The notion of rewards and sanctions was preserved, however: "The policies pursued by this Administration have been designed . . . to build a pattern of relations in which the Soviet Union will always confront penalties for aggression and also acquire growing incentives for restraint."[32] But Arbatov's distinction was now matched by Kissinger's own two-track theory. We need "a dual policy that simultaneously and with equal vigor resists expansionist drives and seeks to shape a more constructive relationship."[33] Confrontation *and* negotiation: the difference with the original doctrine lies in the muting of the hope that negotiation would have results sweeping enough to make confrontation unnecessary, in the recognition of the fragility of détente. Kissinger himself listed a whole series of ways in which "Soviet actions could destroy détente."[34] There is another difference. Earlier, Kissinger had explained that the very stability of the central balance made the quest for marginal gains futile. Why seek to control gray areas whose addition to one's sphere would in no way provide one with any decisive advantage? Later, the Secretary realized that "the strategic balance provides increased opportunities for regional pressure." Since strategic forces are not directly usable, and since "a perceived strategic gap would have only marginal political benefit," "regional balances gain more significance."[35] In other words, there is no end to mutual testing and challenging. Therefore, while "the reality of competition" may "illustrate [the] necessity" of coexistence,[36] one is back at the disheartening inability of containment to carry one to any promised land. And if confrontation remains a permanent necessity, if détente is more like Penelope's tapestry than the spill-over theory of regional integration, what happens to the legitimate world order and the stable structure of peace? If West European Communists are assumed to push policy in the direction of their beliefs, what about Russian Communists?

The Headaches of Primacy   What, in the third place, did the world do to Kissinger's new approach to the preservation of our primacy? While claiming that we were transforming the American world system into a pluralistic "structure of peace," we were merely tinkering with its mode of operation. In some areas, he was successful (although at a cost, to which I shall return). The alliances with Western Europe and Japan survived the shocks of 1971, and the political crisis that followed the "Year of Europe" speech was resolved, to America's advantage, when the Europeans—with France first resisting, then consenting—fled into the American shelter during the oil crisis. After the quarrels of 1971 and 1973, all alliance meetings had turned into lovefeasts by 1976.

Nevertheless, there have been three recurrent headaches. One has been America's difficulty in preventing or solving conflicts between third parties. Here, the record shows three fiascoes and two frail successes. In two instances, the United States found itself on the losing side of the battle (and the U.S.S.R. exploited our weakness). In the Bangladesh affair, we first failed to put any real pressure on Yahia Khan when he started massive repressions in what was still East Bengal, and we continued to arm him, while his men ravaged the rebellious province. Concerning Angola, the Nixon administration began by relaxing the ban on the sale of weapons to the Portuguese and the South Africans. In the rivalry of Black Angolese forces, we kept supporting—in somewhat desultory fashion—a faction that had never been capable of winning. When, early in 1975, reacting to limited Soviet involvement (itself seemingly stimulated to a large extent by Chinese support for "our" side), we began to increase our help (partly at the request of, or in order to reassure, the Chinese), we only provoked the escalation of Moscow's aid to the MPLA. When, in July 1975, we mounted a large covert program (partly in response to "moderate" African states), we found ourselves on the same side as the Republic of South Africa. We gambled on a military stalemate, rather than seeking a political compromise before the defeat of our clients. Such a stalemate would have required Soviet restraint. Instead, the Soviets, eager to ensure the MPLA's control by the time the Portuguese were to depart, mounted their massive lift of Cuban forces. As a searching analysis has put it, "to insist upon defining the Angolan issue in global terms" (once the Soviets and Cubans intervened on a large scale) "to the exclusion of local and regional terms . . . was to exclude the most plausible means of remedying the conditions which had attracted foreign intervention in the first place. And to insist that the only 'chips' were military chips was to play from the weakest suit in the American hand."[37]

If in these two instances Kissinger demonstrated the impotence of military might (in situations where these means were either wrong or necessarily too constrained to be effective), in the third fiasco he demonstrated remarkable political denseness. In the Cyprus crisis of 1974, we first failed to stop a Greek coup aimed at ousting a Cypriote leader whom we did not like but who had kept a precarious peace. Then we failed to prevent the Turkish invasion which that coup had made likely. In 1964 and 1967, United States warnings had deterred the Turks, and the crises could be handled at relatively low or middle levels of diplomacy. In 1974, the Greek coup removed Turkish restraint, and, in the climax of Watergate, the Secretary of State at first could not stop a determined Turkish government incensed by his failure to condemn the coup, and, later, chose not to try very hard to stop the second and more decisive Turkish onslaught—which provoked a spectacular reaction in Congress. Thus, we compromised our alliances with both Greece and Turkey.[38] In all three instances, American mistakes can be attributed in part to Kissinger's exaggerated stress on the connection between the local situation and the great powers' contest, his estimation of the effect a "bad" local outcome might have on the balance of influence between Washington and Moscow (a self-fulfilling prophecy), and his overconfidence in America's capacity to obtain a "good" result. India was Russia's ally; the MPLA was receiving Russian aid; Makarios was distrusted as a breed of neutralist hostile both to our Turkish friends and to the Greek colonels, our allies. Tilting toward Pakistan only helped turn India's victory into a Soviet gain (as happened again when we came to the rescue of the National Front for the Liberation of Angola, the FNLA). American control of the Eastern Mediterranean had no impact on the Cyprus tragedy. In all three instances, we miscalculated the local circumstances—as if we had learned nothing from Vietnam.

The frail successes were achieved by Kissinger in the Middle East after the October war and in Rhodesia after Angola. In both cases, he did exploit favorable local circumstances. In the Middle East, by seizing upon the new, approximate equilibrium of gains and losses between Israel and its foes during the war, the desire of Arab countries for technology and economic progress, and the dependence of an isolated Israel on its American protector, he was able both to reinstall the United States into much of the Arab world and to use this reinsertion to bring some parties a little closer. In Rhodesia, the very fiasco of Angola served as a paradoxical springboard. The fear of more Cuban and Soviet meddling became a common ground for the white regimes in Salisbury and Praetoria and for the more moderate black neighbors of Rhodesia. The worsening economic situation of Smith's government, the prospects of guerrilla warfare, and the assurances Kissinger gave Smith to induce him to accept the kind of plan he had so often rejected before did the rest. But the rest—Smith's conversion to majority rule—was riddled with ambiguities, and, among his adversaries, the radicals had not been neutralized. Thus, by the end of 1976, both here and in the Middle East, all remained in suspense, reversible or (in Rhodesia's case) already unraveling.

A second headache has been a direct challenge to American primacy from a thoroughly unexpected direction: the nations of the Third World. During the months when the triangular relationship seemed to be shifting in the direction Kissinger wanted, there had been much speculation about the advantages (for us) and the dangers (for them) of America's "decoupling" from nations that were likely to cease being important stakes in a muted competition.[39] The grievances occasionally formulated by Third World representatives (or by Western intellectuals who had appointed themselves its champions) were treated with nonchalance. So far was Washington from expecting a challenge, that American officials at first had no objections to, and indeed found good reasons for, a gradual increase in the price of OPEC oil. It would stimulate more exploration to relieve the "shortage" of oil; it would boost the companies' profits; and it would lead to OPEC (especially Saudi) investments in the United States, thus helping the balance of payments.[40] But the offensive that started with the Arab oil embargo, continued with the quadrupling of the price of oil, and unfolded with the claims of Third World countries in a variety of conferences, showed that these nations had many ways of forcing us to pay attention besides reminding us of their strategic value or of the harm they could inflict either on us or on the balance of power if they went over to the other side. Kissinger's reactions varied and changed over time. But for all kinds of reasons that will be noted later, he was not able either to appease the challengers or to blunt the offensive.

What is at stake is more than American primacy. Insofar as there had been a "stable structure" of world economic order after the Second World War, it was a structure created by American primacy. The Third World offensive proved, first, that this order was no longer "legitimate" (what could have been more "revolutionary" than OPEC's moves?) and second, that the chances of establishing a new legitimate order were poor, because in this realm the behavior of nations, industrial or poor, tends to reflect either their ideologies or their domestic needs. Moreover, the persistence of the Soviet-American contest, and the very quest for American primacy, led Kissinger to court and assuage Third World states whose support he deemed essential, yet whose behavior did not contribute to the creation of any "stable structure." Clients such as Brazil and Iran may ratify our political and military primacy, yet their nuclear and energy policies challenge our economic predominace. And if Saudi Arabia seems both to confirm the former and to want to help us maintain the latter, it is not without extorting quite a ransom from the West both insofar as arms and oil prices are concerned, nor without resorting to blackmail in the Arab-Israeli dispute.

The third headache of primacy concerns the preservation of a favorable balance of influence in various parts of the world. Influence is not just a function of military might; it cannot be preserved merely by American military preponderance in the area. It can be affected by economic trends— the political and social effects of recession or inflation. Above all, it can be challenged by political and social developments of a purely indigenous nature, especially by the rise to power of anti-American, or even non–pro-American forces, whether these are communists tied to Moscow, or communists with loose ties to Moscow, or groups that are not communist at all.

Against such threats, neither the resort to military action nor the appeal to the old rallying cry of anti-communism can serve as a panacea. Sometimes, as in Chile, subversion, a combination of external sanctions, and help to internal opposition can bring the "threat" to heel. But—as in Vietnam—it all depends on the local conditions. Events in Portugal and Italy have shown, for all their temporarily (or reasonably) happy turns, that alliances, even shored up by decisive action on the international scene (such as Kissinger's moves in 1974, especially at the Washington conference on the oil crisis), can be undermined from the inside. Ominous threats, such as those President Ford and Kissinger uttered concerning Portugal's participation in NATO,[41] or the presence of United States forces in Europe, can be double-edged and are of uncertain effect.

Once again, one observes the perverse, or at least ironic, effects of détente policy: Far from moderating crises that involve other nations, it may be "destabilizing" insofar as it reduces the fear of communism, or else leads to a slackening of ties between Moscow and local communists (which improves their image and chances), or helps dissolve conservative regimes or coalitions that had drawn part of their power from the cold war. Once again, the impossibility of separating domestic choices from foreign policy behavior, or an international structure from the domestic structure of its members stares one in the face. In fact, in his remarks to American ambassadors in London in December 1975, Kissinger himself dwelt on the evil foreign policy consequences of a "Titoist Italy": a demotion of security issues and unwanted repercussions on NATO and on European neighbors.

There are two reasons why beliefs and behavior cannot be disconnected; both have to do with the relations between the domestic scene and foreign policy today. One, in most countries, foreign policy is in the hands, not of a professional elite often closer in mores and methods to its counterpart across the border than to the rest of its own society, but of men or groups with a distinctive ideology, which may be an ideology advocating an ideal social order, or one that demands a specific international order. (One might indeed ask whether the golden ages in which the transnational elite of diplomats existed were not, either the prenational era before 1789, or, in the nineteenth century, the very brief period between the demise of the Holy Alliance and the new rise of nationalism following 1870.) As a result, the "common code of conduct," insofar as it is more than a transcription of the mechanical operations of a balance of forces, can be only either a deliberate compromise between ideologies or the expression of a dominant one. Two, foreign policy today deals with the external aspects of domestic economic and social issues. One's diplomacy expresses one's internal needs and demands, and, the human mind being what it is, these usually come wrapped in creeds. Hence Kissinger's predicament and the contradiction between his call for a pluralistic "legitimate" order accommodating change in the world and his interpretation of NATO as a kind of Holy Alliance based not only on a common interest in external security, but also on a common constellation of political forces. Indeed, both his failures and his successes in the business of preserving American primacy show an obsession with stability, which puts him far closer to Metternich than to his own criticism of the Austrian statesman, and also quite close to his predecessors' policy. Détente and the new triangular relationship were supposedly to allow the United States to worry more about the designs of its equals than about the tantrums of the pygmies. And yet, even after Vietnam, the United States, in "destabilizing" Allende's Chile and in trying to help its friends in Angola, in submitting to South Korea's corruption and espionage in the United States and to Marcos's blackmail over our bases in the Philippines, in supporting the colonels in Greece, and in sustaining the Republic of South Africa (indeed in using it as a lever in Rhodesia, while proclaiming that it "cannot be regarded as an illegitimate government"),[42] showed that the old equation of stability, anti-Communism and pro-Americanism had survived intact. Metternich's excuse was the fragility of his country, its desperate dependence on the status quo outside. Is the social and political order of the United States equally brittle and tied to conservatism everywhere?

The Limits of Mastery Within

If the world proved unwilling to fit a Procrustean bed built on nineteenth century specifications, the nation, in the Watergate and post-Watergate phase, did not make the pursuit of Kissinger's foreign policy easier. Here again, he was faced with three main problems. First, the new style of foreign policy, the somewhat jingoistic new celebration of the national interest opened the way to a whole series of pressure groups that had remained subdued in the previous era: economic interests eager for protection from foreign competition, a labor movement that was turning away from liberalism out of fear of job scarcity and distaste for multinationals, also ethnic groups—such as Greek-Americans and Jews—determined to be heard whenever American policy went against their passions and their transnational solidarities. As long as the cold war had dominated the agenda, little had been heard from many of these groups, or else, as in the case of the Jewish community, its pressure reinforced official policy, or (as in the Suez crisis) was overcome or deflected by cold war considerations. This was no longer the case. With the cold war no longer clamping the lid down, the pot overflowed.

Second, in his attempt to pursue a complex policy of détente, Kissinger ran into congressional interference. Kissinger, obviously supported by Nixon, had done little to establish a new consensus (see Section Two). This was a misreading of the American political system, of twentieth century foreign policy in any democracy, and of the American mood after Vietnam. For Vietnam had not only destroyed the old consensus, it had also put the government under suspicion. The public and the Congress (was it a psychological device for self-exoneration?) had convinced themselves that deliberate obfuscation, the machinations of the corporate establishment, the arrogance of elitism, had got us into Vietnam (there had been deception, to be sure, but more cosmetic than fundamental; the war was not unpopular, at first). After this, no administration could have asked for "basic trust" for very long. Therefore, it was not surprising that Congress would react. Senator Jackson used "linkage," and he ended breaking an incentive. Congress denied sticks at crucial moments. I shall return below to the significance of this revolt, which far exceeds the dimensions of détente. It compounded the difficulties of the new policy in two ways. It upset the delicate manipulation of diplomatic tools that this kind of a diplomacy required. This raised the question of whether something as difficult as the reestablishment of a "legitimate" world order in a profoundly troubled world is possible without either an almost heroic delegation of authority by Congress, leaving to the Executive the choice of the means and moment (an arrangement incompatible with the American Constitution) or else a previous and thorough agreement between the branches; in other words, domestic legitimization first (see Chapter 5). Moreover, congressional insubordination led to a nationwide discussion of détente, which, although it shook up mistaken assumptions and destroyed delusions, nevertheless—as often happens—overshot the mark and served as a peg on which the most diverse oppositions to or hatreds of Kissinger's person and policy could hang, so that the debate produced far more heat than light.

Third, in one of his attempts at damming the post-1973 flood, Kissinger started defining a policy toward Third World demands that was to some extent ahead of the public. Opinion at large, Congress, business circles, and the Treasury had been neither prepared for nor convinced by the grand attempt at conciliation signalled by the Secretary's speech written for the United Nations General Assembly and delivered by Mr. Moynihan on

September 1, 1975. An irony lies in the fact that the gap between Kissinger's proposals, and the demands of even nonradical developing states, is even wider than that between him and much of the public. And the gap between the public and the Secretary, over so essential a stepping stone toward future "legitimacy," was widened by the antics and popularity of Kissinger's own representative at the United Nations, Mr. Moynihan, whose boisterous pugnacity also overshot the mark. To denounce the hypocrisy and inconsistencies of many Third World attacks on the United States, or the dangerous nonsense of the anti-Zionist resolution, was one (good) thing. To counterattack by denouncing the domestic regimes of some of these nations was far more debatable, not only because skeletons also hang in the closets of the "free world," but also because all Western powers ought to be cautious in the public humiliation of former colonies. To treat the United Nations Charter as a Western liberal document, to use it as a stick with which to beat nonliberal states, and to describe them as fools or dupes of the totalitarians, was hardly diplomatic—not merely in the sense of polite (although there can be no "code of conduct" without some politeness, which means, alas, some restraint on the awful truth)—but also in the sense of effective.[43] In any case, he fed a certain predisposition of the public to dismiss Third World theses as preposterous or as barbaric concupiscence for the hard-won wealth of the industrial West.

PERSONAL FLAWS

The appointment of Mr. Moynihan, a self-inflicted wound, raises the question of Dr. Kissinger's own flaws. The troubles he met in the world and at home were not all his making, although, as we have seen, his moves often worsened them. But other troubles were entirely his own. Some of these affected his domestic base of support. The reliance on a very small number of people, both within the foreign policy machine and outside, sacrificed solidity to immediate efficiency, to the tactical flexibility that was so fervently desired. (Here we are very far indeed from Professor Kissinger's strictures about the need for long-term planning.) At best, these people brought him devoted and competent service, but at much cost. Not only were often equally competent persons left to brood or churn papers in the bureaucracy; but Kissinger displayed a tendency to listen only to reports that confirmed his view of a problem. And, as his hold over foreign policy grew, he often overwhelmed dissident views held elsewhere (such as in the Treasury or Agriculture Departments). Overwhelming is different from convincing, however, and as a result several of his proposals, in

North-South issues, were either half-baked, insufficiently prepared abroad because of a need for secrecy at home (such as the proposal for an International Resources Bank, presented to and rejected by the United Nations Conference on Trade and Development (UNCTAD) meeting at Nairobi in May 1976), or insufficiently backed by other Departments.

Sometimes, as in the case of Senator Fulbright, key influentials suddenly disappeared or, in the case of the Ninety-fourth Congress, found that their influence had been swept away. At worst, as in the case of Mr. Moynihan, the man who was probably supposed to provide a rhetorical cover for Dr. Kissinger's strategic retreat on North-South problems—to throw up tough talk while the boss laid down soft action—Kissinger's cleverness backfired. In the contest of prima donnas the Irishman beat the Bavarian. Running so closed a shop, so concentrated an office, inevitably did little to replenish the drying pond of the foreign policy elite. And when, on land, silence was superseded by high turbulence, Kissinger found himself in possession of too few transmission belts. He had relied heavily on the chumminess of the media. But there is a great danger in turning diplomatic performance into stardom. The popularity of stars is fickle: one flop, and they are out. Moreover, when the currency is power, not image, sooner or later journalists rebel against being used as conduits. Between them and stars, the latter's agents usually serve as buffers. Between them and Kissinger, stood no intermediary. He had taken all the credit when things went well. He got all the blame when they went badly. Of course, in the last year of the Nixon presidency and the years of President Ford, the very vacuum at the top made Kissinger into the most eminent figure. But precisely because of the dangers of such a concentration and personalization of power, he should have resisted his instinct for the limelight and followed his promise to "institutionalize" his foreign policy. He did the opposite. By doing so, he provoked a formidable counteroffensive not only from the media but also from those whom he had pushed aside and who hungered to succeed him. Denigration and discontinuity were the price of his lone dominance.

Concentrated Power, Fragmented Roles We now reach those flaws that affected Kissinger's action abroad. First, that very concentration of power left him with one unbeatable enemy—time. I wrote some years ago that even his days had no more than twenty-four hours, except when he criss-crossed time zones. His mode of operation forced him to take up many issues only when urgency rang, busy as he was with all the intricate details of his dominant concerns. As a result, he paid inadequate attention to problems that later exploded, such as Cyprus or Southern Africa, or relied on improvisation—such as, it seems, the Year of Europe speech and much of the Angola policy in 1975, or the Rhodesia policy of 1976. Nor did he always parcel out his time in the most sensible way: Was all that shuttling in the Middle East indispensable? What happens to other issues (such as SALT II, or the China policy, or indeed Angola) when the Secretary has to haggle over hills and inches?

Here we get into a second problem. It concerns his multiple roles. He was chief adviser to the President, chief policy maker, chief coordinator, chief supervisor of enforcement, and ultimately chief public spokesman, always top negotiator in an era of multiple negotiations. Not only was it too much, but it created conflicts. The biggest of these was that between the negotiator and the foreign-policy maker. Both in the last phases of the Vietnam negotiations (October to December 1972) and in the Middle East, he tended to get caught up in the bargaining. Sometimes, this made him waste time and thus precious opportunities to extend his strategy to other fronts (such as Jordan, while he was bogged down in Syria-Israeli arguments). Sometimes, it made him so eager to conclude that he either underestimated larger difficulties (October 1972), or used drastically over-blown means of pressure in order to force things to an end (the Christmas bombing of 1972). Sometimes it made him so eager to be sole master of the process that his desire for secrecy led him to discount a formidable obstacle (Thieu, in October 1972), or to weaken his official negotiating team and get a worse deal than could have been obtained (as in SALT I),[44] or to dismiss a valuable team (that which had negotiated much of SALT I, in prolonged ignorance of his "back channel" with Dobrynin).

Diplomatic Methods   The prevalence of the negotiator over the policy maker, and even over the "conceptualizer," has had another consequence: the prevalence of tactics over strategy. Here we reach his diplomatic methods. It is not only in the Middle East that he was the champion of the step-by-step and that this choice raised serious questions.[45] Relentless as a critic of past administrations' errors, ambitious but ambiguous as a strategist of innovation, he was cautious and curiously shortsighted and "pragmatic"—a quality that used to find little favor with him—in his more specific suggestions as a writer and in many of his moves as a political dealer. Three examples can be given. In the negotiations on SALT, it remains arguable that the bargaining-chips theory, used to justify first the Safeguard program of ABM, then the development of MIRV, then that of the Tridents, the B-1 and the cruise missile, really did more harm than good. Incentives to agreement are necessary, but the threat of launching a major program if no accord is reached can be just as effective, indeed more effective at getting results at a lower level of absurdity—coming from a nation that remains ahead in sophisticated technology—than starting a program as a prod to agreement. For the latter amounts to actual escalation, and one is thus faced with either having to negotiate a deal that merely restricts the further waste of resources, that will then be called a "political breakthrough" even though it is merely a belated revenge of common sense, and whose discussion will have wasted precious time taken away from all the other aspects of the arms race; or else, as in the case of MIRV and now cruise missiles, failing to stop a genie while it is still in the bottle.[46]

A second example comes from the Vietnam negotiations, where it took extremely long for Washington to clarify to the North Vietnamese its decision not to request them to pull out of the areas of South Vietnam they had occupied. (Although we do not know whether this "concession," if made earlier, would have been matched by the North Vietnamese acceptance of Thieu's temporary survival, as happened in 1972, it would have been worth trying.[47])

Most serious is the case of the Middle East after the Kippur war. Much can be said for Kissinger's initial decision to try limited progress, given the complexity of the Arab-Israeli conflict and the mood in Israel. But it soon became apparent that—as in the case of détente—hopes for spillover, or snowballing, had not materialized; that each negotiation, far from softening the protagonists further, tended to harden them, especially Israel; that almost as much energy had to be spent on wresting a few miles of sand, or heights, or words, than would have been lavished on a far bigger settlement; and that the exercise ended up as a gigantic game of hide-and-seek, in which all the fundamental issues—the future of the Palestinians (the key to a solution), the location of the borders, the terms of Arab recognition, Jerusalem, guarantees—were being postponed. Each negotiation was like the old Chaplin short in which, desperate to earn some money, Charlie sells his services as a snow clearer to the inhabitants of a row of houses and piles the snow removed from each house's entrance onto the snow accumulated next door. As Edward Sheehan has written, tactical success became a goal in itself.[48]

Two effects followed. One, as already noted, was the neglect of opportunities that lay outside the current framework. The other was that the exercise became not merely futile but counterproductive. After the Secretary's failure in the March 1975 negotiation with Israel and Egypt, and his threat to reconsider United States policy, he decided not to change the pace and the scope, but to try again, now that the Israelis had been sufficiently softened up by the threat of a reappraisal. And while he thus obtained genuine political concessions from Egypt in the disengagement agreement of September 1975, this deal, which did not, in effect, amount to an Egyptian decision to drop out of the conflict, not only had to be paid by deeper American involvement and "a moral, monetary and military cornucopia"[49] for Israel, but also sounded sufficiently like an Egyptian defection to provoke Syria's hostility at a moment when, in any case, no second Syrian-Israeli deal could have been obtained. The split in the Arab world that followed, Syria's moves toward a "greater Syria" policy, the Lebanese imbroglio, the radicalization of the Palestinians (both those living on the West Bank and those fighting in Lebanon), the Syrian gradual control of Lebanon, all this, while giving a breathing space to Israel, and perhaps opening new Arab prospects for accommodation, nevertheless also created the conditions for a new war after Arab reconciliation, did not improve (from Israel's viewpoint) the conditions for a settlement, left the Jewish state with a far stronger neighbor on its northern side, provided time for the disintegration of the Israeli Labor government and the rise of the Likud, and began to chip away at the Israeli-American and Egyptian-American relationships. As in the Vietnam debacle, it looks like *reculer pour mieux sauter.*

Kissinger's Middle Eastern policy brought out two more flaws in his methods. One was his general distaste for high risks. He has been unwilling to try, when he was not sure, or even almost sure, of success. He was, of course, right in believing that timing is the secret of success and that dealing with deep-seated conflicts before the apple was ripe enough to fall could mean fiasco. Disputes are not like fruits, however. A ripe apple is better than a green one. A ripe dispute is usually poisonous. Nixon and Kissinger did not, in 1969, give Secretary Rogers the support that could have made his "plan" for an Arab-Israeli settlement less hopeless. In 1973, when both the Egyptians and the Saudis asked for American diplomatic intervention and the latter threatened to use oil as a weapon, no action was taken, except the sale of Phantoms to Israel, even though the election year was over. Kissinger was concentrating on Europe and on the next summit with Brezhnev, and he misjudged the "ripeness" of the Middle East. The same desire not to move too soon can be found in his Rhodesian policy and to some extent in his approach to the Third World in 1975. But in the Middle East, this meant waiting for a war that had, through its effects on oil, disastrous results for the West; in Southern Africa, waiting until after Angola; in North-South affairs, waiting until the Group of 77 had consolidated its front.[50]

Another flaw can be found in Kissinger's tendency to dramatize, thereby putting pressure on a reluctant partner (or foe), which is then usually followed by a compassionate climb down from the high horse and a celebration of harmony reborn. This tactic can be effective as a short-term trick, but it leaves scars even when it does not take the form of the Christmas bombing. In his dealings with Western Europe, thunder from Olympus fell twice: in the Year of Europe speech and at the Washington conference of February 1974, before the grand reconciliation marked by the innocuous Declaration on Atlantic relations of June 1974. In the Middle East, it was the web of off-the-record yet highly publicized complaints by Kissinger about Israeli obdurateness, and the official reappraisal of April-June 1975, that served to heighten tension and suspense. In the North-South drama, it was the period in which Kissinger dramatically summoned the other industrial powers into a common front, launched the International Energy Agency, spoke about the risk of military action in case of "economic strangulation"—and thus set the stage for the subsequent attempts at accommodation. Kissinger was not alone in using such a method. Nixon applied it twice to Japan (over textile imports and during the soybeans embargo), and Nixon and Connally used basically the same technique at Japan's and at the Europeans' expense in August 1971. What matters is not that the trick managed to squeeze concessions from the other side. What matters is that distrust was sown each time.

Possibly more seriously harmful is one of the substantive devices employed by Kissinger to gain time for settlements or, indeed, to strengthen strained or shaky ties. Arms sales to clients became a sort of panacea, a way of keeping both sides of the Arab-Israeli conflict, as well as all sides of the Persian Gulf, if not happy, at least dependent on the United States. In 1974 and 1975, the United States sold, loaned, or gave more than $10 billion of weapons to other nations, as much as the Soviet Union, France, and Britain combined, and compared with $1 billion in 1961.[51] It is certain that an American decision to restrict such sales would not in any way solve the problem of arms proliferation. But one need not feed the flames. Moreover, such practices contradict the quest for a stable world order, even if one believes that one condition for stability is a set of regional power balances.

Providing Israel with the most advanced weapons (even without the Pershing missiles) is a dubious gamble on Israel's greater readiness to exchange concessions for such security and an incentive for the Arabs to find comparable weapons for the eventual battlefield—for instance, from Saudi Arabia, stuffed with American missiles and smart bombs. A comparable inflation of weapons took place in Iran and was promised to Pakistan, Zaïre, and Kenya. Forcing the oil-rich (and those whom they subsidize) to recycle their petrodollars by acquiring United States weapons, making states that are mutually hostile feel sufficiently self-confident about security to envisage even the possibility of bargaining, shutting the Soviets out of certain areas, or reinforcing our friends who feel threatened by Soviet arms expansion may all be valid in the short run. But what could be a prelude to order if each nation merely stalemated its rival, could be a formidable incentive to explosion.

Style versus Substance Finally, the same contradiction existed between the diplomatic style of Henry Kissinger and his quest for "stable structures." A "stable structure" requires at least three elements. At the foundations, one needs states or groups of states sufficiently self-confident, and provided with sufficient leeway, to be willing and able to contribute to the management of the system. The Nixon-Kissinger dealings with allies, until and including 1974, deprived them of confidence and leeway. The European Economic Community (EEC) has not recovered from the joint shocks of the oil crisis and of American haughtiness, including Washington's unwillingness to let the Europeans play a diplomatic role in the Middle East or Cyprus, its decision to preempt the common energy policy and to be the chief strategist for the industrial powers at North-South meetings. (And while Kissinger's indignation at the Europeans' behavior during the October war had its justification, so was their complaint about past American complacency both in the Arab-Israeli conflict and toward OPEC.)

A stable structure also requires relations between states that do not depend, exclusively or primarily, on personal ties between passing statesmen. But the style of Kissinger's diplomacy (including his way of leaving American ambassadors in the dark and of making promises to or reaching "understandings" with foreign statesmen, who then expected deliveries and developments that never came) made for more confusion than stability. The ambiguities that marked his deals (the Vietnam "settlement" or his agreement with Ian Smith) might have been harmless only if his writ had been unchallengeable and permanent at home. Since it was not, the deals often ruined his achievements.

Thirdly, a stable structure requires institutions—such as, precisely, the EEC. Kissinger's style (and the style of Mr. Nixon and Mr. Connally), either undermined established institutions [such as the International Monetary Fund (IMF)], whose director was sacrificed to Washington's displeasure and whose role was affected by the demise of the fixed-rate system), or ignored or even interfered with their attempts (weak enough) at coalescing, whenever we deemed it dangerous (as in the case of the United Nations or the EEC). Bilateralism was the order of the day. Brazil was singled out in Latin America; it was with Bonn, not Brussels, that the United States position at the UNCTAD meeting in Nairobi was worked out. But if mechanical balances of force do not suffice, if common beliefs and common voluntary practices are needed, only international institutions can turn these into programs. True enough, at the end, Kissinger rediscovered some virtues of even the United Nations, celebrated NATO, and blessed European unity; but it was a bit late. There now was talk of multinational fuel-cycle centers and the beginning of a collective approach to the problems of nuclear proliferation. But it came after years of "benign neglect."

It is this combination of miscalculations, unexpected upheavals, domestic obstacles, and personal quirks that have defeated the original design. The key question never found an answer: on what common principle of legitimacy could all the nations of this world agree? The balance itself might have been not merely a mechanism but a creed for the post-1815 diplomats, as Kissinger suggested (but never spelled out) in his book; self-determination may have been the principle in 1919—and it did not exactly lead to a stable order. But today? The quest for order is understandable—it is what any responsible foreign policy is about. But the American conception of order has remained welded to the idea that military confrontation among the great powers is the principal peril. Kissinger was right in seeking a "breakthrough" with our chief rivals. Yet the very cataclysmic character of any prospect of nuclear war among the major states makes other perils more immediate. Kissinger's policy has put on the United States a dubious burden and a dangerous blinder: the burden of teaching others who may not want them the rules of our preferred game, the blinder of neglecting problems that simply were no part of his universe. Before his era, we were told that the world was a single minefield and that we had the responsibility of seeing that no mine blew off. Although Kissinger told us that the time had come to clear out the mines, we were still taught that we were the pacesetters in global self-restraint. Moreover, his style undermined its very achievements.

One is forced to conclude that Henry Kissinger had a road map, but one that failed to describe the real terrain; and he himself often strayed from it, because of his character. And yet, one must add that he reacted to fiascoes with flexibility and resilience: as a man who learns and does not give up. Abroad, he tried to cope with each crisis as it happened. In Western Europe, he attempted to stop communist progression through peremptory warning; in Africa, through a rapprochement with the aspirations of Black African nations. In North-South relations, he shifted from the "consumer front" to dialogue. In East-West relations, he reshaped his theory and consequently restored the priority of Alliance relations, as was shown by the various moves toward tighter economic cooperation (at summits or at OECD), by closer military coordination with Japan, and by a new emphasis on America's need of "a sense of identity and collaboration with other nations who share its values."[52] Even primacy had been renounced, at least in words: "What we have attempted to do was to guide American foreign policy in a period of transition between a time when American strength was preeminent and a period when America will have to conduct foreign policy the way most nations in history have had to conduct it."[53] At home, the "lone ranger" became a tireless speech maker and educator. Even his style evolved: he attended meetings of international organizations and gave up, by necessity, shock tactics and secrecy. This endurance, a gift for focusing the whole force of his incisive mind and all his skills of persuasion on the issue of the moment, and a sense of power that remained intact allowed him to go on, apparently undefeated. But there has been no "State of the World" message since the spring of 1973. After trying to encompass and shape the world, he was, for more than three years, busy keeping the world from sweeping him away. He was still afloat. But his creativity had to be spent on holding operations and on making it easier for his successors to open doors he had only unlocked. His was the loneliness of the short-distance runner. There was no more design. And yet, beyond both his skills and his flaws, he left a double legacy: the priority of the concern for world order (even if it cannot be established according to his ideas and by his methods) and the intuition that it requires the exploitation of mixed interests among states (even if this cannot be turned, as he had tried, to the sole benefit of American primacy).

SECTION TWO: CONDITIONS ON ARRIVAL

In order to judge the state of American foreign policy at the end of the Kissinger era, and to examine the legacy, I will ask the same four questions as for the containment era.

THE STATE OF WAR

The difficulty of assessing power today makes evaluating America's position in the world competition hazardous. How, for instance, can one evaluate the effects on America's position of the rapprochement with China? It does not add to Washington's military capabilities. But because it strengthens the Washington-Tokyo tie, incites China even more to give precedence to anti-Sovietism over general anti-imperialism or aid to Marxist revolutionary movements, and injects extra caution into the North Korean regime, the entente between Washington and Peking, for all its limits and misunderstandings, has improved America's standing in the global contest for influence, which is different from the balance of force. True, the solidity of this improvement depends on the Chinese regime's domestic future and its external calculations, but then any balance sheet of the contest is temporary, any balance of influence fragile.

Let us take a closer look at the relations of power and influence between Moscow and Washington. The Soviets' exceptional effort to increase their military might during this cycle of eight years has led to much speculation. Are they aiming at superiority over the United States? The same factors that explain the American side of the arms race probably account for the Soviets': interaction—in this instance, the will to catch up with the United States so as never to be humiliated again, to break the American monopoly of long-distance interventions, and possibly to provide Moscow with "at least a major edge, if not a decisive edge, in terms of conventional capabilities" on the periphery of the U.S.S.R.[54]—plus traditions, comparative advantages, and bureaucratic pressures. In the nuclear realm, Soviet progression at a time when the American quantitative (but not qualitative) effort had stopped, first led Washington to accept "sufficiency" instead of superiority. Today, there is a heated American debate between the anxious and the confident. The former invent doomsday scenarios: Russia's throw-weight advantage could allow Moscow to destroy America's land-based missiles in a first strike and to keep enough launchers to destroy American cities should the United States retaliate against Soviet urban centers with its bombers and submarine missiles. Their opponents, beginning with Kissinger, reply that United States "strategic forces are superior in accuracy, diversity, reliability, survivability and numbers of separately targetable nuclear warheads. We have a commanding lead in strategic bombers."[55] There has been controversy even over the respective throw-weights[56] and over the degree of vulnerability of American intercontinental ballistic missiles (ICBMs) to a Soviet first strike.[57] The worriers fear that the coming addition of MIRV to Russia's throw-weight advantage might allow Moscow to exploit its superiority either for political gains or, militarily, at levels below the nuclear one (as the United States did in Cuba in 1962). Their critics reply that "new increments of weapons or destructiveness do not automatically lead"[58] to such gains, and that past a certain level superiority brings nothing. Unless the Soviets find a way of neutralizing United States nuclear submarines (whose range keeps expanding) and of making themselves—without antiballistic missiles (ABM)—impenetrable to bombers, they cannot hope to knock out an enemy whose retaliatory force is to a very large extent invulnerable; capable, especially if accuracy keeps improving, of hitting targets other than cities; and able to kill or cripple through radiation a large portion of the Soviet population despite the civil defense effort allegedly undertaken by the Soviets. One is led to sympathize with Kissinger's exasperated reply to a question: What in heaven's name is superiority, in this realm? Thus, the balance sheet is inconclusive, but certainly not disastrous.

It is equally inconclusive for conventional forces, but for a different reason. Here is clear asymmetry, but Russia's undeniable advance may be both partly illusory and reversible. It is obvious in tank production and in the construction of surface ships.[59] But not all the men usually listed as Soviet soldiers are actually assigned battle missions, and the addition of East Europeans to Soviet troops obliterates the essential question of the former's loyalty. United States naval power remains superior in aircraft carriers, tonnage, fire-power range (essential for sea control), amphibious capacity, and numbers of available bases. Above all, Washington has a considerable advance in new precision-guided weapons capable of revolutionizing conventional war, and, if they do not give a decisive advantage to the defensive, they at least return some assets to it, in the unceasing but ever-changing race between the offense and the defense.

To judge the degree to which Soviet military progress has affected the balance of influence, one must examine each area separately. Moscow has gained points in several regions. One is Southeast Asia; but while Saigon collapsed sooner than many Americans expected, the alarmists have not been proven right; dominoes have not fallen outside Indochina. In Eastern and Southern Africa, the United States pays above all the price of deliberate and protracted support for the white regimes in the area and for the conservative Ethiopia of the late Negus. In Somalia, Mozambique, Angola, and later Ethiopia, Russia has fully exploited this opening plus, in 1975, the "no more Vietnams" mood of Congress and the American public. Soviet troubles in the Horn and the reentry of the United States into the fray through the new Rhodesian policy have not yet redressed the balance. The problems of the Republic of South Africa are likely to remain a huge thorn in our side and an opportunity for Moscow, even if Rhodesia's fate should be settled peacefully and by "moderates." That same art of pouncing on the adversary's errors has allowed the Soviets to push American influence back in the Indian subcontinent. To be sure, as Indira Gandhi's rapprochement with Peking already showed before her demise, India is nobody's satellite. But even after her departure, Washington is still far from the days of Kennedy's warm rapport with Nehru, and from the quasi alliance during the Sino-Indian border war.

Elsewhere, American influence is in trouble, but it is not the U.S.S.R. that gains; today's competition is not a zero sum game. We have lost much influence in the Eastern Mediterranean drama; America's loss has, however, been limited by the anti-Soviet inclinations of both the new Greek and the Turkish governments. In Western Europe, the scene is more bizarre. The rise of the left, which disturbed Dr. Kissinger, does not seem to create great enthusiasm in the Kremlin.[60] In Spain, Italy, and even France, the communist parties assert their heterodoxy, not merely on matters of internal behavior (pluralism, intellectual freedom, democratic elections, and the like) but also on matters of defense and foreign policy. The European communist conclave in East Berlin in July 1976 sounded more like a farewell than a reunion. And the West European communists are giving a bad example to their East European comrades. Mr. Sonnenfeldt's famed remarks about the dangers created by the absence of "organic" links between the Soviet Union and Eastern Europe only confirmed the interest both superpowers have in immobility in this part of the world. The Soviets, blunt as ever, rely on military occupation and on a tight net of economic dependencies. The United States and the West European regimes that share its outlook rely on their wealth and on the threat of withholding aid to Italy if the Communist Party should reach the only level of power—the cabinet—to which it yet has no access (and which also happens to be Italy's weakest). Washington has asserted that the evolution of the West European communists could be worse for it than for Moscow. Mere ideological discomfort causes, in our officials' view, less pain to the Soviets than the discomfort produced by active anti-Americanism or neutralism in power would cause to us, should the communists come to power in Western Europe. But Moscow may well be making exactly the opposite bet. A smooth integration of Western communists into the political systems of their countries could be a worse blow to the Kremlin than to Washington; one of the grievances of the French Communist Party against Russia's is Soviet support for Giscard!

In two areas, the American record is clearly positive. One is East Asia. There has been no war in Korea, and Japan's alliance with the United States is now accepted even by a sizable fraction of the internal opposition—which compensates for the decline of the Liberal Party. Here, the United States has taken advantage of Russia's intransigence on the subject of the islands taken away from Japan and its excessive demands for economic cooperation in Siberia. The Soviets have braked their incipient détente with Tokyo, and Tokyo has tilted toward Peking, with Washington's blessing. In the Middle East, as of today, two powers, Israel and Egypt, have put all their eggs in the American basket (a temporary gain, a future headache). The holder of the Arab pursestring, Saudi Arabia, leans on Washington out of anti-communist hatred and economic advantage. Syria, armed by Moscow, maneuvers with Washington's tacit consent. Jordan, a bit neglected, has used gentle blackmail to confirm its armored bond with Washington. Here, Washington has pushed Moscow aside, thanks to Kissinger's exploitation of two huge assets. Only Washington can bring Israel to compromise; Moscow can help the Arab world wage war, but Washington will always prevent any decisive victory. And the United States is in the best position to provide Arab countries with the technological and economic aid they need. To be sure, the returns are not all in: America's game is a gamble on the possibility of a "legitimate" settlement. Arab fragility and divisiveness, Israel's rigidity and toughness, support for Israel in United States opinion and Congress could destroy that possibility, and the U.S.S.R., in no hurry to pour oil on the cinders, seems to wait patiently (but not passively) for the American gamble to fail so that it can spread its influence again.

Nevertheless, the Middle East shows some of America's assets in the world contest. Today's international competition is not reducible to the Soviet-American duel, nor limited to the arena of diplomacy and strategy. And, in the economic arena, the United States has two assets. In bilateral relations the Soviets' main tool of power is military—they can send large amounts of arms to their clients and can now show the flag in much of the world. They can also provide economic assistance but not in vast quantities, and thus they choose to concentrate it. The United States can both match, and indeed surpass, Soviet weapons transfers if it chooses to meet Moscow on the Soviets' preferred terrain and resort to economic aid on a scale and of a kind Moscow cannot equal. We have a double advantage in this respect, and, so far, greater demand—more states still turn to us for aid than to the Soviet Union.

Moreover, economic relations are not limited to bilateral interstate transactions. As a market economy, we can play a much larger role than Moscow in multilateral economic relations (still shunned, to a large extent, by the Soviets) and an extensive role in private transnational relations from which the planned economies are absent. Thus, here again, we have a double advantage: our resources—precisely those that make the U.S.S.R. dependent on grain imports from the United States and eager to buy the latest American technology—and America's presence in all organizations, negotiations, and markets. The United States may not be able to break Soviet autarky and force the Soviets to compete on world markets. But the need for American life-jackets felt by all those who *do* swim in the stormy waters of the international economy, and the preference expressed by most of the new states for such a swim rather than for autarky as the best way toward development, give the United States possibilities that Russia does not have. Moscow would gain them only if it modernized its civilian industry and thoroughly transformed its agriculture. But such reforms, as well as full Soviet participation in the world economy, might, in the long run, destroy the regime's foundations.

PATTERNS OF ORDER

World order, as we have seen, was the great, if vague idea of Kissinger's reign and allegedly the highest priority. Clearly, the new triangular relationship did not help enforce the design. The Big Three have not succeeded in defining a scheme of world order acceptable for all three and capable of accommodating their ideological differences. There have been two additional causes of failure. The United States itself, despite its commitment to stability, has not contributed to it either through its leaders' methods or through its substantive moves. And above all, the capacity of any or all the great powers to shape the content of world order has been curbed by the autonomous and turbulent rise of all the others.

Regional attempts at order have made little progress. The OAS has shown growing resistance to Washington, and several of its members want to organize without the United States. Kissinger reacted with a mix of bilateralism and proposals for institutional reform. The record of the EEC has been poor, both because of growing differences in the economic situation and the policies of its members following the oil crisis and the recession, and because most of the issues with which they are concerned cannot be solved within the framework of the Community, whose capacity for autonomous action has been shrinking drastically. The OAU has been racked and almost wrecked by its members' fights over Angola, the fate of the former Spanish Sahara, and the future of Djibouti. As for worldwide order, there has been only one small advance—one that tried belatedly to curb a major peril of regression: the beginning of a common nuclear export policy by the leading and potential exporting countries. But this attempt at slowing down the spread of nuclear weapons remains precarious.

The United Nations has stopped playing the world order role once assigned to it by American preferences. Here is a dramatic change. On the one hand, resort to the United Nations as a buffer or fire extinguisher has become rare since 1967; the days when one dreamed of generalizing United Nations Emergency Forces are far away. United Nations soldiers are stationed on the Golan and in the Sinai, but the direct involvement of the United States is more important than these forces. Washington has lost control of the General Assembly. The resolutions adopted by it under the leadership of the Group of 77 underdeveloped countries are more remarkable for their ideological effervescence than for their capacity to create a balanced world order. Mr. Moynihan's imprecations, Mr. Waldheim's modest role and discrete warnings, reveal how much has changed. Between 1946 and the early sixties, the typical alignment had been the coalition between the United States, its automatic allies (including the states of Latin America), and most of the new nations, sometimes against the colonial powers, sometimes against the U.S.S.R. and its allies. Today's typical coalition is that of the Third World (including many Latin American countries) and the communist states against the liberal industrial powers.

Most interesting have been the tribulations of the economic and monetary order. They began with American efforts at making it serve more closely the immediate interests of the United States, not at destroying it. United States exports were suffering from allied competition, partly because of American inflation and the overvaluation of the dollar, partly because of a decline in American competitiveness. Unemployment was rising. The deficit of the United States balance of payments had resulted in an accumulation of dollars held by the allies, hence a threat to America's gold reserves, should these nations have wanted to reduce the overhang. Capital was fleeing. In order to improve the situation, American actions exploited the basic economic strength of the "rogue elephant in the forest,"[61] the dependence of its allies on United States military protection, the quasi-universal need for United States technology, the role of the dollar in international settlements. What Nye and Keohane[62] term the underlying power structure was called upon to wipe out the weaknesses of America's current structure of influence. To reshape world order, Connally and Kissinger moved in three directions. They changed the rules of the game (through the August 1971 decision ending the convertibility of the dollar, unilateral imposition of a surcharge on imports, and subsequent devaluations), obtained new rules (i.e., floating rates) deemed superior because they preserved America's earlier advantages without further exposing the United States to costly constraints, and prevented the adoption of new rules that would hamper the freedom of action of American enterprises (concerning the exploitation of the seabeds and the two-hundred-mile economic zone between the territorial sea and the high seas).

Far from reshaping world order to American specifications, these moves have resulted in a series of disruptions. Two important lessons have emerged. First, action by the preponderant power risks chaos. Floating exchange rates may have allowed the industrial powers to cushion the effects of the oil crisis and recession. However, they do not constitute a regime or a lasting monetary order, and they have helped cripple one attempt at partial monetary order, the poor European currency "snake." Moreover, there is the risk of setting a bad example, of giving others ideas, of contagion. The United States is not the only power that can unilaterally exploit key assets in order to get better rules of the game. Although the rules of trade among advanced industrial nations, while a bit dented, have managed to survive Mr. Connally and to prevail over the protectionist temptations induced by the recession, the rules of North-South relations and indeed the economic prospects of the oil-poor developing nations have been ravaged by OPEC's decisions and by their snowballing effects. True, the catastrophes predicted in 1974 did not occur. The interdependence of economies, America's smaller dependence on oil imports by comparison with Japan and Western Europe, what could be called the Washington-Riyadh axis, the interest OPEC countries have in investing in the United States and in attracting American investments, above all the recession itself, which reduced oil imports, the tensions between rich and poor states in the Third World, all this has allowed the United States to keep turbulence from turning into tempest and to organize recycling. Still, the old rules have collapsed, and no "new international economic order" is in sight.

The second lesson of these years is that even a power as well endowed as the United States can no longer shape world order by itself, even by defining its interest in an enlightened way, taking into account the special concerns of its allies and clients, and rewarding them for participation. In other words, not only did the attempt, in 1971, to practice esthetic surgery on the features of economic order, to replace the old lines that expressed a concept of the long-term interest with new, narrower, and more aggressive ones, not work, but the earlier idea that the preponderant economic power can be hegemonic as long as it is not too selfish or exploitative no longer works either. Hence the reaction—polite but unenthusiastic—of most of the developing countries to the proposals made, from September 1975 to May 1976, by Kissinger on North-South relations. At the General Assembly, at Nairobi, at the conference on the Law of the Sea, he tried to take their interests into account: hence his proposal for a dual system of exploitation of seabed minerals, for an International Resources Bank facilitating these countries' access to capital markets, his acceptance of generalized preferences, his endorsement of the idea of stabilizing the income derived from the export of primary products, and so on. But on commodity agreements, on debt reduction, on the link between special drawing rights and aid, on the key question of the South's share in the decision-making process (at the IMF, or at the World Bank, or in the new institutions being proposed), the content of his offers has remained slight. As a result, even initiatives that aimed at accommodating the new demands seemed more geared to improving the safety of investors and the exploitation of Third World resources in the interest of the advanced countries, than to improving the capacity of the developing ones to reach their own economic objectives or to gain a greater say in world affairs.[63]

We have moved from the age of supremacy based on one nation's enlightened interest to the age of compulsory bargaining and compromise. This does not mean abdication: the final deal will certainly have to reflect in part the assets of relative preponderance. But the preponderant power must make concessions. Washington can tell its challengers that if they go too far, there will be a jungle, and in the jungle it is the strongest, not the weakest, who prevails. But when a scorpion knows that the lion does not want to be stung or to fight even against less formidable beasts, because he needs their support in other contests, the lion's threat is a call for a compromise. And a compromise is likely to chip away at the quasi monopoly exerted in the past by the liberal industrial powers, and above all by the United States, in the international monetary system; to reduce the autonomy and the role of American multinationals; and to curtail on behalf of interstate agreements that famous rule of the free market still seen by most Americans as the golden rule of international trade and national development.

SPECTACLE INSTEAD OF CONSENSUS

This raises the problem of consensus and another paradox. For a long time, the statesmen of this second era acted far more than they explained. They worked as if the domestic lowering of tensions necessary after 1968 (though compromised, briefly but ardently, by the invasion of Cambodia in 1970) entailed giving up the old techniques of consensus engineering, as if the very substance of the new policy was incompatible with the earlier mobilization of public opinion, elites, and Congress for the "cold crusade" of containment. In this period the clearest explanation was provided by the somewhat prissy, yearly State of the World messages, pedagogical but not widely read. And yet, in this period support for the administration's policy was strongest (if we leave aside the Cambodian episode and the final crisis of the Vietnam negotiations). After the end of 1973, explanations got more frequent, more frantic, and less coherent; but support receded, and Kissinger complained bitterly about the sabotage of his diplomacy by politicians and legislators.

The first half of the cycle substituted slick spectacle for the noisy free-for-all into which the old consensus had degenerated. Like Eisenhower, Nixon wanted a hush, not a shout. His passion for secrecy, his fear of crowds, his distrust of the Eastern Establishment, his hatred of the media, his bizarre use of an entourage of public relations experts to insulate himself, meant that the quasi demobilization that followed his narrow electoral victory suited him well. Vietnam still stirred passions, but he tried—with uneven success—to defuse the bomb by withdrawing troops and ending the draft. Kissinger did not have much respect or use for the tired and discombobulated foreign policy elite that had nurtured him, and Secretary Rogers played golf. At moments of crisis (the A.B.M. decision, Cambodia), the influentials in Congress came in and gave in. The Executive asked Congress and the public to leave it alone and to judge the results. When, after Kissinger's trip to Peking in July 1971, the results flashed like fireworks, the public applauded the fiesta, and reelected the chief fireworker. "Pragmatism" rather than consensus prevailed. Détente with Peking was achieved with panache and without humiliation; heaps of beneficial agreements were being signed with Moscow; the American war in Vietnam ended without the sell-out of one's ally; Israeli superiority continued without a new war; the Third World seemed to cease being a stake for the great powers and to stay quiet; so why worry, why complain? Only a few radicals muttered about the new friendship with South Africa and Rhodesia, or the hostility shown to Allende. Only the Old Establishment grumbled about the tone in which allies were charged with having fattened on America's generosity or about Connally's economic nationalism; others loved it.

It was too good to last. While Kissinger, having become Secretary of State, still enjoyed diplomatic immunity by contrast with his embattled President, Congress voted the Jackson and Stevenson Amendments and broke one of the spokes of the wheel of détente. The deluge came. The forced ending of war operations in Cambodia and in all of Indochina, the limitation of presidential war powers, sanctions against Turkey, discrimination against Latin American members of OPEC, the denial of help to Thieu and Lon Nol *in extremis,* the refusal to authorize arms transfers to anti-Soviet factions in Angola, the investigation of the CIA, a ceiling on arms sales abroad, a tougher antiproliferation stand, resistance to negotiations with Panama, all this formed a turbulent, and politically incoherent, counterweight to the Secretary's own centralization of foreign policy making power. In part, it can be called, or dismissed as, the Watergate effect. Watergate's enormous stone provoked ever-wider ripples in the political pond and ended up splashing Kissinger himself. His call for "compassion" to schemers and liars, his impatience with the spectacular and protracted "desacralization" of Nixon, and his own involvement in wire-tapping, cost him some of the sympathy his charm, wit, cunning, and successes had earned him. Watergate also led to the revolt, in Congress, of the new boys against the old influentials, which was a major factor in the Angola affair, Kissinger having consulted only those he deemed sufficient, but who were no longer "safe." Indeed, Watergate, which symbolized the use by the Executive of methods deemed normal in the contest abroad, against its domestic foes ("deviants," dissenters, and political rivals) could not fail to bring forth, gradually, a reaction against the use of these methods abroad, i.e., against the "imperial Presidency" itself.

But the crisis was far more than a consequence of Watergate, or of the fact that to proclaim the advent of détente and the "age of negotiation" was to remove the reason for congressional patriotic obedience, or of the intimate connection between domestic concerns and the new economic agenda of world affairs. It also resulted from a triple hiatus between foreign policy and the domestic base of support. In the first place, a neoclassical or neo-Bismarckian policy of balance, a policy that also claimed, with limited sincerity, to aim at a pluralistic world order rather than at an order flying the American flag, would have had a chance of digging roots into the domestic turf only on certain conditions. The national soil was used to monochrome pluralism, accustomed to distrusting a multipolar world as a quicksand in which the United States could be trapped by cunning foreign leaders, and to pining for world harmony under a common rule of law: ours, the only guarantee of moderation. It was traditionally hostile to balance of power diplomacy with its closets full of partitions, compensations, secret treaties and gunboats. Therefore, that soil ought to have been systematically explored and prepared. If the cold war was over and the agenda of world politics changed, Congress would try to recuperate some of its powers that it had abandoned or muted during the long years of the crusade (indeed, as is usual in such cases, some of the moves of Congress did show a mix of retrospective remorse for abdication, of prospective determination to restore proper checks and balances, and of sheer partisan posturing). Hence close coordination with Congress should have been a high priority. Once one gave up simple or simplistic ideas that drafted good consciences behind a flag, once one replaced patriotic calls with ambiguous formulas, it became doubly essential to go beyond the small circle of influentials—and to obtain the support of ethnic and economic groups, if only not to be overrun by them. It was a Herculean task. But it was not undertaken until the descending phase.

There is no middle ground between mobilization and bargaining. Nixon and Kissinger tried to find one. But the "solution" that was preferred for so long to such a dreary effort at persuasion—trying to get acclaim for the performance—was bound to backfire. It could not fail to induce the artist to inflate the value of his feats, and this in turn could not fail to provoke the disappointment of the public and to turn the bravos into boos. Nixon had a special talent for exaggeration. Whether it was the late Smithsonian monetary agreement, or the deals with Russia, or the visit to Peking, and especially of Vietnam treaty, he always managed to describe dubious metals as pure gold. The Secretary of State later got the backlash: adversaries untroubled by hyperbole, an impatient public, now systematically took all such metals for sheer dross.

Third, and most importantly, one might ask whether even a more serious and thorough effort of internal explanation and negotiation would have succeeded in marshalling the indispensable domestic support for a policy that needed to be perfectly modulated and considerably flexible. Throughout 1976, politicians of both parties and writers of all kinds declared that a Kissingerian policy was incompatible with American democracy—and this incompatibility might explain why he himself may actually have felt that the nurturing of an active domestic constituency might even be a burden, because the game abroad demanded such good timing, subtlety, and concentration as to rule out unprofessional kibbitzers. But the problem goes much deeper than Kissinger, and it extends to the future. It does not only arise from the fact that once one sends the crusaders home, democracy risks putting its nose into its secret services, indulging in an orgy of "leaks," and turning a diplomacy of maneuver into a heap of open secrets. Above all, the dexterous use of sticks and carrots that such a diplomacy entails, the proper dosage of concessions and resistance, does not survive such dualities as Executive versus Legislature, or administration versus interest groups—or intelligence activities and the public's right to know—

i.e., the American Constitution and politics. To threaten the Soviets with military reprisals as long as Congress frowns at interventions or the cost of weapons programs; to push OPEC into a mood of compromise by reducing America's oil imports as long as Congress, fearful of inflation, of imposing sacrifices on the public, or of turning to nuclear energy, refuses any stringent domestic program restricting the consumption of oil, is to expose one's nakedness. In other words, such a policy demands, in the absence of a mobilization of public opinion and elites that is incompatible with its essence, a kind of abdication that is incompatible with American democracy. Whereas Metternich's foreign policy was dictated by his concern for Austria's internal vulnerability, Kissinger was a practitioner of the primacy of foreign policy. But one can say of him what he said of Castlereagh: his own country defeated him. His policy had turned out to be simultaneously too complex in execution for the domestic forces whose support he needed, and too simple in design for the present-day world, despite its being far more subtle than the earlier simplicities of containment. Can a more adequate, i.e., even more complicated policy, gain internal support? At the end of the cycle, there was a nostalgia for the old days when the cold war made things perfectly clear if not easy, a contradictory desire not to go back to them, and a fear of being duped by countries more unscrupulous or less inhibited.

"REALISM" AND REACTION

The first cycle of American postwar policy had been the period of American exceptionalism, near the activist pole of the pendulum. The second cycle may not have tolled the "end of exceptionalism," but it certainly marked its crisis. The troubadours of containment may have seen in it the advent of Realism. But Kissinger's brand of Realism was much closer to European *Realpolitik* than to his predecessors' Americanism. While he paid lip service to the pursuit of America's values, he tended to see in them fuel for the foreign policy drive of his diplomacy—an asset to be used—rather than a direction or a compass for it; he never ceased pointing out the difficulty of projecting moral judgments and criteria abroad. With his sermons on the difficulty of foreign policy choices and the unavoidable necessity for imperfect solutions,[64] he seemed to want to relegate to past history both isolationism and the crusades, to warn against either expecting harmony or relying on brute force. And yet, the message does not seem to have made many converts.

Anti-Communism had appealed to all the varieties of American impatience: those who believe that there is no substitute for victory—that the alternative to world disarmament is escalation—and those who believe that the purpose of America is to promote American ideals all over the world. But anti-Communist containment, being negative, had been bound to disappoint both the jingoistic believers in the drastic efficiency of toughness, and above all the idealists for whom activism must be a means of doing good. However, the "stable structure of peace," more positive a goal, still sounded too vague and too cold to appeal either to the wounded idealists, shocked by Kissinger's methods across the world, or to those hard-nosed toughies whose activism was geared to the simpler vision of an American century. The new nationalist tone could satisfy these, for a while. But they had their eyes on the one contest—with Moscow—that mattered to them, and there they were distressed. A policy that gave up both the most extreme claims of force and evangelism, that tried to curb both the rhetoric of confrontation and the rhetoric of universalism (used, in the recent past, by a diplomacy whose imperial strivings had been licensed by idealism) struck an unresponsive chord. Moreover, it had trouble achieving its own synthesis. On the one hand, at times it unleashed force, or the threat of force, with the same disproportionate frenzy as the predecessors it criticized, whether into Cambodia, over Hanoi, during the military alert of the Kippur war, or à propos the Mayaguez. The public was bound to be struck by the meagerness of the results. On the other hand, insofar as it tried to describe America's purpose for the voters, it still resorted to moral attributes rather than to a political rationale, despite its emphasis on political realism; and it resorted to spectaculars to celebrate its "breakthroughs," despite its promise to restore diplomacy. In the American context, such shows and such words reawaken the never-dying aspiration for harmony, the illusion that friendship among peoples is around the corner because deep down we are all alike; and in some quarters, they revive the lingering paranoia that fears the trickery of foreigners and reveals a fascinating conviction that Americans abroad are born dupes.

Therefore, just as Vietnam had become a symbol of the moral bankruptcy of containment and destroyed the ethical base of the contained crusade, all the disappointments—domestic and external—of the descending phase of this era came to symbolize the moral deficiencies of *Realpolitik*. It was simply too cool for the heated nationalists and too indifferent to tap the huge reservoir of American idealism. To the former, and to many of the idealists, Kissinger's "realism" meant either a loss of national muscle and will or a lack of inspiration. To other idealists, his "realism" seemed, despite his protestations, nothing but an ideology, but the wrong one—an ideology of conservatism worthy of Metternich and Bismarck, and expressed both in that search for stability on the basis of the status quo which was called détente (cf. the "Sonnenfeldt doctrine") and in the repression of radicalism in the Third World.

Interestingly enough, after the liquidation of the Vietnam war, this revolt against the new realism only partially took the form of quietist idealism. McGovern's "Come home, America," the call for a populist contrition that radicals and revisionists initiated, the idea of retiring from a world one could only corrupt, did find an echo, and the number of isolationists increased. But it is still below 25 percent.[65] Neo-isolationism neither spread widely nor lived long in its moralistic form. It lingers only when presented as a refusal, derived from basic American values, to apply abroad methods deemed degrading at home, even if they have a long diplomatic pedigree: the corruption of foreign clients, as in the Lockheed case, or the assassination of foreign leaders. Isolationism today is, more often than not, a traditional form of nationalism, a conviction that self-interest must express itself in noninterventionism, in the refusal to commit America blindly. However, most of the moral splintering has occurred around the activist end of the pendulum, around and away from Kissinger's policy. This confirmed the divorce between a public looking for quick, demonstrable results—foreign demons daunted, evil entanglements eliminated, enemies driven back, brotherly love triumphant—and a policy that was a game of patience, with uncertain results and ever-shifting patterns, and risked being a game of solitaire as well, both because of the way in which it was formulated and because of its inability to meet such expectations.

So one heard once more the impatient activists of unilateral toughness, who pointed out that the world was still above all a duel between us and communism, that the policy conceded our contraction and their expansion, that it smacked of appeasement. Here, old suspicions of the United Nations felt at last fully vindicated. The neo-Darwinian formulations of a William Buckley, the cartoon-like (or Hollywood Western) machismo of a Ronald Reagan have demonstrated their appeal to a sizable fraction of a befuddled public. Next were the nostalgics of the cold war crusade, idealists, not nationalists, who do not come from the far right: the neoconservatives, gloomy, grumpy, or flamboyant, of *Commentary,* the *Public Interest,* and the later Committee on the Present Danger. Here, a violent anti-Sovietism (which brings closely together such men as Moynihan, Senator Jackson, Eugene Rostow, Paul Nitze, and James Schlesinger) merges with a bitter critique of the divagations of American liberals, the so-called excesses of American democracy, the "radical chic" intelligentsia, the fall of traditional values. In part, it is a call for a new cold war (Jackson claimed to be Truman's heir), for a reawakening of American moralism. The critique of détente borrows from Solzhenitzyn and tries to provoke a spiritual revolt. But what is new, by comparison with the earlier versions of anti-Communism—cold war moralism or Goldwaterism—is the judgment of American democracy and the contempt for the Third World. It is a double sourness that once was the privilege of the foes of activism, and which they reserved, at home, for the munition makers, the fat cats and the government (rather than for the intellectuals, the young, or the minorities) and, abroad, for the cynical Europeans (rather than the "savages").

Next—or rather, far away—come the neo-Wilsonians, except that they see themselves as radicals or progressives, not liberals.[66] These would like the United States to purge itself of all the evil forces that have led it into corruption—the "industrial military complex," the greedy businesses that waste resources and spoil the environment, the vested interests, in the bureaucracy or in the labor movement, that have no stake in reform. They also want America to lead the endangered planet toward a new moral and political order, based not on a balance of power and on the common legitimacy of statesmen, but on justice, the promotion of human rights, the satisfaction of human needs, a new equilibrium between national self-sufficiency and global institutions. Their touching faith in the overwhelming power of the common aspirations of peoples everywhere, and in the possibility of sprinting to the millenium by dropping the heavy load of weaponry and interventionist diplomacy, testifies to the durability of angelism and faith in clean harmony.

Finally, there is another chorus of somewhat less exalted voices, which sounds like a third attempt at a synthesis or overcoming of national tensions and traditions. After cold war "realism" and Kissingerian *Realpolitik,* they seem to want to return to the idealism that the former had somehow perverted and the latter somewhat neglected, and to eliminate the hubris that had marred both. It is a chorus of moderate activists, without hegemonic pretenses, eager to draw on the reservoir of American moralism on behalf of international cooperation. Like the progressives, these voices insist on the importance of transnational and international forces, an old liberal dream; on the importance of the common problems of mankind, an old inclination to apolitical thinking; on the need for the United States no longer to confuse conservatism and stability, anti-Communism and democracy, again, the critique of American support to tyrannies, as in Kissinger's Chilean policy; on the need not to mistake the defense of capitalism and political democracy.[67] Here, by comparison with the radical idealists, is just as much confidence in America's capacity (despite Vietnam and other blemishes) to show the way to rectitude and concord, much less emphasis on internal social change, less pessimism about the structures of domestic power, more faith in inspired leadership without overhaul, which may be a kind of inward-looking angelism. But there is more awareness of the inability of even a rejuvenated United States to reshape the world alone. Many of these people have rallied around Jimmy Carter; he came prepared with little more than an idealistic mold, and they were eager to pour in the content.

The Kissinger Legacy

Thus, the legacy of the second cycle to the third is complex, and not without paradoxes. On the substance of foreign policy, while both the post-1947 and the 1969 designs are dead, much of what has been undertaken in recent years is widely seen as beyond challenge. But a new rationale is needed, to provide United States diplomacy, on the one hand, with a road map less imprecise than the "stable structure," more adequate to a complex world than the imperfect and limited notion of triangular détente, but also, on the other hand, to save it from mere acrobatic improvisations aimed at overcoming crises (often provoked by our fumbling) with the minimum of damage. Such a rationale should help in the main domestic effort: obtaining broad support, an indispensable task, even if the public is wary, if Congress is unlikely to return to automatic approval, and if the necessary intermediary elite is shrunken and split. Can such a rationale be found? Can a repudiation of Kissinger's decision-making methods and diplomatic style, the return to a less centralized and more open process, the concern for internal persuasion and bargaining, meet the external needs for flexibility and cohesion? Can internal pressures and external interests be reconciled? Can the reservoir of idealism be used again, yet kept from overflowing? Henry Kissinger left a double heritage to his successors. Abroad, he had rescued enough bits and pieces from the shipwreck of his design, to allow them to build a new one with those pieces. But his weakest spot in this design as well as at home had always been the relation between domestic structures or beliefs and foreign policy, the relation that had ruined Metternich, and the European concert after Bismarck. His successors will have to innovate most profoundly on this point, both to cope with world order problems and to provide American democracy with the institutional, emotional, and intellectual foundations without which it cannot act effectively abroad.

Meanwhile, the ends of the two cycles were oddly similar, despite the differences in concepts, tactics, and domestic bases, despite the fact that the main attack had come from the far left in 1968, from the far right in 1976. The barricades of the cold war and the quagmire of Vietnam had made way for an apparent siege of the United States by a "hostile world," recurrent rhetorical battles with the Third World, renewed confrontations with OPEC and the Soviets. As in 1968, a worried American people, led by the very scope of their leaders' ambitions to react to often minor setbacks as if they were doomsday's dawn or proof of decline, demanded that the nation's defenses be strengthened. But at the same time, a nation tired of doing battle against enemies or "ingrates" wished not to get involved in external complexities capable, or so it seemed, of overtaxing its resources or of eroding its institutions. As Richard H. Ullman has put it, "it wants not so much . . . withdrawal or isolation . . . but . . . greater detachment" and "a national interest more narrowly construed."[68] This is not so much isolationism as a kind of aggressive divorcement from a treacherous world. The number of internationalists has diminished. One sees converging those who want no more Vietnams arising from military or countersubversive ventures, and those who would like the United States to behave as a fortress counting on its strength alone, with its leaders hurling imprecations at its assailants from the top of the wall. And yet, such divorce is not possible. And the thirst for a more idealistic stance, however contradictory with the fear of involvement, shows a continuing desire to affect the world—if only to make costly involvement unnecessary. But in order to influence the world, and even in order to set the goals toward which one wants America and the world to move, one has to understand both the nature of the present system of states and the limits America's own nature imposes on its actions.

NOTES

CHAPTER TWO

1. See especially Stephen R. Graubard, *Kissinger: Portrait of a Mind,* Norton, New York, 1973; Bruce Mazlish, *Kissinger,* Basic Books, New York, 1976, part 2; and John Montgomery, "The Education of Henry Kissinger," *Journal of International Affairs,* vol. 9, no. 1, 1975, pp. 49–62.

   For general assessments of Kissinger's diplomacy, see also Roger Morris, *Uncertain Greatness,* Harper & Row, New York, 1977; John G. Stoessinger, *Kissinger: The Anguish of Power,* Norton, New York, 1976; George Ball, *Diplomacy for a Crowded World,* Atlantic-Little, Brown, Boston, 1976; George Liska, *Beyond Kissinger,* Johns

Hopkins, Baltimore, 1975; and Richard A. Falk, *What Is Wrong with Henry Kissinger's Foreign Policy,* Center for International Studies Policy Memorandum No. 59, Princeton, N.J., July 1974.

2. Quoted in Graubard, ibid., p. 70.
3. *A World Restored,* Grosset and Dunlap, New York, 1964, p. 1.
4. Ibid., pp. 145 and 318.
5. Ibid., p. 318.
6. "Reflections on Bismarck," in D. A. Rustow (ed.), *Philosophers and Kings,* George Braziller, New York, 1970, p. 338.
7. *A World Restored,* op. cit., p. 320.
8. Ibid., p. 322.
9. Ibid., p. 329.
10. Ibid., p. 328.
11. Ibid., p. 326.
12. Ibid., p. 317.
13. Ibid., p. 328.
14. *United States Foreign Policy for the 1970's,* 1972, p. 3.
15. Ibid., p. 4.
16. *United States Foreign Policy for the 1970's,* 1973, p. 27.
17. *United States Foreign Policy for the 1970's,* 1972, p. 16.
18. *United States Foreign Policy for the 1970's,* 1973, pp. 27–28.
19. Ibid., p. 7.
20. For a more detailed analysis, see my essay, "Uneven Allies," in David S. Landes (ed.), *Western Europe: The Trials of Partnership,* vol. 14 of Critical Choices for Americans, Lexington Books, Lexington, Mass., 1977.
21. *The Kissinger Study of Southern Africa,* Lawrence Hill and Co., Westport, Conn., 1976, p. 105. See also Anthony Lake, *The 'Tar Baby' Option,* Columbia University Press, New York, 1976, chap. 4.
22. "Reflections on Bismarck," op. cit., p. 369.
23. Cf. Jerome Alan Cohen, "A China Policy for the Next Administration," *Foreign Affairs,* vol. 55, no. 1, October 1976, pp. 20–37.
24. Remarks to United States Ambassadors in Europe in December 1975, as reported in a State Department nonverbatim summary, *International Herald Tribune,* Apr. 12, 1976.
25. See, for instance, the articles of Paul Nitze, "Assuring Strategic Stability in an Era of Détente," *Foreign Affairs,* vol. 54, no. 2, pp. 207–232; and "Deterring Our Deterrent," *Foreign Policy,* no. 25, Winter 1976–77, pp. 195–210.
26. "Appeasement and Détente," *Commentary,* January 1976, pp. 27–38.
27. Department of State, Bureau of Public Affairs, Secretary Kissinger's Statement on United States–Soviet relations, Sept. 19, 1974, p. 6.
28. Cf. Kenneth Jowitt, "Images of Détente and the Soviet Political Order," unpublished paper.
29. Marshall I. Goldman, "The Soviet Economy Is Not Immune," *Foreign Policy,* no. 21, Winter 1975–76, p. 79. See also his *Détente and Dollars,* Basic Books, New York, 1975.
30. Cf. Kissinger's speech, "The Cohesion of the Industrial Democracies," *Department of State Bulletin,* vol. 75, no. 1934, July 19, 1976, pp. 78–79.
31. Sonnenfeldt, op.cit.
32. Kissinger in *Department of State Bulletin,* vol. 74, no. 1913, Feb. 23, 1976, p. 204.
33. Ibid.

34. See footnote 27: ibid., p. 16.
35. Kissinger's remarks to United States Ambassadors in Europe in December 1975, *International Herald Tribune,* Apr. 12, 1976.
36. Kissinger, "The Western Alliance: Peace and Moral Purpose," *Department of State Bulletin,* vol. 75, no. 1935, July 26, 1976, p. 110.
37. John A. Marcus, "Lessons of Angola," *Foreign Affairs,* vol. 54, no. 3, April 1976, p. 418. See also Tom J. Farer, "The United States and the Third World," *Foreign Affairs,* vol. 54, no. 1, October 1975, pp. 85–87.
38. See Laurence Stern, "How We Failed in Cyprus," *Foreign Policy,* no. 19, Summer 1975, pp. 34–78.
39. Cf. Werner Levi, "Third World States: Objects of Colonialism or Neglect?" *International Studies Quarterly,* vol. 17, no. 2, June 1973. See also the quote from John Kenneth Galbraith ("such nations have no vital relation to the economic or strategic position of the developed countries") in Robert W. Tucker, *The Inequality of Nations,* Basic Books, New York, 1977, p. 46.
40. Cf. V. H. Oppenheim, "Why Oil Prices Go Up," *Foreign Policy,* no. 25, Winter 1976–77, pp. 24–57.
41. On Portugal, see Tad Szulc, "Behind Portugal's Revolution," *Foreign Policy,* no. 21, Winter 1975–76, pp. 3–62.
42. *Department of State Bulletin,* vol. 75, no. 1943, Sept. 20, 1976, p. 354.
43. If, as Senator Moynihan writes in "Abiotrophy in Turtle Bay" (*Harvard Journal of International Law,* vol. 17, no. 3, Summer 1976, p. 480), "the process of decolonization brought into existence a United Nations majority made up of countries for which the assertion of racial equality was scarcely to be distinguished from the assertion of manhood," the style of his United Nations campaign could all too easily be seen as an involuntary denial of such equality, given the contempt with which many of the new nations were treated.
44. See Raymond L. Garthoff, "Negotiating with the Russians: Some Lessons from SALT," *International Security,* vol. 1, no. 4, Spring 1977, pp. 3–24.
45. For a defense of step-by-step, see Kissinger's speech, "Moral Promise and Practical Needs," *Department of State Bulletin,* vol. 75, no. 1951, Nov. 15, 1976, p. 7601.
46. See in particular the articles by Graham T. Allison and Frederic A. Morris, and by John Steinbruner and Barry Carter, in *Daedalus,* "Arms, Defense Policy and Arms Control," Summer 1975.
47. See Tad Szulc, "Behind the Vietnam Cease-fire Agreement," *Foreign Policy,* no. 15, Summer 1974, and Gareth Porter, *A Peace Denied,* Indiana University Press, Bloomington, 1976.
48. See Edward Sheehan, *The Arabs, Israelis, and Kissinger,* Readers Digest Press, New York, 1976. See also my essay, "A New Policy for Israel," *Foreign Affairs,* vol. 53, no. 3, April 1975, pp. 405–431.
49. Sheehan, op. cit., p. 192.
50. And when, despite all this caution, the carefully planned move failed (South Vietnam, October 1972; Europe, April-Summer 1973; Israel, March 1975), Kissinger's fury at the obstacle was tempestuous.
51. "The International Transfer of Conventional Arms," a report to the Congress from A.C.D.A.; 93d Congress, 2d session, p. 4. See also Leslie H. Gelb, "Arms Sales," *Foreign Policy,* no. 25, Winter 1976–77, pp. 3–23.
52. *Department of State Bulletin,* vol. 75, no. 1935, July 26, 1976, p. 106.

53. *Department of State Bulletin,* vol. 74, no. 1923, May 3, 1976, p. 566.
54. James Schlesinger, "On Making Too Much of Our Present Discontents," *Foreign Policy,* no. 24, Fall 1976, p. 36.
55. Cf. footnote 52, p. 108.
56. See Lee Aspin, "How to Look at the Soviet-American Balance," *Foreign Policy,* no. 22, Spring 1976, pp. 96–106, and the controversy that followed in no. 23, Summer 1976, pp. 32–52.
57. See John D. Steinbruner and Thomas M. Garwin, "Strategic Vulnerability: The Balance Between Prudence and Paranoia," *International Security,* vol. 1, no. 1, Summer 1976, pp. 138–181; also, Thomas J. Downey, "How to Avoid Monad—and Disaster," *Foreign Policy,* no. 24, Fall 1976, pp. 172–201.
58. See footnote 54.
59. Assessing the two navies seems even more difficult than evaluating the nuclear arsenals. See Michael T. Klare, "Superpowers Rivalry at Sea," *Foreign Policy,* no. 21, Winter 1975–76, pp. 86–96; Admiral Bagley and Rear Admiral La Rocque, "Superpowers at Sea: A Debate," *International Security,* vol. 1, no. 1, Summer 1976, pp. 56–76; Admiral Turner, "The Naval Balance: Not Just a Numbers Game," and Michael Krepon, "A Navy to Match National Purposes," in *Foreign Affairs,* January 1977, pp. 339–367.
60. In his book, *Le Mal Français,* Plon, Paris, 1976, pp. 432–433, the French Minister Alain Peyrefitte tells about a visit by the Soviet Ambassador to France during the presidential election campaign that followed Pompidou's death in May 1974: he came to declare that Moscow favored Chaban Delmas (and would, on the second ballot, favor Giscard d'Estaing if he prevailed over Chaban on the first ballot) against the candidate of the left.
61. See Raymond Vernon's article by that title in *Foreign Affairs,* vol. 51, no. 3, April 1973.
62. *Power and Interdependence,* Little, Brown, Boston, 1976.
63. See my analysis, "Les Etats-Unis: Du Refus au Compromis," *Revue Française de Science Politique,* vol. 26, no. 4, August 1976, pp. 684–695.
64. See for instance the speeches "Moral Promise and Practical Needs," op. cit., and "The Moral Foundations of Foreign Policy," *Department of State Bulletin,* vol. 73, no. 1884, Aug. 4, 1975.
65. "Nationalism, Not Isolationism," a report from Potomac Associates, *Foreign Policy,* no. 24, Fall 1976, p. 20.
66. See Richard A. Falk, "Beyond Internationalism," *Foreign Policy,* no. 24, Fall 1976, pp. 65–113.
67. See in particular Richard H. Ullman's "The Foreign World and Ourselves," *Foreign Policy,* no. 21, Winter 1975–76, pp. 97–124, and Joseph S. Nye, Jr., "Independence and Interdependence," *Foreign Policy,* no. 22, Spring 1976, pp. 129–161.
68. Richard H. Ullman, op. cit. in footnote 67, pp. 110–111.

PART TWO

THE NIGHTMARE
OF
WORLD ORDER

What is this world, what are its perils?

Few people still believe that the United States can disentangle itself from the world. The author of a distinguished plea for a new isolationism, written a few years ago, has since moved on to schemes for the American invasion of the Persian Gulf and, as a way of reducing Israeli dependence on the United States, for a nuclear Middle East, which is easier to see as a recipe for a disaster involving the great powers than as a panacea for their disengagement.[1] And yet, there remain vast differences between those who think that the United States should keep its power "latent" and drastically restrict the scope of its activities in an increasingly unmanageable world, and those who believe that having pursued the mirage of hegemony for so long should not divert it now from providing some leadership toward world order. As usual, prescription and description are mixed. Those who want the United States to cut commitments and concentrate on its own problems see the world as black. Those who want the United States to show the way to a new global order, whether they see themselves as liberal realists in the Establishment tradition or as radical populists, tend to assume a manageable world, or rather a world that could be managed if they advised or became princes.

What is this world? An assessment of its main features cannot fail to suggest whether a United States retreat is possible and, if not, the scope of America's choices and the nature of the imperatives we must heed. I shall proceed in two stages. First, I shall analyze the present international scene,

103

not to point out the main issues, crises, alignments or institutions that form the stuff of daily politics, but to explore the underlying dynamics and the most original characteristics of the international system. The international system is constituted by the political units that act and interact in the world. These interactions form patterns and lead to outcomes that can be understood if one examines the structure of the system (i.e., the distribution of power), the features of the principal actors, and the nature of the forces that operate across the borders. These patterns and outcomes, in turn, influence the behavior, create opportunities for, and impose restraints on the actors. I shall try to assess the extent to which world politics today differs from what we have known in the past, and to find out whether we are witnessing fundamental differences or merely a new choreography for the traditional ballet of states. Second, I shall discuss the problem of order in the present international system, i.e., whether, given its features, it can obtain the degree not only of moderation (which may be purely temporary), but of resilience that the concept of order entails. This depends on sufficient security and flexibility being provided to the actors and on their assent to the rules of the game.

CHAPTER THREE

A World
of Complexity

Communism and anti-imperialism are still on the ideological offensive against the liberal industrial powers. But one of the most bitter rifts of all opposes the two leading communist states; the former Mecca of Communism, Moscow, and the Rome of the capitalist world, Washington, negotiate on military matters; and the anti-imperialist nations show a remarkable ability at double bookkeeping. They denounce the unfair order imposed by the rich nations of the West, yet they deal profitably with several if not all of these, and they pursue their own rivalries and grievances in ways that turn the common front of the developing nations into a mass of bitter conflicts. A given country can, depending on the issue, be a member of a host of coalitions. Brazil is both a military ally of the United States and, occasionally, a champion of the Third World; the same is true of the Philippines. Military alignments seem reasonably stable: United States forces have not left Europe, Japan has not denounced its alliance with the United States, there is still no West European defense system, the Arab-Israeli stalemate persists. But there has been frenzy over economic matters. Not only has their politicization put them on top of the statesmen's agenda, but it has been accompanied by monetary crises, energy warfare, collective confrontations, cycles of inflation and recession, anguish over limits of growth or resource shortages, and the like. Can one make sense of all of this?

SECTION ONE: CHANGES

One way of trying to understand the present is to try to fit it into, and to compare it with, the analytic models of international politics that we find in classical political theory.[2] Classical philosophers may have reflected more often on the good state than on the right international order, but they did have views on it and on how it might come about, and they had implicit or explicit interpretations of the dynamics of world affairs.

CLASSICAL MODELS

We find two radically different interpretations. The first is the model of the imperfect community, which prevails in Christian political thought from Augustine to Grotius at the end of the sixteenth century. It treats mankind as a community ruled by princes who are themselves submitted to the rule of law, and not arbitrary and willful masters. There is God's law and there is Natural Law, the product of human participation in divine reason. Behind this model lies a double postulate: the princes' community of spirit and sense of obligation, the decisive role of the Church in interpreting and enforcing the norms of Natural Law. Being human, this community is imperfect. Hence the ever-present risk of a violation, by princes or by their subordinates, of the dictates of Natural Law, i.e., the possibility of war. Since mankind is deemed a community—a group welded, not by mere ties of mutual interest, but by common beliefs, values, and goals, and ruled not by wills but by higher law—the use of force is not a morally neutral act. In modern parlance, it is either a delict or a sanction, a delict when it violates the conditions of Just War laid down by theologians, a sanction when it meets these criteria, which deal with the prince's intention, the cause (or goals), and the means. In this conception, in which the princes are not the shapers of separate sovereign entities, but the shepherds of the various flocks that form mankind, the obligations of Natural Law and of the Just War theory apply not merely to states but to all individuals.

A second model prevails in modern political thought, from Grotius (whose work shows traces of, and contradictions between, the earlier and the new conceptions) and from Hobbes to the present. But its real Founding Father was a historian, not a philosopher or legal theorist: Thucydides, whose study of the Peloponnesian war not only aimed at making future readers understand a singular event, but also and above all at laying out the necessary logic of a certain kind of human behavior. For while his impeccable staging of the principals describes the singular through such universal concepts as honor, interest, fear, or power, he was most eager for, and proudly conscious of, reaching the universal through the singular. His ambition was to show how the combination of human nature, a certain structure of power, and the specific properties of rival states creates an inescapable logic characteristic of a vital and permanent realm of human affairs: world politics. It is the model and the dynamics of fragmentation. There is no world community; there is the domestic order and the international order, and a double contrast exists between them. The citizen's allegiance is to the state; the state's highest allegiance is to its own survival, security, and power. The state has at its disposal a domestic monopoly of force. But there is no force superior to the state's. Hence, the ever-present possibility of war was conceived, not as a punishable revenge of human wickedness over Natural Law, or as the marshalling of human violence for a rightful cause, but as an inevitable outcome of human nature uncorseted by the norms and force of the state.

Hence also the very special problems of order in international affairs.[3] First, in the realm of politics. Within the state, power, whether it is exercised by political leaders or by social groups, is often at the service of common ideals; this restricts the scope of "power politics," and indeed the essence of the polity is—ideally—the prevalence of cooperation over conflict. The opposite is true in world affairs. There is no aspect of interstate relations that cannot be claimed or reclaimed by politics, even if it appears "depoliticized" (i.e., as not requiring for its management or solution the intervention of the wielders of political power, due to the intrinsic importance of the issue for their policies, or to the concern expressed by domestic political forces). Moreover, politics here means generally "power politics," the politics of confrontation, for in this realm even cooperation exists only because of conflict (allies coalesce against an enemy), or evolves primarily through conflict (as, indeed, in most alliances). The fundamental cause is psychological: domestic affairs are the realm of mutual understanding and predictability (even among adversaries); world affairs is the realm of mutual suspicions, misconceptions, and projections.[4] Second, in the realm of Law. The domestic order is a domain of vast regulation; its members are the subjects of commands and of sanctions imposed directly on them by the state with the help of justice and the police. On the international scene, rights and duties apply only to the states, and they result from contracts, not from superior rule; there are vast gaps and ambiguities in the regulations, the authority of the world judge is limited, and enforcement is a polite word for self-help. In institutions, in authority, in substance, international law is weak. Third, in the realm of ethics, international politics suffers particularly from the lack of integration. The range of moral conflict, i.e., of conflicts between moral conceptions, is a frequent threat to whatever solidarities survive across borders. The state's range of moral opportunities is narrow, since its first priorities are survival and security, not the good life—without survival, there can be no quest for it—yet the requirements of survival often clash with the requirements of ethics.[5] Hence a tragic separation of order and justice. The existence of order in the state gives license to the quest for justice, and the order reflects—or imposes—a dominant conception of justice. But in world affairs, order has to be achieved first; it is often established at the cost of justice—international law is a frequent consecration of state might, the balance of power is the rule of the great powers, the balance of terror is the threat of the unthinkable—and attempts at establishing justice often breed utter chaos.

A second distinction has to be made, for there are two different models of fragmentation. One might be called the model of troubled peace. It sees in the contrasts between the domestic and the international realms differences in degree rather than essence. The international milieu is not pure anarchy. There are forces capable of ensuring a minimum of order. They result from common sociability (Locke's notion) or mutual interests (Hume's); and they can result in common norms. Therefore, there remains a distinction between the international "state of nature" and the state of war. The former finds its cause in the absence of central power and is responsible for the weakness of the common norms: each state interprets them itself and resorts to self-help. But a state of war is a state of general malevolence and will to dominate, with no common norms. The state of nature is inferior to a well-ordered civil society, but preferable to a common despotism.

The other model is precisely that which sees international politics as a state of war. Not the absence of a common superior, but the existence of war is the essence, for everything in world affairs is the struggle, or its preparation, or its sequels. Thus, whatever common norms appear to exist, are but fragile and temporary products of a momentary configuration of power or convergence of interests backed by power. The many authors of this model never agreed on the cause of the state of war. Is it human nature itself (Hobbes, Kant)? Is it civil society which has corrupted human nature (Rousseau)? Is it a certain kind of civil society: capitalism (Marx)? Is it fragmentation itself, i.e., the structure of power, or all these factors acting together (Thucydides, Raymond Aron)?[6] And there is a final disagreement. Some deem this state of war ultimately bearable, like Hobbes, who saw in the existence of the state—long before nuclear weaponry or mass terrorism—a cushion for the individuals, hence in the international state of war less of a calamity for them than a "war of all against all" among equally weak and puny individuals. Others such as Rousseau and Kant—and Marx—thought the state of war would be unbearable.

Where does the present international system fit? The systems of the past centuries—what has been called the post-Westphalian order of nation-states, although the treaties of Westphalia (1648) merely crystallized trends that had existed for a long time—have all corresponded to the model of fragmentation. Sometimes they have vindicated its more optimistic version. In periods of international "legitimacy," when states agreed on the rules of the game, practices developed that moderated state ambitions, and international law flourished. Sometimes, in the revolutionary periods, fragmentation meant the "state of war." This distinction fits Clausewitz's notion of two types of wars, depending on how the "remarkable trinity" of "primordial violence, free play of the creative spirit, and pure reason", i.e., the mix of instinct, skill, and political control, turns out: there are limited wars and wars of annihilation.[7] The greatest contemporary Clausewitzian, Aron, in his magnum opus on the Prussian theorist of war, argues that the old model of fragmentation still applies. The decisive actors are still the states, the game is still a contest of separate units endowed with the means of violence and saddled with survival as the necessary overriding goal. International relations is still an arena of conflict. There remains something distinctive about war (i.e., collective, organized, armed violence), which characterizes the world scene, and it should not be drowned in an undifferentiated notion of social violence, lumped together with either social coercion or social control.[8] Thus the problem of world order remains, as before, that of creating troubled peace rather than a "state of war."

This may be true, but at so skeletal a level that it tells us nothing about the new flesh and blood of world affairs. In order to appreciate the degree of novelty (and without deciding yet whether novelty means merely greater complexity, which would affect the *varieties* of behavior on the stage, or a radical transformation of the *logic* of behavior itself), let us begin with the ideal-type of interstate relations that one finds in most of the texts of the fifties and sixties, particularly in Aron's own *Peace and War*.

1. The game is played by a small number of actors: independent states, in control of their instruments of action (dependent states who had, in effect, transferred some of these instruments to their masters were pawns, not players). This does not mean that there was no interconnection between states, or no interpenetration between societies; but the connections were voluntary and removable, and the penetration (by trade or travel) did not affect the sphere of political decisions, i.e., the realm and tools of power available to the state for action abroad (military might, economic aid, regulation of trade or investments, subversion, and so forth) or at home (fiscal, credit, welfare, industrial and agricultural policies, thought control, educational policy, and so on).

2.   The actors define their national interest, not on the basis of domestic political concerns but by giving primacy to their foreign policy needs and greeds: in terms of the geo-political situation of the country, its external rivalries, ambitions, and drives, and its diplomatic traditions. For the main objectives are possession goals, i.e., the effective control of territories, populations, resources, and markets capable of increasing the overall power, of improving the geo-political position, and of raising the rank of the player.

3.   They play in a single international system, dominated by the possibility of armed conflict. Their game is the strategic-diplomatic contest, whose main structure is the military alliance, a concert or coalition of forces aimed at deterring and eventually defeating an enemy. The key distinction is that between adversaries and allies, even if they change over time.

4.   Consequently, the decisive means is military might or strategic power (often identified with power altogether). Power as a set of resources is defined above all in terms of military supplies (men, material, and bases) and of the capacity to mobilize the society for war production and combat. Power as a relation of control is seen as the ability to wrest from others the possessions one wants, or to protect one's own possessions from their grasp.

5.   The hierarchy of the system is geo-military. The great powers are those that have the greatest military capabilities (such as France and Russia in the eighteenth and nineteenth centuries, Austria in the eighteenth, Prussia and later Germany in the nineteenth) or (as Britain did) an inexpugnable home base, the power to conquer and protect key positions across the world, and the financial and economic power to support allies in a military coalition.

In other words, it is a tournament of distinctive knights. Their alliances do not jeopardize their independence; they are supposed to preserve it. They may need to acquire their resources abroad, but these are either brought in from areas under the player's control, or else they are bought on the free market, in a depoliticized trade protected by classical international law (even interstate war was not allowed to interrupt it). To be sure, reality was always more complex. Yet this ideal-type did schematize rather than distort reality's main features. Today, however, the distance between this ideal-type and world politics is enormous. And the drama lies in the following points. One, since the states remain the main actors, there is still a prevalence of conflict and a poverty of common norms. Two, technology and the universal quest for economic growth have created, if not a world society, at least an unprecedented interdependent milieu. Three, the combination of an interdependent world economy and an international system without central direction means an entirely original tension between the "objective" need for global solutions to problems that threaten the future of mankind, and the uneven splintering of the centers of decision. In other words, what operates at present is not a mere juxtaposition, but an interplay of the old and the new. This can best be understood as a series of changes, contradictions, and races.

THE OLD AND THE NEW: AN OVERVIEW

There are five major changes. They concern the actors, their goals, their power, the international hierarchy, and the international system itself.

Actors and Objectives   One, there is a change in the number and nature of actors. This is one of the reasons why a purely "structural" analysis of the international system that focuses only on the number of great powers and on "the distribution of capabilities among units" tells us little.[9] On the one hand, there are more than 150 states. This means, of course, that the "group" that comprises the main players, or the main subjects of rights and duties, is still small by comparison with a domestic society. But it represents a considerable increase by comparison with international systems of the past (which, in fact, were usually limited to parts of the globe). Some of these actors have limited resources; but other factors of the system, such as the role of "collectives"—international organizations and groupings—and the relative decline of force (to be discussed below), compensate, to some degree, for such weakness, and make even more formal sovereignty an asset: intangible assets are a form of power.

On the other hand, nonstate actors, even though they may not be "sovereign," which means essentially that they are not constituted according to the principle of territorial organization characteristic of the state system, can nevertheless be players. As such, they can be considered part of the system's "structure" and not merely of the "processes that go on within it."[10] They are not merely members of a transnational society separate from the interstate system, whose behavior may affect a given state insofar as what happens in its society affects the state's policy. They are endowed with power over resources essential to the state; they can bargain directly with the legitimate wielders of political power (or try to undermine them); and even when they are the mere emanation of a state, or a creation of states, they have a de facto autonomy within certain ranges. It is true that they are not "a new phenomenon in world politics, and no present-day corporation has yet an impact comparable with that of the English East India Company, which employed its own armed forces and controlled territory."[11] But the question is not whether they are new. It is whether their importance in world affairs has increased sufficiently to require their inclusion even into an ideal-type of present world politics, whereas they did not need to be so included in the past.

If we use a traditional definition of actors (or of power also), we shall not understand what is happening. Yesterday, it was roughly true that only states were actors; hence, we defined the actors as those endowed with a legitimate monopoly of force over a territory and population. If we define actors as those whose autonomous decisions affect resources and values, and who interact with other similar players *across* state lines,[12] we shall be able to take changes into account. The definition creates two difficulties, however. It introduces heterogeneity into the category of actors (some have a territory and population, others do not), and it raises a problem of ambiguity: are the nonstate actors as autonomous as the states, even within their range of jurisdiction? One can answer, first, that the heterogeneity is an essential fact of life today. Second, although it is of course true that nonstate actors can operate "only in conditions in which a modicum of peace and security has been provided by the action of states,"[13] the problem of ultimate autonomy (which could always be raised even in the relation among states, given their uneven power) is one for empirical research. What matters for an analysis of world politics is that the actors behave *as if* they had such autonomy, even if, in a crunch, some will discover that they do not. A third problem—the fact that a nonstate actor can be both largely autonomous and used as an instrument by (or bring advantages to) a state— is, again, in the nature of present world affairs.

These nonstate actors are, first, such transnational agents as multinational enterprises, and also Internationales of religion, ideas, interests, or scientific organizations, or private groups operating across borders (whether they are airline companies, terrorists, or foundations).[14] Secondly, there are international and regional organizations endowed with powers and secretariats capable of initiative or management. One consequence of this increase and diversification in the nature of the actors is the intensity of contacts, both among governments and among societies, in world affairs today. Needless to say, one would need a map describing the unevenness of these contacts, for the world of transnational agents is not the whole world, and a society's degree of penetration or openness is still controllable by regimes determined to preserve their impermeability.

The nature of the states' objectives has also changed. The old ones still exists, of course. But foreign policy has ceased being the preserve of the diplomat and of the soldier. It is no longer a specialized activity, and what used to be its essence—the integration of force and policy, the use of coercion on behalf of external goals—is now only one of its aspects. Foreign policy has never been divorced from domestic politics. (Bismarck's diplomacy was aimed, in part, at preserving the power of conservative forces in Germany, and he knew how to manipulate the internal affairs of others.) Insofar as the old ideal-type assumed such a divorce, it was merely normative—it was a prescription, not a description, an ideology, not an analysis. But what used to be a connection has become a fusion. Foreign policy has become the external dimension of the universally dominant concern for economic development and social welfare. All economic and social issues have an external dimension, since, with few exceptions, none of the state actors is self-sufficient and all the other actors still depend on the states for their operations. The old definition of the national interest is far too narrow: international politics becomes a collision of economic and social policies, in addition to being what it has always been. This means an end to specialization, and a second cause of the huge increase in scope. Every ministry, every agency, has its foreign policy, and the constituencies of foreign policy have broadened along with the sphere of decision makers; they include not only the foreign policy establishments or the "industrial-military complex," but all the groups whose interests are affected by what happens abroad. It is therefore not surprising if coalitions of interests, ideas, or even bureaucratic fragments appear across borders. The old "primacy of foreign policy" loses much of its meaning under these conditions, for that imperative assumed specialization and separation.

While possession goals have not disappeared in a world in which the "struggle for the world product"[15] is intense, one notices a double shift. Possession goals become, so to speak, repatriated—states want *domestic* control over their resources, or aim at increasing self-sufficiency, or define their national ambition as the development of their economy. Abroad, states, as well as nonstate actors whose means of power are usually less complete, less blunt, or more fragile, seek milieu goals: an atmosphere in which multinationals can operate safely, or a set of rules allowing for the stable promotion of exports or for the security of supplies. Moreover, who gets what possession depends on the rules of the milieu. These goals require a modicum of cooperation, for the coveted possessions can best be enjoyed if there is common consent. In other words, *influence* rather than *control* is at the heart of the process. There are too many actors for any one of them to exert a decisive importance on all fronts or for very long, especially as (see below) the use of force is limited.

There are immediate, or intermediate, stakes. Procedural goals must be reached if the ultimate objectives are to be attained. First, there is the determination, or the transformation, of the rules of play, i.e., the balance of burdens and rights, advantages and costs that will accrue to the various players and their powers of control. Second, the framework in which a given issue will be discussed must be set. It can be more or less favorable to a given actor or group of actors, depending on this framework's degree of specificity or generality, on its degree of openness, and on its degree of democracy or oligarchic control. Lastly, once the framework of discussion or decision has been settled, the agenda itself must be set, which often slants or even shapes the outcome. These immediate stakes are means to the end—the modeling of the milieu—and are substitutes of the traditional means, the use or threat of war, toward possession ends.

The Transformation of Power   Power remains the capacity of affecting the behavior of others, or the outcome of an issue, whether or not its use was deliberately aimed at doing so.[16] But there has been a radical change in the nature of power. One is in its *diffusion,* which has resulted from the increase in the number of actors and from the immense increase in foreign policy issues. A second change is the *diversification* of power. The kinds of supplies needed to exert influence are so varied that the old quasi identification with military might has become absurd.

A third change is a fundamental *heterogeneity* between two ways of using these supplies. One is the use of power according to the logic of separateness and the rules of interaction; the other is the use of power according to the logic of integration and the rules of interdependence. In the former, the central assumption of the contest is that, ultimately, "my gain is your loss," even if it is so only ultimately, i.e., if we pursue mixed interests for a while. What is distinctive is that the moment may always come when the gain I am after will be perceived by you as an unacceptable loss, and the only "compensation" you would get if you accepted my gain is the absence of war. The even greater losses that you might incur if you fought my gain you may well deem worth risking, if you think my gain too dangerous or believe that war could bring a gain for you. The perspective is that of the *ultimate* test of strength, of the zero-sum game, which requires a constant calculation of force. My interest consists either in preventing or eliminating your gain, or, should the costs prove too high, in extracting a concession in return for my acceptance of your gain. I have to take your power into account because of what you might otherwise do to me, not because I could not live without you—indeed, I wish you did not exist. Two powers cannot be number one simultaneously. Since I am in control of my instruments of power, how I react to your moves is my sovereign business; your moves may constrain my choices, the way a city's maze of streets constrains my walk to a destination. Some choices may thus be costlier than others. But they are still mine. This is the traditional logic of interstate politics.

The "modern" logic does not deny conflict and competition. It starts from the awareness of increased contacts and mutual vulnerability. Even if my first concern is my absolute gain (for instance, the industrialization of my country), I may want to gain at your expense, or I may seek my gain in a way that inflicts a loss on you (cf. Iran's oil strategy versus the industrialized world). There are elements of a zero-sum game here; there is assuredly no permanent premium on "constructive" cooperation, and nothing necessarily benign about the interdependence of sovereigns. But the *ultimate* perspective is one of solidarity; the dynamics of the world economy, of world science and technology, is, for better (growth and welfare) or worse (population explosion, pollution, depletion, inflation, and recession) a dynamics of integration. If I push too far, your loss risks becoming mine. And we may all lose, if we all become victims of inflation, recession, shortages, or an epidemic of protectionist moves. The only difference may be degrees of loss. (This explains why a world economy dominated by a hegemonic state, such as Britain in the nineteenth century, may be more advantageous, say, to a middle or small power than a world in which the hegemony breaks up; a hegemonic state, if it is enlightened, may take the interests of others into account in setting the rules, but as its power declines and insecurity grows, all the participants in the world economy may suffer from the breakdown of the rules, the deficiencies of the international financial and monetary system, speculative capital movements, or the loss of national control over credit or monetary policies.) Inversely, even when there is a test of wills, there is a joint incentive, not merely to split the difference, but somewhat to "upgrade the common interest."[17] The best way for me to maximize my gain, even if I inflict a loss on you, is to see to it that you gain something, too—either because this will give you an incentive to help me increase my gain, or because you will otherwise be tempted to erase it. So, what is distinctive here is not so much the quest for absolute gains,[18] but the interest in a joint gain: Your loss (or my gain) will be at least partly compensated by some gain for you.

To be sure, this need not be the case in situations of extreme dependence, where one side's domination results in actual and total exploitation. Nor does the "compensatory" gain need to be equal to the loss. It merely has to be sufficient to prevent the actor that suffers the loss from seeking revenge. In the kinds of relations that theorists of imperialist dependency usually describe, the imperialist actor obtains his gains less often by inflicting a loss on his colony or client, than by preventing the development of his dependent, or by slanting it in a way profitable mainly to himself. But the situation lasts only as long as at least one important group in the colony or client state makes a gain—the "comprador" group, the social elite tied to the ruler of the imperialist actor. Thus, the notion of a joint gain says nothing about the evenness of distribution, the fairness of the game, or the possibility of better alternatives for one or even both partners. But it points to a game *different* from the traditional one.

Interdependence results not merely from the interpenetration of societies, but from the way in which this interpenetration concerns and constrains the actors. It is "policy interdependence"[19] that matters, and it results from both the very scope of "societal interdependence," which cannot fail to affect the actors, and the increasing control governments try to exert over society, given the predominance of economic and social issues in the domestic political agenda. The consequence is clear: the loss by state actors of some instruments of control, such as monetary, credit and taxation policies.[20] Choices are not merely constrained, they are sometimes eliminated—a state like Japan cannot "choose" economic self-sufficiency—either by external or domestic imperatives. Thus, the "interdependent" use of power is both less free (or full) and follows a different strategy than the traditional one. In the conventional logic, if my enemy became my friend, I would no longer have to worry (see the relation between the United States and Canada). In an interdependent world, the more intensely you are my friend, the more I may have to worry (think of the propagation of recessions, or United States–Saudi or United States–Iranian relations). There was some truth to a statement made, around 1973, by Sonnenfeldt: we had more difficulties in relations between Washington and its partners than in those with the U.S.S.R. and China, to which the logic of interdependence does not fully apply.

Obviously, the ideal-type of the first use of power is the diplomatic-strategic game, the ideal-type of the second, the modern world economy. But reality is more complex. The uses of power form a continuum, and they can be subtly mixed. Moreover, because today's military power has a large economic component—arms industries—some of the second type of logic appears in relations between military allies, or arms buyers and sellers; and because the open world economy is not as extensive as the planet, there are states that, to protect their separateness even in the economic realm, refrain from following the logic of solidarity, prefer autarky, or may even prefer to use the logic of interaction in the old mercantilist tradition. Conversely, even a state that observes the logic of interdependence in the world economy has two series of choices.

First, it can choose a more or a less cooperative strategy, by trying to maximize its relative gain, or to preserve a sizable joint gain even if its relative advantage is smaller, because it hopes that future benefits will be greater thereby. Secondly, it can try to improve its position in the sphere of interdependence by bringing to bear on it the assets it enjoys in the realm of interaction, such as military might others may want to draw on for their security. The mode of operation depends on the components of power at one's disposal. (Indeed, one may have no choice if one is ideologically committed to separateness and surrounded by foes, or, at the other extreme, if one is in a condition not merely of interdependence but of one-sided dependence on another nation). In most instances, the choice is largely determined by one's objectives.

To sum up: in the traditional usage of power, states were like boiled eggs. War, the minute of truth, would reveal whether they (or which ones) were hard or soft. Interdependence breaks eggs into a vast omelet. It does not mean the end of conflict: I may want *my* egg to contribute a larger part of the omelet's size and flavor than *your* egg—or I may want you to break yours into it first, etc. . . . But we all end in the same omelet.

A fourth change of power lies in the existence of new *restraints* that affect the old logic of interaction and are built into that of interdependence. They make power less calculable than ever, for there is an increasing difference between supply and usability and a growing distance between uses and achievements. I shall return to this later.

New Hierarchies and Multiple Systems These transformations of power have also affected the nature of the international hierarchy. There is no longer one hierarchy based on military or geo-military power. There are separate functional hierarchies, and in each one the meaning of being "top dog" is far from simple. Here again, the restraints on power operate, and their effects range from an attenuation of hierarchy to an outright subversion. In other words, it is a trying world for the top dogs, because of the general difficulty (the interference of other actors and one's own domestic accidents) of using one's might to achieve desired results, because of the difficulty of making might in one area affect outcomes in another (linkage), and because of the handicaps proper to each area.

The international system itself has been transformed. For the first time there is a single international system, symbolized by the United Nations, in which all state actors have to take, or pretend to take, stands on huge quantities of issues. This singleness is also illustrated by the way in which action on one issue—such as oil—affects the military and financial capabilities of states, their stands and claims on the world monetary system, on other raw materials, on aid and technology transfers, and so on. And yet, the very intensity of contacts, number of issues, and transformations of power allow one to establish two distinctions. One, there is still a distinctive strategic-diplomatic system, dominated by the possibility of violent conflict and characterized by the threat or the use of force. The same actors, however, participate in other systems, or games, where the threat or use of force is remote—a *distant* possibility, not a merely *latent* one (as it often is in the strategic-diplomatic arena), an improbable event even when the game's framework reflects the hierarchy of force. This improbability results from the costs of a resort to force, which would exceed by far any likely gain, or, even more, from irrelevance (force simply not being the means to the desired end), or from both. America's abstention from force against OPEC resulted from the political and economic losses such an expedition would have entailed, from the doubt that even a "successful" conquest would force a lasting reduction in the price of oil, and from the obvious fact that there are more appropriate ways of securing supplies of oil than through military conquest. (It also resulted in part, from ethical restraints, although their reach is not universal.[21]) Finally, the United States, the greatest possessor of military power, could afford to restrain this might because it depends much less on imported oil for its industrial production than countries insufficiently endowed with military supplies. The two superpowers, despite their different choices with respect to interdependence, are not in desperate need of external resources.

Second, there are many different functional systems in the nonstrategic realms, and it is not easy to produce an inventory. There are nonstrategic games of economic interaction (but not interdependence) between East and

West, for instance. Mainly, there are specialized games of "complex interdependence," to use Nye's and Keohane's expression.[22] Some crystallize around an issue—territorial, such as the oceans, or functional, such as international trade. Others crystallize around an issue and an international organization, such as the world monetary system (IMF) or food [Food and Agricultural Organization (FAO)]. Other games seem to have as a primary object the creation of the framework in which they will take place. For instance, should energy problems be dealt with separately or along with other raw materials? Should each commodity have its own arena? Thus, there is both some fluidity and room for additions, because some issues are not yet the objects of real collective games, even if they are put on the international agenda either for symbolic reasons, or, like the matter of human rights, as weapons in the diplomatic-strategic contest. Thus the unity of the international system contains a bewildering differentiation.

The Diplomatic-Strategic Chessboard

A survey of the changes cannot stop here. One must take a closer look at the "traditional" diplomatic-strategic chessboard and at the "modern" systems. In the traditional one, power remains above all a stock of national capabilities and forces that each state uses as it sees fit, to preserve or acquire the maximum possible freedom of action. The states are practically the only actors, along with groups (such as terrorists) struggling to form or to control states. The game of power remains what it has always been: My aim is to increase my ability to harm you and to decrease your ability to harm me; and this game is played with alacrity by many states, quite noticeably the new ones.[23] The structure of the game is still the military alliance. A partial *and perhaps temporary* transformation, however, has been brought about by the nuclear revolution. It has introduced into the competition of those states that now possess nuclear weapons an element of solidarity that tempers the very logic of separateness that gave rise to the nuclear race in the first place: It is solidarity for survival. The rules that apply are no longer the old rules of interaction, but it would be excessive to say that we are now in the same realm as that of economic interdependence, which entails not merely the vulnerability of one actor to the other's moves, but also a certain volume of transactions. "Policy interdependence" results from "societal interdependence." Nuclear solidarity does not come from the interpenetration of societies, but the effect is somewhat similar, and we can therefore talk about nuclear interconnection. It means that, for each of the present nuclear powers, the supreme form of military might is not usable in the daily course of world politics; given the risks of escalation, this also dampens their resort to conventional force among themselves. Hence the prevalence of oblique, indirect, or latent uses of force; the concern for arms control and the phobia of nuclear proliferation; and the desire, even when the struggle for influence unfolds in the traditional mode, to prevent third-party disputes from triggering a state of war between themselves. In other words, this fear of force not only makes the "minute of truth" more hypothetical, but also privileges other kinds of power.

This has, in turn, led to three changes. The first is a change in the rules of the "game of power," now a strange blend of arms race and restraints. On the one hand, at the nuclear level, the old Clausewitzian formula, "war is the continuation of state policy by other means," has become invalid. The peril of escalation is such, one, that the search for limited nuclear war strategies that might bring the formula back as a guideline is still most likely to fail or merely to reinforce deterrence;[24] and, two, that even at the conventional level, only limited, not "knock-out" wars make sense. For the nuclear level, the blend has produced the paradoxes of deterrence: I stop you from wanting to attack me by threatening suicide. We must both be concerned about injecting some stability into the race, and thus formally or informally coordinate our separate contributions to it, to allow ourselves to pursue our ordinary competitive pursuits without risk of annihilation. And we must respect some Alice-in-Wonderland precepts to protect deterrence's foundations. I must make sure that your retaliatory force can survive any attack by me, and I shall leave my population exposed to your retaliatory blows. Thus we have not only an exclusion of the old logic of the zero-sum game from the nuclear and even the large conventional war levels, but also the introduction of mixed strategies at the nuclear level.

On the other hand, the nonnuclear actors experience two kinds of restraints. One is traditional: Insofar as they are members of a great power's network of alliances, or as their enemies are protected by another network, they are inhibited in their resort to force by the need not to antagonize their guardian or the guardian of their foe. The other restraint is more original. Because the agenda of world politics is now crowded by issues that do not involve the use or threat of force, and because there are many games with varied alignments, the total hostility that usually brings reality closest to the model of the zero-sum game, and antagonists closest to the minute of truth, may be less frequent (although we still find it in the

Middle East). Even states that are on opposite sides on some issues, may be on the same side on others or be sufficiently interdependent economically for violence to be suspended (see the relations between several Black African nations and Praetoria).

The second change affects the hierarchy of states. The strategic-diplomatic game is the only truly bipolar one. But there are now different levels of strategic action. At the nuclear level, since atomic weapons are so far only weapons of deterrence, there has been fortunately general abstention. Large numbers of wars have been waged at the level of conventional conflict, however: interstate limited wars, wars of national liberation that remain limited on the defender's side, and all-out civil wars. Finally, there is the new level of terrorism. It all amounts to a decline in the actual ability of those who have the biggest supplies to use their military power, and the very inhibitions that weigh on them give greater opportunity to smaller states and nonterritorial groups to resort to violence. Moreover, the well-endowed states compete to sell arms to, or to license arms production by lesser ones. Thus, in various ways, the hierarchy is being subverted.

The third change concerns the structure of the game. On the one hand, the classical structure—the military alliance—has shown far greater resiliency than, say, General Gallois' prediction of their dissolution by the purely national character of nuclear weaponry would have led one to believe. This is because alliances have usually not been fusions but additions. And yet the formidable issue of the credibility of deterrence for the protection of an ally, the steps taken by nuclear powers themselves to replace deterrence-by-the-threat-of-doing-the-irrational with deterrence by-the-threat-that-leaves-something-to-chance, to use Thomas Schelling's terms, and to replace even the latter with elaborate strategies of war fighting, all this has created serious strains among allies. Unless one nuclear power places its forces at the service of another (as Britain alone has done or rather has had to do, given the technological dependence of its "independent" deterrent), alliances between nuclear states are difficult. The weaker one's asset lies precisely in its independence, i.e., in its forces' eventual use *not* being aligned and merged with the planned use of the superior one's. One such alliance has exploded: that between the U.S.S.R. and China. For alignment or merger makes the smaller deterrent unnecessary and creates no special problem for the potential enemy. But nonalignment, separateness, creates one both for the enemy and the senior ally. And alliances between a nuclear power and nonnuclear states become means by which the former controls the behavior of the latter. On the other hand, as Kissinger has recognized, the stability of the central nuclear balance has led to a splintering of the world into partial military balances along regional lines or around specific conflicts. There are, in effect, two kinds of fragments in the strategic-diplomatic puzzle: those that remain subdued, because an explosion there might lead to general war, given the sizable and direct involvement of superpower's forces (the prime example is Europe); and those that, so to speak, can afford turbulence.

THE GAMES OF INTERDEPENDENCE

Modern games, those in which the use of force is unlikely, are also extraordinarily complex. This is partly because of the far greater variety of economic capabilities and of the ways they can be used. There are many natural resources and all the means to exploit them (technology, skilled labor, fleets . . .). There is real capital and financial capital. There is what has sometimes been called the *force de frappe* of a nation's exports and also that of investments abroad—portfolio investments or enterprises. One can use economic power as a stock to be kept under one's control or use it to gain control over others without giving up anything of one's own freedom (see Soviet sales of natural gas). Or one can weave with one's economic power a seamless web made of inextricably intertwined national threads—indeed, not merely national threads, since these are games played by nonstate actors as well. This latter possibility becomes a necessity for a state whenever the level of transactions and the actor's sensitivity to them create that web, and for nonstate actors, which cannot usually resort to the logic of strategic and diplomatic interaction.

This use of power, which is not universal, interests us most here, both because of its originality and its importance. With the end of empires—the subjugation of needed resources or markets—with the sweeping internationalization of economies because of the communications revolution, the worldwide spread of technology and entrepreneurship, and the projection of the effects of consumption and production outside the nation's borders; with the resulting disappearance of the radical separation between interstate affairs and international economic transactions that was characteristic both of liberal theory and of much nineteenth century practice, and given the role played by the state in economic development and welfare, the states themselves are interdependent. This explains why the debate among experts about whether the ratio of foreign trade to GNP or the level of foreign investments have much increased since 1914,[25] misses the point. Even if the figures are not higher, the political significance of such interdependence is entirely different.

The Rules of the Game   This interdependence, the possibility or obligation to weave one's power into the web, is both an opportunity for and a restraint on the actor. It is an opportunity to exert influence almost literally on a global scale. It is a restraint, not only on domestic autonomy, but also on the hostile use of economic power, not just because of the actor's interest in promoting joint gains, but for three other reasons. One has to do with objectives. Let us take the case of a state actor whose aim is to maximize economic development, however defined (whether in terms of aggregate growth, or with priority given to those components of national power that can best be used for gains on the world scene, or in such a way as to overcome a rival, etc.). The level and nature of interdependence may well be such that this state could not reach its goal unless others (its rival included) reach their own development and welfare goals. Thus a joint gain is not only in the actor's interest; it is a necessity. This is the case, at present, among the nations of Western Europe, the United States, and Japan. Even the U.S.S.R., which in the traditional strategic-diplomatic game tries to reduce America's power and does not play the games of complex interdependence, is sufficiently in need of American wheat, technology, and credits to have been highly ambivalent about the recent "crisis of capitalism." And some East European countries, far more eager to play these games to escape from Russia's clasp, were not ambivalent at all about wishing capitalism well.

The second reason has to do with the impact of foreign policy on domestic affairs in a realm where the old, partial separation has vanished. An actor's hostile or aggressively competitive use of his economic power may well backfire at home. De Gaulle's accumulation of gold reserves in his fight against the privileges of the dollar, his determination to keep wages from rising too fast so as to improve the competitiveness of French industry in the Common Market, created social frustrations that led to the explosion of 1968.

This points to the third restraint, which results from the game itself: A state's uninhibited use of economic power could hurt it, for it might backfire internationally. In monetary matters, de Gaulle himself, far from waging an all-out war on the dollar, "was (contrary to much popular mythology . . .) pulling punches."[26] He wanted to dethrone the dollar; he did not want to destroy the principles of Bretton Woods—fixed rates, convertibility—which he approved and which he accused Washington of undermining. Similarly, he pulled his punches in his effort to limit the entry of American multinationals, for if they had been kept away from France, they would have invested their capital in the economy of France's EEC partners, and their products would have been imported into France.[27] Thus, the motto, quite different from that of traditional interaction, becomes, "You can harm me, and I you, but neither one of us can retaliate fully without harming himself." The recognition of the capacity to harm acknowledges, so to speak, the conflictual part of the process. After all, even among interdependent "partners" whose might is not drastically imbalanced, interdependence, being divisible, is seldom homogeneously even, and, being constraining, it is often resented. But the formula also acknowledges the ultimate non–zero-sum game aspects. Even when I try unilaterally to increase my share of the pie, I should not endanger its existence; even when I resort to conflict to exploit my advantage, ultimately I need, if not your cooperation, at least your consent.

Hence, here also, a triple change. First, in the rules of the game of power. Its name becomes the manipulation of interdependence: I pull on your thread, you pull on mine; I need you, but you need me—even when you are, either generally or even in the area that concerns us specially, much stronger than I am. The stakes of the games are multiple: specific gains (for instance, a certain level of oil prices, or an agreement to protect exporters of raw materials against losses resulting from price fluctuations, or the wiping out of the debts of certain nations); but also the determination of the rules of a game (who has the power to license the exploration of the seabeds? Who controls the IMF?), and the possibility of linking separate games to redress one's weakness in one through one's strength in another. Clearly, the calculation of power, always a difficult exercise, becomes almost impossible.

One can weigh capabilities of power, but whether, and on how broad a front they will be usable, and with what results, is largely a function of one's own skill, that of one's opponents, one's internal cohesion, the circumstances, and so on. The pace of technology, the ups and downs of the world economy, and monetary fluctuations make even the evaluation of capabilities difficult. Power tends to be disaggregated, abroad, into the various functional systems of interdependence. Each one tends to involve only a certain element of power (money, a given raw material, source of energy, and the like). At home, it is fragmented into a variety of bureaucratic services. Moreover, to make calculations even more complex, the formal power of governments or public institutions to deal with issues is divorced from the substantive power of private actors to empty that formal power of much of its content. For example, the oil multinationals thwarted the Arab embargo of most of its effect, with Japan receiving far more oil than before.[28] The irrelevance of using force to reap benefits or erase disadvantages also introduces vast uncertainties about the outcomes of contests, by removing one traditional trenchant way of ending them. Finally, the very nature of the web makes an accounting of power difficult: You and I may be so entangled that we do not clearly know where your power ends and mine begins. Or else, whether my power (defined as my capacity to reach my goal) exceeds yours, depends on third party reactions. For instance, in the contest between Saudi Arabia and Iran (the two chief antagonists in the split over oil prices among OPEC members in December 1976), whether one camp prevailed over the other depended in large part on how many of the consumers' orders switched to the cheaper oil. All of this in turn becomes an incentive to further testing one's power and that of one's rivals—or partners.

A Twisted Hierarchy of Players Second, there is a change in the hierarchy of players. As many hierarchies exist as games, and none of them is bipolar, since, on the whole, the U.S.S.R. remains absent or hesitant. On top of each, one finds not necessarily the state that has the greatest amount of overall power, but those states that, in this particular realm, individually or collectively enjoy a monopoly or oligopoly. Thus, the United States was able to change the rules of the monetary system in August 1971, because of the international role of the dollar. In a monopoly or oligopoly of a sufficiently vital resource, those states that depend on it may be forced to accept the linkage even of a game in which they are stronger, to that in which this monopoly or oligopoly operates. For years, the United States has obtained economic concessions from the EEC and the Federal Republic, or prevented them from making "unfriendly" decisions about the American multinationals or the Eurodollar market, by linking its military protection to the economic issues. OPEC not only changed the rules of the world oil game, but forced—in alliance with other developing nations—the United States to accept, in 1975, the linkage of energy to all the other economic demands raised by the Third World. And Saudi Arabia, more subtly, is coaxing a linkage between the realm of oil and the Arab-Israeli conflict.

This has the following effects on the international hierarchy. The games of interdependence obviously favor the United States; its economic capabilities are huge, its threads are all over the tapestry. Moreover, the loss of its external sources of supply, of its outlets, of its means of action abroad, while dealing a serious blow to its influence, would not be fatal—in contrast to the situation of Japan, West Germany, or the OPEC countries. And yet, serious inhibitions on the use of America's power limit its capacity to obtain outcomes proportional to its capabilities (and provoke dismay in a public that is not used to vulnerabilities, dependencies, and forced restraints). These inhibitions also weigh on the power of other "monopolists." Here are some instances:

▢ "I could theoretically use my advantages at your expense on a given issue, but must refrain from doing so because I need your support on another." This could be called "self-deterring linkage," as opposed to "enforced" linkage. For instance, both in the International Energy Agency and in the huge recycling facility Kissinger proposed in 1975, the United States could try to impose its technology on partners eager for substitutes for oil and its preferences for economic policies to be followed by them, in exchange for its help. But the United States, in turn, needs their support in dealing with the oil-producing countries, and it therefore has to behave more like a senior partner than a hegemonic master, if a common front of consumer countries is to be achieved. Similarly, the Third World countries cannot stabilize their export earnings if the United States refuses to, but the United States, or at least its multinationals, needs, sooner or later, an agreement on the rules of the game: the great power's interest in predictability and order operates as a restraint. And the oligopolists of OPEC, in turn, need the support of the oil-importing states of the Third World, both in order to resist the pressure of the rich oil-importing countries eager for guarantees of supply and concessions on price, and in order to wrest a larger share of the management of world economic institutions. This puts some brakes on the pricing policies of OPEC, and obliges the cartel to provide at least some aid to the poorer victims of its price increases.

▢ "I cannot push my advantage too far, because my power is partly your hostage." Multinationals have an incentive to respect the laws and customs of their host countries; otherwise they risk expropriation. The OPEC countries cannot increase the price of oil beyond reason, not just because this might provoke a military response, but because of their own interest in investing their huge revenues in the economies of their clients and in receiving goods and services from them. Their ambition for power and economic growth will force them to help their clients remain prosperous and will certainly refrain them from inciting their victims to confiscate OPEC investments or wiping out their debts to OPEC. In this respect, an oil embargo is a perfectly sensible strategy *before* mutual entanglement has gone too far, that is, as long as your short-term need for oil exceeds my short-term need to earn revenue. But once I have begun to put my earnings into your domain, a new embargo could hurt me as much as you. And if some oil-producing countries propose new price increases that could further depress the world economy (and perpetuate the vicious cycle, since the proposed increases are partly aimed at compensating for the failure to earn as many petrodollars as had been expected, due to the consumers' slump), then the common front risks splitting, as it did in December 1976.

□ "If I push my advantage too far, you can copy me, and thereby wipe it out." This might be called deterrent linkage. It is, for instance, the problem of competitive devaluations, or export subsidies, or import restrictions. (To be sure, there is not always perfect reciprocity. The United States has been able to change the rules, to devalue twice, and to force others into a system of floating rates. But this meant, in exchange, the end of the United States privilege of obliging its partners to absorb unlimited amounts of inconvertible dollars.)

□ "I cannot go too far, because I fear unwelcome domestic consequences both on your turf and mine." There are, unevenly distributed over the world, striking inhibitions on the use of force over economic matters. In the United States there is growing opposition to the use of food as an instrument of foreign policy, or even to the use of economic aid to shore up politically shaky and dubious allies. In other words, there is a restraint that comes from a somewhat inchoate, not always fair, but undeniable sense of legitimacy. In a very different vein, having to do not with moral scruples but with political prudence, Washington could not encourage an unlimited expansion of its "cosmocorps," without fomenting a revolt of labor unions and domestic industries within the United States. It almost happened with the Burke-Hartke bill. It would also foster a reaction from the "penetrated" foreign societies. Here we come to the impact on foreign turf: If you are a friend, I must make sure that I do not behave as a rogue elephant, for instance, that my anti-inflation policy does not induce a recession that could cripple you and aggravate my own. Even if you are an opponent, I must be careful not to bring about the advent of an even more intractable regime. Thus, arguments in favor of a United States military intervention in Arab countries to force a reduction in the price of oil left conveniently aside the issue of the regime that might take over, were the Saudi King overthrown or humiliated. And Saudi Arabia has pleaded for restraint in oil pricing, lest radical regimes rise over the depressed economies of Italy and France.

Thus the capacity of the strong to exploit fully the favorable asymmetries of interdependence is limited. The United States may be at the top of almost every hierarchy of economic power, but here, as in the strategic realm, it is a Gulliver tied, not a master with free hands. And insult can be added to injury: I refer to what might be called the *revenge* of the weaker. All those aspects of the new game can be seen, if not as factors of egalitarianism, at least as correctives to overall asymmetries.

The most obvious example is that lesser actors, devoid of military might or vast industrial resources, yet endowed with an asset (such as oil, bauxite, copper, or uranium) indispensable to the most advanced nations, can, through cartels and coalitions, extract a price that will help them narrow the gap in the race for development. The same relationship exists among unevenly powerful advanced countries: de Gaulle's great skill lay in exploiting such French assets as geography, or France's veto power in the EEC, to wrest advantages from NATO without losing the American guarantee or to obtain a Common Agricultural Policy (CAP) maximizing French advantages.

Other assets of a weaker power eager to block policies of a larger one reside in what Joseph S. Nye calls "the asymmetry of attention" and the "greater cohesion and concentration"[29] of the weaker government compared to the more powerful state. The latter has to disperse its attention over a huge number of chessboards and players and cannot always keep its own internal bureaucratic coalitions together. The examples Nye gives come from United States–Canadian relations.

In the cases of Canada and France, *in*dependence allowed a weaker state, by exploiting its assets, to decrease an "asymmetrical interdependency." But such a state can narrow the asymmetry another way. It consists of accentuating the *inter*dependency, even if it entails an apparent loss of autonomy or "separateness." For in certain relationships the stronger state is in fact obliged to transfer wealth or other resources to the weaker. Thus, the United States and its allies are transferring technological know-how to Iran; the United States is selling to Arab countries weapons that will provide them with a military panoply capable of reinforcing their economic *force de frappe*—and of making United States military intervention more difficult. In a world of interdependence, your desire to influence me may force you to help me get stronger. There is yet another way to accentuate interdependence in favor of the weaker partner. Keohane and Nye have found that Canada has done better than Australia in its relations with the United States because of the greater role played, in Canadian-American affairs, by transnational actors (auto, oil, and car companies) whose interests "did not always coincide with the United States government's."[30]

There is a corollary: The new games provide new opportunities for a very old exercise, the blackmail of weakness, or, "since you need me, and since my collapse would hurt you, you have to save me." For your possession of assets that are in demand (for instance, America's and West Germany's currencies, American weapons, grain, or technology, Bonn's current surpluses) turns out to be double-edged. It gives you some power, but you cannot either refuse to give (or sell) what your partner desperately needs, or impose such conditions that your partner in trouble would try to get help from your opponents. Thus, Bonn's interest—political and economic—in preserving the Common Market has led the Federal Republic to keep financing the CAP, to keep Italy afloat, to establish a regional fund, and so on. Washington, despite its hostility to gold, has had to allow its European allies to revalue their stocks to meet their new financial obligations to OPEC. Similarly, one can expect the OPEC countries to increase their aid to the Fourth World, whose support they need in their own contest of wills with the industrial nations.

The players who are in the most uncomfortable position are the industrialized middle powers. They have no monopoly or oligopoly, and, separately or jointly, they cannot force either linkages or changes in rules of the game (hence the anemia of the EEC). Nor do they have the weapons of the weak: they are stopped from fully exploiting the assets they *do* have— technology, capital goods, or financial resources—by their need to get the potential "victim's" support in another game, or by the fact that their might is another's hostage, i.e., they suffer the same inhibitions as the strong. And their economies are too entangled in the web of interdependence to allow them to choose the Soviet or the Chinese way.

Indeed, the refusal to play power-as-entanglement, still characteristic of the two main communist states, is, for them, a source of embarrassment as well as a strength. If a nation plays the game of entanglement and bargaining with all the other players, it creates both great chances for self-enhancement and great risks in a contest of constant uncertainty, where no gain is ever final, no setback fatal. A loss may be a gain at the same time (as when the United States "lost" power to OPEC, yet "regained" power toward Western Europe and Japan). Conversely, an undeniable gain (such as the obtention, for instance by Iran, of all the traditional trappings of power, weapons, factories, investments abroad, and the like) can also become a trap, since the preservation of power now means permanent and universal worry about the other actors' welfare and resources. Most nations, not being self-sufficient, have no choice: they must play, if only to try to increase their margin of self-sufficiency or their measure of control over the uncertainties of insufficiency. On the other hand, if a nation tries to be self-sufficient to preserve itself from the risks of the game, the compromises of the bargains, and the contagion of the other players' diseases, then it may well be able to increase its power by its own means, but its influence abroad is likely to be limited. Even Moscow's military cornucopia, and its skillful political exploitation of quarries of radicalism, are no substitutes for the influence derived from interdependence. The power of example may be its own reward, but it is not a tangible one, especially since it is not an example many countries can follow. Thus, playing the game of power on the world scene means an endless chase after elusive achievements, but trying to build power away from that scene means a temporary abdication from, or limitation of, an impact of events.

To be sure, there is ample room for half-way houses. China can try, so to speak, for discrete effects—without entanglement—for instance, through oil exports to well-selected targets of influence (such as Japan). The U.S.S.R., while trading with the rest of the world, tries to reduce the risks of interdependence by buying goods and technology only if the transaction creates no lasting dependence on a supplier, or no foreign right of overseeing Moscow's domestic policies. But such half-way houses are not stable. And the Soviets, in order better to control their satellites, do practice entanglement in Eastern Europe, where its inconvenience is discounted by the presence of Soviet military force. Yet it is not abolished thereby: force can be used or brandished only at exceptional moments, and entanglement involves some constraints for the U.S.S.R. (for instance, in the matter of East European oil supplies). Raw materials delivered to Eastern Europe are not available for export to Western countries. And just as the West often has to subsidize its exports to Russia, Moscow has to grant credits to its East European partners, or else import from them industrial goods it does not badly need.

And a New Structure   Third, a change, or rather a double innovation, has transformed the structure of the game. On the one hand, many more actors and a new type of game also bring with them a new grouping. As ever, indeed even more than before, the contests—those of interdependence as well as those of interaction—are fluid bets and plots among shifting partners. But there is now a generally recognized need for structures of bargaining, such as institutions, agencies, and organized coalitions. The actors need them to maximize *their* disaggregated or dispersed power and to minimize mutual interference, or at least make it predictable and maybe even beneficial; the issues require them because of the mixed interests of the players. (This, in turn, creates another restraint on an actor's itch to use his economic power aggressively. Some of the partners he needs are likely to cool him down or to thwart him: witness Kissinger's gradual shift to conciliation in North-South affairs, due to West European and Japanese misgivings about the earlier hard line, or Iran's difficulties with Saudi Arabia in OPEC.) To be sure, part of the contest is *about* such structures. In areas where I alone am strong, it is in my interest to dodge the harness; in areas where I alone am weak, it is in my interest not only to join those whose alliance with me will add up to collective strength, but also to slip a harness on you. But this in itself is a new element. And—again—it contributes to uncertainty. Will the structure last? If it rests on a mere convergence of different calculations, how solid will it be? Moreover, it consecrates a kind of power that, to be sure, requires a "stock" or ingredient of some kind to be more than a *trompe-l'oeil,* yet, like most modern economies based on paper currencies, depends more on trust, reputation, or faith than on any fixed ratio of gold to banknotes: the power to organize coalitions, define acceptable rules of the game, change these and force linkages. And states are unevenly skillful at cementing a beneficial coalition, or dissolving a hostile one. The choice of an actor for one alignment over another often depends not only on its interests in the case at issue, but also on its regime at a given moment. The very disaggregation of power may lead the same player to belong to diverse coalitions, depending on which game is being played—Harold Wilson once joked (was it a joke?) about the future British membership in OPEC, but when it comes to raw materials, Britain is surely not a member of the Group of 77. Thus, these groupings contribute to a certain defusing of world politics—states group to bargain, not to shoot—and to its complexity. They can be no more than interstate pressure groups, but they can also, like OPEC, become cartels controlling prices and quantities, or they can become even a mix of cartel and alliance, like the Arab members of OPEC. They can be highly specialized and deal with just one product, or be very general (like the Group of 77) and aimed, a bit like a political party, at putting some fire under a collection of demands. They can be ideological groups, like the Islamic Conference, or institutionalized groups, like the EEC. This brings us to the second structural innovation.

On the other hand, in world affairs, as in domestic societies in the earlier part of this century, the magnitude of the issues as well as the concern for some stability or moderation now brings about a shift from a system in which the management of interdependence was sought through the observance by states of a set of rules (such as those of GATT or Bretton Woods), to a system in which joint management will be required through international institutions, the pooling of sovereignties, and the coordination of policies and goals. Rules prescribing states what to do and not to do are no longer enough; yet governments remain unwilling to let, for instance, indicators determine automatically when to eliminate their payments surpluses or deficits. Whether one considers the regime of the oceans, the problem of food, or the future international monetary system, one sees no way of avoiding the establishment of international organizations with considerable powers either of administration or even of policy making.

Coalitions and international agencies mean an enormous expansion of the scope of multilateral diplomacy; and this, in turn, contributes to the transformation of the international hierarchy. Multilateral diplomacy boosts the influence of small states, both because of their numbers and because of the ability of even very weak states to obtain vicarious power through coalition. This is a fact which the smaller members of the European Community discovered long ago, and which the Soviets know, fear, and resist. On the traditional chessboard, small powers can exploit, at Washington's expense, either the security link or the ties created by the existence of an ethnic pressure group within the United States (as in the case of Israel). In the arenas of interdependence, it is multilateral diplomacy which dilutes the full use of American power because Washington faces not discrete weak players but groups of actors tied together by convergent interests. Saudi Arabia has known how to exploit both the security link and multilateral games.

THE POSITION OF THE NATION-STATE

All these transformations affect the position of the state in international affairs. They can be understood by looking at three terms of the traditional diplomatic vocabulary: sovereignty, the national interest, independence. Sovereignty, the state's privilege of carrying no obligations other than those it has accepted (whether this acceptance is truly voluntary or the result of a *Diktat*), the state's mastery of its own territory, population, and resources, is at the same time bolstered and undermined. It is bolstered by the rise in the number of states and by their attempts to control all their resources; it is undermined by the mutual and constant interference of the players. Everyone, from the lowliest to the most eminent, tries to find, develop, and exploit some asset either to maximize his influence or to ensure his security, but when all do this simultaneously, the outcome is, inevitably, frustration for many and a threat of chaos for all. With hierarchies constantly reshuffled, with an unprecedented proliferation of pieces moving all at once on the board, the exercise of safe external or even internal control is difficult, evanescent, and shaky. Although each state tries to make itself less, and others more vulnerable, or to turn the relation of interdependence into one in which it will be less, and others more dependent, these "neomercantilist" strategies collide with the current world economy, which has invalidated two key premises of old mercantilism: that the economic contest among states is a zero-sum game and that the right policy for each is autarky. Moreover, they collide with a highly nonmercantilist phenomenon: the loss of national control over essential ingredients of power or over vital tools of policy. This loss is experienced not merely (as in the relations between oil-importing countries and OPEC) by some states to the advantage of others, but by all (witness Iran's economic troubles). It is due partly to the role of actors that are not states and partly to phenomena: short-term capital movements, speculations against weak currencies, the spread of inflations and recessions, which the international economy conveys and which states either do not know how to check, or else fear trying to control by unilateral measures that might cut them off from the international economy on which they depend. National measures to curb inflation and payments deficits easily boomerang: the West German and American moves to cut demand created a deep recession because they were simultaneous. Or one's own policy-making autonomy can be ravaged by the moves of others: Japan's post-OPEC limitation on imports restored its balance at the expense of other nations' exports, i.e., of their payments balance. As a result, sovereignty becomes both a frantic quest for extending control wherever it is still possible (see the oceans and the new wave of creeping protectionism) and a last defense against the thrusts of all those forces that have turned the old armor into a sieve.

The concept of the national interest was inseparable from a relatively hard, calculable, and stable idea of power and the international system. There was always something oversimplified and wrongheadedly dogmatic about it. But the old uncertainties about physical survival and military safety look simple next to the new ones. The modern games offer so many alternatives, mysteries, and complexities that an "objective" definition of the national interest makes even less sense than before. In the first place, although many nations—especially among the newly rich—obviously act on the belief that their *interest* lies in behaving in a traditional way, that is, to imitate the patterns of the past by maximizing their military might and by becoming industrial powers, this may not be the wisest path. Military might may turn out to be hard to use—given the restraints watchfully observed or imposed by the great powers—as well as dangerous to the domestic stability. And while industrialization, investments abroad, and a large trading role, allow one to splash in the sea of interdependence, one's lifejacket is tied to those of the other swimmers, there remains a permanent peril of sinking, and the longer one stays in the water the less one can break out of the chain and reach the shore where one could be tranquil, if alone. In the second place, the old concept of the *national* interest is clearly being dissolved, so to speak, from below, from the side, and from above. From below, it is dissolved through the transgovernmental bureaucratic alliances along functional lines that recent studies have begun to describe; from the side, through the subversion of sovereignty either by transnational alliances of barons and bureaus or by transnational agents, especially corporations that often create in the host country a dilemma between regulation on behalf of the "national" development of priorities, and openness or even incentives to penetration on behalf of rapid growth; from above, through interstate or transnational bargaining solidarities (which it would be a mistake to describe as mere clusters of material interests, for ideological and psychological factors often determine the alignments), or through international or regional organizations that the state must either enlist or enfeeble.

The concept of the national interest was supposed to provide the state with a compass for an independent course. There seemed to be a clear choice between independence and dependence. But today the fluidity of games without any necessary single minute of truth or clearcut boundaries, played by so many players over so many issues, gives each player a choice among several strategies. Each one has its risks. Each one corresponds to a different priority (for instance, independence as the maximum of impenetrability compatible with welfare, or independence as the maximum of influence abroad) or to the preference for a particular kind of solidarity. Material solidarity alone does not explain, for instance, why in the winter of 1973–4 eight out of the nine members of EEC preferred Henry Kissinger's strategy to Michel Jobert's, or why, in most of the North-South meetings, the oil-rich and the poor nations of the Third World have tended to vote together. Or else the choice depends on the internal balance of political and social forces, which can shift. Precisely because very few nations are able or eager to be self-sufficient in every realm, even a country eager to maximize its independence, to eliminate one-sided dependence on a single "big brother" on all the playing fields, and to fragment its dependencies would have a variety of alternatives. (Is it more important to spend resources on military autonomy, or on the creation of a heavy modern civilian industry? To give top priority to reducing imports of energy or to reducing dependence on foreign computers? Who should be one's partner in the effort? And so on.) Thus each state is adrift on a sea of guesses.

Sovereignty as Sisyphean abstraction, a battle against loss of control, yet waged over a broader front than in the days when control was safer but politicization less prevalent; the national interest splintered into many alternatives, yet with no assurance that any one course would lead the state to the Erewhon of independence: does this mean the decline of the nation-state? Let us, once more, be prudent and observe that the present scene is the triumph of ambiguity. There are nonstate actors, but not, on the whole, in the traditional arena. In the modern ones, the very perils of loss of control, the determination of new states to assert themselves, the fear of most states to have interdependence turn into costly dependence on a master or on an extortionist—all this and the politicization of economic issues give the state enormous resilience, the will to curb the nonstate actors, and the desire to curtail one's vulnerability even by reducing the openness of the society. International interdependence may frustrate a state's ambition, but it is not irreversible. It provides opportunities for manipulation and rebellion, and the nature of the issues often gives to the state's action abroad, however handicapped, the dynamism that comes from domestic needs. Thus, the state has been neither superseded nor tamed. Many states are threatened by secessions, but these would create more states. Individuals or groups may not agree on the limits of the national community, but it is still to the state that they turn for protection, welfare, and justice.

SECTION TWO: PROBLEMS

Any international system has three dimensions: horizontal (the relations between major players), vertical (the hierarchical aspects), and functional (the subject matter of international political transactions). As in a surrealistic dream the three dimensions move at once and into each other. To what extent are the current restraints among the big powers tied to a long period of growth and prosperity? Would they survive the centrifugal domestic pressures toward autarky or aggressive nationalism that worldwide economic dislocations might provoke? What would be the effects of a frequent reshuffling of the hierarchy or, rather, hierarchies of power, since different pyramids of players correspond to different kinds of assets? Can there be a reasonably stable system with inconsistent hierarchies, that is, wildly disparate "top dogs," depending on the component of power? Are the same principles of management and rules of bargaining valid on all the chessboards? Is there, as Alastair Buchan had suggested in the 1973 Reith lectures,[31] a domain for balancing power and a distinct one for collective management? Is the traditional strategic-diplomatic chessboard still the decisive one? How extensive are linkages between games likely to be? The fact that one can not yet answer these questions suggests that the outcome of the struggle between the separate drives of the players and their groping toward joint management is far from clear. Before we return, in the next chapter, to the question we asked at the beginning of this one—where does the present world fit?—let us draw some conclusions from the preceding analysis.

The present international system is a theater of three contradictions and three races.

CONTRADICTIONS

A first contradiction exists, quasi-universally, between ideologies and interests. It is not total, since interests tend to wrap themselves in ideological rationalizations. A good example is anti-imperialist ideology, especially the so-called theory of *dependencia,* with its view of a world periphery bled white by the centers of industrial and financial power. It reflects and elevates the interest in emancipation of those "peripheral" areas most subjected to foreign investment, most devoid of local entrepreneurs, and least endowed with modern technology and industry. Also, ideologies, when they provide the basis of a regime's legitimacy, literally create interests—as in the case of Soviet political dominance in Eastern Europe. Similarly, as George Kennan has pointed out, Soviet ideology requires "the protection of the image of the Soviet Union as the central bastion of revolutionary socialism throughout the world,"[32] and therefore dictates support for "progressive forces" in the Third World. Still, ideology and interests are often in conflict. As development proceeds, especially when it does so according to a capitalist model and through reliance on the world economy, anti-imperialist ideology conflicts with the need for cooperation, bargains, and imports of advanced technology. Opposition to a traditional law of the seas that served the interests of the most advanced nations no longer overcomes the clear difference in interest between coastal developing nations and landlocked ones. Soviet ideology suggests alignment with the Third World against the liberal industrial nations, but nuclear interconnection puts the Soviets and the Americans on the same side of the proliferation issue. The competitive yet convergent interests of the world's two largest fleets lead to joint Soviet and American stands for an unimpeded right-of-transit passage in the territorial sea or in straits, and for freedom of scientific research within the new 200-mile economic zone. The interests of the U.S.S.R. as an industrial society, joined with its internal economic difficulties that would in any case curtail the contributions Moscow could make to the development of the Third World, have incited the Soviets to remarkable abstinence in general North-South discussions.

Many of the world's regional organizations are founded on some ideological solidarity and have foundered on clashes of interests among their members, the OAU being the most recent example. OPEC itself is torn between states with huge oil resources and small populations, whose first concern is the profitability of their huge capital abroad, and states with smaller oil reserves and large populations, whose first concern is to maximize resources for their internal development. A world of highly conflicting interests is not orderly per se. But a world of self-righteous and uncompromising ideologies would be literally hopeless, even if physical annihilation were avoided. Some nations (Algeria, for instance) are very good at pragmatic dealing behind unfurled ideological banners. But nothing, except obtuse faith, guarantees that pragmatic leaders will everywhere prevail over romantics or revolutionaries. Nothing tells us that pragmatic deals aimed at making economic interdependence hasten national development, will not put more potent fuel into the motor of ideological strife. And if the world's multiple tyrannies have to show some material progress to their peoples, they also often need to cover pure and simple meanness with an ideological fig leaf. For every Nasser or Sukarno who disappears, there seems to be a Khadafi who comes, or a Kim il Sung or a Park who stays.

A second contradiction exists between the various kinds of fragmentation and the unity of the international system. We have mentioned regional fragmentation, produced by the very multiplicity of players, and the central balance of military power, functional splintering that corresponds to the different games played, and the different functional hierarchies. These partitions can easily be seen as providential safeguards against worldwide disasters, a tentative, haphazard equivalent of the federalist system, which sees (by contrast, say, with French centralization) that every local trouble, far from leaping to the top of the world agenda, clogging channels, or spreading into chaos, remains well circumscribed, Unfortunately, two forces work the other way. One is miscalculation. A local war or act of terrorism can spread beyond regional bounds through the dialectic of the commitments made by extraneous powers, along the lines described by Thucydides, or through the reprisals of the terrorists' target state. Or the failure of states to agree on the rules of the game in one functional area— the monetary system, say, or the oceans—can lead to a snowballing of conflict into other economic realms (trade) or even to armed conflicts (e.g., Greek-Turkish tension over the respective rights of the two nations in the Aegean sea).

The other force of reescalation is quite deliberate state will. Not only interdependence, but the willed manipulation of it, makes "decoupling" the global system from its fragments difficult. Remember that what could be called the oil spill from the Arab-Israeli war of October 1973 was provoked first by the Arab countries, then by OPEC. Similarly, the attractiveness of military might—including its supreme form, nuclear weapons— for states that are weak in the strategic-diplomatic game but on or near the top of the hierarchy in other games may lead to a kind of rapprochement between these hierarchies on the plateau of greatest peril. Less dangerous, but still of an escalatory nature, is the desire of poorer states or states with limited assets to compensate for their weakness in some of the functional areas by exploiting international egalitarianism.

Whether it takes the form of miscalculation or of a deliberate decision, this risk of contagion shows that the beneficial effects of fragmentation—its potential as a way of ordering a complex world and in cushioning its members against the excesses of interdependence—are neither assured nor unlimited. On the traditional chessboard, each great power is torn between its desire for stability and domestic progress which induces caution abroad and the worldwide involvement dictated by its ideology as well as its interests. Whenever the latter prevails, fragmentation fades. In the modern arenas, the very logic of the world economy makes fragmentation, if it should lead to protectionist goals and beggar-thy-neighbor policies a peril, not a buffer. Remember the 1930s.

These dangers point to a key flaw of the world system. Unity exists, not at the top in the guise of a superior, but only at the level of the actors—one might say at the level of (potential) mischief making. It is they who decide how to distribute their efforts and whether to try to create links.

A third contradiction follows from another kind of heterogeneity. On the one hand, the players participate in a simultaneous set of games. On the other, they belong to different ages of world politics. I am not referring again to ideological splits. I am trying to describe something that results from a mix of differences in economic levels, degrees of nationhood and statehood, dates of formal independence, and content of ideological dogmas. I am also referring to basic attitudes, tested more by crisis situations than by daily behavior, in which routine or practicality often prevails.

Some actors seem to live, more or less schizophrenically, in the world I have tried to describe: a potpourri of conflict and cooperation, anxious interaction and confusing interdependence, national selfishness and vague concern for a wider order. Others, even when caught in the economic web, or remote from the great powers' strategic maneuvers, seem to live in an age that seems past to the "sages" in the first category, but is very much the present to their leaders. They have just emerged from subjugation; they are still struggling to reduce dependencies; or they believe in philosophies of revolution. To them, the nation-state is not a familiar structure whose recent inadequacies are revealed in ever-growing cracks, but a new shelter and a new springboard.[33] One group sees national control waning, the other grabs it at last, whatever its imperfections. This is true even for states that are not new—like those in Latin America—yet are trying for the first time to act on the world stage and to develop their economies. Our nineteenth century is very much their twentieth, and consequently their view of order is unlikely to be the same as ours. It is often less concerned with long-term problems (population growth, pollution, depletion of resources, preservation of "commons") than with the achievement of power and autonomy. At worst, this achievement is seen as the triumph through battle of the righteous over the miscreants, at best the final flowering of Wilsonianism, a world order of harmony through self-determination and rather little collective management, unless they can control it and use it against the big and rich. Another consequence is that the problems of borders, the difficulties of social integration (with the risk of an external diversion of internal troubles), the festering of traditional rivalries, in other words, proneness to violence, have to be given different weights depending on the area.

I am not suggesting that there shall be no peace or order until those whose present is our past have been lifted to our lofty level. After all, we too carry the past into our present, for the simple reason that the past lives on both in the logic of much world politics and in our own minds (hurrah for the Mayaguez! And the beatitudes of Wilsonianism are not unknown in Washington). I am merely suggesting that different ranges of experience raise one more obstacle. Even though there is a growing economic differentiation in the "new" group—between rich and poor, almost industrialized and backward—and a bewildering variety of regimes, there is no comparable mental diversity insofar as the approach to world politics is concerned. Here, it is difficult to skip stages (and let us remember the fragility, or even reversibility, of our own mental stage).

RACES

The future of world order may well depend on how these contradictions will be smoothed out. It may also depend on the outcome of three races, besides the race, described throughout the last section, between the logic of conflict, whose range has been widened by the increase in the scope of international relations and by the intensity of interstate contacts, and the new restraints of nuclear interconnection and economic interdependence. Even though the latter do not constrain actors to cooperation, and even though de facto solidarity is not a solidarity of commitments, there are imperatives of prudence that dampen at least interstate conflicts; and all of world politics tends to become the testing of the uncertain and shifting limits of these restraints.

Domestic Politics, Technology, and World Order There is a race between the domestic priorities that govern the political life of states, and the external imperatives of order. Everywhere, domestic pressure groups, parties, such public services as the military, or the guardians of official orthodoxy do their best to influence or control the definition of the nation's policy, to capture, so to speak, the national interest. Leaders, whether tyrannical or democratic, have to take care, if not of the needs of their people—a concept as vague as that of the national interest—at least of the demands of those from whom their power comes or on whom its survival rests. When this happens to fit the interests of world order, it is a happy coincidence. At any rate, the criterion of national policy remains, at best, the interest of the nation or of a fragment of mankind with which it identifies; more usually it is that of a group within the society, whether this interest is primarily material ("the American farmer") or ideological. Either the global interest is not taken into account at all (for it remains an abstraction): what is peace, or peaceful change, next to the drive for black self-determination in Southern Africa or the defense of shrinking white supremacy? Or the global interest is not yet a felt reality—say, in matters of population control. Or it is more or less candidly equated with the national interest—see the American ideology of the free market for world develop- ment. Or it clearly clashes with a state's or a group of states' conviction about its own interest—as when OPEC pushed an (admittedly low) price of oil so high that not only was a serious blow administered both to the industrial nations and (even more) to the poorer developing countries, but the earnings of the oil producers outran their capacities of absorption or induced excessive development plans that dragged them into debt. Thus, the breakdown of the great divide between foreign policy and domestic politics turns out to be, like so many other changes, a mix of good and evil. It is good insofar as it results from a change in the political agenda that has brought to the fore issues that ordinarily can not be resolved by violence; bad, insofar as the late, unlamented and partly mythical primacy of foreign policy, for all its brutal consequences, had the uncelebrated virtue of sometimes protecting diplomacy from the parochialisms and the contradictory passions of domestic politics—whereas interdependence today provides the leaders and interest groups of one state with countless opportunities to manipulate domestic forces elsewhere.

There is a second race, this one between technology and the capacity of the fragmented international milieu to master it. In the realm of nuclear energy, both among the nuclear powers and among those states that are on the threshold of or are tempted by the status of nuclear statehood, the progress of technology, military and peaceful, has already outstripped diplomacy. I have mentioned it apropos of SALT. The current arguments about slowing down the spread of the capacity to produce nuclear bombs through the development of peaceful nuclear energy often have a tone of desperation. The progress of peaceful nuclear power and the bomb can, no doubt, be slowed down. But mastery, in the sense of curtailing the harmful potential, seems increasingly difficult. Technological progress also risks putting increasingly more accurate missiles at the disposal of the superpowers, with dangerous consequences for the taboo on direct military contests between them (see Chapter Four); it risks putting sophisticated conventional technology at the disposal of many states; it risks blurring the essential distinction between conventional and nuclear weapons (as it does in the case of cruise missiles), a distinction that has been crucial for the self-restraint of the nuclear powers. Inversely, in many other areas—the exploration of the seabeds, techniques for improving food production, or for reducing population growth—the beneficial potential of technology is being held back both by the nature of international politics and by domestic political or social obstacles.

Dimensions of Insecurity   A third race exists between the universal desire for security—nourished by the abundance of means of mass destruction and by a fear of a scarcity of resources (or of restriction to their access)—and what might be called the proliferation of insecurity. I shall not mention at length the obvious insecurity of terrorist groups, international agencies submitted to the financial whimsy and political pressures of states, and multinational enterprises coping with monetary fluctuations, demands from their parent state, and restrictions imposed by their host states. Let us concentrate on the state's three dimensions of insecurity. There is, as before, physical unsafety, the product of the risk of war, the need to protect oneself from it, or the urge to wage it. Despite the worldwide interest in survival, and the inhibitions observed by the present nuclear powers on the use of certain kinds of force in direct confrontations, this fear has been heightened by all the new ways in which violence can either penetrate the "inviolable" state, or subvert it from within. It is intensified by the spread of nuclear weapons (and the risk of theft of nuclear fuels), the surge of terrorism, the universality of intelligence work, espionage and covert operations, and the ideological, financial, and often overtly symbiotic links between domestic forces and foreign foes.

Second, economic unpredictability,[34] the newest and most insidious of these dimensions, may appear less deadly than military unsafety, but may well be even more unsettling insofar as it is less manageable and calculable. The ingredients one needs to develop one's economic power may depend on someone else's good will: the industrial world, and part of the developing world, have discovered the cost of dependence on imported oil. Or they may depend on someone else's wisdom: the Third World (rich and poor) has discovered the cost of having to import manufactured products from the industrial world at a time of inflation.

Some of the new, interdependent power is passing almost by essence, because whoever exerts it at the moment has little control over how long he will be able to exploit it. This is particularly true of the ability to bargain and forge coalitions. Thus, for several years, French policy consisted of trying to build, in the EEC, a structure whose base would be a de facto alliance between France, aiming for common policies, and the EEC's, eager to extend the scope of its activities. But that alliance collapsed in the mid-1960s because de Gaulle was forced to choose between, on the one hand accepting Britain's entry or else reinforcing the supranational aspects of the Community—two very different developments, yet both leading to a loss of French control over the common policies—and, on the other hand, the pursuit by France alone of some of the objectives it had tried to get its partners to share. He chose the latter course, which led to a blind alley both for France and for the EEC. The alliance of France and the Commission was forged again under Pompidou, thanks to his decision in favor of Britain's entry. This time, the energy crisis broke it up, when France's eight partners chose, in effect, a United States–led structure, the International Energy Agency (IEA), rather than the EEC as the framework for that overarching issue.[35] Bargaining power and the art of shaping coalitions also depend heavily on individual leadership skills that may not be transmissible.

The lack of control over one's momentary power is not limited to bargaining situations. One's investments abroad can be confiscated. One's surpluses or reserves may be wiped out, by a sudden external action that one could not affect (cf., the effect of United States devaluations, in 1971 and 1973, on Washington's allies; or the impact on Britain, France, Italy, and Japan of the quadrupling of the price of oil); by a sudden domestic drama, such as May 1968, in France; by internal mismanagement, as in Italy; by the domestic policies of a major client (cf., the impact of United States inflation and recession on its trading partners, or the effect on French economic growth of the failure by Bonn and Washington to stimulate their economies sufficiently in 1976); by the perfectly "rational" calculations of huge private companies moving their capital from one place to another; or even by the boomeranging outcome of one's own external policy (cf., the ultimate impact on America's inflation of America's monetary practices of the 1960s and early 1970s, leading to the deterioration of the international monetary system). Technologically based assets—such as a nation's aeronautic or electronic industry—are susceptible to obsolescence and to the superior competition of latecomers. Inversely, the exploitation in America of domestic oil reserves and of alternatives to oil that were unprofitable before the OPEC decisions has become a potential source of increased power for the United States, for reasons entirely independent of American will. Finally, there is insecurity even when one's bargaining power rests on a tangible asset, if it is nonrenewable. Algeria's resources of natural gas and Iran's and Algeria's oil reserves are limited, and the difference between them and Saudi Arabia in this respect puts a question mark on the future of OPEC.

When I no longer know where your power ends and mine begins; when yours is partly my hostage; when the more I try to force you to depend on me, the more I depend on you; when world politics becomes a test of vulnerability, and degrees of vulnerability are not identical with power supplies, who can feel secure? There is, as before, yet in far more complex ways, psychological uncertainty. It is partly due to the depth of ideological cleavages, to the abysses of miscomprehension between opposed camps, and to the resulting tendency to see in the other side a devil rather than a part of mankind. It is partly due to the elusiveness, fragmentation, and frequent ineffectiveness of power, to the complexity of the games nations play, to the dilemmas of choice among possible strategies. Not only do we live in a world full of enemies, but we cannot rely entirely on our friends, because those who are "on our side" in one arena may play against us in another game. It is partly due to the existence of a single international system, which obliges each state to cope with issues far beyond its reach and, indeed, beyond its psychological resources. It is partly due to the rapidity and uncontrollability of social change. It is partly due to the importance of milieu goals, which, almost by definition, can never be reached in their entirety or for long by anyone. It is partly due to the rules of nuclear deterrence, which requires states to search for "credibility," to test their will even in unlikely places, and to replace iron with image. Very often, therefore, a statesman who tries to chart his nation's course for the various games of world politics does not know what cards he has, what his cards are worth, or for how long. Cards on which he may count heavily could turn out to be liabilities (think of Britain's Blue Streak and Sky Bolt missiles, the Concorde's misadventures, the troubles of the European space programs, or the European monetary "snake," once a key French objective). Cards that may have been treated with indifference turn out to be assets (think of German or Polish coal). New cards may appear out of the deep blue sea (think of the North Sea oil). Conversely, foreign statesmen trying to predict a friend's or a rival's behavior are often left with question marks. Precisely because many alternative strategies are open, can one be sure that the next government will follow the same approach, or that even a few changes in the top bureaucracy will not lead to a different way of using whatever power may be available? And yet the statesman must act, and neither he nor the average citizen has the time to look at all the implications of these acts constantly.

Let us return to our original question: Which of the models of international politics does the present system resemble? One thing is clear. The model of community is as irrelevant as it has been for more than four centuries. There is no equivalent of the universal Church: "nonterritorial central guidance"[36] remains fragmentary and controlled by modern Princes of highly divergent faiths. There may be some universal norms, such as self-determination, but they are so vague and so distorted by self-interpretation as to be pathetic. There are some imperatives of prudence—no nuclear war, no economic disaster, some aid to development—but they correspond to calculations and convergences of interests rather than beliefs. As Robert W. Tucker has pointed out, wealthy citizens of a nation may feel some sense of obligation to the poorer ones, but rich nations feel no such duty toward the poorer countries, partly because of the vast difference between individual equality and the equality of states, which may never benefit their members.[37] There may, in some parts of the world, have been a decline in the acceptability of force, a result of liberal values, but it remains limited in scope and depth. The highest allegiance of each actor remains either to himself or to a fragment of humankind—a bloc he belongs to out of necessity or conviction.

We are still among the models of fragmentation, then. But which one? State of war or troubled peace? The originality of the postwar bipolar system was that it blended the two. The bipolar contest seemed straight out of Thucydides, but nuclear weapons, the legitimacy of the nation-state, the obstacles posed by the heterogeneity of the world to the annexation of all other issues by the cold war served as moderating factors in the strategic-diplomatic arena, while the restraints of economic interdependence developed in the other ones. Where are we now, and where are we going? The present is still a blend of the two ideal-types. Precisely because of the fragility of common norms, the prodigious progress of weaponry, the multiple ideological, ethnic, tribal, and national hostilities, the uneven distribution of power, there are still many features of the state of war. The modern games themselves are, to a large extent, conflictual. They are struggles around the two key issues of all politics, who benefits and who commands—struggles in which, as we all know today (and as the truly dependent or exploited have always known) blows are inflicted and losses imposed. Nevertheless, because of the restraints on the use of force and those that result from mutual economic interests, because of the need to blend hostility and cooperation, or to move from hostility to cooperation, which nuclear interconnection and economic interdependence induce, it would be excessive to speak of universal malevolence or a complete absence of common rules, even if those that exist are "rules of the game," not moral commands. But can such a blend be stable?

So far I have listed changes, contradictions, races, ambiguities, all facets of an increasingly complex world. One must not only analyze, but also evaluate. What do the dynamics of this intricate system portend for world order?

NOTES

Chapter Three

1. Robert W. Tucker, *A New Isolationism,* Universe Books, New York, 1972; "Oil: The Issue of American Intervention," *Commentary,* January 1975; "Israel and the United States: From Dependence to Nuclear Weapons," *Commentary,* November 1975.
2. For a comparable but more thorough exercise, published after this one had been drafted,

see Edward L. Morse, *Modernization and the Transformation of International Relations,* The Free Press, New York, 1976, especially chaps. 2 to 4.

3. See, for further elaboration, my *State of War,* Praeger, New York, 1965, especially chap. 2.

4. See Robert Jervis, *Perception and Misperception in International Politics,* Princeton University Press, Princeton, N.J., 1976.

5. See Arnold Wolfers, *Discord and Collaboration,* Johns Hopkins Press, Baltimore, Md., 1962.

6. See Kenneth N. Waltz, *Man, the State and War,* Columbia University Press, New York, 1954; and my *State of War,* op. cit., chap. 3.

7. Clausewitz, *On War,* Pelican Books, Baltimore, Md., 1968, vol. 1, chaps. 1 and 2. See Raymond Aron's monumental two-volume work, *Penser la Guerre, Clausewitz,* Gallimard, Paris, 1976, especially vol. 1, chap. 3.

8. Aron, ibid., vol. 2, chap. 6.

9. Cf. Robert Keohane and Joseph S. Nye, Jr., *Power and Interdependence,* Little, Brown, Boston, 1977, chap. 3. This is at the heart of my disagreements with Kenneth Waltz. In his incisive essay, "Theory in International Relations" (in Fred I. Greenstein and Nelson W. Polsby, eds., *International Politics,* vol. 8 of *Handbook of Political Science,* Addison-Wesley Publishing Company, Reading, Mass., 1976), he indicts my conception of the international system for being "so rigged" as not to explain anything. This may be true. But on the one hand, I find his "purely positional" definition of structure (pp. 46–47) too narrow. To understand a structure requires that one know, not only "the principle by which a system is ordered" (coordinate units versus super and subordinate ones) and "the arrangement of parts," but also whether those parts are, so to speak, all apples, or a mix of apples, oranges, and stones. Power as capabilities cannot be assessed otherwise; hence the importance of knowing whether the actors are all states, and, even if they are, whether they are of the same type. On the other hand, to limit one's concern to showing how the level of the structure (A), narrowly defined, and the level of the interacting units (B) "operate and interact" (p. 45), "how A and B affect each other," is also much too narrow. I agree with Waltz that "to define a structure requires ignoring how units relate with each other" (even if "concentrating on how they stand in relation to each other"— his definition of structure—demands, in my opinion, more than a "purely positonal picture," since I need to know *who* is "positioned"). But "how units relate with each other" results not only from the structure (defined in his way, or even in my broader one), but also from other elements, such as the domestic regimes and the transnational forces, and in turn affects not only the structure, but also these elements. Moreover, changes in those regimes and forces affect the structure, insofar as they also change the "distribution of capability among units" (think of the passage from Weimar to Hitler). I have other, minor quarrels with Waltz's critique of my writings. For instance, when I say that the existence of a system is certain, I do not mean that the system is a reality. I mean exactly what he does when (pp. 8–9) he talks about theories as being instruments to apprehend some part of the real world. In his critique of my notion of structure, he confuses homogeneity or heterogeneity of the structure (i.e., is it composed only of nation-states, or of a mix of empires, nation-states, and city-states?) with homogeneity or heterogeneity of a given state. Whether "outcomes" are "unit determined" or "system influenced," is, for me, a matter of empirical research. Obviously, a superpower usually can affect the system more easily than a tiny actor; but the superpower can also be mightily "system influenced" (see below). (Incidentally, to say, as he does in his critique

of Morton Kaplan, that what Kaplan calls a "subsystem dominant system," i.e., one in which the units determine the outcome, is "no system at all," is as absurd as saying that a domestic system shaped by a "subsystem" such as a dominant party or institution, is no system.) And while Waltz now (by contrast with his analysis in *Man, the State and War*) interprets Rousseau correctly, he thoroughly misreads my interpretation of Jean-Jacques—to which he has come around.

10. Waltz, ibid.. p. 74.
11. Hedley Bull, *The Anarchical Society*, Columbia University Press, New York, 1977, p. 271.
12. Cf. the definition given by Keohane and Nye in *Transnational Relations and World Politics*, Harvard University Press, Cambridge, Mass., 1972, introduction and chap. 4.
13. Bull, op. cit., p. 272.
14. These forces are not to be deemed "actors" unless they meet the definition given above. If they do not have autonomy (i.e., they are merely the tool of a totalitarian state), and if they have no power to make decisions affecting resources and values across borders, but merely that of making suggestions that can influence governments because of the interaction between each society and its state, then we are still in transnational society, not in world politics.
15. See Helmut Schmidt's article, *Foreign Affairs*, vol. 52, no. 3, April 1974.
16. Cf. Susan Strange, "What Is Economic Power, and Who Has It?" *International Journal*, vol. 30, no. 2, Spring 1975; and Jeffrey Hart, "Three Approaches to the Measurement of Power in International Relations," *International Organization*, vol. 3, no. 2, Spring 1976.
17. Cf. Ernst B. Haas, "International Integration: The European and the Universal Process," *International Organization*, vol. 15, 1961; and *The Uniting of Europe*, Stanford University Press, Stanford, Calif., 1958.
18. Here I differ slightly with Keohane and Nye (see their "World Politics and the International Economic System," in C. Fred Bergsten, (ed.), *The Future of the International Economic Order: An Agenda for Research*, Lexington Books, Lexington, Mass., 1973, p. 127.
19. Ibid., p. 122ff.
20. Cf. Morse, op. cit., p. 104ff.
21. Cf. my essay, "The Acceptability of Military Force," in *Force in Modern Societies*, Adelphi Paper No. 102, *International Institute of Strategic Studies*, 1974; and the discussion in Klaus Knorr, *The Power of Nations*, Basic Books, New York, 1975, chap. 5.
22. It is characterized by multiple channels connecting societies, an absence of hierarchy among issues, and abstention from the use of force.
23. Cf. Klaus Knorr, "Is International Coercion Waning or Rising?" *International Security*, vol. 1, no. 4, Spring 1977, pp. 92–110.
24. Whether this will be the case forever is not sure. See the discussion below, pp. 152ff.
25. Cf. Kenneth Waltz, "The Myth of Interdependence," in Charles Kindleberger (ed.), *The International Corporation*, Harvard University Press, Cambridge, Mass., 1970; Peter Katzenstein, "International Interdependence: Some Long-term Trends and Recent Changes," *International Organization*, vol. 29, no. 4, Autumn 1975; and R. Rosecrance and A. Stein, "Interdependence: Myth or Reality?" *World Politics*, vol. 26, October 1973.
26. Susan Strange, op. cit., p. 213.
27. On the respective effects of domestic policies and international interdependence on

foreign economic policy, see Peter Katzenstein's brilliant essay, "International Relations and Domestic Structures: Foreign Economic Policies of Advanced Industrial States," *International Organization,* vol. 30, no. 1, Winter 1976.

28. Cf. the issues of *Daedalus* on the oil crisis, Fall 1975.
29. "Transnational Relations and Interstate Conflicts: An Empirical Analysis," *International Organization,* vol. 28, Autumn 1974, p. 992. See also Keohane and Nye, *Power and Interdependence,* op. cit., chap. 7.
30. Ibid., p. 207.
31. Cf. Alastair Buchan, *Change Without War,* St. Martin's Press, New York, 1975.
32. *The Cloud of Danger,* Atlantic-Little, Brown, Boston, 1977, p. 187.
33. Cf. Morse, op. cit., p. 111ff.
34. See Wolfgang Hager, *Europe's Economic Security,* The Atlantic Papers, 3/1975, Atlantic Institute, Paris.
35. See Robert J. Lieber, "Oil and the Middle East War: Europe in the Energy Crisis," *Harvard Studies in International Affairs,* no. 35, 1976.
36. Cf. Richard A. Falk, "The Sherrill Hypothesis," unpublished.
37. See his "Egalitarianism and International Politics," *Commentary,* September 1975, and *The Inequality of Nations,* Basic Books, New York, 1977.

An Unmanageable World?

Are there, in the international system described in Chapter Three, patterns, rules, or institutions that ensure order? Later, we will try to define order with some care; here, let us simply use a rudimentary definition: order is what provides the states and their subjects with security of life and possessions. I shall again begin by trying to answer the question in terms of the models of classical thought. Later, I shall examine the chances of formulas of order derived either from past experience or from political philosophy.

SECTION ONE: DISORDERS

When we think of the future, we can again evoke two contrasting models. There are those who believe that international relations will remain, at best, the blend I have described, or become again a state of war, and there are those who think that world politics will become more like domestic politics. The former think that, regardless of any process of restraint that moderates international anarchy, security concerns, especially physical, will continue to dominate. The latter believe that world affairs will become a complex set of processes with no inherent essence (such as the state's security dilemma

149

in the traditional model), no dominant concern determined once and for all by the structure of the milieu. Let us call this a debate between the classical and the *modernes,* remembering that some of the former are very much alive today, and that the latter have a distinguished ancestor in the Enlightenment.

The model of continuing fragmentation points to the persistent importance of the nation-state, inhibited, entangled, but still the supreme decision maker, endowed today with enormous domestic responsibilities. It stresses the lasting role of military power—especially at a time when troubled areas are being stuffed with weapons by avid sellers and when the defensive or status-enhancing function of nuclear weapons may prove contagiously attractive. It shows the new perils of economic power in a world in which the past inhibitions on its mercantilist abuses were linked to the dominance of one economy, America's, but in which there may be increasing tensions between the United States and other industrial nations, mounting challenges from the developing countries, a cumulative loss of state control to private transnational agents, unmanageable inflation and other threats to growth, yet no stable, authoritative, and wide-scoped institutions for joint management. At worst, one ends with an apocalyptic vision of a planet on which scarcity could lead to war and chaos. The global triumph of the zero-sum game would be due to the fragility of mixed "external" interests and to the fact that the reassuring priority states supposedly give to absolute domestic gains rather than relative external ones would no longer hold in a disrupted or stagnant world economy. At best, even if the apocalypse is avoided by the miracles of technology and a surge of reason, one still ends with a continuing and prolonged difference between politics among armed actors without a common superior or common legitimacy solid enough to tame self-interpretation and self-help, and the internal politics of actors restrained by common values or the superior force of the state.

The other model is the Kantian vision of world pacification through the dynamics of mixed interests: harmony brought about by fear and greed, by the increasing irrationality of modern war (in Churchill's memorable phrase, "safety the sturdy child of terror and survival the twin brother of annihilation"), and the inescapable interdependence of trade. Or maybe it is a Comtean bet on the pacification of the world through industrialization. It points to the stability of the nuclear balance; to the collapse of the distinction between state acts and the moves of private forces, sub- or transnational; to the blurring of the distinction between domestic and foreign affairs; to the end of the old specificity of interstate relations. It emphasizes the gradual tying up and emptying out of state sovereignty. It foresees a slow march from convergent military self-restraint to a joint international security system, a taming of the economic jungle by the combination of material solidarity and the sobering fear of chaos, the preservation of an open economic world system resting on the enlightened leadership of the United States and on growing institutions of collective management.

With bureaucrats colluding across borders; with speculators, operators, and corporations destroying the economic autonomy of states; with the increasingly obvious irrelevance of force to most of their goals, or the increasingly lopsided ratio of costs to benefits entailed by its use, international affairs, like domestic affairs, turn into a host of problems of administration, bargaining, pressures resulting in trade-offs, and games of skill rather than fights. There may be no world state, but there will be more world institutions. There may be few substantive common values, but there will be common concerns and procedural values. There may be conflicts, but the antagonists will behave like a government and its opposition in a reasonably liberal society or like parties competing for power in it.

FOUR REASONS FOR CONCERN

The "good" model requires great wisdom for its vindication. It exudes a good deal of optimism and complacency. The "bad" one is a warning. The fact is, the present blend does contain multiple perils that make one skeptical about the realization of the *modernes'* ideal-type, unless deliberate efforts are made in that direction: to rely on wisdom, to trust existing processes, is not enough.

No Pacification Through Economic Development   First, there is no evidence so far to support the old contention about pacification through economic development.[1] One of the great hopes of nineteenth century liberals as well as non-Marxist socialists, inherited from Montesquieu and Bentham, was the idea that the benefits of trade, or the costs of conquest, would deter nations from going to war. But economic calculations are not the last word. At present—as in the world of 1914—the strategic-diplomatic arena seems indifferent to, or separated from, all the good things that are allegedly happening in the world's stock or trade exchanges. In a sense, for many of the states that play the games of economic interdependence, there is enough quasi-global solidarity, the world market provides enough opportunities for domestic gains, to allow one to forsake solidarity with that neighbor with whom one is in conflict over survival, borders, or first principles. In the traditional domain of world politics, there is still room for applying Rousseau's metaphor of the stag hunt (in a competition for scarce goods, the separate interest of each hunter prevails over the common interest). And as for the other states, either they do not play these economic games anyhow, or else they find them so unrewarding that they have very little to lose in pursuing old rivalries. The factors that have pacified some old ones, say the France-German enmity, or that between China and Japan, or muted some current ones, such as the Soviet-American or the Soviet-Chinese duels, or the Indian-Chinese contest, have remarkably little to do with the gold of interdependence. They are all contained within the traditional arena. Sometimes, this pacification or moderation makes possible the weaving of the cloth of economic interdependence, as in the case of the EEC, or in Japanese-American relations; but it never happens the other way around. After all, even religious, cultural, or ethnic solidarities—pan-Islamism, pan-Africanism, pan-Arabism—do not overcome conflicts between Morocco and Algeria, Ethiopia and Somalia, or Syria and Iraq.

What is true is another paradox: the "relations of major tension," precisely because they survive in the strategic-diplomatic game, often restrain the tensions in the other games. "No longer can all issues be subordinated to military security."[2] But formal or de facto alliances created by military (in)security can dampen the contests which, in the economic games, often oppose such allies: the United States has refrained from challenging too vigorously, in the oil game, its OPEC opponents, Iran and Saudi Arabia, that are "bastions against Communism" and from turning the *issue* of human rights into an *arena* of world politics, because many of those who would be on the defensive are America's allies.

In short, economic cooperation does not pacify, although security concerns may dampen economic or humanitarian hostilities. However, should the major tensions in the traditional arena escalate into actual hostility, for reasons of their own, it is not only unlikely that this breakdown of moderation would be limited by the criss-crossing of economic alignments, but also probable that the state of war would seriously disrupt the economic arenas. In the Middle East, Arab hostility to Israel became the springboard of an economic embargo and of OPEC's later actions, and thus served as the fuse that set off mines in different realms. The fragmentation of the international system into separate games depends on the traditional one not degenerating into critical violence.

The Perils of the Traditional Chessboard   Indeed, in the second place, there are multiple sources of possible breakdown in the traditional arena. We all assume that the central balance is stable and will remain so, but let us not forget that, in the absence of a sufficiently comprehensive agreement covering both the quantitative *and* qualitative arms race, each side keeps working at measures, such as antisubmarine warfare, that could destroy the balance and make even nuclear war appear again like a plausible "pursuit of state policy by other means."[3] While mutual first-strike conditions are hard to reach, they are not unachievable, as one study has pointed out, if the ratio of invulnerable launchers to accurate, hard-target warheads drastically decreases—and the multiplication of warheads through MIRV and cruise missiles is occurring. To be sure, instability in the arms race is not doomed to lead to actual military and political destabilization, as long as the fear of a holocaust deters each side from a first strike. But it could erode the fragile psychological basis of moderation. The most serious danger may well lie elsewhere: in the development of accurate and small warheads. A first strike against the enemy's land-based missiles would still leave its retaliatory force of submarines (and bombers) intact, while appearing to be the launching of an all-out war. But accurate, small warheads can be aimed at industrial or military facilities and could either promote the idea that nuclear weapons can be useful, not merely for deterrence, but for war fighting, or suggest that the superpowers could fight a nonnuclear, "limited" war, since the warheads do not have to be nuclear.[4] Thus, the recurrent dream of counterforce, which technology and traditional military thinking seem to provoke, could undermine the principles of superpower restraint. And while the "attractiveness" of the dream lies in the alleged limits and controllability of counterforce, even the return to "limited" war between the superpowers, and of course the risks of escalation, would amount to a breakdown of the postwar order, which has rested on the nonuse of nuclear weapons.

Next is the whole issue of nuclear proliferation, which is justified by formidable political reasons. Some of them can be found in the intensity of a specific survival problem, as in the case of Israel or the Republic of South Africa. Sometimes, it is a matter of regional contagion among rivals. If China becomes a nuclear power, can India be indifferent? And if India has the means of producing the bomb, can Pakistan be far behind? Sometimes, it is a matter of status, a mark of local preponderance, an expression of the will to align the hierarchy of might with the new hierarchies of wealth, as exemplified by Brazil's and Iran's policies. Moreover numerous technical possibilities are now available: plutonium reactors, new methods of uranium enrichment, new reactors with natural uranium, the development of fast breeder reactors. To be sure, there is a difference between proliferation and use and between use in a local conflict and world incineration. If there ever was a subject about which generalizations are wrong, it is this one. But this also applies to the general proposition, often associated with General Gallois, that the possession of nuclear weapons ensures peace through wisdom, thanks to balanced or proportional deterrence. For no assurance can be given that in certain circumstances, nuclear weapons would not be used offensively or preventively against a nonnuclear foe undeterred by the mere presence of nuclear weapons on the other side. Nor can one assume that nuclear weapons on two sides of a regional abyss are tantamount to stable deterrence. The technological conditions and the costs of achieving invulnerability to a first strike are prohibitive, and the temptation to strike first because of mutual vulnerability would be strong. The conditions that have vindicated Gallois so far are not universally replicable.

Below the nuclear level, one finds a world overflowing with opportunities for conventional conflict. Regional tensions, particularly in Africa, the Middle East, and the Persian gulf, are being fueled by the competitive arms sales in which the superpowers indulge and which other states promote often for more crassly commercial reasons. A report to Congress from the United States Arms Control and Disarmament Agency suggests that "arms transfers are inherently neither stabilizing nor destabilizing": it all depends on "precipitating political forces and events."[5] A safe truism; but such transfers risk "precipitating" the balance of political forces toward disaster. Superpower involvement, even if limited to arms sales, always risks crossing the thin line between the mutual stalemating that prevents either side from wresting a "marginal advantage," and the test of strength through proxies in which the quest for great-power credibility multiplies local tensions. Moreover, the capacity of nations to produce weapons indigenously has spread, either in full independence or under licensing and coproduction arrangements, and the apparently coming revolution of precision-guided weaponry may expand low-cost, high technology inventories across the globe. Finally, nobody has yet found a way of mastering the problem of terrorism. Too many frustrated causes—national liberation, the oppression of minorities, revolutionary social change, anti-imperialism— have desperado champions ready to strike across borders. One also has to remember what might be called officially sponsored terrorism, whether it consists of Khadafi's goon squads or in CIA-licensed assassination attempts. And points of vulnerability to terrorism are so numerous, methods of retaliation so risky, weapons so cheap and accessible, that no end is in sight.

Now, none of these prospects of local breakdown, even if encouraged by the great powers, is tantamount to a vision of world chaos. As long as the central nuclear balance is stable, the likelihood of a final "minute of truth" is small. But the very assurance a stable balance seems to provide can become a license for sorcerers. Nuclear weapons might save the world from total nuclear war, perhaps even from all-out conventional war between the superpowers (assuming they resist the appeals of counterforce war, or succeed in containing it). But the idea of a world condemned to a series of partial or regional minutes of truth, with, at best, the superpowers alone, in Clausewitz's words, able to live indefinitely on credit while all the others would have to pay cash, is not reassuring. The most serious peril remains an escalatory involvement of the superpowers in regional crises in which their stakes are high. Although this involvement has dampened the fires, in past Middle Eastern wars for instance, this may not happen if one of the great powers was confronted with the possibility of one more humiliating defeat for its clients or of the annihilation of its champion. Less dramatic but not negligible would be the effect of successive regional crises on the fragile rules of prudence that have kept the use of force within limits since 1945. Reasonably orderly international systems die not only when one actor deliberately kills them, but also when the common practices of mutual restraint, which frustrate great and small powers, collapse under the weight of repeated tests that make these frustrations unbearable. This is what happened to the system that collapsed in 1914. And a world of nuclear deterrence and of arms spread aimed at inducing mutual restraint is a world of denials inhabited by gain seekers: a dangerous condition.

The Perils of Interdependence   Thirdly, there are sources of trouble in the various games of economic interdependence. The idea that, given the new "nature of international power . . . those with the most influence are likely to be those which are major constructive participants in the widest variety of coalitions and partnerships, since such countries would have the largest supply of usable political currency" (the power to "support you on this issue, if you support us on that issue")[6] is far more attractive than it is accurate. So much of the game tends to be about making, unmaking, avoiding, or emasculating coalitions; and in a world of uneven power, many countries with specific grievances or revisionist ambitions will choose strategies of obstruction and exploit their nuisance value. Even pseudosovereigns, who feel threatened by more powerful states or transnational agents, still have the power to destroy the tenuous network of functional solidarity, or the capacity to exploit the domestic strains of others, and therefore the aptitude to get rewards for not doing so. Even if one assumes the continuing irrelevance of force in these games, two serious dangers could make "troubled peace" a condition in which the first word deserves emphasis.

One is the problem of coherence, at two levels. At the national level, foreign policy risks becoming a mystifying process, from which emerges more a sum of disparate decisions (or omissions) for which a galaxy of services and interest groups may be responsible, than a deliberate, if diversified, strategy. The very magnitude of the issues, the lack of control any one actor has on monetary and technological processes, the pressure of a calendar filled with meetings and negotiations that require stands, not to mention the limits on the skills of statesmen, the routines of bureaucrats and the blinders of functional bureaus, all of these may reduce statecraft to a short-range "management of the unforeseeable," in Giscard d'Estaing's words. There is just too much for it all to be centralized in one department or in the head of one leader. The race between domestic demands and external necessities therefore risks being won by the former. As a result, and given the possibility of different, equally sensible strategies aimed at maximizing a nation's autonomy and influence, several such strategies— involving different coalitions, the use of different markets, and the exploita- tion of different resources—might be tried in different arenas at the same time, the contradictions appearing only later to the country's great embarrassment.

At the international level, incoherence may result from a multitude of factors. Some actors (such as the communist powers) choose to play only a few games, while others play them all, and the alignments, hierarchies, rules, and stakes vary with each. Uncertainties abound about linkages of issues. A state may create confusion by wishing fully to exploit the oppor- tunities of interdependence in one area and to restrict them in another, according to its assets or degree of vulnerability. The same state may want high prices for a commodity it produces and low ones for a raw material it imports. Major actors may suddenly shift their strategy, for instance from a strategy of relatively limited involvement to a strategy of entanglement, or from liberalism to protectionism, or from cooperation to conflict. Some games are shaped by a small cartel, others are closer to the free market model, and still others to that of collective bargaining. All this is likely to obstruct the progressive moderation of world affairs called for by the *modernes*.

Indeed, there is a peril of immoderation. To go back to an earlier metaphor, breaking eggs can produce a fine omelet, if a pan is on the stove, and the right herbs are provided, and the eggs have been well beaten. But if the eggs are dropped on the floor, one has a mess. And there are many messes in the world economy. One occasionally results from the fact that the theories of economics do not make it a science. We have become sharply aware of the limits of our knowledge, not only in the matter of the development of the poorer countries, but in that of continuing growth, full employment without inflation, external disutilities, and monetary disturbances for the advanced countries. While the current recession is being sluggishly overcome, many societies keep experiencing inflation *and* high unemployment; public and private funds used to cushion the impact of the recession (such as through unemployment compensation) cannot be used for productive investment. Keynesian certainties have been shaken but not replaced, and the divagations of the advanced economies (partly due to their fragmentation into separate national entities with different priorities, credit, tax, and monetary policies, and so on) have served as a cover and rationalization for the revolt of the less advanced nations. Muddling through is no guarantee of future wisdom, and the present monetary "system" of floating rates manipulated by the actors themselves removes one of the factors that used to constrain domestic policy.

Moreover, our shaky understanding is matched by our moral uncertainties. There is no common standard for the distribution of economic goods among nations, once the rule of the market is rejected by many of them and political interventions multiply. The diffusion of influence through wider participation in the decisive organs of international economic organizations is at once an attempt at defusing discontent and a cause of trouble. For if those who, for reasons of wealth or common beliefs, had formed an interstate elite in charge of world economic management could no longer operate alone, those who represent drastically opposed viewpoints could not operate together.

Another source of trouble lies in the nature of economic activity. As we have seen, economic games are not zero-sum, but not all governments can achieve a surplus in their balance of payments simultaneously. Yet, for a variety of reasons, they seek to achieve one and to avoid deficits that could force them to choose between dependence on creditors and drastic domestic restrictions. This means, not only that even "this game is partially conflictual,"[7] but also that when the measures taken to obtain a surplus or avoid a deficit are decided unilaterally and aimed at a specific group of competitors, we are indeed in a "neomercantilist" universe of discord, especially if such moves are made during a recession or very slow growth. Finally, this universe risks being messy because of the very absence of "central guidance." Moderation means predictability and the ability to cope with issues before they fester. But many of the issues that require global care do not really figure on the international agenda, because of widespread resistance derived from domestic taboos and external suspicions (like the case of population, for instance). Others appears only when there has been a quantum jump in seriousness, i.e., when the nations' tendency to help themselves and hope for some manifestation of the Invisible Hand has created a mess already (as it has in the case of the oceans and nuclear energy). Others reach the top of the agenda when there has been the international equivalent of a domestic coup d'état, i.e., when a nation or a group of nations is powerful enough to create a world crisis, as Nixon did for the dollar in August 1971, and OPEC for oil at the end of 1973.

Thus, a world in which the autonomy of states is threatened by transnational trends of uncertain origin and direction, which may end up benefiting some nations far more than, or even at the expense of, others; a world whose states' policies reflect internal wants and bargains, is permanently threatened by "statist" rebellions against global integration and outside intrusion. One could make a long list of state moves that intentionally or not damage interdependence for domestic reasons. Some are actions of national self-enhancement (such as OPEC's decision of 1973 or the export of dangerous nuclear technologies). Others are reactions against the shackles of interdependence (floating rates can be so interpreted; and both the United States and the EEC have indulged in genteel protectionism lately). And there are cases of state inaction that threaten interdependence, such as our "benign neglect" of our payments or trade imbalances, which puts undue burdens on others for redress.

So far, the peril of immoderation has been conjured, but there are reasons for pessimism. The successful management of the world economy was dependent on regular growth and tied to American preponderance. Now the latter is being challenged, and growth has led to inflation, which in turn has pushed states to measures which threaten growth yet fail to curb inflation. The willingness of states to accept the costs of interdependence is being eroded both by the uncertainties to which permanent manipulation exposes them and by the inequality of power: the strong resenting the demands of the weak (the South blaming the North for its plight), the weak seeking to change the rules of the game. And the capacity of states to resist domestic drives against interdependence is challenged both by the huge increase in the functions of the state and by the aggressiveness of groups or elites seeking priority for factional or national goals. As a result, the agenda of governments are overloaded, and they tilt toward internal priorities. The world economy effects permanent, haphazard redistribution of wealth and power within and among states, but it is not acknowledged as legitimate by the victims of these shuffles.[8]

This world, torn between the unifying forces of science and technology (which operate unevenly, unpredictably, and carry political flags), and the traditional reflexes of competing sovereigns, remains under the curse of immoderation and instability, but in an original way. It is not (or not just) the use of force that is the daily peril; it is, literally, chaos. It is not war that brings the moment of truth, it is economic or environmental disaster. For instance, if the recovery of the industrial powers is slow, they cannot absorb the exports of the poorer developing countries that have suffered huge deficits because of their need to import oil at OPEC prices.[9] The peril also lies in the failure to clarify and to understand the new rules which govern the relations between different games, the transfer of power from one to the other. After all, these have only recently become major arenas of world politics; scholars are in the dark, and statesmen experiment in ignorance or by analogy. And peril lies in the failure of states to agree on new rules of delimitation, which would prescribe how far they and other actors are allowed to go in the exercise of political control and economic maximization. This is at the heart of the problems of contemporary international law: It has to deal with areas formerly beyond its reach, such as space, or to try to replace previous rules that no longer apply because of technological change and of the growing greed of states and economic interests, as in the case of the oceans. It is also at the heart of multiple confrontations of recent years, at UNCTAD, the United Nations, or the North-South conference in Paris. Can producers who enjoy a quasi monopoly pretend both to set prices and to regulate production? How can the interests of foreign investors and those of the host state be reconciled? Should the same rules of trade apply to the developing as well as to the industrial nations? Also to be feared is the inadequacy or breakdown of those few rules of cooperation and joint management that have been devised, and the absence of rules of cooperation in a variety of areas in which no state can be successful in isolation, from environmental protection to the regulation of short-term capital movements, or in which unilateral state action might invite trouble (the exploitation of the seabeds). Chaos is already a real threat.

A Return to Force?   Thus we come to the fourth cause for concern. Can chaos or anomie be guaranteed not to lead to a return to force? As I have pointed out before, economic power is both a stock of resources and a web. The most successful weavers happen often to be those with the biggest stock. It is therefore not surprising if states, however wiser now about the costs of distant conquests, remain perfectly capable of using force either to protect what they deem to be their stockpile of threads from someone else's attempt to weave with it, or to fight about whose stock of threads it is. The recent conquest by Morocco of the potash-rich Sahara despite Algeria's outcry, the cod war between the British and the Icelanders, the grabbing of vast economic zones next to the territorial sea by a large number of states, should warn us away from the premature temptation to hail peace. "Complex interdependence" may be characterized by the small role of military force, but its games are best played by those who have something to play with, and seizing or holding is one way of having that something. If interdependence does not get braced by firm rules and effective international regimes, unbridled competition for the goods of the "global commons" could lead to a surprising resurgence of gunboat diplomacy.

There are other risks of violence as well, which lie not purely within the economic sphere itself, but in the link that exists between all spheres at the level of national policy making. Is it absurd to believe that the militarily more powerful states would resort to force to prevent drastic economic losses or to impose favorable economic terms—for instance, for access to certain resources within another's economic zone or for guarantees of safe supply of certain materials—if the countries against which this action would be launched are states that are, on general political and strategic grounds, already considered foes? At the time of OPEC's decision to quadruple the price of oil, had the Soviets been farther away from the Middle East and had the prime movers of OPEC been Libya and Iraq, would the United States have reacted as prudently as it did? And is it absurd to believe that, as in the past, states may resort to force as a diversion from domestic economic and social problems, for whose lack of solution they could pin the blame—often quite rightly—on the unfairness of the world economic system and on the machinations of some of its beneficiaries? It may be true that the rich have little to fear from the poor and that—OPEC being an exception—there is no "threat from the Third World." Yet in the political systems of industrial powers, the threat posed by the poor was not economic but political—the threat of violence. The poorer nations of the Third World are quite capable of resorting to force. This would create a risk of escalation either by provoking military reactions by the advanced states if these should feel threatened or by inducing each great power to support its clients. Moreover, even if one admits that this risk remains limited, the same cannot be said about eventual resorts to force by some of the richer developing countries. They too have formidable domestic problems; the control of resources is of great importance to them;

and their elites, whether out of nationalism or Marxism, do not have the same inhibitions on the use of force that exist in much of the advanced capitalist world. And the capacity of the great powers to dissociate themselves from these countries' moves is small.

ENDURANCE AND LIMITS OF THE CLASSICAL VIEW

Thus, for the present and near future, we reach the following conclusions. Despite all the changes listed in the previous chapter, the international system still fits the model of fragmentation; it is not likely to escape from it easily, or by mere reliance on the processes of science and technology that would make common interests prevail or curb the excesses of separate ones. Traditional security issues have remained essential for states (the most essential may not always be the most pressing). Western Europe's military insecurity, and its nations' different reactions to it, have persistently slowed down not only the strategic-diplomatic unification but also the economic integration of the half-continent. The protection provided by the United States has allowed Japan to become the "economic animal" admired or deplored all over the world. Western and Japanese attempts to use Russia's and East Europe's need for technology to obtain concessions in the realm of European security have been in vain. The Third World's offensive against the existing world economic order coincides with the relative decline of America's conventional preeminence and Washington's acceptance of nuclear equality. Much of the booty from OPEC's raid into the industrial nations' treasury, as well as a huge share of the revenues of even the poorest states, goes into weaponry. While economic gain has become an almost obsessive goal, it does not repudiate the "game of nations," however much it may affect its chips, alignments, and rules. For wealth and welfare can be both ends *and* means—to greater status, security, and autonomy on the world stage, immemorially ancient ends that the older states have never given up and the newer ones pursue with zest. And this explains why economic unpredictability, even if it usually leaves little room for force, and economic competition, even if it seems to be sheathed in cooperation, may confirm the traditional distinctive feature of world politics: the prevalence of conflict in a system with no effective common values or central power. In the days when domestic politics and foreign policy were not yet fused, when the traditional game was the only one, states fought because the statesmen played for stakes not all of them could win simultaneously. Today, the players clash because the much longer list of stakes, imposed by internal political dynamics, cannot all be won by all players in the short run. It may not be a zero-sum game but this is still a world of material and psychological scarcity.

In a blend of troubled peace and state of war, the hard features of the latter always threaten to break through the soft make-up. Thucydides is still relevant. A world divided into sovereignties is a coercive universe, even if sovereignty is leaky, and coercion is more sophisticated than before. The jungle is given a semblance of order by the search for alliances or coalitions—and by empires. Domestic conflict feeds interstate contests. In the motives of states, fear, honor, and interest are one bundle, the dialectic of commitment versus appeasement still reigns, offensive and defensive moves are inseparable. Clausewitz is still relevant, except in the upper reaches where war is at present no longer an instrument of policy. His model of absolute war, the war of annihilation, serves not only as a warning, but as a reminder of its having happened twice already in this century. Even if the central balance holds, even if the American economy remains the strongest, let us not forget that the relative moderation we have enjoyed, the success of the restraints we have analyzed, have been due to features that are vanishing. In the traditional arena, these are the very small number and special constellation of the nuclear powers and the mix of invulnerable retaliatory power and fear of escalation, as well as the relative limitation of conventional weaponry outside the possession or control of the nuclear powers. In the new arenas, these features were the wide acceptance of American predominance and the relative smoothness of economic growth. This suggests that however valid or profound the classicists' analytic insights remain about the persistence of force as the *ultima ratio* of world politics, the state as the power of last resort, and the purely marginal importance of nonstate actors (many of which turn out to be quite national), a world of nuclear weapons and problems that cannot be solved within national borders transcends the classical conception. For the game it describes has no other goal than its own perpetuation or its resurrection after a breakdown. Today's game must aim both at avoiding such a breakdown and at solving the problems that the traditional game can only exacerbate or, at best, contain.

SECTION TWO: ORDER?

Let us return to classical thought and historical experience, however. Do they provide lessons for today's world? If the new complexities and restraints only distort and diversify the old dynamics of world politics, but do not change it fundamentally, and if indeed the dangers are both huge and familiar, it may not be absurd to look back—not to produce a capsule history of political thought about world politics, but to see how past writers promised to overcome the fragmentation of mankind or to reconcile it with the need for order.

HISTORICAL PRESCRIPTIONS

When we look back, we find six sets of prescriptions, some with subsets. The first is the old Just War theory, worth mentioning because it continues to incite efforts at modernizing it. The attempt is admirable. The Covenant of the League of Nations and the Charter of the United Nations have reversed the post-Grotius practice of treating the use or threat of force as morally neutral, as a legitimate act of sovereignty. Again, as in the Christian tradition, the use or threat of force is supposed to be either a delict or a sanction. At the same time, exceptions through which whole armies can pass, such as the right of collective self-defense or the right to self-determination, are recognized by the recent United Nations definition of aggression. Moreover, the almost metaphysical nature of such a concept as the "first use" of armed force in situations like the Middle East and the uncertainties of many borders, on the one hand; the lamentable state of pre-1945 rules that tried to regulate the means and to protect the victims of war on the other hand, impel one to find modern equivalents of the Catholic precepts about causes, intentions, proportionality, double effect (evil effects should be neither willed nor disproportionate), or the immunity of noncombatants.[10] As long as armed conflict exists, it is important to try to define both a code of legitimacy and a code of usage.

The trouble, however, is that it cannot work. Let us leave aside the obvious inability of this attempt to deal with the specific troubles of complex interdependence—that is not its function. But even within its realm, it runs into two obstacles. One is the incompatibility between the nature of the international milieu and the basic assumption that a common and meaningful code outlining the legitimate uses of force is possible. When there is no universal code of values, and no Church endowed with spiritual authority and secular means of enforcement, self-interpretation produces either total looseness (what would be a "community cause" recognized as such by all today?) or incessant violations wrapped in hypocrisy. Or else there would be a risk of real danger if the code should actually be applied. As in the doctrines of collective security that were so popular after 1918 and 1945, the result could be the generalization of just conflicts rather than the localization of any conflict.[11] The second obstacle is the incompatibility between the attempted restrictions on the use of certain means and the technological conditions of modern conflict. The Just War theory was worked out for a very different type of violent conflict, and in an era of sharp distinction between peace and war. Deterrence has blurred this distinction. It is now the permanent preparation and threat of war in peacetime that aims at avoiding war; hence the thorny questions, which theologians like to debate but cannot resolve, about its moral validity.[12] Moreover, in modern wars, the stakes grow with the means; this makes nonsense out of the rule of proportionality. As for the double effect rule, if one interprets it only as a ban on the intentional killing of civilians, it still leaves a huge loophole: unwilled, "incidental" massacres. But if one interpretes it as a strict ban on these, too, one sweepingly excommunicates modern war—with no way of enforcing the ban. This does not suggest that restraints should not be sought; but they must rest on different foundations.

Philosophies of History and Liberal Prescriptions   A second direction is provided by philosophies of history that promise us peace under certain conditions. I have already mentioned Kant's brief and intriguing essay in which he seemed eager to prove to himself that peace was not only possible, hence a moral duty, but inevitable. Hegel explained that war was historically and morally necessary and good, that the idea of perpetual peace was therefore absurd, restraints were always temporary, and the precepts of international law merely "normative"; and he described world history as the world court that decides about the worth of states according to the outcomes of their agonistic confrontations. Yet he assumed optimistically that war, during the unfolding of history, would be creative and assure the spread of civilization, rather than a drive for extermination. And he also predicted that once Universal History—the worldwide triumph of the modern state—was achieved, the competition of states would become purer. This prediction was an act of fatih, thoroughly wrecked by the history of modern war. How could what had been presented as essential to the moral health of the state, necessary to its triumph over the centrifugal and corrupting tendencies of civil society, as well as expressive of the state's individuality, have so easily faded away?

Marx, the deviant disciple of Hegel, replaced his master's view with a "cataclystic optimism" (Aron) that promised peace through the abolition of class conflicts. Peace thus presupposed, first, acceptance of the view that the state is the expression of one class's supremacy, and second, universal revolution.[13] (Meanwhile, wars and imperial expansion were not only acceptable, but possible agents of progress.) History has treated both notions roughly. Given the often considerable autonomy of politics, even when the state rests on a given class, it can pursue concerns that have little to do with the class struggle; and nobody, including Lenin, has succeeded in reducing modern war to the struggle that breaks out when capitalism, fragmented along national lines, spills over these lines.[14] Moreover, as long as the socialist revolution remains arrested in one part of the globe, there is obviously no way of putting an end to war, except through more war.

Marx made a change in the domestic social order a prerequisite of world peace. Other such prescriptions constitute a third direction, the difference with Marx being that, here, the normative element prevails over the philosophy of history, the prescription over the prediction. One example is Kant's essay on perpetual peace (in which he does not proclaim it inevitable). The state of war is to be overcome through a League of Republics, whose purpose would be the abolition of war and the adoption of "cosmopolitan law," a world law of hospitality and comity. This would have been comparable to modern international organization, except that, as in Wilson's idea for a League of Nations, only governments based on consent would have been members, and world peace depended on the universal presence of such regimes. But the League was a half-way house, a concert of states, not a world state. Such half-way houses, as we know from experience, are stakes, arenas, and instruments more than autonomous forces; the big powers want control, the small ones independence. As for constitutional regimes, we know that—as Rousseau had foreseen—both the structure of the international milieu and the corruptions of the general will could drive them, too, into violence. Moreover, at present, their chances for spreading over the globe are slim indeed. If no world order can be established until and unless all tyrannies have been superseded, we are in serious trouble.

Abolition of war through a league is a dream; but another doctrine sees the domestic society as the key. Liberalism entails the notion of world moderation, to be reached in particular through the gradual extinction of war and to be achieved thanks to the spread of liberal principles. In its political version, it is little more than a reprise of Kant, and it suffers from the same failing: this kind of proliferation has not taken place. More interesting is its economic version, from Cobden to Norman Angell's Great Illusion. War is a curse, because it violates the laws of economic harmony. Civilization means the decline of reliance on physical force, the diversification of interests within each nation, the replacement of wars with fights against nature, of military society with industrial society. Peace would be assured, in a world of nation-states, by the mere functioning of the free market, supported by enlightened public opinion and some legal institutions and rules among nations. The fundamental assumption is the existence of universal laws leading to harmony, due to the complementarity and convergence of interests that result from the division of labor. The fundamental concept is welfare, not power. The basic unit of activity is not the state but the individual; the state should be no more than a collection of public services; and borders are irrelevant for economic purposes. "Whoever does not forget the political separation of states will never deal correctly with questions of political economy" (Turgot). Another Frenchman (J. B. Say) stated that "wise nations foster with all their might the progress of their neighbors."

Obviously, those who hold this view enjoy some kinship with some of our *modernes,* who point to actors other than states and to the oozing of sovereignty through the pores of economic interdependence. Yet the *modernes* are, on the whole, less sanguine about economic liberalism and pacification of the international system through the market. As critics of this view showed more than a century ago, the classical model of international free trade gravely oversimplifies economic reality. It makes unwarranted assumptions about the characteristics of nations (fixed endowment of factors of production, similar levels of technology). It neglects all the noneconomic considerations that so often turn governments away from its prescriptions, such as the social and cultural side-effects of trade, or the frequent neglect of public goods, collective equipments, and education, or the development of consumerism amidst misery. Above all, it ignores factors of inequality: the benefits from free trade spread slowly, if at all, and unevenly through the formidable barriers of privilege, class, and status within societies (in which small groups often monopolize the rewards) and the obstacles of unequal endowments and levels of development in the world.[15] Hence the counterattack launched—by intellectuals and politicians—against such countries as nineteenth century England and the postwar United States, accused of having indulged in the "imperialism of free trade." It can of course be shown that this "imperialism" has helped the emergence of rivals,[16] but these also helped themselves, through some protection, and many did not rise at all. For these reasons, and many others having nothing to do with trade, the state has not become a mere "administration of things." It is still a "government of people" with a will of its own, including, when this serves its interests, the will to promote free trade.

Today, the United States and West Germany still cling to the idea of the free market as the greatest force for efficient development. But the notion of pacification through trade is not widely held; free trade is supposed to work its miracles in the modern arenas, not in the traditional game. On the other hand, today's risks of chaos or anomie partly result from a *revolt* against the deficiencies of the free market—both the "ideal" free market, and the "real" free market, which often turn out to be anything but competitive (given the monopolistic or oligopolistic power of key multinationals or states), and whose rules often reflect the interests of the advanced nations, especially of the United States. It is not so much a revolt against efficiency, as a will to balance the need for efficiency and the desire for national identity. The advanced states have comparative advantages in technology and technicians, but the new nations want to be able to develop their own cadres and tools. Today's revolt asks the key political questions that the theory has left out by dealing with ultimate, problematic results satisfactory for all. In the meantime, who gives the orders, who reaps the benefits? Efficiency for whom? It is a revolt led by the very forces that the theory dislikes and whose nuisance value it denounces: the states. The theory never guaranteed efficiency if there were market imperfections and an unstable political environment—it gave itself ideal conditions. The state *is* a market imperfection, often the most formidable one, and it owes its strength sometimes to its identification with the privileged groups that want to stay in power and restrict the spread of economic benefits, sometimes to its refusal to let international trade become a lever for political exploitation by advanced foreign states. In other terms, in today's world, the market, given its reality, not its ideal conditions, is the problem—not the solution.

Finally, the free market system, in its international dimension—the free trade world economy—has always been achieved, not by the conversion of all nations to the ideals of liberalism, but by the will of a dominant economy. Britain, and later the United States, had an interest in the maintenance of an international division of labor, in investing capital abroad, and in running the international monetary system. The dominant country, through a combination of military and economic assets, imposed the "two-track" method of managing world affairs—one track for the strategic-diplomatic relations of states, another for the economic interdependence of private markets, i.e., for a relatively "depoliticized" world economy functioning within a political framework set by the dominant power. This regime can last only as long as the dominant economy remains unchallenged by nations seeking to change the rules. Indeed, the interdependence of the states, not merely the markets, makes the exercise of domination far more difficult: a free market world economy presupposes an interstate compact. Robert Gilpin has analyzed the postwar international economic order in such terms. Today, even though America's relative power remains great, it has decreased, it suffers the restraints described above, and it is being challenged by competitors and by nations eager to change the nature of the international division of labor and benefits.

THE BALANCE OF POWER

The fourth direction takes us away from the promise of world order through domestic reform. It points to the nature of the international milieu and to the need to arrange it so that it accommodates the maximum of "peace" and the minimum of "trouble." The most prestigious scheme is the theory of the balance of power.[17] It has two assets. It rests on the nature of world politics, rather than requiring a utopia. As long as there is a fragmented structure, with power unevenly divided among the states, whatever their own nature or their social or economic systems, the states will block each other's ambitions and attempts at domination, and, either through deliberate creation or not, balances of power will occur. Indeed, the second asset of the theory is historical confirmation. There have been balance of power systems, i.e., systems in which the basic "law" of politics just mentioned operated in specific conditions (concerning the number of major players, the relative homogeneity of the structure and domestic regimes, and so on). These resulted in certain methods, peaceful or coercive, for the maintenance of the balance, and in the moderation of violence. These two advantages explain why the model has to be treated seriously. Nevertheless, its relevance to the present world is limited. For there is a difference between the maintenance of the central nuclear balance, which provides, so to speak, the steel framework of the whole construction and which results from the two superpowers' policies, and the establishment, in order to moderate conflict, of a balance of power *system* inspired by such systems of the past.

The balance was essentially a technique for the management of the strategic-diplomatic arena, which constituted, if not the exclusive, at least the principal functional realm of interstate politics. (In the days of mercantilist economic policies, economic gains and losses were treated exactly like stragetic gains or losses, since economics was regarded not as a net of transactions but as a mass of goods to be seized or held in a zero-sum game; the logic of the power struggle, what I have called above the logic of separateness, and the rules of conflictual interaction, applied across the board.) Now, the idea of a new balancing system has many of the same attractions as the Kissinger design, which it certainly inspired. But the traditional arena, in the present world, does not lend itself to the restoration of a balancing system for a variety of reasons, many of which we indicated when we discussed the fate of this design. The "game of nations," even though it is still played in a decentralized milieu, has changed and does not fit the model.

For such a game to be played according to the rules of the balance of power, various conditions had, in the past, to be met. First, there had to be a number of major actors—it usually was around five or six—of comparable if not equal power. Today's distribution of power among the top actors is quite different. Only two states are actual world powers, militarily present and influential over most of the globe, and indispensable for all important settlements. China is still mainly a regional power, more concerned with breaking out of encirclement than with active involvement outside. While Chinese leaders assert that China will never want to become a superpower, there is no way of predicting that this will be the case. Even if both dogma and growing power should push Peking toward a world role, given its enormous internal problems of authority and development, the transition will be long. China is bound to remain in the meantime a potential superpower, i.e., a major player presently limited in the geographical scope and in the means of his activity albeit exerting considerable attraction on the global scene. There are no other two "poles." Both Japan and Western Europe are military dependents of the United States. Neither, despite huge but fragile economic power, behaves on the strategic-diplomatic chessboard as if it intended to play a world role under the American nuclear umbrella. Japan, so far, does not have even a clear regional policy. Western Europe is a perpetual promise—a tease—not a real political entity.

A second condition for the functioning of past balance of power systems was the presence of a central balancing mechanism: the ability of several of the main actors to coalesce, in order to deter or to blunt the expansion of one or more powers. This corresponded to two fundamental realities: the inability of any one power to annihilate another and the usefulness of force. Aggressively, force was a productive instrument of expansion; preventively or repressively, the call to arms against a trouble maker served as the moment of truth. The invention of nuclear weapons and their present distribution have thoroughly transformed the situation. The resort to nuclear weapons can obviously not be a balancing technique. Indeed, the central mechanism's purpose in a nuclear world is the *avoidance* of nuclear conflict. This central mechanism of deterrence is likely to remain bipolar for a long time. Only the United States and the U.S.S.R. have the capacity to annihilate each other—a capacity distinct from that, which France, Britain, and China possess, of severely wounding a superpower but suffering either total or unbearable destruction in return. Only the superpowers have an oversupply of nuclear weapons to deter each other not merely from nuclear but also from large-scale conventional wars and from the nuclear blackmail of third parties. Their quantitative and qualitative advance over other nuclear powers remains enormous. It is doubtful that Peking could find the indispensable short-cuts to catch up with Moscow and Washington. Nor is an eventual nuclear Japan likely to outstrip the Americans and the Russians; political and psychological inhibitions in the Japanese polity are likely to delay a decision to join the nuclear race and to limit the scope of any nuclear effort. Western Europe continues to have an internal problem not unlike that of squaring a vicious circle: the British and the French deterrents remain separate; they are threatened with obsolescence and unlikely to grow much. But a genuine "West European" deterrent would require a central political and military decision-making process of which there are no traces. Nor is there a willingness of Bonn to consecrate the Franco-British nuclear duopoly, or a willingness of London and Paris to include Bonn.

A pentagon or hexagon of nuclear powers is not necessary and could be dangerous. The deterrence of nuclear war is not a matter of coalitions. What deters Moscow, or Peking, from nuclear war is the certainty of destruction. To add the potential nuclear strength of a Japanese or West European strategic force to that of the United States may theoretically complicate an aggressor's calculations, but it does not change the picture. Furthermore, a world of several *major* nuclear powers would be of dubious stability by itself and would probably foster further proliferation. Maybe five or six strategic forces of comparable levels could be "stable": each would-be aggressor would be deterred, not by a coalition, or by a third party's guarantee of the victim, but by that potential victim's own force. But here we are talking about very uneven forces. The balance of uncertainty that up to now has leaned toward deterrence and restraint could begin oscillating furiously. Even if it should never settle on the side of nuclear war, it would promote an arms race among the five or six. The very argument that stresses that nuclear guarantees are not credible would incite more states to follow the examples of Western Europe or Japan. Some would have a second-strike capacity against each other, and a first-strike capacity against others. It would be difficult to devise a "moderate" international system under these circumstances.

What of a return to a *conventional* balancing mechanism comparable to that of the past? It has been asserted that the very unusability of nuclear weapons actually restores the conditions of traditional war. But the model does not apply any better. Against a nuclear power, conventional forces are simply not a sufficient credible deterrent. Deterrence of nuclear attack, or of nuclear escalation by the side that finds its conventional forces stopped or beaten, depends on either the possession of nuclear forces or on protection by a credible nuclear guarantor. In a nuclear world, even if conventional war provides moments of partial truth, ultimate truth is either nuclear war or its effective, i.e., nuclear, deterrence. Moreover, from the theoretical viewpoint of a conventional balance, a world of several major actors would not resemble the great powers system of the past. The balance of power was predominantly about Europe. All its members sought a world role. It is difficult to imagine either a West European entity or a conventionally rearmed Japan seeking such a role. Each one could become an important part of a regional balance of power—not more. There is no central, worldwide, balancing mechanism: the logic of fragmentation operates.

In this arena, then, three phenomena are likely. First, only the two superpowers are likely to remain, for a long time, capable of sending forces and supplies to distant parts of the globe. The world conceived as a single theater of military calculations and operations is likely to stay bipolar. Second, as long as the fear of nuclear disaster obliges the superpowers to avoid deliberate military provocation and direct armed clashes, and as long as China, Western Europe, and Japan remain at least partly hemmed in, endowed only with modest conventional means, and largely neutralized militarily by their very connection to the central nuclear balance of deterrence, other states, independently (like India) or, more likely, equipped or protected by a superpower, and in pursuit of objectives that are of vital importance to them, will continue to be able to provoke their own "moment of truth" and to build themselves up as regional centers of military power, as Israel has done in the Middle East, or North Vietnam in Southeast Asia, and as Saudi Arabia, Iran, and Brazil are doing now. A coalition of states with great power but limited stakes is not enough to stop a local player with limited power but huge stakes. For the superpowers and for such local players, conventional force used outside their borders still has considerable productivity (although, paradoxically, the superpowers can use such force only in small doses, through proxies, or in limited spheres). For France, Britain, or China, however, the greatest utility of conventional force is likely to be negative: its contribution to deterrence. Third, the fragmentation that results both from the impact of nuclear weapons on world politics and from the regional nature of several of the present or emerging military powers suggests that a future conventional balance of power would have to be regionalized some more. A strong Japan or a strong Western Europe could not ensure a sufficient balance in the Middle East, or in South Asia, or in the Western Pacific.

Nuclear weapons have obviously not abolished war, they have displaced it. The central mechanism of the past was aimed at the problem of large military intervention by the main actors. Their restraint now depends less on a global mechanism than on a local one. No amount of military coalition building would have saved Czechoslovakia. No adversary coalition could have prevented the United States from moving into the Vietnam quagmire. Moreover, because of the fear of escalation, much of international politics on the diplomatic-strategic chessboard becomes a game of influence—less violent but more intense. There is an art of knowing how to deploy force rather than to use it, how to exploit internal circumstances to dislodge a rival. Whereas the traditional balancing mechanism may not work against war, it still functions where the stakes are influence, not conquest; for military strength in an area can deter or restrict the subtle access that influence requires. A strong Western Europe still associated with the United States would be guaranteed against "finlandization," for instance. Yet there are grave complications even here. Precisely insofar as violence is curtailed, a coalition aimed at stopping a great power may actually goad it into expanding its influence by "leaping" over the coalition and leaning on local parties determined to preserve their own freedom of maneuver (a United States–Chinese coalition in Asia or Africa is not sure to stop Soviet influence, for instance). Also, a superpower has other ways of strengthening an area against the influence of a rival than by military build-ups. Most importantly, much depends on the internal circumstances in the area. Neither military build-ups nor coalitions may compensate for domestic weakness. There are too many local balances for the great powers, singly or jointly, to be able to control them all, as was shown in Southeast Asia. Finally, moderation at a global or even at regional levels is compatible with occasional setbacks.

The traditional mechanism, geared to different stakes, is too gross for the modern variety of the old game. Indeed, the logic of the traditional mechanism, as applied to the present international system, is a logic of arms races, nuclear or conventional. A game of influence partly played with weapons supplies in a world in which many statesmen continue to see in force the only effective way of reaching vital goals risks—as balance of power systems did before—leading to multiple wars. In past centuries, global moderation was compatible with such explosions; but in a nuclear world there is no assurance that they would be as limited as, and more localized than, before.

A third requirement for an effective balance of power used to be the existence of a common language and code of behavior among the major actors. This did not mean identical regimes, or the complete insulation of foreign policy from domestic politics, or a code of cooperation, but a diplomatic Internationale capable of reducing misperceptions, if not miscalculations, and of coping with crises. But today, summits too are fragmentary—our presidents meet either with our allies, or with Brezhnev, or with Chinese leaders. Even if we look only at the major powers, we are still very far from a common language. Even a tacit code prescribing how to handle conflicts, how to avoid or resolve crises, how to climb down from high horses, and how to save one another's face remains a dream, for several reasons. There is still the Sino-Soviet conflict, deepened by mutual charges of heresy; it makes the triangular relationship something quite different from a moderate balance of power. Next, neither Moscow nor Peking subscribes to a code of general self-restraint. In the past, an effective balance of power required either agreements on spheres of influence and dividing lines, or hands-off arrangements that took the form of neutralizing or internationalizing certain areas. Of course, today, some spheres of influence are being respected: the Soviet's in Eastern Europe, ours in Latin America. But Moscow and Peking both apply to the world a conceptual framework that dictates the exploitation of capitalist weaknesses and contradictions whenever possible and safe. Regimes in which the state molds the society are better at granting priority to foreign affairs than regimes in which the impulses of the society actually control the state's freedom of action.

Further, the heterogeneity of many nations split along ethnic, class, or ideological lines, makes it impossible even for an angelic diplomacy dedicated to the principle of nonintervention to carry out its intentions. But it offers irresistible opportunities for diplomacies tied to a strategic (which does not necessarily mean warlike) vision of politics and to a dynamic reading of history. Prudence, yes; the simple preservation of the status quo, no. Indeed, the very delicacy of the status quo in the one area where Moscow most assuredly tries to perpetuate it—Eastern Europe—the Soviet Union's inability, for domestic and external reasons, to separate security from domination there, the fact that, however (in its own eyes) unideological, the West cannot easily accept an equation that enslaves half of Europe, all this is likely to oblige the Soviet Union to keep trying to weaken the West in Europe, or at least to prevent it from strengthening itself, because even after the Western nations' recognition of the territorial division of the continent, their power and prosperity could serve as magnets. In the Middle East, in South Asia, in Southern Africa, on the world's oceans, the Soviets, without encouraging violence where it would backfire, but supporting it where it works, behave as if any retreat, voluntary or not, of the United States and its allies, or any weak spot created by Western diplomacy, constitutes a vacuum to be filled or a position to be held. This is not the code of behavior we would like Moscow to observe. But multipolarity is not Moscow's game, or interest.

Such tactics, if skillfully used, do not destroy moderation. But they test self-restraint. Of course, Moscow could be constrained to adjust its behavior to *our* code, should we encourage, in balance of power logic, other actors to fill the vacuum and to strengthen the weak spots. But we are caught between our desire for a détente and the fear that it would be compromised if we built up the power of those allies whom our adversaries most suspect. Our rivals' game is to improve their relations with us insofar as we tend toward disengagement without substitution—in which case, our self-restraint could benefit them. In other words, two requirements for a new balance of power—relaxed relations with former enemies and greater power for former dependents—are in conflict. Such will be America's dilemma as long as our interest in "flexible alignments" is matched by our rivals' search for clients; as long as their revolutionary ideology (not to be ignored just because their vision is, literally, millenial, their means are prudent, and their tactics flexible), as well as their great-power fears or drives, result in an extensive demand for security tantamount to a claim for either permanent domination where it already exists or regional hegemony to exclude any rival. Indeed, regardless of whether Western Europe and Japan become major actors, Eastern Europe and East or Southeast Asia will remain potential sources of instability.

Multiple asymmetries are at work, therefore, insofar as moving toward a common code is concerned. There is the asymmetry between the dynamic ideologies of the communists and our more static conceptions, which envisage order as a set of procedures rather than as a social process, as a web of norms rather than as the ever-changing outcome of struggles. There is an asymmetry between the active policies of the superpowers and the still nebulous ones of Western Europe and Japan. Far from being two poles of diplomatic-strategic power, they are stakes in the contest between the United States, the U.S.S.R., and China. There is an asymmetry between the exhausting global involvement of the United States and a Soviet (and potentially, Chinese) strategy that has to do little more than move into the crumbling positions on our front lines or jump across into the rotting ones in the rear. Order and moderation used to be organic attributes of the international system, corresponding to domestic conditions within the main states, as well as to the horizontal ties between their diplomatic corps and codes. Today order and moderation tend to be more complex and mechanical, corresponding to necessities of survival and to opportunity costs.

A fourth condition for an effective balance of power system has to do with the international hierarchy. While the world was a much wider field in days of slow communications, the international system was simple: There were few actors, and the writ of the main ones covered the whole field. In Europe, the small powers had no recourse other than to entrust their independence to the balancing mechanism. Outside Europe, the great powers carved up the world. Today, the planet has shrunk, and the superpowers are omnipresent. But there are more than 150 states. The small—thanks to the nuclear stalemate, or by standing on a bigger power's shoulders—have acquired greater maneuverability and often have intractable concerns. Any orderly international system needs a hierarchy. But the relations of the top to the bottom, and the size of the top, vary. In the future, if we want a moderate world, these relations will have to be more democratic, and the oligarchy will have to be bigger. As some of Kissinger's troubles have demonstrated, it is a mistake to treat issues in which third parties are embroiled as if these countries were pawns in a global balancing game, instead of dealing with the issues' intrinsic merits and the nations' interests. The very difficulty of bringing a *theoretical* balancing game no longer sanctioned by the minute of truth to bear on the local situation dooms the old-fashioned approach.

The proliferation of nations in a highly heterogeneous world, like the impact of nuclear weapons, suggests a fragmentation of the traditional scene. The old balance of power system assumed that peace is *ultimately* indivisible—although perhaps not every minute, as pure bipolarity does; more tolerant of minor shifts, it saw any expansion by a great power as a threat to others. Our analysis, however, suggests a greater divisibility of peace and a more evanescent character of influence, as long as the central nuclear equilibrium lasts. What will have to be balanced, so to speak, are that equilibrium and the regional balances. Each one of these has its own features, its own connection with (or disconnection from) the central balance. The contest for influence between Washington, Moscow, and Peking tries to exploit and to shape these balances—we have seen it in Southern Africa and in the Middle East; but their own specificity exposes that contest to their hazards. Thus, in the traditional arena, the *model* of the balance of power provides no real prescription, however wise the *idea* of balance remains. For the model, and the reality on which it was based, essentially rested on the following assumption. A crisis would be kept under control by the mechanism of the balance—i.e., the possibility of a limited war to stop a trouble-maker—and settlements would be ensured or imposed by the great powers. Force was thus both a threat, when used against the balance, and the heart of management, when used by the concert of the great powers. But today, the great powers are hampered by the nature of their rivalry, and demonstrably incapable of imposing their writ (either because they cannot "collude," or even when they do, as the issue of nuclear proliferation shows). This is so, because force in the hands of the great powers is no longer a management technique. Limited war against a superpower is too risky, and there is too much competition between them for joint action against small trouble-makers. The focus of the mechanism was the prevention of forcible action capable of upsetting the delicate balance of the great. Today's balance, being as much one of influence as of might, can easily be upset by domestic, political, and economic trends that neither great-power force nor great-power summits can crush: witness the rise of the Southern European left, which worries Bonn, or the emancipation of South European Communist parties, which troubles Moscow.

Anyhow, the balance of power is not a relevant mechanism in the new arenas of world politics. In games of "complex interdependence," the first or the only imperative of a state is rarely to limit the capabilities or gains of a rival, and even when this is its goal, coalition building is not by itself the most effective method. The rival will have to be restrained, either by building up superior capabilities oneself or by the coalition's ability to manipulate interdependence, not by threatening the use of force. To be sure, groups are formed as in all politics, for instance, the IEA versus OPEC. But not every form of coalition mongering is a balance of power policy, not every network of bargaining coalitions is a balance of power system. The latter term refers to a system in which military might, and the ambitions carried at the point of the swords, are stopped by equivalent or superior military might. In the realm of interpendence, the excessive power of a state or group of states in one currency (oil, food, technology) is to be neither balanced nor necessarily curtailed, but prevented from reducing others to dependence and turned to mutually beneficial uses, thanks to the assets available to other states or coalitions. These assets usually consist in countervailing but complementary chips. The peril in this realm lies neither in the failure of the balance to beat down the excessive ambitions of one sovereign that even force will not stop, nor in the rigidity of the balance when it splits the world into rival, frozen coalitions that lead to general wars. It lies in anomie: the failure of the groups to agree. To paraphrase Kissinger's style, the essence of the successful balance is stalemate, the essence of successful politics of interdependence is a bargain.

In the golden age of the Concert, the international economy was managed, not by the balance of power, but by largely transnational private markets, in a framework established and preserved by the hegemony of Britain, the guardian of a global system that ran to its advantage. When the rise of rival economic powers, and the beginning of Britain's own decline, put an end to this hegemony, the result was not a balance, but growing chaos.[18] Today, the application of an irrelevant concept to the fields of interdependence would be dangerous. It can, of course, be tried: As we have seen in Chapter Two, the Nixon administration's proclamation of the "primacy of national interest" in these matters, and its attempt to link the strategic realm to them to extract advantages from our allies, has had unexpected effects. For the very policies that often succeeded in restoring self-restraint and moderation in the traditional game threaten to breed antagonisms in the new ones. To apply the logic of separateness in fields of integration invites disintegration. A universal balancing of power there would actually mean a break-up of the world economy into independent economic blocs with fluctuating relations based on nothing but bargaining strength. This would not be a source of order. The flexibility the world economy needs is not that of shifting alignments and reversible alliances. Such shifts can be beneficial, to be sure, when they prevent a break-up into rigid blocs and facilitate compromises. But once these are struck, rules adopted, and joint regimes set up, one needs committed partners.

FUNCTIONALISM AND RADICALISM

With an eye both on the new games and on the traditional arena of contest, students and practitioners of world politics discouraged by the balance of power have turned to another technique of moderation: what is sometimes called *neofunctionalism*. It hoped to take advantage of interdependence so as to promote deliberate integration, i.e., the gradual transfer of resources, power, authority and allegiance to new central institutions created by the partners, or at least the gradual pooling of resources and acquisition of "new techniques for resolving conflict," of new "institutionalized procedures devised by governments for coping with the condition of interdependence."[19] It was also hoped that these processes would spill over into the realm of strategy and diplomacy.[20] Actually, the testing ground of neofunctionalism has been limited to Western Europe. While some progress, thanks to some linkages of issues, has been made in the learning of new habits and techniques and in the development of transnational contacts, there has been only little "upgrading of common interests," and the common institutions have remained weak. The impact of outside events has been more disruptive than integrative.[21] The resilience of each of the nations, their capacity to remain bottled up in their problems and priorities has been remarkable. Internal necessities and external pressures have increased the discrepancies between the members' policies. There has been little spill-over into diplomacy, none into strategy. Neofunctionalism has not been a failure as a regional experiment aimed at substituting cooperation for conflict in the realms of interdependence, but it is certainly not a formula for world order. Conditions that have made it a limited success in Western Europe are hard to find elsewhere.

Neofunctionalism wanted to improve the chances of world order by getting the states themselves, deliberately or under the pressure of sub- and transnational forces, to give up "the factual attributes of sovereignty."[22] It suggested a way to manipulate the attributes of present-day world politics to change gradually its structure or at least its processes. But there are those who see the only chance for survival in a real mutation of world politics; they are the radicals who propose a fifth approach. Unfortunately, different mutations are conceivable. The most daring, impractical, and gloomy by implication was suggested two centuries ago by Rousseau. Peace depends on the creation of an ideal world of small democracies, ruled by the general will (we are here at the birth of the idea that regimes based on popular consent are the precondition of peace, which Kant endorsed) *and* sufficiently self-centered and autarkic to avoid being dragged into the familiar competition. For the rivalries of ambitions could bring about the return of violent conflict and the corruption of the ideal regimes. It is fragmentation carried so far as to mean the end of the international milieu. It is based on the idea that as long as the latter exists, such mitigating techniques as the balance are no shelters, interdependence is but a name for mutual envy and the quest for comparative gains, and half-way houses are too fragile to be taken seriously.[23] But since the requirements of autonomy, i.e., the existence of communities of fully participating citizens who do not delegate their will, rule out world federation and entail small nations, total disconnection becomes the only salvation.

There would be little point in reviving this stark utopia, if it were not for the way in which it exposes the other remedies suggested for the state of war, and also for its concordance with some contemporary critiques of the international system. Those who, among *dependencia* theorists or analysts of structural violence and imperialism, such as Johan Galtung,[24] denounce present built-in violence, poverty, repression, and environmental destruction as necessary ingredients of capitalist and "social" imperialism, often sound like disciples of the author of the *Discourse on the Origins of Inequality,* who would have transposed his indictment of man's enslavement by man into the language and categories of international relations. And it comes as no surprise to find among the key strategies advocated for the creation of a new and better structure, moves by which the exploited "periphery" would gain control over its economic life through self-reliance and disconnection from the political clutches, economic control, and business cycles of the "center." There is the same distaste as in Rousseau for trade and the international division of labor, seen as sources of exploitation and dependencies. Indeed, the measures advocated for the "peripheries" come close to Rousseau's ideal of frugality, egalitarianism, and citizen mobilization (general will and civil religion). And yet, the modern epigones of Rousseau, often as high-mindedly censorious as he was, are not able to follow to its—to his—extreme end the logic of self-sufficiency and "decoupling." Johan Galtung, for example, not only acknowledges the usefulness of trade (as long as it aims at the collective self-reliance of the periphery), but demands continuing technical assistance (even if it is as "reparations" for structural damages) as well as the internationalization of the world's commons, of "world production for fundamental needs," and of multinational corporations. He is vague on these points, both because he explicitly wants self-reliance to receive more emphasis than collective international jurisdiction, and because he fears that the latter might be controlled by the wrong interests. But clearly, he senses the tension between the two opposite directions—centralization and drastic decentralization—and realizes the necessity of the first.

There is certainly more than a grain of wisdom in the plea for self-reliance and lesser dependence of the periphery. States can choose among alternative models and strategies of development, each with its own priorities and costs; there are states that find horrendous the social costs and the external political dependencies entailed by the capitalist model. If their primary concern is social justice or national identity, not aggregate growth, then this model is obviously wrong. Insofar as the world is concerned, the total manipulation of all by all would likely be unbearable, especially because of unevenness, but also because of the dazzling and damaging variety of strategies states have at their disposal to make interdependence more profitable or less costly. Some disconnection may be a prerequisite for order, since total interconnection is a recipe for complete insecurity. If states do not have a reasonably safe and predictable measure of domestic autonomy, the internal backlash from the constraints of the international system could lead to highly disruptive foreign policy reactions. And yet, today, collective self-reliance and increased economic autonomy for the developing nations cannot be ensured merely by the nationalization of the resources of one's territory. They, too, require the manipulation of interdependence: connectedness is the way to possible, and limited, disconnection. How else will the Third World obtain the financial and technological aid, the earnings from exports, and the imported equipments that alone would allow it to start meeting its basic needs?

Moreover, the theory addresses three major problems only obliquely. What about issues, such as food or the environmental ones (the conservation of natural resources, for instance), which, even after every state has taken the "right" measures, still require cooperation not only across borders but also across the great divide that separates the "center" and the "periphery" (a divide that is becoming more fuzzy in many areas)? What about countries so badly endowed that collective self-reliance would not provide them with any real gain in autonomy? For autonomy is meaningless unless it is exerted over a certain stock of capabilities. What about the fact that most states do not want to follow the imperative suggestions? The rich would have to sacrifice some of their living standards, jobs, and earnings to the "periphery" and lose control of or advantages from their multinationals. Many of the poor want to apply the capitalist model, and remain unimpressed by the progress of less "interdependent," and yet not ipso facto more just and honest societies.

The two key weaknesses in this uneasy compromise between two orientations are these: one is an implicit, grandiose, and often less-than-candid reliance on quasi universal revolution as the way of chasing or chastening the "parasitic elites" at the "center of the center," or at the center of the peripheries, and of making the peoples of both center and peripheries want what is good for them—recognize, so to speak, their true needs. The other is the almost complete neglect of the noneconomic causes of conflict, the reduction of strife to conditions of exploitation and dependence, which explains the advocacy of "solutions" which, in the traditional arena, could easily turn into disasters. In nuclear matters, self-reliance might all too easily mean proliferation; here, what order ideally requires, if it is too late to obtain abstinence from all nuclear power by all states, is preventive or deterrent centralization, rather than disconnection.

The true logic of radical reform leads to centralization. This is indeed the path of the World Order Models Project, which seeks to eliminate war, poverty, injustice, and ecological disaster by the creation, on the basis of national self-determination, of a world polity, with a world assembly as its chief policy-making organ.[25] One recognizes, in the heavy garb of pseudo-scientific language and post–Torrey Canyon, post-Vietnam, post-Watergate idealism, the old model of world government and world peace through world law. As usual, it rests on an impeccable critique of the dangers of the present and of the wishful thinking of limited reformers and liberal exhortations. As usual, its own radicalism leaps over a breath-taking number of abysses. The generous assumption is made that the four values[26] that ought to become the world's priorities are, or can be made to be, universal imperatives—to which all the components of the global community would give not widely divergent meanings. It is a very American assumption, and it shows a Wilsonian tendency to claim universality and self-evidence for American values that the radicals share with the liberals they lambast. Global legitimacy is thus assumed, although some recognition is given to the possibility of conflict between the four values. Next, there is a tendency to believe that the perils of scarcity and the rising demands of equity will somehow provoke a transition to a post-Westphalian order, rather than exacerbate conflict, as long as public consciousness is heightened. Finally, excessive reliance is placed on transnational populist coalitions. Not only are populist forces weak or impotent in many countries, where they are either kept down by repression or under firm establishment control, but populism often tends to be more parochial than enlightened, more driven by internal fears than drawn to global solutions. The biggest obstacles remain today's actors: the states whose "war-system" and selfishness thwarts the four holy values, the multinationals that put their own profits ahead of "needs-oriented development." Opposed to violence, the radical design does not recommend their overthrow by force. But short of it, how will Utopia be realized?

Radicalism, whether revolutionary or peaceful, assumes wrongly that economic injustice among and within nations is the principal factor of instability (Galtung dismisses the Soviet-American conflict as a sham). But in the past, order has been compatible with high degrees of economic injustice; one of the chief forms of order was imperial. In the real world, as opposed to an ideal one in which the beneficiaries of injustice would meekly yield, and its victims gently gain, the elimination of injustice can all too easily become a tornado.

WHAT SHOULD WORLD ORDER BE?

Looking back has not helped us much. It has alerted us against inadequate analogies, warned us against unwarranted assumptions, and sharpened our assessment of the originality of the present international system. And it suggests two conclusions, one analytic, one normative.

World Politics versus Domestic Politics   First, current world affairs may begin to resemble our idea of domestic politics because of the very scope and nature of the issues, the collapse of the distinction between domestic and foreign affairs, the logic of economic interdependence, the kinds of cooperation required by the material solidarity on which it rests, the relative retreat of force, and the growth of global institutions. But however different the new international relations may be from those of older international systems, the current world system remains very different from domestic political societies. It is far more fluid than either. Fluidity means insecurity; I have mentioned some reasons for it, as well as its main varieties; another reason is the very coexistence of the old, latent, or partial state of war and the old forms of national power bound to it, with the new contest of interdependence and its forms of entangled or captive power. To use an analogy (like all analogies, not to be carried too far), the international milieu displays some of the same neuroses as domestic societies did when they passed from the age of rigid hierarchy and feudal-rural economies to the age of democratic social relations and industrial economies. Each such society has tried to cure those neuroses through its system of social and political institutions, its formula of legitimacy. We haven't really begun on the world scale.

In domestic political societies, interdependence and bargaining are channelled by a constitution, by a network of reasonably stable institutions, by traditional patterns of behavior and of organization. When bargains are struck, they have a chance to last: a common legislator sets their terms, a judge controls their interpretation, the central government's police sanctions their violation, and the basic consensus of the citizens or the state's monopoly of force prevent an easy breakdown or a frequent lapse into group violence. Battles against injustice or inequality have often been at least partly won, because of the power of the ballot, as well as the mobility of workers and capital. In world affairs, means of redress, especially ways of decreasing inequality by common consent, are exceptional; the mobility of labor is limited; and the mobility of capital often increases inequality. In a tyranny, injustice and privilege can long be preserved by central force. In today's world, the restraints on the mighty and their need for the puny shake up hegemonies. Interstate bargains always carry, in fact, the *rebus sic stantibus* provision, and last only as long as either the balance of force that underwrote them or the balance of reciprocity that made them possible. When there is no common principle of distributive justice that could serve as the criterion for an agreement, and when force does not shape the attribution of benefits, deals are neither easy to reach (as the negotiation on the law of the seas has shown), nor likely to last.

Moderation Plus Second, we need to refine our concept of order. As long as the main arena of the international system was its strategic-diplomatic one, discussions of order turned around the issue of war, and were locked in exchanges between those who, aware of the weaknesses of most techniques for the limitation of force, argued for a ban, and those who, pointing to the incompatibility of such self-abnegation with the nature of the milieu, and to the unlikelihood of any mutation, sought the best ways of reducing the inevitable violence. If idealism was the badge of the abolitionists, realism was on the side of the moderators. And in the traditional realm, this is still the case. But moderation is not enough, in two respects.

First, as was suggested at the close of Section One, it has always come to a bad end. When the balance of power broke down or when, as in the 1930s, it never managed to operate at all, a general war reshuffled the cards, helped some players, wounded or even killed others, and the game went on. This time, a general war would mean the end of the game. As long as there is no sure way of preventing limited holocausts or regional slaughters from dragging in the rest of mankind into a nuclear or an escalating war, the assumption of a disconnected world in which packs of players might be annihilated, but the big gamblers would remain around an increasingly Russian-like roulette, is a bit unsettling—especially as the latters' instinct for prudence, driving toward disconnection, conflicts with their universal concerns, which tempt them into involvement. I am reminded of Buñuel's masterpiece, *L'âge d'or*. Once in a while, on a quiet street, a house blows up. After a while, there is no more street. On the strategic-diplomatic chessboard, the directive for world order becomes: provide incentives to, and mechanisms for, the moderation of violence, such that the risks of escalation are reduced to a minimum. By escalation, I mean two things: the spread of violence (in geographical scope, weaponry, or numbers of players involved) within the traditional arena, and its snowballing effect into the other arenas (a world safe from large conventional wars, yet safe for universal terrorism could hardly be termed moderate). The directive, then, begins to sound like a call for the kind of moderation that *tends toward* abolition. Of course, since we are and will long remain far from abolition, such a strategy is perfectly compatible with, indeed requires, measures to prevent local violence from spilling over globally, i.e., measures of disconnection. But these will have to be taken: automatic "decoupling" or fragmentation cannot be assumed.

In the modern arenas, moderation is, again, only part of the answer. It entails worthy objectives, such as no "large-scale economic disruptions, either in the relation between the rich and the poor, or, more generally, in international financial mechanisms and through balance of payments problems," or in world trade.[27] But such disruptions, as we have seen, cannot be avoided merely through the combination of self-restraint, balancing techniques, and collective processes of negotiation and peace keeping. The condition, here, would be, in Miriam Camps's sober formulation, the "more efficient use of global resources" (efficiency including "social and ecological as well as economic criteria") and "improvement in economic welfare, . . . in quality of life, some narrowing of the disparities in wealth as between countries, some narrowing of the disparities of power as between states."[28] Moreover, all these objectives, even if they entail occasional "disconnection," require in varying degree doses of collective management. Given the stakes, building a moderate international system will have to coincide increasingly with building a "world community" (utopian in the other arena). Moderation is a negative goal: it is organizing the coexistence of players with hugely different regimes, ideologies, levels of development, histories, time perspectives, and processes of decision making. It has, in the past, permitted a variety of woes—assaults on the quality of life, arms races, wars, internal massacres, and a vast amount of domestic and international inequality. It is true that even now "an international system holding the promise of reasonable order and stability can become more egalitarian only within rather closely circumscribed limits."[29] But it is difficult to conceive of a future international system remaining moderate if the inequality among its members and internal turmoil in some of them incites recurrent violence. While, especially in the traditional area, sovereignty will continue to manifest itself through unilateral moves or concerted diplomacy (although it will have to make its mark more through restraint than through self-assertion), there is a growing need for shared powers, joint policies and effective institutions in all the new realms of international politics—precisely because the changes described in Chapter Three concerning the number of actors, their agenda, power, and hierarchies, threaten otherwise permanent chaos.

Two kinds of essential tasks present themselves: those which, if neglected or bungled, could lead to the ultimate disaster, and those which the very postponement of the "moment of truth" and the realities of a materially interdependent planet push into the daily agenda. This is a world full of active self-fulfilling memories: states that behave *as if* nuclear weapons and the increasing costs of conquest had not sharply reduced the positive productivity of military power and *as if* might were still the yardstick of achievements; and by behaving in this way they carry the past into the present. There ought to be equally active self-fulfilling prophecies—states moving on the conviction that on the seas of interdependence we are all in the same boat and should worry more about maximizing common benefits than about national achievements. But community-building raises formidable questions of its own.

One, does community mean spreading and intensifying interdependence deliberately? The answer is no. We have to remember that in every community (including the most elementary one—the family), order and concord reign only if each element or unit has, so to speak, its own breathing space, its measure of autonomy, its protection from total interdependence (i.e., total dependence). Community-building in world politics will have a chance only if, simultaneously, ways are found to reduce the burdens and increase the benefits of interdependence for the actors not only through cooperation but also through individual measures to reduce insecurity and vulnerability. In other words, room must be made, not only for more ambitious central management, through collective institutions and international regimes, and for the reconciliation of divergent domestic objectives, but also for some emphasis on self-sufficiency whenever reachable (in food, for instance, and other basic human needs). A partial "delinking" between some poor states and the richer ones will have to be made possible. The objective would be not unattainable autarky, but the lessening of one-sided dependencies: the encouragement of policies of selectivity[30] that allow a state to provide itself with the economic and political means (whether acquired through trade, domestic control, or collective international bargaining), of reducing the dose of unavoidable dependence.

For just as, in the traditional realm, one must distinguish between the utopia of "abolitionism" and the imperative of pushing the definition of moderation toward abolition, in the modern arenas one must distinguish between the utopia of global welfare-and-justice and the imperative of gradual economic and social progress. The former, exactly like abolitionism, ignores the constraints of the international milieu and proceeds from the implicit model of a (suitably decentralized) world state, the ideal nation-state writ large. Hence admirable suggestions for a worldwide war on poverty and the worldwide protection of human rights. Again, a formidable critical thrust lies behind these proposals. They point out that the less radical world order schemes, which rely on the actors themselves for moderation and progress, merely pin the sheriff's medal on the bandits and confuse steps that tame the *states* (and multinationals) with steps that serve *mankind*. Would social justice be served merely by a bit more state-equalitarianism in international organizations? In other words, shouldn't one go beyond a "moderate international order" toward a just world order reaching destitute or oppressed individuals?

My answer is that the best is the enemy of the good. These ambitious goals are excellent. But, as with abolition, the whole problem lies in reaching them. Let us be lucid. If our goal is economic and civic equality for people, not equality for the states, at best the road will be very long, and it will most likely require violent upheavals in many places. Because domestic turmoil tends to spill into foreign policy and because one aim common to revolutionary and to counterrevolutionary regimes is to foster abroad the replacement of hostile governments with friendly ones, the chances for moderation would be slim. Does this mean that moderation and order require the domestic status quo (the very notion I criticized when reviewing American foreign policy)? It does not. It only means that one has to make the goals of equity and world order compatible. There shall be no world order unless some progress is made toward worldwide equity, interstate and internal; but equity at the cost of world order is unacceptable for at least two reasons. Revolutions are no guarantee of internal equity (or if they succeed in promoting greater social justice, it is often at a formidable price). And a world of confrontations between the revolutionaries and the die-hard champions of the status quo would be not only violent and chaotic, but far from assured of leading to more justice.

The old Kantian or Wilsonian question remains valid and disturbing. Can one expect a moderate world order unless the domestic regimes are themselves founded on the principle of consent and on the rule of law? But all the tyrannies and all the regimes of social injustice simply cannot be suddenly whisked off the face of the earth. To make their elimination an explicit *goal* of world order would be slightly suicidal: any attempt at world order must, initially, try to enlist them. Their elimination can be a desired effect, not an open objective. One cannot reason as though the actors— bandits or victims—did not exist. The question is, how does one get them to change their policies? Or how does one create, from the outside, conditions that will lead to the elimination of the bandits without too heavy a price for world order? The distinction between domestic politics and international affairs is still with us in one important respect: a nation's choice of regime is not yet a matter of international concern, despite the exceptional case of white minority rule in South Africa. It is international affairs we must order, but precisely because its scope extends to most issues of domestic politics, such ordering should have an effect on internal conditions. The present international system has only some rudiments of order. To ask for perfection now is to forget, first, that the institutions needed to achieve it do not exist; second, that the actors do not agree on its goals; and third, that our knowledge of how best to reach them is shaky.

This does not mean that a concern for international order excludes preoccupation either with extremes of domestic inequality or with viola- tions of human rights. Nor does it entail the illusion that adequate, even enlightened management of international functions (trade, financial mar- kets, monetary transactions, the world's commons, etc.) will by itself assure political democracy and economic justice. But, as before, some order in the international realm is a precondition for internal justice: an insight Rousseau had expressed and liberals have often picked up. Interna- tional violence provides pretexts for tyrants or dominant elites to exercise their power, and it wastes resources. And, more than ever before, order in the international realm *is* inseparable from a modicum of justice, however imperfect due to the actors' self-interests and to the difference between justice among states and justice among human beings. Thus, the modern arena must accommodate two kinds of provisions for world order. Substan- tively, it will have to address itself to issues (for instance, the role of multinationals and commodity agreements) that would not have been on the agenda some years ago and that the demands and moves of Third World countries have put there. Procedurally, it has become inconceivable to try to build effective institutions without the participation of all those states that want to participate in them. A few years ago, statesmen and experts in the advanced countries gravely debated the respective advantages of "effi- ciency" (as demonstrated by the World Bank or IMF) versus such partici- pation; they stressed the risks of paralysis, corruption, waste, or sloth present in more "democratic" institutions. Today, it would be difficult to proceed in a way that community building would appear as a mere neocolonial device through which the rich perpetuate their hold on the poor.

Thus, traditional concerns and community building will have to be pursued together. Yesterday's dialectic may have been that of a central balance between a handful of powers and imperialism, which pushed back the limits of the diplomatic world. Tomorrow's dialectic will have to be that of a complex balance, both global and regional, allowing for a fragmentation of the strategic-diplomatic contest under the nuclear stalemate, and an emergent community in which competition will, of course, persist, but where mankind ought, perhaps, slowly to learn to substitute games against (or with) nature for the games between what Erik Erikson has called "pseudospecies." A world of complexity allows for no universal solutions, and the imperatives of moderation and community building, defined, respectively, with the additions and limitations described above, will have to be heeded in ways that will sometimes appear in conflict with their goals. Thus, in the traditional realm, the need for moderation points both toward more arms control agreements between the superpowers to prevent unilateral breakthroughs and competitive escalations or imitative proliferations into the absurd, *and* toward the preservation of the superpowers' nuclear stalemate as the essential condition; toward regional arms control systems *and* a multiplication of regional balances of power; toward some centralized measures to limit nuclear or conventional arms races *and* the possibility of "decoupling" from local disasters. In the economic realm, community builders will have to remember that interdependence can be positively exploited only if the nations caught in the web have a modicum of autonomy.

The term *world order* is used so often, and so loosely, that it may be worthwhile to sum up what I have said so far. One, (like integration), it refers both to a condition, and to a set of processes. World order is, or rather would be, the state in which violence and economic disruptions are tamed; it is, or would be, a state of moderation among the actors, plus the kind of economic progress described by Miriam Camps, plus collective institutions. It is also all those processes, of negotiation as well as deterrence, of balancing of force as well as of managing the economic bonds, that could lead to such a state.

Two, a condition or state of order is above all a set of procedures for the settlement of disputes, the administration of joint programs, the transfer of resources. I do not equate world order with the universal triumph of a particular political philosophy, such as liberalism or Marxism. To assume that order cannot exist without it is a counsel of despair, a postponement of the necessary until utopia is realized, or a call for trouble. The problem is to make possible the coexistence and cooperation of actors with different dogmas. However—and this is where the problem becomes even more difficult—the set of procedures world order entails rests, like any set of procedures anywhere, on certain assumptions, values, and beliefs that are not universally shared. In domestic societies, the citizens' consensus and the force of the state are usually sufficient to oblige dissenters to respect these procedures even when they reject the principles on which the procedures are based, even when they would like to replace them with methods and institutions reflecting their own principles. When this is not the case, the domestic order breaks down. The squaring of the world order circle is, how to obtain what is the norm in domestic affairs without a comparable consensus or superior force.

Three, the establishment of world order is not a deliberate creation comparable to that, say, of the United Nations. It must be a long-term effort by many actors. It would result from a series of measures: in this sense, like peace according to Kissinger, it would be a by-product rather than a direct goal. However, it ought to be at least the ultimate goal. (Let us go back to the analogy of peace: what was wrong with the appeasers was not that they wanted peace, but that they believed appeasement would secure it.) And order would be a criterion in the evaluation of methods and moves in every realm of policy.

Four, the process of world order has to be evolutive. Despite some connotations of the word *order,* it is not a formula for managing the status quo, especially because the status quo contains the seeds of its own international and (in many places) internal destruction. Nor is it a formula for world revolution, for the reasons I have given. It is a formula for a profound, gradual, yet controlled transformation of world politics, and thereby of domestic politics as well.

World Order Politics versus Politics as Usual

Given the irrelevance of past models, we have no choice but to innovate. World order is the field that so ardently requires the creativity which Kissinger required of statesmen. There is no substitute for universal bargaining, issue by issue, deal by deal. A double revolution is called for: in the scope of diplomacy, and in the process. The scope will be huge; the process must be more collective. For in economic matters as in nuclear ones, exclusive clubs—of producers, consumers, or suppliers—are useful in defining their members' common stands, not for reaching a generally acceptable, hence effective, solution. Thus the process will resemble the coalition building of domestic politics. Which brings us back to a point raised before: we are *not* in the realm of domestic politics; we are in a realm where everything remains open and unresolved. The imperatives of order consist in trying to move the international realm in the direction of domestic political systems, to turn it from the model of Hobbes to that of Kant's historical fantasy. Now, this task, which, it seems, we have no safe way of shirking, meets two formidable obstacles, which the fate of Kissinger's design for world order has already revealed. The first is the universal priority of the domestic outlook, an inescapable effect of the nature of the milieu. This priority has several meanings, all of which amount to saying that the state remains a pump of collective self-righteousness. It means, at times, a low-level chauvinism, which often makes states indifferent to the establishment of international rules, or at least unwilling to contribute to their operation and safeguard if any costs are involved. It also means excesses of protectionism, unjustified by "infant industry" arguments or by temporary serious payment problems. It means, above all, either the pursuit of inexpiable hostility or the unwillingness to let the risks of violent conflict or the waves of interdependence erode the sharp edges of an ideology or of a "pseudospecies" solidarity. The key problem remains, then, that of legitimacy: of obtaining assent to sets of rules from actors who display every conceivable type of heterogeneity—ideological, political, economic, in their constitutive principle (states versus nonstates, multiracial versus national states, etc.)—in a world where the nature of issues makes a separation of belief and behavior impossible. Many of these actors will continue to be political leaders determined, by nationalism, Marxism, or a mix of both, to erase at home and in international relations all the marks of what they consider to be imperialist exploitation. Such a drive makes the adoption of common rules both more necessary, as a bulwark against chaos, and more difficult—unless the rules take the likely prevalence of this ambition into account.

Second, in order to obtain and to safeguard such rules of predictability, moderation, and progress, states would have to follow strategies that run counter, not only to their outlooks on the world, but also to the traditional logic of behavior in the international competition. Nothing less than a genuine conversion is required, in four respects:

☐　The actors would have to give priority to what is collectively important in the long run over what is individually attractive in the short term. One can see how much of a revolution would be involved if one thinks of sales of nuclear reactors, or of weapons to African, Middle Eastern, or Latin American clients, of the attraction of financial benefits and the argument, "if we do not give it, our rival will." One can also think of the urge to exploit the seabed's natural resources now, and of how the exploitation affects pollution, the fisheries, and the oil deposits under the seas. Or one can think of how the OPEC countries and the United States have handled the problem of oil.

☐ The actors should be willing to commit, in advance, certain kinds of resources—money for aid or for stabilizing export earnings, stocks of food products, reserves of important raw materials, and also soldiers and weapons for peace-keeping forces—to decrease insecurity and to contribute to moderation. The traditional logic, however, makes such resources national tools for the extortion of a momentary advantage or submits them to the hazards of domestic pressures. True, "commitments" are a staple of world affairs, but they are always antagonistic. One commits one's forces or resources *against* a foe, and the peril then becomes a shield against domestic complaints.

☐ Given the intolerable burden of excessive and uneven interdependence and the risk of chaos involved in the constant manipulation of it, each actor ought to take internal measures to reduce his vulnerabilities and to reinforce areas of genuine autonomy. And he ought to help other actors to do the same. For only actors who do not feel threatened by the many insecurities I have described will be able to cooperate effectively, i.e., in such a way that their compacts will be lasting, because their transactions will be fair. (There will still be enough dependencies and vulnerabilities to make compacts necessary.) In this respect, Robert L. Paarlberg's argument for "domesticating global management"[31] deserves a wide hearing. The domestic measures of management he calls for, concerning food, population, and energy, are the only alternatives to the conflictual international politicization of every issue and to the search for outside escapes from internal reform.

Each actor should be encouraged, for instance, to adopt a sound policy against inflation, to stockpile food, fuel, or raw materials of critical importance or, in the case of developing countries, to carry out at least in part a "basic needs" strategy. He should also reduce his dependence on the access of his industrial products to the markets of advanced nations, on national development through foreign multinationals, or on food aid which the donor can manipulate for political objectives. Yet states frown on, and often try to thwart, actors who move in this direction. They condemn it as a retreat from interdependence or as a way of shifting burdens to others. The reason for such hostility is clear: a policy of reduced vulnerabilities is exactly the opposite from the politics of blackmail or external diversion that is of the very essence of traditional foreign policy. Incentives to blackmail ought to be removed, so that a new order can be established on the basis of the complementarity of interests rather than on uneven vulnerabilities or *Diktat*. (Only in the rules of deterrence, through "mutual assured destructions" has one so far succeeded in going in that direction, but because nuclear interconnection is the domain of supreme paradox, each actor has protected himself by making his retaliatory force at least partly invulnerable, and has also tried to reassure his rival by keeping his population vulnerable; in this respect vulnerability is the guarantee of moderation.) Elsewhere, the domestic base does not encourage such efforts any more than do outside powers. Either, as in America's oil nonpolicy, vulnerability to outside blackmail appears less objectionable than the measures one would have to take at home to eliminate it, or else, as is so often the case with quotas, tariffs, and capital export controls, domestic pressure groups want to protect themselves from foreign competition by manipulating international trade rather than by taking internal measures to improve their efficiency.

☐   Moderation, predictability, and progress require a major effort at institutionalizing world politics, even if the agencies remain half-way houses. They will be needed not only in the realms of interdependence, where many of them function already—yet many more are called for (for peaceful nuclear energy, the seabeds, or the management of commodity agreements, energy, and industrial policy), and far greater coordination is indispensable—but also in the traditional arena, for the enforcement of global and regional arms control deals, which will not be able to rest on "national means of surveillance" forever, or for the arbitration of disputes. This also goes against the logic of the international milieu, which gives preference to unilateral action or bilateral diplomacy, and treats institutions as fields of hostile maneuvers rather than as forces to be strengthened. For instance,both the misuse of a variety of international bodies by the crusaders of the anti-Zionist resolution, and the replies delivered by Mr. Moynihan, have weakened already creaky structures.

The politics of world order requires that the old view of international affairs exclusively as a contest between "us" and "them," as a struggle in which others are treated as friends only as long as one needs them against foes, be gradually discarded. And yet this view is the product of what might be called the normal way in which each national community internalizes and deepens its specificity, and of the logic of the milieu. We find it today among many of the new nations, born admidst hostility and bitterness, among nations kept by iron or bamboo curtains from intense intercourse with others, and among the advanced nations of the First World, whose tendency—in the media, popular literature, and the minds of public officials—is still to look at the world scene as a stage for grand confrontations. This is neither a plea to discard conflicts, since they are the stuff of politics, nor a request to substitute cooperative solutions for all other modes of human activity. There will still be room for unilateral action and for competition; cooperation itself, in domestic affairs, is a method of conflict resolution at least as often as it is an expression of partnership. I am only arguing against the prevalence of hostility, which leads, at worst, to the very disasters world order cannot survive and, at best, to the fragile stalemates that can no longer sustain it.

We can thus better understand why this analysis has been, so to speak, torn between two opposite but equally pressing moods. One is the mood of urgency. Before one can speak of the management of interdependence or of world order, interdependence has to be turned into a force of order, and order has to be created. The other mood is pessimism or, perhaps, awe at the unprecedented nature and magnitude of the task. We have to create order out of heterogeneity, and do so without illusions about common values. Moreover, a prerequisite to success is an awareness of the new conditions of international affairs, a knowledge that world order tomorrow will not resemble, and may well require the opposite from world order in the past. Are citizens and leaders really prepared for such imperatives? Are they willing to stop listening to familiar clichés, fixed ideologies, and self-righteous harangues? Will the need forge a way?

NOTES

CHAPTER FOUR

1. See Raymond Aron, *War and Industrial Society,* Oxford University Press, London, 1958.
2. Robert Keohane and Joseph S. Nye, Jr., *Power and Interdependence,* Little, Brown, Boston, 1977. p. 26.
3. David C. Gompert, "Strategic Deterioration: Prospects, Dimensions, and Responses in a Fourth Nuclear Regime," in Gompert et al., *Nuclear Weapons and World Politics,* McGraw-Hill, New York, 1977.

4. Cf. Henry S. Rowen, "The Need for a New Analytical Framework," *International Security,* vol. 1, no. 2, Fall 1976, p. 142ff.

5. *The International Transfer of Arms,* Report to Congress from the United States Arms Control and Disarmament Agency, 93d Congress, 2d Session, Apr. 12, 1974, p. 64.

6. Seyom Brown, "The Changing Essence of Power," *Foreign Affairs,* vol. 51, no. 21, January 1973, p. 289.

7. See Edward L. Morse, *Modernization and the Transformation of International Relations,* The Free Press, New York, 1976, p. 94ff.

8. For further elaboration, see my essay on *"Domestic Politics and Interdependence,"* prepared for the Marshall Plan Commemoration Conference, Paris, June 1977, to be published.

9. Cf. Robert W. Tucker, "Oil and American Power—Three Years Later," *Commentary,* January 1977, pp. 34–35.

10. Cf. my essay, "International Law and the Control of Force," in Karl Deutsch and Stanley Hoffmann (eds.), *The Relevance of International Law,* Anchor Books, New York, 1971.

11. The best discussion of collective security remains I. L. Claude, *Power and International Relations,* Random House, New York, 1962, chaps. 4 and 5.

12. Let us use traditional categories: deterrence obviously follows from a "right intention" and aims at a good cause. But it is the threat of doing evil, which depends, for its effectiveness, both on a credible firm intention of carrying it out if necessary, and on a kind of permanent escalation of means, which would make the evil even worse if deterrence fails.

13. On this point, and particularly on differences between Marx and Lenin, see Miklos Molnar, *Marx, Engels et la Politique Internationale,* Gallimard, Paris, 1975.

14. See the critique of Leninist theories of war in Raymond Aron's *Century of Total War,* Beacon Press, Boston, 1954; and *Peace and War,* Doubleday, New York, 1966.

15. Cf. the discussion in Klaus Knorr, *The Power of Nations,* Basic Books, New York, 1975, chaps. 8 and 9.

16. Cf. C. Fred Bergsten, *The Dilemmas of the Dollar,* New York University Press, New York, 1975, chap. 4. See also Robert Gilpin's incisive unpublished essay, "Economic Interdependence in Historical Perspective."

17. See I. L. Claude, op. cit., chaps. 2 and 3; Martin Wight, *Diplomatic Investigations,* Allen and Unwin, London, 1966; and my essay on it in the *International Encyclopedia of the Social Sciences,* vol. 1, Macmillan, New York, 1968.

18. See Benjamin M. Rowland et al., *Balance of Power or Hegemony: The Interwar Monetary System,* New York University Press, New York, 1976.

19. Cf. Ernst B. Haas, "Turbulent Fields and the Theory of Regional Integration," *International Organization,* vol. 30, no. 2, Spring 1976, p. 210. See also Robert Keohane and Joseph S. Nye, Jr., "International Interdependence and Integration," in *Handbook of Political Science,* vol. 8, the best introduction to this complicated and jargon-ridden field.

20. Cf. Ernst B. Haas, *The Uniting of Europe,* Stanford University Press, Stanford, Calif., 1958.

21. Cf. my essay "Obstinate or Obsolete? France, European Integration and the Fate of the Nation-State," in Hoffmann, *Decline or Renewal? France since the Thirties,* Viking Press, New York, 1974, chap 12.

22. Ernst B. Haas, "The Study of Regional Integration," in Leon N. Lindberg and Stuart A. Scheingold (eds.), *Regional Integration: Theory and Research,* Harvard University Press, Cambridge, Mass., 1976, p. 6.

23. See my essay "Rousseau on War and Peace," in *The State of War,* Praeger, New York, 1956, chap. 3.

24. See his "A Structural Theory of Imperialism," *Journal of Peace Research,* vol. 8, 1971, pp. 81–117.

25. See Richard A. Falk, *A Study of Future Worlds,* The Free Press, New York, 1975.

26. V_1, V_2, V_3, and V_4 are the minimization of large-scale collective violence, the maximization of economic and social well-being, the realization of fundamental human rights and of conditions of political justice, and the maintenance and rehabilitation of ecological quality. See Falk, op. cit., chap. 1.

27. From my essay "International Organization and the International System," *International Organization,* vol. 24, no. 3, 1970, p. 407.

28. *The Management of Interdependence,* Council on Foreign Relations papers on International Affairs, 1974, pp. 15–16.

29. Robert W. Tucker, *The Inequality of Nations,* Basic Books, New York, 1977. p. 170.

30. See Carlos F. Diaz-Alejandro, "Delinking North and South: Unshackled or Unhinged?" in Albert Fishlow et al., *Rich and Poor Nations in the World Economy,* McGraw-Hill, New York, 1978.

31. *Foreign Affairs,* vol. 54, no. 3, April 1976.

PART THREE

AN AMERICAN POLICY FOR WORLD ORDER

What are our limits, what should we do?

Many will answer that American leaders, if not all Americans, are ready. Stable structures of peace may be out, but Henry Kissinger called for a "new international system which adds to security the needs of economic cooperation and political consensus on a global scale," and Jimmy Carter has called for "a more stable and more just world order."[1] World order politics is obviously "in."

Two hundred years after the birth of the United States, so ambitious a set of goals for American foreign policy deserves a domestic consensus. And yet, one has good reason to doubt that the task has been properly understood. There is, first of all, the power of irrelevant analogy. As candidate Carter's speech revealed, Americans often equate the needed effort to manage world order with a "thrust of creativity," like that of the years that followed the Second World War. But this thrust began by overlooking the absence of a common "legitimacy" among the winners, by looking backward to prevent new Hitlers, and by producing a United Nations whose inadequacy was demonstrated within a few months. And although our foreign policy soon shifted course and built the walls of containment that still surround us, the world we face today is neither the world in the black and white of the cold war, nor one in which Washington can indulge its economic preferences.

Next is the pressure of idealistic activism. The "framework of peace" requested by Carter is one "within which our own ideals gradually can

199

become a global reality.''[2] This identification between world order and us, this assumption that the best in us is what "they" must want—or that what "they" want, we should want also—is a bit disturbing. The more one is convinced that the United States needs a policy for world order, the more important it is to understand that it cannot be an *American* world order policy. So let us examine both why we must have a world order policy, and what that policy cannot do. Next, I shall discuss what we should do.

This examination of the limits and imperatives of American foreign policy in today's world should not be read as a commentary on the Carter administration's diplomacy. The remarks that follow were written almost entirely before its advent. If there is congruence between the thoughts expressed here and the ideas put forth and carried out in Washington, it is a happy coincidence. Every new administration (especially a Democratic one) needs several months to settle down and reach its cruising speed— months during which it seeks new paths and often accumulates contradictions or mistakes until it realizes the boundaries of renovation and the need for a hierarchy of priorities. It would therefore be entirely premature, and unfair, to grade its performance. But some of the suggestions that are presented here can properly be used as criteria for evaluating its present and future course.[3]

CHAPTER FIVE

America's Predicament

SECTION 1: NO CHOICE

There are three reasons why American foreign policy, in quest of a new road map after the somewhat circular and bumpy route of the Kissinger era, should make world order its chief priority. No matter is more important; we have no alternative; and the time is right.

THE REASONS FOR A WORLD ORDER POLICY

Every aspect of Amercan foreign policy is a part of the problem of world order. There is no topic familiar to foreign affairs specialists that does not have a world order aspect, however much we may be used to looking at it from another angle. When we ask whether American companies will be able to explore the seabed and exploit manganese modules; when we discuss whether to invest in alternative sources of energy or increase our imports of oil; when we argue about subordinating aid to Italy to exclude the Communist party from the Italian cabinet; when we protest the West German nuclear deal with Brazil; when we worry about Soviet arms in Somalia, Soviet tanks behind the Iron Curtain, Soviet fleet buildup in the Mediterranean, or Cuban soliders in Angola, we raise world order issues. This does not mean that world order is a new catchword for foreign policy—at least not yet. It does mean that every separate issue, even if

201

couched in traditional terms of antagonism, raises the problem of world order along with the problem of "our" influence or "their" threat.

Let us go back to the domestic misanalogy. In a nation like the United States, not every crisis or example of untidiness raises a problem of domestic order; a strike, even if it involves a major industry and lasts a while, does not ordinarily pose questions of overall consensus, legitimacy, or the like. But this would not be true in two cases: in a highly centralized country, such as France (where a chain reaction provoked by the police evacuation of the Sorbonne courtyard led, in Ionesco-like fashion, almost to the fall of the Fifth Republic in May 1968), and in a thoroughly disjointed one, with weak central authorities and a creeping civil war—say, Lebanon before its final disaster. The international milieu is close to the second end of that spectrum. At one time one could, say, not "bother" about the Hottentots. Today, a massacre in Burundi or Uganda has repercussions on inter-African affairs, therefore on the great powers, and so on.

The Lebanese example raises the second question. Even if world entanglement is potentially disastrous, can U.S. foreign policy simply turn its back on the world? It is now being argued that of "the many types of interdependencies to which we are subject . . . most are unwished for and represent vulnerabilities that we should certainly hedge against . . . I think," writes Earl Ravenal, "our government would be protecting our security far better by eliminating vulnerabilities than by creating interdependencies."[4]

I, too, have argued for "eliminating vulnerabilities," but doing so to make the interdependencies bearable. Ravenal argues for giving up commitments, cutting down forces, and playing hedgehog rather than lion. He rejects the label of isolationism, even though he would like us to move "toward the capacity for self-sufficiency"; he claims the label of noninterventionist. He is right in stressing domestic and external constraints on America's ability to control the world. But, like earlier isolationists, he forgets that, however protected the American economy may be, a heavy price tag would be levied on U.S. exports and imports in a hostile world (and the price of alternatives would be exorbitant.) Ravenal forgets that no great power defines its interests in terms of strategic control or physical security alone. Influence is the name of the game, especially when the blunt play of power is too risky and the player stands, or thinks he stands, for certain ideals or principles of behavior.

Similarly, George Kennan reminds us of the multiple internal "limitations that rest upon the United States government" and tells us that neither America nor the international community is "organized in a manner as would conduce to effective action through international organization on a global scale"; indeed, he pleads for "the reduction of external commit-ments to the indispensable minimum," given "our general helplessness"[5] in the face of most problems. But he forgets that the U.S. network of influence in the world, which he wants to dismantle because of the perils to which it exposes a domestically half-paralyzed United States, is simply too vast, too intricate, and crystallizes too many interests in the United States and abroad to be discarded in so sweeping a way. Even if demolition is desirable, impatience is not. The very scope of American power, both as a stock of resources and as a strand in the web of economic entanglement, prevents Washington from using the risks of world unmanageability and new quagmires as a reason to drop the quest for world order.

The argument of the noninterventionists is that a drastic reduction in military production, presence, and sales, and a decline in illusions about cooperative efforts in world economic affairs would contribute to world order. Cutting down and toughening up does not mean opting out, but giving in to necessity. "Something has to give." The costs of control, of commitments, are financially and psychologically too high. So let us not ask what will happen to Western Europe or Japan if we reduce our risks and costs. Let us ask whether it makes sense to carry these risks and costs.

One must reply that the real question is not what the costs of having to carry out our commitments would be (because the very commitment may save us from having to deliver), but what the effects of any cuts would be, not merely on the United States, but on the various components of world order. What would be the chance of further nuclear proliferation, of more violence breaking out? Could the United States avoid being dragged back into the messy world (as in 1940–1941), especially if the Soviet Union should be the main beneficiary of our withdrawal? Would our exit have no effects on the various economic games? For even if their outcomes are not determined by the distribution of military might, even if the great military powers do not win them automatically, they are not totally unrelated to the central balance—insofar, for instance, as confidence in the dollar, or the position of American multinational enterprises, or the rules of trade in the First World are concerned. To argue that certain kinds of American buildups, interventions, and sales are detrimental to world order is one thing; to argue that a drastic retrenchment would be necessarily beneficial is another.

There are three facts nobody can ignore. One, the United States *does* confront hostile powers whose views on world order are not compatible with its own. Their behavior is not merely a response to American hostility;

to believe that it is, is one more example of reverse hubris. Two, for reasons for which Washington bears some responsibility, but which cannot be eliminated instantly, there are, at the moment, no partners who can "shoulder the burden" significantly in the military realm. Three, the United States has an interest in giving its own views on world order a fair chance, if not of controlling, of at least affecting the collective agreements and regimes that will shape it. Indeed, this third reason explains why many who share Kennan's and Ravenal's conviction about the excesses of the defense establishment and the exaggerated fears of Soviet preeminence, suggest that the resources saved by bugetary cuts at the military's expense be used not merely or primarily at home, but in a world campaign against poverty and for radical change.

At any rate, only by an effort at creating world order will the United States be able to reduce vulnerabilities—if not without pain or risk, at least with less damage than the retrenchers would provoke. For only within a framework that receives wide assent and provides for some "devolution" will the United States be able to trim its sails without sinking. Some retrenchment might be a goal. Some world order is the condition.

THE MOMENT FOR A WORLD ORDER POLICY

Finally, the time for a world order policy is right. We are, to use an inescapable cliché, at a moment of transition in world politics, and not only in U.S. foreign policy. Leadership in the Washington-Moscow-Peking triangle is changing. We may be at the threshold of an era of nuclear proliferation. The Bretton Woods regime is dead but has not been replaced. The law of the sea is being negotiated. The search for a new international economic order has begun, with more breakdowns than breakthroughs. In other words, something may well happen to the bipolar strategic chessboard, and the other games are in search of rules.

The nuclear balance between East and West and the effect of nuclear weapons on the use of force have given to the traditional game a certain viscosity; it is the result of removing from whole ranges of world affairs, or at least of inhibiting, what used to be the most decisive tool of change. The fundamental post-1945 configurations around the superpowers have held remarkably well. For all the turmoil accompanying decolonization, for all the repercussions of the 1971 to 1975 economic storms, what the French (a bit unfairly) call the Order of Yalta has been resilient. Would this relative solidity survive rapid nuclear proliferation, the massive return of force in the affairs of much of the world, or the shock effects of rising regional hegemonies?

On the other hand, those storms have temporarily abated. We have emerged from them in less battered shape than post-OPEC hysteria would have made one expect. The revolution in oil prices has triggered no financial collapse, even in the so-called Fourth World. The petrodollars have been recycled, and if the oil-rich have shown some "impudence," it has not been in trying to use their wealth to manipulate Western states politically, as was feared, but in improvising development plans that exceed their capacity. The recession has been handled without a "general crisis of the capitalist system." Rich and poor nations are at least engaging in dialogue. And in the absence of a monetary regime, the Jamaica agreements of January 1976 amount to a stopgap armistice. This may well be, as one writer has suggested, because the troubles of the 1970s, unlike those of the 1930s, owe more to a general inability to cope with new problems than to major conflicts between the leading economic powers. "Thus the system has broken down but the will to economic cooperation has not."[6] The armistice is also partly due to the continuing, if relatively decreasing and widely challenged, economic preponderance of the United States. Also, sometimes nations learn something from history; one could sense the ghosts of the 1930s behind the statesmen of the 1970s. Despite an upsurge of protectionism, the recession did not lead to an unraveling of international trade or to an orgy of neomercantilist revenge, any more than the shrewd OPEC gamblers wanted to destroy the economies they shook up.

The relative tranquility after (and between) the storms provides another favorable element. In a world without any consensus on the ideal polity or the ideal scheme of world order, there is at least one quasi-universal trend: the race for economic growth. Only a handful of nations have selected insulation to preserve traditional society, rural values, and the balance of nature. As for the states that have chosen "self-reliance," most use it to develop without, or out of, dependencies, not to stay at their present level. They want to avoid the social costs of the capitalist model of development even at the cost of some growth, but not at the expense of growth altogether. Opting out of the world economy does not mean opting out of the race to develop. Thus, we must guard against two errors. The first is to mistake development strategies that put priority on the agrarian sector as antimodernization strategies. In very populated countries, agrarian development is both a formula for employment and for feeding the needy. When self-reliance, in addition, is a national policy, as in China, such a priority become inescapable. But the debate that seems to have raged in China between the left-wing Maoists and those whose investment priority was in heavy industry, was a debate between strategies of growth (and their political effects), not a clash between modernizers and traditionalists.

Even in those countries that have chosen the capitalist model, a new awareness of both the economic and the "social limits" of growth[7] has arisen. But it only warns us against the physical impossibility and the unbearable strains of a perpetual growth that pays no attention to the environment and places no restraints on the competitive, meritocratic, and bureaucratic features of modern society.

Second, one should not mistake the popularity of certain countercultural themes—about the ecology, the misery of large cities, alienation, and so forth—for an incipient revolt against industrial civilization despite the awareness of its perils and excesses, especially among the "haves." A desire to redress the balance of wealth, to provide a better "quality of life," to make work more fulfilling, to exploit resources more rationally, or to create counterweights to the huge corporate structures that control one's life is not the same as the invention of a new "social project."

Only among Western intellectuals does one find, for reasons rooted in the troubled relationship between the intelligentsia and capitalism, an indictment of industrial society that amounts to a celebration of all those happy pastoral societies that most of mankind want to escape from. Only there does one witness a tendency to tell others that growth just is not good for them—see what it has done to us—and a capacity to believe that there actually is a worldwide movement against what the bulk of mankind— West, East, and South—is obviously rushing into, whatever its divisions about who should lead the way and how to get there. It is sometimes difficult to decide who is more obnoxious: the intellectual who tries to tell people that most of their desires are inauthentic, that their wants are largely "false needs," that there exists a group that knows what is authentic and true, and that this group should be empowered to reshape society accordingly—or the intellectual who peddles the latest pseudoscientific fads of the "applied social sciences" and seems to believe that mankind's future can be entrusted to technetronic trickery.

This quasi-universal trend toward development provides the United States with an opportunity for influence—but not because the United States is or is not the "social laboratory of the world" and the great stabilizer.[8] For one thing, the United States has often been destabilizing, not only through its policy mistakes, but also because its economic dynamism, corporations, and consumerism have been forces of massive change; for another, what matters is whether others recognize one as their laboratory and stabilizer. The United States is widely seen as the prime example of economic growth, prosperity, and power, even when the social and political forces of the United States are deemed repulsive or unreplicable.

The gloomy themes of the Club of Rome have created a public awareness of the dangers of unexamined growth. But both the flaws of the model it used and the recent recession have confirmed the conviction of most people that growth—regulated, oriented—not stagnation, was the only chance of solving mankind's problems. Scarcity, or zero growth, would generate even worse social frustrations than the fast growth of the period before 1973. In world affairs, zero growth would turn every economic contest into a zero-sum game and promptly bring the scourge of wars of conquest and "resource interventions" back into the economic arena; i.e., carry the old logic of separateness and the "state of war" back into the realms of interdependence.

None of this is said to minimize divergences, which cover every possible corner in discussions of the ends and means of growth. But it is important to point out that the task of seeking world order is not merely essential; it is also not a quixotic task, although it may prove to be impossible to push it through. The twilight of the 1970s should be used as a prelude to more light, lest there be nothing but darkness in, and no end to, the proverbial tunnel.

One other objection needs to be faced. Have I not written that world order cannot be deliberately created? Is not order more a matter of improvising rules by trial and error, finding the best way to resolve each problem in its own terms, and muddling through intelligently? We have seen the fate of the original Kissinger design, vague as it was. Would not a scheme even more ambitious and complex fail even more completely? Is not some messiness, both in the process and in the institutional map, inevitable? These questions form a plea for what is often called *incrementalism*—the marginal corrections of mistakes, the minimal adjustments to new conditions—or for what Ernst Haas has christened "fragmented issue linkage,"[9] a learned expression for a procedure more ambitious than incrementalism and far untidier than "rational-analytic" planning. But incrementalism simply will not do. Not only are there too many issues, but each one requires a degree of foresight (incrementalism with respect to nuclear proliferation, for example, is a form of myopia). Because issues of world politics are interrelated, part of the strategy used by many dissatisfied states today consists precisely in refusing issue-by-issue increments. "Fragmented issue linkage" may well be a result of failed planning or messy details; it can hardly be called a strategy. The same could be said of muddling through.

The strength of the objection lies not in what it proposes to do, but in what it warns us against—the familiar American game of all-encompassing designs that appeal to engineers, lawyers, and academics. World order is not a matter of architectural efforts. It will not issue from a simple design the way a house seems to come out of an architect's blueprint. As George F. Kennan once said, gardening—not engineering—is needed, and there is no master gardener. (We know how Ibsen's *Master Builder* ended.) The lesson from Kissinger's attempt should be, not that world order policy is wrong, but that his particular one was too overbearing and too tight, too made-in-Washington, and too obsessed by stability to succeed. But we have obviously reached the other side of our argument: why we can't, by ourselves, do everything.

SECTION TWO:　NO ILLUSIONS

If the biggest *world* problem is how to produce order out of heterogeneity, harmony out of cacophony, the biggest *American* problem is how to devise a policy capable of receiving domestic support, yet avoid the illusion that our *idea* of world order *is* world order, that the United States can not only contribute to it but actually shape it. "Leadership without hegemony"[10] is both a good motto and a slightly tricky one for a country that likes to think of itself as a leader, not a hegemonic power, and in a world that likes to believe that American hegemony is the willed product of American leadership. Having tried to reply to those who argue that a world order policy could or should not be tried, one must now face the far larger and enthusiastic crew of those who argue so convincingly that we must try, and that we are uniquely qualified to do so, or that we have a moral duty, that they forget our limitations or the preconditions for even limited success. Thus, unwittingly, they sow the seeds of new disillusionments and the subsequent reactions toward "toughness"—the blunt nationalism of the self-righteous patriot—or toward isolationism—the refuge of the disgruntled idealist—or they lay the groundwork for more Vietnams.

The predicament is understandable. How can one call one's compatriots to arms, so to speak, for world order—i.e., for something both vague and complicated—unless one reduces it to a handful of slogans and explains that its aim is to reshape the world in one's own image? My point is that this is a dangerous and arrogant procedure, and a recipe for internal as well as external failure. "Moderation plus," a shorthand description of the kind of world order I feel we need, calls for "modesty plus" on the part of the United States: modesty in claims and expectations, plus skill in execution. What should be stressed here, meanwhile, are two sets of limits on American action: obstacles the United States faces in trying to move toward world order, and internal preconditions for a chance at external success.

OBSTACLES TO WORLD ORDER

The obstacles can be listed in three categories: those Washington encounters because the United States is a great power; those generated by its own special characteristics as a great power; and those that arise from certain domestic peculiarities of the United States.

The Great Powers' Contest and the Great Power Blues   A great power today encounters a double series of constraints. Some result from the superpowers' contest, some from the frustrations that plague the great in the present international system—what might be called the "great power blues." In the first place, the United States cannot bow out of the contest with its chief rival. Even détente was only a way of regulating and taming the contest. The radical critique of U.S. foreign policy all too often avoids discussing the "relationship of major tension"; or it assumes that it has settled the problem by pointing out that the cold war is not a zero-sum game and that not every U.S. retreat means a Soviet advance, or by exorcising the "war system" rhetorically one more time. But one cannot wish away problems that are written into the very essence of world affairs and into the very nature of one's chief rival.

One can, as some "peace researchers do," explain that imperialism capitalist-style and imperialism socialist-style are really twins, and that their duel is a sham or a way of keeping one economy and one political or police system going, thanks to the industrial-military complex. Alas, the horizontal dimension of world affairs—conflicts between states for ideological, ethnic, or national interest reasons—is as real as the vertical dimension—the struggle of the oppressed against their oppressors. The proportion of the world product devoted to military expenditures, from 1865 to 1965, rose from 2.6 to 6.8 percent, with the great powers' part increasing from 1 to 5.4 percent.[11] Nor can one assume that an American decision to follow a policy of peace-and-justice, to dismantle our imperial apparatus, to stop new weapons systems, and to invite others to join us in a worldwide campaign against nuclear energy and weaponry or for human rights, would provoke a contagion of converts and a wild proliferation of the Golden Rule.

Those others who, citing the weakness of Russia's economy and the vast uncertainties of China, keep telling us to downgrade that triangular relationship, to stop worrying about every Soviet move, and to concentrate on relations with our friends are often right in their critique of our obsessions. But they tend to make three mistakes. They minimize the potential mischief our chief adversary could make if we were to try to shut him out of realms he deems of primary concern to him or if we were to act as if he did not matter and he then refused to cooperate with us in areas where his participation is essential. (Even George Ball wants us to involve the Soviet Union more closely in our effort to settle the Arab-Israeli conflict.)[12] They forget that much of what our allies want us to discuss with them, is how we can keep protecting them from our common adversary—especially now that Russia's military capacity for meddling has mushroomed, and our very "world orderly" and perfectly rational tendency to try to limit the risks of escalation by decoupling general nuclear war from controlled forms of violence seems to encourage opportunities for such meddling. Finally, they fail to realize that the very cost of keeping our adversary from achieving, in nuclear or conventional weaponry, advances that would be destabilizing, sharply limits the financial *and* the intellectual resources available for all other world order tasks.

One does not have to be an old cold warrior, one can indeed be an appreciator of détente, to realize that the four imperatives of state behavior listed at the end of Chapter Four, which world order would require and which go against the traditional logic of the international milieu, are difficult to heed when one plays against an adversary whose own strategy consists mostly in not heeding them, in behaving in the traditional way except for a few well-circumscribed areas (such as negotiated strategic force limitations and nuclear proliferation). Giving priority to what is collectively important in the long run is exactly the opposite of what has happened so far in the qualitative nuclear arms race between the United States and the Soviet Union.

In another matter, the collective good requires, for instance, that the major powers agree to prevent more states from acquiring uranium enrichment plants and reprocessing facilities, perhaps by giving up competitive sales in this matter or by setting up multinational or regional processing centers. But progress has been pretty difficult, since it requires either revising or refusing deals with states (such as Iran or Brazil) on whom one counts in the contest for influence with the Soviet Union, or else putting the screws on allies (such as France and West Germany) whom we provide with nuclear fuel—and whom we need in this contest as much as they need us. Similarly, we shall continue to be tempted to gain friends, or at least clients, in the competition by selling our weapons to the neighbors of those to whom our adversary sells his, or to use our military hardware to entangle important developing countries (such as Saudi Arabia, Brazil, Indonesia, Zaire) in the American economy. To apply self-abnegation could easily be denounced as an act of folly—handing over to the "enemy" a golden opportunity for advance or throwing away an opportunity to gain some control over the behavior of third parties.

It is hard to find the line that separates arms sales necessary to establish regional balances from the kind of arms pushing that incites escalation and tempts Soviet intervention. One is once again caught in a contradiction: the quest for political advantage at the expense of a rival versus the logic of world order. In the late 1960s and early 1970s, the half-hearted American attempt to move Israel toward a settlement was partly due to the fear of enhancing Soviet influence in the Middle East—of what, in more recent hyperbole, would be called "making the world safe for Communism." After the brief springtime of détente, the shock of the oil crisis, and Angola, Washington has pursued the "normal" logic with greater vigor than the logic of world order.

Let us look at the fourth imperative: increasing institutionalization. Is it really to our advantage to push the Soviet Union into agencies when its absence has, so far, appeared to make them more manageable, even if these bodies should deal with issues (such as oil or aid) whose solution is hard to imagine without Soviet participation? And would not the institutionalization of post-Helsinki cooperation between the two halves of Europe actually amount to giving the Soviet Union a right of supervision and veto over the affairs of the Western half?

I do not suggest that the intensity and duration of the Soviet-American contest reduces a policy of world order to whatever steps these two contenders agree to take in their common interest as superpowers afraid of immoderation, or to whatever areas are "safe" because of a complete Soviet lack of concern for them or of means to interfere in them. But the reader should take note of the contradiction and reflect on the fact that not every form of containment is good for world order.

However much American leaders decide to embrace the logic of world order, they will suffer from the "great power blues": the frustrations engendered by the disparity between might and achievements. In discussing the restraints that weigh on states in the traditional strategic-diplomatic arena and in the new economic games and in analyzing the fate of the international hierarchy in each of these realms, I have tried to show how the assets of a great power can turn into burdens. Thus, the great powers have to be prudent in their resort to force outside their imperial domains. (Even when they use it successfully, as the Soviets did in Angola, they cannot be sure they can control the aftermath, short of outright occupation.) Their use of military and economic rewards gives them influence, not mastery. Their resort to subversion has produced a mixed record in which failures and festering resentments balance what were often pyrrhic victories at best.

America's situation in the wake of World War II was exceptional. Since then, the inevitable rise of Soviet military might; the decline in the relative size of the U.S. economy; the fact that physical security fears have become both more diffuse than in the days of the all-encompassing Soviet menace and less dominant over other kinds of fears; the increasing role of Third World countries in the daily contests; the interest that even (or perhaps especially) the most powerful economy has in the existence of a network of rules that would protect its operations abroad yet cannot be imposed unilaterally by it—all this means giving up the hegemonic dream. And it is psychologically so difficult to accept because there has been no corresponding decline in capabilities. The United States, like the Soviet Union, has enough resources to be less affected by outside events than most other states; the two great powers remain capable of affecting others more by their own acts (deliberate moves or policy mistakes) than they are vulnerable to the acts of others. This perpetuates the illusion, not only of relative immunity but of mastery. And yet, in the not-so-long run, both illusions are wrong.

The great power blues has three themes. One, what Joseph S. Nye calls the "power to control outcomes"[13] is not proportional to power-as-resources, even in a given functional area (nor, I would add, to power-as-supplies, i.e., as resources multiplied by the state's capacity for collective action). In other words, neither overall military might, nor the supply of power available in a given area—food power, the power of one's fleet and technology in the ocean, or one's communications technology in space, etc.—suffices to produce results commensurate with one's resources. The results depend largely on the peculiar structure of each game, and on game skills that are hardly determined by might or size: the skill in shaping coalitions, in linking or in decoupling issues, in achieving compromises.[14] Now, in any case it is hard to resign oneself to the rule of nonproportionality. But because skill plays so large a role in the outcome, any failure to achieve something close to the theoretical best—i.e., proportionality— may well be seen at home as a failure of will, that miraculous cure-all that is supposed to do for the United States what spinach did for Popeye.

The second theme, what I have elsewhere called the prevalence of denials over gains in the strategic-diplomatic realm, describes the lack of opportunities for a great power across the board. Especially in games where force or the threat of force cannot easily be used, where states can choose among competing would-be rewarders, and can, in the last resort, retreat to the blackmail of the weak, a great power is often reduced to preventing others from imposing their wills (for they need its contributions), while it is unable to impose its own. Recent North-South discussions, as well as the bargaining on the law of the seas, have confirmed this. At the Conference on International Economic Cooperation in Paris, in June 1977, Washington could not get the oil-producing states to accept any institution in which they might have to share their power, or even submit it to review. Kissinger reminded the nations that argue about the oceans that, "if the deep seabeds are not subject to international agreement, the United States can and will proceed to explore and mine on its own." But this muscle flexing was aimed at preventing the conference from establishing an international authority, run by the developing nations, that would control the right of access to seabed minerals. "From a practical standpoint, no one recognizes more clearly than American industry that investment, access, and profit can best be protected in an established and predictable environment."[15]

The third theme is this: a great power's very need for order in the safe pursuit of its special interests and competitive concerns (a need fully reflected, for instance, by the Soviet stand on the law of the sea), means that it is in its interest to compromise. Thus, the outcome of a negotiation will be less favorable than the one the great power would have obtained had it been able to impose its will, yet a mediocre result will be preferable to the absence of order. There are exceptions. In the monetary realm, American views have prevailed, since "there is at present no clear, feasible alternative" to the role of the dollar.[16] But what marks this realm is not a definitive American success in reshaping order; it is the absence of an agreed-upon and established regime, the perpetuation of an interim, made necessary by disagreements about alternatives to Bretton Woods and made tolerable by the role and relative strength of the dollar.

On the whole, however, as was demonstrated by the misadventures of the tough "national interest" policy followed by Richard M. Nixon and John Connally, world order today requires not merely a broad, long-range view of the national interest, as in the late 1940s and throughout the 1950s, but compromises between competing interests, genuine concessions to interests opposed to those of the United States. Instead of a choice between two ways of calculating American benefits—a long-range and a short-term definition—we will be faced with a choice between such compromises and the risks of chaos. This is a major shift, because it entails bargaining (instead of laying the groundwork oneself) and accepting far less than the theoretical best. And the United States will have to make such sacrifices of interests while lowering its expectations of control. Still, this assumes that compromises are possible, that the genuine acceptance of divergence will lead to tolerable bargains. This is far from sure, not only because there may be issues on which conciliation will appear impossible, or states whose intransigence will be implacable, but also because of purely American handicaps, independent from but added to general great power predicaments.

Drawbacks to American Preeminence The second class of obstacles could be defined as follows: Not only does the United States, as a great power, not get rewards as large as its assets, but it suffers from the drawbacks of its advantages. By contrast with the Soviet Union, Washington plays every game; and by contrast with some of its main allies, it is at or near the top of every hierarchy of power. This presence and eminence create trouble as well as opportunities.

First, there is embarrassment. Our assets permanently threaten to reduce the flexibility, impede the mobility, and deepen the commitments of the United States. When a marcher has huge, leaden shoes, every mud bank may become a quagmire, and inevitable involvement tends to turn into inextricable entanglement. In the new international system, with its elusive or shifting gains for the players, an omnipresent great power, such as the United States, may easily find that its responsibilities far exceed the rewards. Its "privilege" is to be concerned lest local violence or functional chaos threaten the framework of the world order it needs to protect its interests and promote its influence; and its physical safety and material advantages are paid at the high price of permanent fear, not only *for* that framework, but *of* excessive entanglement.

Developing nations need American resources for their progress, a condition of world order. But the great powers' contest will continue to limit U.S. contributions, except in the mischievous form of arms sales. The dissatisfaction of the South with the scale of our efforts contributes to putting us on the defensive. Our good conscience about telling other nations far poorer in sources of energy that they need not push into a plutonium economy is troubled by evidence that we have not always been reliable suppliers of enriched uranium for the reactors we deem acceptable, and whose sales we have long monopolized. Similarly, even in the stragetic-diplomatic realm, Washington, seeing itself (in contrast with the scheming Soviets) as being both a fighter in the contest and a high priest of order, has tried to mediate large numbers of disputes in the non-Communist world. We have often failed: Kashmir, Cyprus, the Middle East, the Franco-Tunisian clash in 1958. . . . (The Soviets have tried it at Tashkent, between India and Pakistan, and succeeded, thus exploiting a Western failure. But they failed in the Somali-Ethiopian conflict.)

Then, there is our familiar plague, inhibition. The United States offers maximum hostage surface to others. Its economy is entangled in the economies of a large number of clients; its need for their support limits its ability to exploit fully the advantages of "asymmetrical interdependence." Having decided that world order requires the observance of at least minimum universal standards of human rights, we find ourselves in trouble with several allies of considerable military and economic importance to us as well as with our chief rivals, whom it is in our interest to prod into greater moderation and cooperation, not into greater secretiveness and hostility. In other words, we must accept restraints that do not hamper actors with less opulent but more concentrated assets or strategies.

Finally, there are contradictions. The more Washington wants to build elements of order close to its preferences, the more it has to pay for their financing and also to allow others to take part in their management. Hence a paradox: Washington may have to choose between underwriting institutions or agreements that threaten to slip out of its control, or completely lose grip on them by refusing to support them. This is the choice we have with respect to the international authority for the seabeds. It is one we resolved in the usual way—by making concessions—when the International Telecommunications Satellite Consortium (Intelsat) was established.[17] Similarly, we have had, so to speak, to spread the right of veto at the International Monetary Fund. There are now three veto groups: the United States, Western Europe, and the developing countries. Hence a potential paradox: a great power interested in institutionalization for the sake of world order may have to pay cash in exchange for a promise of future order, even though, at present, international agencies are fields of contest and often flooded by demagoguery. This does not make a world order policy easier to explain or to "sell" at home.

THE VALUES GAP

Its Nature   Thus we come to the third, and most serious, set of obstacles: those which result from America's domestic peculiarities. These are of two kinds: American values different from those of other nations; and the gap between practices derived from America's past and its present necessities. The first kind creates what the French writer Jean-Marie Domenach once called America's "incommunicability." It could be christened the "values gap," but this would be partly misleading. The United States is not the only nation whose values are not universally shared and are fought or rejected in much of the world. The problem lies rather in the American expectation of universal relevance (the outward-looking and expansive form of American exceptionalism), in the disappointment of that expectation, and in the consequences of that disappointment for America's action in the world. This expectation is, at present, unique. To be sure, our communist rivals also claim universal relevance—but with two differences. Marxism-Leninism, however distorted by conflicting glosses, however distorting of social complexities, nevertheless suggests that not every country is ripe for revolution. An element of time is built into the dogma, along with hosts of classifications and distinctions. There is, on the other hand, something timeless and abstract about America's deep conviction that the principles, practices, and institutions that have made America great can be used with similar effect elsewhere, that even when the backgrounds are profoundly different, either determined American action or satisfactory compromises will allow the survival and spread of these ideals and patterns. The ways in which ethnic groups and races have been integrated into a common framework (except for those who were exterminated, and on these one does not dwell), the ways in which the original values have not only withstood but shaped enormous economic changes, cannot be exported and turned into recipes. But acknowledging this remains difficult, for its spells defeat.

Furthermore, although for different reasons, the two leading communist states have currently given up the propagation of their model. China gives precedence to the containment of Soviet power. Russia gives precedence to the weakening of Western power and seems to have had second thoughts about the proliferation of communist states beyond its direct control. But the United States, even in its more blatantly cynical moves inspired by pure and simple anti-Communism, has never ceased being embarrassed by the contradiction between some of its values and its acts: paying lip service to the former (such as Kissinger's homilies on human rights when in Brazil or in Pinochet's Chile) while guided by the conviction that part of the American experience—if not the idealistic, at least the materialistic—had to be "sold" abroad on its merits.

Hence a profound disillusionment. Just as America's immediate postwar predominance was not a promise of perpetual domination, the triumph, in the early postwar years, of the principle of self-determination and of the "Western" model of development, did not mean the multiple replication of

America. Americans saw in decolonization a triumph for their principles, and they are now bitterly disappointed. They discover that while America's popular culture and techniques are in great demand, what foreigners want is not the "American model," just its benefits; not the system, but the goods. (On the contrary, the immigrants came largely for the system: the gains came as a reward.) This is a disjunction that scandalizes Americans—just as many are scandalized today at the thought of quotas for women or minorities, which are seen as violations of the system of individual ascent based on merit and hard work, rather than as initial correctives to collective inequality of opportunity. Indeed, they tend to see the world not merely as alien—a frightening thought already—but as hostile.

And yet, it is necessary, when one analyzes the "values gap," to distinguish between two components, first of all because they have very different—indeed, sometimes almost antagonistic—implications and, second, because different Americans stress one or the other of these components. Let us begin by dismissing a myth.[18]

Nothing in the American experience makes us incapable of endorsing a demand for equality. This is not where "philosophical isolation" lurks. Liberty was not an American monopoly. To men such as Montesquieu, Voltaire, or Tocqueville, liberty was to be found in England, and it was seen either as an aristocratic legacy or as the by-product of a commercial society. It was English liberty the American rebels demanded from George III. It was *equality* that Tocqueville found in America: the rejection of caste and privilege, and the faith in universal suffrage; and it was the conciliation of equality with liberty that fascinated him, since it had eluded France. What the United States is facing in today's world is mainly a demand for "state equality." Some of the states that push this claim are oppressively inegalitarian at home. This is not enough reason to resist their demand. And by itself, resistance does not demonstrate an inability to grasp equality; it only shows an unwillingness to make the *state system* more democratic—i.e., to accept a decline of one's privileges as an actor on the world stage. Insofar as the equality of individuals is concerned, the demand for it takes many forms. There is legal equality, equality of opportunity, equality of results. Americans, because of their attachment to the market economy and their distrust of the state, are suspicious of the demand for the latter; because of their wealth, they tend to forget that equality of opportunity works only above a certain level, and that the poorest individuals (or nations) do not have the means to reach this level, i.e., to grasp the opportunities. But even insofar as equality of results is concerned, the American political record is not one of constant or total hostility. And insofar as class stratifications and elite preserves go, the United States is by no means the world's worst delinquent.

"Philosophical isolation" threatens elsewhere. First, it has to do with the spread of tyrannical regimes in the world, the mutilation of human rights, the stifling of dissent. Some of these regimes are indeed hostile to the United States. But others, many others, while either contemptuous of American political institutions (such as the Shah of Iran) or quick at explaining why the American political model cannot be exported (such as South Korean, Filipino, or Brazilian leaders), have been among America's "best friends" in world affairs. What many liberal Americans resent is not so much isolation as betrayal. Others are, uncomfortably, possessed of a virulent anti-Communism—which makes them accept the alliance of tyrants as long as they are the right ones (or of the Right)—and, at the same time, obsessed with defending our system against certain (not all) oppressive regimes, not because these are oppressive, but because they challenge American positions in the world arena. It is a mix of displacement, diversion, and contradiction. The problem is not one we face alone. We are not the last of the democracies, even as we deplore their shortage. Moreover, a viable world order will, at the start, have to accommodate (to us) unsavory and imperfect regimes.

Far more serious is the second component: the divorce between America's economic system and much of the rest of the world. Again, the United States is not the only capitalist power, the only parent of multinational corporations, the only market economy. But except for West Germany (and even here the similarity is only partial), the United States is the only nation in which the state's role in the economy is so deprecated ideologically (even if its actual importance is vast) and in which the market is not merely a process but a divinity, not only a criterion of efficiency but a guarantee of value. Here, we must carefully distinguish two very different sorts of hostility, even if they converge on a single target: the United States. There are critics abroad who attack, not the model itself, but what they see as the dominant role of American capitalism at the expense of their own nation's development—the repatriation to the United States of profits and royalties, the exploitation of raw materials at the expense of industrialization, or the import of capital-intensive technology. This attack is a power struggle, not a fundamental challenge. What these critics want is an opportunity for national capitalism (often more inegalitarian and exploitative than America's). Others, however, reject the model itself and want national development to take a very different form—more closed, planned, collec-

tivist, and egalitarian. It is true that both kinds, if in power, might nationalize American companies and demand a "new international order." But,
obviously, compromises will be far more difficult to reach with the second
group than with the first.

Americans must not confuse the maintenance of certain positions of
economic power with the defense of a cherished model of economic life.
And we must also understand why foreign supporters of that model come to
challenge an American exercise of control over their future, and why the
inherent flaws of the model—and the grip its export abroad has given to
Americans (i.e., foreign masters) and to narrow national elites tied to
them—explain the rejection of the model itself in many parts of the world.
American universalism, plus the irresistible tendency to confuse one's
power with one's values, make this double adjustment difficult. To sum up:
the risk we face is not "capitalism in one country,"—i.e., that we end up
isolated—but that we mistake our somewhat mythical view of capitalism
for the only one, that we believe that the future of capitalism in the world is
tied to the unlikely chance of capitalism *by* one country—propagated and
controlled by us alone—and that we treat as foes of the United States all
the enemies of the capitalist system. The market economy of an advanced
industrial society is not the essence of America, and all these enemies (for
instance, within left-wing parties and unions in Western Europe) are not
ipso facto agents or dupes of Moscow.

Its Effects   The double "values gap" strengthens what is, in any case,
the greatest obstacle to world order: the risk that the very diversity of
idological, political, and economic systems will make the definition of
common rules and international regimes impossible, or their survival
unlikely. Far more is at stake than America's popularity, its place in the
world's hit parade, and therefore its influence.

The "values gap" can have two conceivable effects on American behavior abroad, and both would be bad for world order. One would be a policy
of reaction and resentment. Frustration is bred not only by the lack of
proportion between assets and profits, but also by the ineffectiveness of
America's traditional tool of problem solving: the apolitical pragmatism
that stresses efficiency above all (and hence has a strong conservative bias
in social and economic affairs) and tries either to fragment obstacles or to
leave the hard core of disagreement for the end. This works well only when
the political and social values of the contenders are compatible (or made

artifically compatible by the existence of a common enemy), or when, as after the Second World War, one of the actors enjoys so overwhelming a superiority that he can remodel his enemies according to his own values and can select the means of recovery for his friends. But we can, in today's world, neither "convert the non-democratic countries of the non-Communist world into democratic societies,"[19] as we did in West Germany or Japan, nor convert nations fundamentally opposed to the free enterprise and free market models.

There is therefore a risk that those Americans, say, who resent Pinochet's Chile for its onslaught on human rights—and our support of it—and those who resented Allende's Chile for its attack on our economic power and model, will unite behind the kind of policy that Patrick Moynihan called "the United States in opposition." Such a policy would wreck any chances for world order. It would also be absurd: the two components of the "values gap" are not comparable and should not be confused. To treat as equally important the humanitarian values that inspire the U.S. political system, and the economic processes of American capitalism would be doubly wrong. Tactically, this confusion would put us in opposition against much of mankind (for if tyrannical regimes abound, it is not in response to popular demand . . .), and it would create formidable contradictions in places such as southern Africa, where the Republic of South Africa and Rhodesia symbolize both Western capitalism and racist rule. Philosophically, there simply is no necessary link between liberal democracy and free enterprise capitalism. The former is incompatible with totalitarian forms of socialism; it certainly is not with other forms. Democracy is compatible with mixed economies, and it should not be equated with social immobility and the fear of experimentation.

The great flaw of "the United States in opposition," whether its opposition results from moral revulsion at the practices followed by certain regimes or from indignation at the attack leveled on United States capitalism, is its utter impotence. It is a modern-day version of the old quietest idealism, which consisted of renouncing *action* in the world, while hoping to improve it by a stern refusal to recognize what one did not like. Rhetoric is not policy. Indeed, it could all too easily lead to abdication, to a dropping of all the levers of influence the United States can still use. The danger of that policy exists primarily in the realm of economic values because it is difficult for us to impose our economic principles and practices on hostile nations. It exists also in our relations with communist regimes; as the episode of the Jackson amendment and more recent developments have shown, it is impossible for us to force the communists to liberalize their societies (the price of which would be a breakdown in the quest for "moderation plus" on both fronts). But the mere rhetoric of constant denunciation makes this quest more difficult.

The danger of an opposite American reaction to the "values gap" also exists: not withdrawal covered by remonstrances, but militant activism that could take two familiar forms—tough nationalism and expansive idealism—and create trouble in two domains. On the one hand, even in the realm of economic values and policies, we may, as in the past, be tempted by what could be called the Cuba-Chile syndrome. We might interpret the expropriation of American investments, moves aimed at decreasing dependence on U.S. capital and trade, and explosions of anti-American feelings, as attacks on our values and influence. We would then self-righteously convince ourselves of having two reasons, one ideological and one derived from the power contest, to intervene—especially if our challenger should be politically linked to our main foe, or if the challenger should possess resources whose denial could threaten ("strangulate") our prosperity or that of our allies. Such interventions, overt or covert, are dangers (for reasons to be examined below). Yet a residual faith in gunboat machismo and, above all, the strong connection between American private interests and the U.S. government, always argue in favor, if not of blatant violations of the hapless norm of nonintervention, at least of forms of retaliation that range from subsidies to "friendly" forces, and other dirty tricks, to the use of American influence in regional and world bodies to deny credits and diminish flows of aid to the delinquent—measures that hardly contribute to "moderation plus."

On the other hand, a different "activist" reaction could occur in a realm where it has rarely appeared in the past: in the defense of our political values versus those of the non-Communist world—the realm of activist idealism, pure and simple. For two brands of indignation are currently brewing against Third World, and First World, tyrannies: the angry, "tough," defensive variety and the newly proposed crusade for justice and progress. One explicitly denounces the crimes of those who denounce us— the leaders of Uganda, say, or Cuba, or Cambodia. The other attacks the horrors of those whom we have embraced—Iran, say, or Brazil, Chile, or South Korea—and wants us to use our connections and to acknowledge our responsibility to effect change. Among the crusaders, we find the radical idealists,[20] whose shrewd insights into the obstacles our domestic system puts up against any such crusade somehow do not restrain them from advocating it with enthusiasm or from hoping that a surge of populism would sweep the United States and, for once, favor the new world mission instead of parochial chauvinism. We also find the liberal idealists, who reject the "amoral" foreign policy of the recent past, speak of basing the future on "a community of the free," call peace "the unceasing effort to preserve human rights," and human rights "a fundamental tenet of our foreign policy."[21]

Alas, a *crusade* for democracy and basic rights is for many reasons neither feasible nor desirable. Even if we agree on their importance in the hierarchy of values; even if we believe that repression cannot be explained merely by reassuring theories about stages of development (forced-draft capitalism in poor countries with turbulent masses,[22] or forced-draft socialism in its revolutionary phase); even if we believe that some of our alliances are disgraceful and that the need to prevail or hold our own in the contest with Russia cannot be the alpha and omega of our policy; even if we realize the domestic popularity of an appeal to American moralism (but also to some smugness about the superiority of our institutions) and the usefulness of this appeal in providing a foundation of support for our foreign policy— temporarily at least, for there will be disappointments and disputes later— idealistic militancy ought to be resisted as a general guideline.

On moral grounds, it contains an often unconscious paternalism. Because we know what is good for everyone, and because they cannot achieve it themselves, we shall take their salvation into our hands. Moreover, there is a formidable self-serving hypocrisy here. Shouldn't we first put our house in order? Like charity, well-ordered crusades should begin at home. We have neither the competence to forge revolutionary fronts abroad, nor, in countries where political life has been crushed by years of nihilistic centralism, can we often find champions. To carry on a crusade, we would, therefore, as often before, have no choice other than to ask the factions in power to be good enough to reform in exchange for our help or at the cost of losing it. And we would end up, as we did in South Vietnam or in the colonels' Greece, at their mercy, having sacrificed our vaunted values for the sake of minimal, token, or purely cosmetic reforms.

Moral modesty and political prudence converge to make one suspicious of the practical judgments such as outsiders' crusade would involve. Should we look only at the way governments observe, or violate, public liberties? Or shall we also take into account their performance in trying to fulfill what might be called public needs, what the French call economic and social rights as distinct from political ones? We have rarely done so in the past, and yet people deprived of the former rights are in no condition to take advantage of the latter. Can one demand human rights of a Park or Marcos, yet have no misgivings about communism in Italy and France, or China? If the answer should be yes, can it be for reasons other than pragmatic? And if, indeed, pragmatic considerations are indispensable in the application of moral judgments to political issues, what, then, is left of the crusade? If, as Patrick Moynihan has argued, we need a single standard, we are in a dilemma: if it is too low or too partial (leaving out human needs, for instance), we shall look hypocritical; if it is too high, we will collide with most states and be ineffective. In other words, we must remember that our power, when it is misguided, has for all its limits a vast capacity for harm.

None of this is a plea for moral relativism, moral indifference, amoral realpolitik, or "the premise that our moral values and policy objectives are irreconcilable."[23] While peace is "a moral as well as a political objective" (in Kissinger's terms), it is perfectly obvious that *any* peace, *any* order—such as that of the Soviet empire in Eastern Europe—is not a justifiable goal. Some injustices are better than some orders. It is perfectly obvious that some regimes are pure evil. But whereas fighting their expansion is a valid foreign policy goal, and not helping them tighten their grip can be one, forcing their internal demise becomes one only when, as it was in Hitler's case, there is no other way to stop their expansion. Their destruction or radical reform can be a perfectly sound objective of private groups and individuals outside its borders—a distinction between state and citizens that should not be declared hypocritical too soon in a world where the state, aiming at order and justice abroad, risks either producing chaos or corrupting morality. A world in which human rights would be trampled under the feet of military and ideological despots would be one in which order, relying on the mutual balances of fear and the fleeting balances of interests alone, would be fragile indeed.

The problem of moral action is one of methods and timing. I have no doubt that an American policy for world order cannot avoid including such moral concerns for deep internal reasons, that it should include them for external ones, and that it ought to try to share these concerns as widely as possible. The problem that remains is essentially one of degree. Where, when, and to what extent can and should what Richard Ullman calls "the quality of political life"[24] become a part of an American policy for world order? Honest persons can differ on the answer, but to turn this problem into an absolute is to turn the "values gap" into an abyss.

DOMESTIC PRECONDITIONS

The "values gap" itself is not new. The difference between America and the world has, for two centuries, inspired American faith in America, the unique and the exemplary. What is new is the divorce between expectations and intentions we have inherited from our past, and the necessities of the present. What is new is the irrelevance of the two traditional manifestations of exceptionalism. The American people and their leaders can no longer swing from an insulation, aimed at protecting their institutions from external corruption, to a crusade aimed at spreading American values (and power) over the world. They must also curb the aggressive nationalism that expresses itself in a mix of protectionism and unilateral toughness, and that often appears in reaction to the frustrations of the crusade as a substitute for impossible isolation. Separation, monochrome globalism, and "Americanism" are out. And yet, even after thirty years of involvement, these are still the terms of the political discussion.

One can see why. It lies in the very depth of America's self-image, in the persistent hold of the experiences that have forged the American nation over more than 200 years. The passion for control, so deeply rooted in American history, the universal moralism, so deeply expressive of America's civil religion, must now yield to an external policy of extreme delicacy. To be sure, its strength will reside in the outlets it will provide for American idealism. But this idealism, with its tendency to oversimplify through projection, to overwhelm through self-confidence in American know-how, and to manipulate other societies to make them more familiar and more accessible, will need to be curbed. Sharp restraints on idealism are the only safeguard against its own corruption. Yet the experience of the recent past—eight years of "amorality" tacked onto the long immorality of Vietnam—will make the curbing difficult. If historical activism is strong, historical memory is weak. The instinctive desire to save the former creates the legend that Vietnam was merely a product of cynicism and elitism, rather than a catastrophe resulting largely from misplaced idealism.

The Plight of the Executive   What we need today are not only technical skills, given the intricacy of many of the functional issues of world order, but a central political will that assures coherence and guidance for the necessary tests, compromises, and deals. This means a difficult blend of some qualities that not even the most partisan critic can deny Kissinger—flexibility and resilience—and of some qualities he did not display at all—such as openness or, at the end of his cycle, the ability to present others with a clear road map. Some of these skills are also required for success at home—for getting from the domestic political system the support without which, as we have seen, no foreign policy can be waged well. Here, too, a clear road map is indispensable. Here, too, candor will help. And yet, here again, are formidable obstacles.

First, will the kind of flexibility needed for pursuing simultaneously a host of bargains while maintaining America's strength be understood and approved? The combination of toughness and willingness to negotiate, which American policy toward the Soviet Union will continue to require, is a hard one for American opinion to grasp. In atavistic fashion, negotiation implies the end of hostility, and toughness the opposite of compromise. The same combination will be needed in other realms; for instance, toughness against the total and angry politicization of international conferences, but readiness to discuss concrete issues. Without the former, world bodies might well lose their usefulness; without the latter, one can expect nothing but battles between blocs along ideological lines—blocs that tend to dissolve only once one reaches, in negotiation, the often divergent interests concealed behind the lines. Will Congress take the domestic measures that would improve America's bargaining position abroad? (The case of energy is hardly reassuring). Will the Executive have the authority to make deals (for instance, with countries that have shown ideological hostility to the United States, such as Cuba, Vietnam, or Mozambique) or to use the threats and sanctions that toughness will at times demand? Kissinger's revival (or modern adaptation) of the old balance of power play did not work well on the home stage. But an even more complex drama of multiple bargaining, however much it can be wrapped in a "progressive" rhetoric of world order rather than the off-putting jargon of manipulation for stability, will not be more readily applauded by divided and suspicious audiences. Nor will it be easier to reconcile with the duality of the executive and legislative branches and of the administration and pressure groups.

Second, it is futile to hope that the executive branch will receive the authority it needs, if it only, from now on, "levels" with Congress. The lessons of the recent past create a quandary. The executive branch enjoyed maximum, indeed excessive, leeway in those years (1952 to the mid-1960s) when it successfully drafted the entire nation in the battle against communism. But such a mobilization cannot be repeated. Communism has splintered. The apparently permanent tension with the Soviet Union dominates only one of the arenas of world politics, and even in this one a two-track policy will have to be pursued, if only to limit the horizontal and vertical arms races. Nor can one mobilize the nation around an abstraction such as world order. On the other hand, the abdication of Congress and public opinion that Kissinger at times called for (and indeed would have needed for his policies) can simply no longer be obtained. Thus, there is no substitute for doing at home what must also be done abroad: constant persuasion and bargaining—an appeal not to patriotic or crusading instincts, but to common sense. Given the nature of the issues, pressure groups of all sorts will demand to be heard, will resent being hurt by this or that "adjustment," will appeal to basic American values, will evoke the insecurity that involvement in the world contest has imprinted on American minds. Congress can be expected to reflect these pressures. Its members have neither the background nor the means to develop a coherent and adequate foreign policy of their own.

It may be that the American political system simply magnifies what other democracies also experience but manage to contain better. It can give its Executive more support than almost any other democractic system, but it can also apply more brakes and breed more confusion. At present, this clash between the internal need for support and the external necessity for action (between what is widely preferred at home and what seems wise abroad) is already visible in three important areas. One is the Arab-Israeli conflict. Here, American policy has been hampered by the difficulty of obtaining internal approval for any moves bolder than the step-by-step approach, which has run its course and has had some bad long-term effects along with its good short-term ones. Another is southern Africa, where the United States had found itself opposing political and social evolution, yet experiences domestic resistance to the shift of its policy. The third area includes all the North-South issues that challenge both America's interests (as the leading capitalist nation and as an advanced industrial society) and its belief in the market or free enterprise—that challenge, that is, both America's power and its self-image as a progressive, even revolutionary, experiment.

Making reason prevail over passions and cool imagination over fears; putting events into perspective so that temporary turmoil in Portugal, glacially slow political evolution in Italy, or a bad but local defeat in Angola will cease being equated with radical disaster, or a happy summit with momentous progress; getting certain pressure groups to accept the sacrifices involved in, say, reducing arms sales abroad; getting other groups and congressional committees to resign themselves to generalized preferences, commodity agreements, or broader Third World participation in the management of economic regimes—measures that will hurt American interests—will require a major effort in two domains. The two domestic preconditions to a possible (but not assured) external success are the rooting of American foreign policy and a reform of foreign policy making in the executive branch.

The Rooting of American Foreign Policy—the Public and the Congress   By far the most important is the rooting of American foreign policy. Where, as in the areas just mentioned, foreign policy and domestic politics

seem to point in opposite directions; where, as in so many other areas—
Western Europe, Japan, the triangular relationship with Moscow and
Peking—the consensus of experts and politicians is not shared by the
public, the American foreign policy of world order must be rooted in the
American soil to have a chance of internal solidity.

The rooting of foreign policy presents a triple challenge. There is, in the
first place, the need for a rationale, both for the ouside world and for the
citizens at home. U.S. policy had such a rationale during the cold war era.
During the Kissinger years, fuzziness about "stable structures," the clash
between the goal of stability and his personal style, the thrust of his major
efforts, meant that détente was widely seen as the chief rationale. (Hence
many of the troubles that beset him at home, once it became clear that its
beneficial effects on East-West relations, as well as on all the other world
issues, had been either oversold or overestimated.) For the past four years,
there really has been no rationale.

It is not easy to define in clear and comprehensible *political* terms a
policy of great complexity. And it would be as perilous as in the past to
compress its necessary diversity into a few simple *moral* slogans. But it
should not be beyond the intellectual resources of American leaders to
explain what the main trends and dangers in the world are; why the
challenges faced by the United States are more subtle, more numerous, and
less concentrated than before; why military safety, economic predictability, and psychological security require a world order yardstick; and why
certain policies might bring us closer to that goal. Nor should it be impossible to preach a sermon of modesty; to explain that America cannot "save"
mankind any more than it is responsible for all the world's miseries; or to
warn against the oversimplification of grand designs, charters, and architectural metaphors. The message will have to be that the United States cannot
expect to gain from its foreign policy more than "most nations in history"
(outside of imperial interludes) have been able to get, yet has to move
toward its goals in ways different from those of most nations in the past. Its
goals must be a world that will not be the United States writ large, but in
which a measure of world order might improve the chances for those
institutions (political and economic) that Americans deem of universal
value, and in which the prevailing methods will reflect the bargaining and
compromise characteristic of America's past experience.

This may sound like a naïve plea to turn American leaders into Sunday
school teachers of international relations. Who has ever heard a president
or premier go beyond the sensational? But we come back to a constant
theme: the need to innovate and, particularly, to rescue world order from
the heroic mode, whether the latter takes the form of "blood, sweat, and

tears" or "new eras of peace." Discussions of domestic issues have been framed in a far different, more complex, and more mature fashion for a long time now, except during these regressions in the service of democracy— election campaigns. But that which has never been tried—either because the institutional system, such as Britain's parliamentarism, allows for fairly sophisticated debates and subtle rationales since the relevant public is that of the representatives and the establishment; or because the constitution gives the president very broad powers in foreign affairs, as in France, whose parliament is far less potent than Congress; or else because national involvement in world affairs has tended to take the simple and sweeping form of a crusade, as in America's recent past—cannot be declared hopeless at the start.

Are mature discussions of foreign policy "hopeless" because of an inherent distrust of the people's competence and maturity in foreign affairs, which turns even Jeffersonian presidents into Hamiltonians in that realm? Do the presidents' own instincts reflect what I have called "education in the heroic mode"? Have we misinterpreted President Wilson's fate, the tragedy of a man who let his ideals exceed his grasp and whose immodesty for America led to his fall? Are slogans the product of the media's hunger for the quick and the flashy? The President does not have to sound like a Brookings report or an academic policy paper. But he should be able to make complexity understandable so as to make insecurity bearable.

Next, American foreign policy needs far more intimate congressional-executive coordination than has been the case in the past. Since the Constitution cannot be changed, and since attempts at de facto modification through executive fiat backfire, the system of checks and balances must be made compatible with the requirements of a foreign policy of world order. Joseph S. Nye, Graham Allison, and Peter Szanton have made some useful suggestions in this respect.[25] The measures a policy of world order will entail all require congressional approval, because of their price tags, because they take the solemn form of treaties, or because, as in the past, they involve the use of those familiar tools, U.S. economic and military assistance.

If one wants (to use Nye's words) the cooperative involvement of Congress, two kinds of measures are essential. There will have to be an understanding, a kind of gentleman's agreement, on the boundary between the domain of legitimate congressional intervention and the area of necessary executive autonomy. The former must consist of the general definition of policy (for even though, under the Constitution, especially as interpreted by the modern judiciary, the Executive has a pretty free hand here, the legislative branch could cripple policy all too easily). This domain must also, of course, cover the specific measures that require the express consent of the Senate or of both Houses. It must, finally, include periodic reports to Congress about, and oversight by Congress of, the main instrumentalities of policy, with no more secrecy than is absolutely necessary.

Again, I seem to be requiring an unnatural act, both insofar as the definition of policy and the CIA and other forms of counterintelligence and countersubversive activities are concerned. But the participation of those members of Congress who play key roles in the various committees concerned with foreign policy (not merely the Senate Foreign Relations and the House Foreign Affairs committees) in the setting of the main courses of action is the best way of ensuring cooperation and of educating the members of Congress about the necessities of world affairs.[26] To wait until bills are on the floor of the House or the Senate is to expose the policy to setbacks, the nation to embarrassment, and the President to a piecemeal waste of his political capital. As for intelligence, a regular procedure of the sort that the Senate adopted in the spring of 1976 to oversee U.S. intelligence activities has the double advantage of making unnecessary the exuberant leakage that always follows the excess of secrecy and of putting strong deterrent pressure on the agencies.

On the other hand, the Executive must have a margin of flexibility in daily negotiations. Only if directions are defined in cooperation with Congress will the Executive be in a strong position to ask for the approval of initiatives and for the transformation into commitments of promises offered within the limits of the policy. Only if Congress is involved in this definition (as it was during 1947–1949) will it tend to refrain from perpetual kibbitzing. I am not saying that the joint definition will be easy or that Congress will never interfere in policy making—only that Congress will certainly interfere if no such attempt is made, and that a presidential effort to give a political rationale and to explain it to the public would facilitate the joint exercise. Again, it is no more than transposing to foreign affairs what is standard operating procedure between the Executive and Congress in domestic affairs (transposing, not applying, since the Executive plays different roles in those two realms).

In addition, each of the services and offices of the executive branch that take part in the formulation and enforcement of policy will have to devote considerably more time and effort than in the past to domestic persuasion. There will be a need for policy integration; its purposes will be multiple. The external imperatives of action for world order must be given precedence over internal pressures. These imperatives are often contradictory

(Can one curb both nuclear proliferation and arms sales? Can one promote détente and reassure allies about America's commitment to their security?); they must be made compatible, so that these contradictions cannot be exploited by special interests. A more effective and farsighted policy of adjustment to economic losses resulting from the pursuit of long-term foreign policy goals is necessary. One would want to avoid the confusion of cross-pushes and pulls that has marked American policy toward Turkey since 1974, or toward Vietnam since 1975,[27] or the evolution of the American stance on the law of the seas, for example, and particularly the retreat from its perhaps fuzzy idealistic position of 1970 on a "trusteeship zone" beyond the territorial sea, under the pressures of oil interests, coastal fishing interests, and even scientists.[28] But preventing this confusion, or a further retreat of labor and business from trade liberalism, will make it only more necessary for the different departments to try to "convert" their respective clienteles, including congressional committees, to the wisdom of the courses chosen. Just as every domestic department now has a foreign policy, every service involved in foreign policy will need to have a staff especially charged with obtaining domestic support without appeasement. This will require a considerable change in organization and habits. And it will have to be matched by a similar determination by Congress to impart a foreign policy perspective to its "domestic" committees.

Here also, fragmentation is a peril, and the integrative steps already taken (with respect to the budgetary functions of Congress, for instance) will have to be followed by more (Allison and Szanton suggest a "Committee on Interdependence," drawn from all the appropriate committees, in each House). The responsibility of the congressional leadership will be considerable; it has not always been effective, and electoral considerations, especially in the House, have often defeated good intentions. But such a change could be presented as an integral part of a policy that associates Congress much more to the definition and enforcement of foreign policy.

The Rooting of American Foreign Policy—a New Elite　　Finally, the United States needs a new foreign policy elite. The formidable establishment that gave U.S. foreign policy its roots for the 1950s and early 1960s has been decimated by Vietnam and old age. Today, a kind of expectant establishment has come back to power with Jimmy Carter, but it arouses two concerns. One is the heterogeneity of the establishment, for it comprises two different elements: survivors of the cold war era, saved either by having been more right than wrong on Vietnam or (more frequently) by having occupied minor positions of limited visibility; and younger men with even more limited public experience, or none at all. The first group tends to slip into a slightly brushed-up version of the old imperial, patronizing idealism, and the second one is a bit at a loss as to how to go beyond such imperatives as "no more Vietnams," "no more shady deals and dirty tricks." One group is too positive, the other too negative. One tends to overestimate America's clout abroad, the other to be stupefied by domestic priorities and constraints. And both seem more concerned with stance than with substance, with "posture" than with policy. Another cause for concern is the small base of support this new, would-be elite provides. The media, academia, the business community, and the law firms (let us, for once, forget about public relations firms) have shifted their interest from the outside world to domestic problems. As a result, today's foreign policy elite is both narrower and more specialized, both more fragmented internally and less deeply rooted in American society, than its predecessor.

This is surely one of the most serious problems facing us at the beginning of America's third postwar cycle. True enough, what Brzezinski calls "the coherence of values" and "the social confidence" of the past elite had its drawbacks, as Vietnam proved. But a broad elite capable of bringing to the administration the reasoned consent of the public and the cooperation of Congress is indispensable. Without such an elite, and in the absence of a single compelling threat, foreign policy risks being the plaything of bullies. Without it, the most important task of the future—educating the citizens and the future leaders for world order—will not be undertaken. And yet, the very shift of attention, which causes the present vacuum, also prevents its being rapidly filled.

The amount and quality of information American citizens receive about the outside world are seriously deficient. Television coverage, inevitably, cherishes crises and climaxes—wars, riots, floods, hijackings, state visits, and the sampling of Chinese food by presidential palates. Often, it has been daring and provocative, but, again, mainly around "hot" issues, like Vietnam, or in the dizzying form of simplified pro-and-con arguments precariously balanced on the top of an issue. As for the press, with the exception of a small number of fine papers and magazines, both the quality of reporting and commentary, and the quantity of space devoted to the outside world, have been declining, even though earlier levels were never high. Is it because a world that is obviously not our oyster and whose complexities defy analysis ceases being interesting? Whatever the reason, the fact is that outside a thin geographical area—the Northeast—this country has, materially, become almost insulated again. Even the press that deals with the outside world gives an overwhelming priority to the marshalling of facts. This has two effects. It induces an unhealthy closeness between journalists and officialdom, because officialdom has, and often creates, the facts. Hence the reluctance of many correspondents to criticize their sources and the ease with which in this field even as free a press as America's can be manipulated. This, in turn, worsens the second flaw: the two other functions the press should perform are not adequately fulfilled. There is little analysis of the bewildering harvest of facts each day brings in, and there is far less evaluation. The intellectual and the civic roles the press ought to play thus go begging, or remain the somewhat musty preserves of uninfluential academics.

The disarray of the councils and associations that served as relays between the administration and the enlightened public in the cold war days; the shift in foundation concerns; the failure of academic centers of foreign policy studies either to grow, or to broaden their fascination with cybernetic models, simulation, or computers to include the real world; the discredit that has, not always unfairly, fallen upon think tanks at the service of the government or upon academics whose itch to advise the Prince has often subverted their values and deadened their language—all of this makes the creation of a new consensus, the education of a general public that has come through two cycles of frustrations and does not know what to expect, the shaping of a concerned elite, and the training of an adequate foreign policy personnel an extremely difficult task. As long as it is not undertaken, the uncertainties of the outside world are likely to feed the anxieties to which Americans have so long been addicted.

How, then, can it be done? As usual in the United States, not by fiat from the top, but through a host of initiatives in different circles. The media will have to devote more attention to long-range international issues, rather than focusing on easy dramatizations. The schools will have to find more room for the outside world in their curricula. Universities and colleges will have to rejuvenate theirs(in which world affairs are often but a dreary collection of data) and show the inseparability of domestic and international issues, their historical and cultural roots, and how these world problems raise all the important questions of traditional political and moral philosophy. Foundations will have to accelerate their new, still timid encouragement to the study of world order problems. The shocks of 1973 may have produced some stirrings. As one political scientist has pointed out, the capacity of the "undirected and semi-directed processes" of the international system "to produce unanticipated consequences" has been extraordinary; he lists the population and energy crises, the proliferation of nation-states, the growth of multinationals, global pollution, and the monetary and payments crises.[29] These trends are beginning to reawaken interest among the citizens of a nation of "doers."

To be sure, firm and wise leadership can also powerfully contribute to reawakening, in the various segments of American society, a concern for the problems of the world. But leadership is no panacea. A new awareness must come from the American society itself. Today, it oscillates between exaggerated anxieties about America's present strength and a lackadaisical attitude about the perils of the future. The opposite is needed: confidence in America's continuing assets, but an acute consciousness of "catastrophies too apocalyptic to contemplate," and of time "running out on all of us"[30] insofar as the fate of mankind is concerned. This, and the ability to distinguish between the need for world order and the claims of American world leadership—the ability to distinguish between unavoidable disappointments and real national failure.

FOREIGN POLICY MAKING

Let us return to leadership. The other domestic precondition for possible effectiveness abroad concerns the organization of the "foreign policy machine." It is a dreary subject, no less arid for all the passions it arouses among former practitioners and all the reports produced by political figures, academics, and management experts.[31] But it is not a trivial subject. As Allison and Szanton show, "organization matters": faulty organization can cause incoherence, incompetence, and imbalance among the interests and outlooks that policy decisions express. All too often, writers and officials have been primarily concerned with fighting the abuses of the recent past, just as founders of international organizations and diplomats at peace conferences always try to prevent the previous war from reoccurring. In the early sixties, the Eisenhower staff system of mushy consensus was being exorcised. Nixon and Kissinger reacted against the paralysis of the Johnson machinery. Today, the enemy seems to be the Kissinger system (as if so personal a technique were easily repeatable anyhow).

Rather than beginning with what one wants to avoid, one should start with the goal one wants to reach. A foreign policy dominated by the security dilemma, as it was in the cold war era, can afford to give the defense interests a central role in decision making (for instance, through the composition of the National Security Council). A foreign policy greared to a neo-Bismarckian design requires the flexibility and personal control that

Kissinger demonstrated. A foreign policy that aims at putting world order concerns on top of the agenda must devise a process that provides for coherence, a capacity of long-range action, and the integration of domestic considerations into foreign affairs (both in the preparation and definition of foreign policy, and in its enforcement). I shall not discuss organization charts. The specific organizational details are at any rate ultimately governed by the preferences of the President and his chief foreign policy advisers. But a few fundamental points ought to be stressed.

The first is the need for long-range scanning and planning. Nothing is more obvious, especially if world order becomes a goal and a criterion of policy. One could assert that in security matters statesmen can advance only one step at a time and that a worldwide set of controlled security relations can emerge only gradually; it is enough that each step taken be the right one. Even so, long-term thinking might have helped devise a "more right" step. (The ABM has been contained just in time, but was MIRV really necessary? And what about nuclear proliferation, or cruise missiles?) The pattern of "correct" short-term thinking here has consisted essentially in trying to drag back into the barn wild horses that one had let escape. Moreover, in most of the newer arenas of world affairs, a crisis approach can be not merely second-best, but outright awful. Measures taken only when they can no longer be postponed put an enormous strain both on international cooperation and on domestic politics, as in the attempt to cope with the effects of the energy crisis of 1973; or else they may be highly detrimental to international cooperation, such as those of August 1971. The same is true of domestic measures taken without an assessment of their effects on others (I think of the embargo on soybean exports in 1973).[32] And while policy makers may be right in saying that no set of institutions can be repaired *à froid* (i.e., before it is time), to wait until they have collapsed does not seem the best way of building new ones: it may well be the moment when antagonisms are sharpest.

The inter- and transnational economy that has developed across the Atlantic and the Pacific, and in particular the huge amounts of capital in search of maximum profit, have undermined the autonomy of national economic policy so thoroughly that a short-term or crisis approach allows governments only to draw belated consequences from their impotence, and to try to limit the wreckage and thus give themselves some respite until the next onslaught. Also, the short-range atavism of bureaucracies prevents a timely approach to a host of problems that only a handful of experts identify as major potential headaches. By the time bargaining begins, interests have crystallized, frenzy may have set in, and alignments that have very little to do with the issue may be entrenched. This has been the world's experience with environmental problems, the oceans, oil, commodity trade, and so on. Finally, the planning and, later, the operation of global regional institutions for joint management will require a far greater capacity for long-term action than any government now possesses.

Resistance to such a change is partly due to a necessity. Most governments, especially in advanced (i.e., complex) and democratic societies, can only move with small, incremental steps. Crises—often provoked by those less burdened, or even more hard pressed at home, or more ambitious— may actually be welcome, for they provide governments with the means to cope with issues which they had been obliged to leave unresolved: a costly method. But resistance to long-term planning is also due to a paradox: long-term thinking about almost any important issue in world affairs takes one "beyond the nation-state," or at least beyond autonomous nation-states. Even if one does not believe that transnationalism is the wave of the future, its expansion creates for the states problems that can be solved only by joint management; but the horizon of every bureaucracy remains parochial. This—especially at a time of strong domestic priorities—has been a far more potent obstacle to European integration than is usually acknowledged. Long-term thinking and action do indeed run into domestic obstacles; bureaucracy's inertia and the momentum of domestic pressures, demand immediate intervention by the state itself when things go wrong, and technocratic plots are suspected to be behind all schemes for long-range planning. For these tend to increase the distance between domestic producers or consumers, and inter-, supra- or transnational decision makers, and to make the latter look at the world as a single unit rather than as "us" versus "them." Thus, the built-in unresponsiveness of any bureaucracy to future or potential headaches is buttressed by a tension between the highly resilient domestic legitimacy of the nation-state (reinforced rather than weakened by the government's increasing role in welfare) and its inadequacy to cope with major issues. All these issues require a *fuite en avant*, a leap into the future; yet the states' feet are leaden.

Before 1969, no writer had criticized more acidly the U.S. foreign policy machine for its inability to put the important ahead of the urgent, than Henry Kissinger. In office, he was not modest about celebrating his administration's "profound enterprise" and "philosophical, as well as . . . practical reorientation of our foreign policy."[33] One of the weaknesses of his approach, however, deriving from traditional balance-of-power policy, was that, being all process, it told one nothing about substantive undertakings, and it relied on mechanisms (essentially unilateral shocks and interstate negotiations) that were inappropriate to twentieth century issues. One of the problems with his call for a "new Atlantic Charter," for instance, was that, while it correctly saw the danger of a series of irritating, disconnected, short-term negotiations aimed at shoring up old alliances, it had nothing better to offer by way of an overarching, long-term, joint political directive than a list of common *problems* and promises of good mutual *behavior* (something that is more significant in U.S.-Soviet relations than in inter-Allied ones).

The monopolization of foreign policy by a small staff under Kissinger, first at the National Security Council, later at the State Department, resulted—as so often before—in actually dissolving planning into operations. Some years ago, I argued against the division between planners and performers, which dooms the former to a choice between insulated irrelevance and self-betraying immersion. If "the policy-makers must also be the planners," then the precondition for long-range thinking is nothing short of a revolution in the training of the foreign policy personnel. As long as colleges and universities do not provide an adequate preparation, it would have to be done in the Foreign Service itself. Once trained, the personnel's attention could be kept on long-range issues if the process recommended by Nye and Keohane were adopted:[34] the establishment of a regularly updated list of problems and opportunities, identified by a variety of research centers and academies, and a White House–centered coordination system based on that list (and on regular reports on the State of the World).

This raises another issue: centralization versus decentralization of the policy process. There is now, inevitably, a reaction against the extreme centralization of the Kissinger years. His appointment as Secretary of State did not make the State Department the fountain of policy. Decisions continued to flow from the same small group, whose geographical location had been shifted. In the future, despite the "rehabilitation" of the State Department, other departments will most likely be unwilling to abdicate their responsibilities in foreign affairs in favor of State. It is hard to imagine that even a much-reformed State Department would be capable of enclosing within its walls all the expertise required for the joint management of a global system—unless State itself becomes even bigger and more unmanageable. At a time when almost every domestic function of the state has an international component, the only real alternative is a *less* centralized system in which the various departments provide functional expertise, and in which the State Department's role is radically transformed. Its relative demise was not due solely to the prejudices and practices of Dr. Kissinger; those practices derived from his experience with it—and, alas, did nothing to eliminate its flaws, while doing a lot to destroy its morale. "Elephantiasis," long years of either disconnection between the Secretary and the department, or else policy direction bypassing State, and the increasingly shameless application of the spoils system to ambassadorial appointements have led to the prevalence of paper over thought, to the waste of some of the most highly talented people in the government, and to the debasement of a career service at a time when the noncareer elements were bespattered by scandal.

The real mission of State ought to be to provide what functional departments rarely possess: skill in *political* analysis and *synthetic* ability—the capacity to study in depth the political conditions abroad (a very different task from reporting the latest public news and the latest private chit-chat), and the capacity to show to the President, to the public, and, of course, to Congress (with which the State Department has to deal) how the functional pieces of the puzzle fit or conflict. The State Department, thus slimmed and stiffened, could present to the President and his special assistant the main alternatives on a steadier and broader basis than have the National Security Councils. In all likelihood, the final decisions will remain at the highest level. Only there can the viewpoints of other departments on questions of foreign policy relevant to their subject-matters be reconciled with those of State. Only there can domestic necessities be properly drawn into the picture. But even so, such a system would make a better use of the varieties of expertise than was the case in the Kissinger years, and the State Department would have a far greater share in the preparation and enforcement of decisions.[35]

A third issue concerns precisely the integration of policy. If each department or agency has access to the President, will not policy be decentralized before and after the final decision, and will there not be a functional disintegration, a separation between security affairs (at the Pentagon), intenational economics (back at the Treasury, Agriculture, Commerce, and Energy), with a residual category, traditional diplomacy, left to State? Can one pursue both balance (or decentralization) and coherence? Will not a wide and complicated process—especially if it involves bargaining with Congress—result in delay, rigidity, or half-baked compromises, or give domestic considerations a stranglehold on foreign policy? Actually, contrary both to appearances and to recent practice, an integrated treatment of all foreign policy issues, one that would give to the problems of international economic interdependence the continuous attention they require, needs a more decentralized process than that of the Kissinger era. If either the State Department, even revived and reorganized, or a NSC system such as that which functioned from 1969 to 1973, were to evoke and annex even only the major issues of interdependence, the seams of policy making would burst. On the other hand, the more decentralized the process, the greater the chance of mere incrementalism and crisis-coping.

Integration and coherence first require the transformation of the State Department, both along the lines I have suggested and along those recommended by the Murphy Commission. The intellectual emphasis on long-range political analysis and synthesis must be combined with a strengthening of its economic ability. "The aim would not be to place the Department in a dominant position with respect to foreign economic policy formation" (for it would become "so entwined with the warp and woof of domestic policy as to jeopardize its primary mission")[36] but to make it better able to fulfill its missions: the formulation and the execution of foreign policy, and negotiation. Hence the commission's suggestion for four new functional bureaus (and the additional plea by Nye and Keohane to entrust to them the task of defining America's policy in the various international organizations that deal with these functions). Next, integration and coherence require a coordinating body more representative of the full range of issues than the National Security Council set up in 1947. Hence various proposals for either replacing it altogether (Allison and Szanton) or creating next to it a new council in which the economic departments would figure.[37] Of course, the heavier such a body, the more difficult reaching the supposed "solution" would become.

Therefore, integration and coherence require, at the top of the pyramid, a presidential assistant with responsibilities covering, not merely "national security," but all foreign policy issues (including economic—here I disagree with the commission's preference for a separate senior assistant charged with all economic policy, foreign and domestic) and a staff dealing with interdependence issues as well as traditional ones. The assistant and the staff would have an essential role, but a limited one. They would be, so to speak, the watchdogs of coherence and consistency, the guardians of balance, and the sentinels alerting the departments to problems the bureaucracies failed to pick up. But they would not be the shapers of content: the substance of policy would be the responsibility of each department, under the control of the President—insofar as the issues fell within the department's jurisdiction and the responsibility of the President himself—in all matters of importance and especially on all issues requiring the participation of several departments and affecting domestic politics. The assistant and the staff would help the President prepare his decision—no more. The assistant's role would be one of discretion, administrative efficiency, and analytic talent—not advocacy, and certainly not activism. These are the preconditions. What about the policy?

NOTES

CHAPTER FIVE

1. Henry Kissinger, "The Future of America's Foreign Policy," *Department of State Bulletin,* vol. 75, no. 1936, Aug. 2, 1976, p. 150, and Carter's acceptance speech at the Democratic National Convention, July 15, 1976.
2. Carter's speech at the Foreign Policy Association luncheon in New York, June 23, 1976.
3. For an evaluation written after this book, see my essay "The Hell of Good Intentions," *Foreign Policy,* no. 29, Winter 1977–78.
4. Earl C. Ravenal, "Soviet Strength and U.S. Purpose," *Foreign Policy,* no. 23, Summer 1976, p. 51.
5. George F. Kennan, *The Cloud of Danger,* Atlantic-Little, Brown, Boston, 1977, pp. 51, 228–230.
6. Fred Hirsch, "Politicization in the World Economy and Necessary Conditions for an International Economic Order," unpublished paper of the 1980s project of the Council on Foreign Relations, April 1976.
7. See Fred Hirsch's *Social Limits of Growth,* Harvard University Press, Cambridge, Mass., 1977.
8. Zbigniew Brzezinski, "America in a Hostile World," *Foreign Policy,* no. 23, Summer 1976, p. 92.
9. Ernst B. Haas, "Turbulent Fields and the Theory of Regional Integration," *International Organization,* Spring 1976, pp. 173–212.
10. See Marina v. N. Whitman, "Leadership Without Hegemony," *Foreign Policy,* no. 20, Fall 1975, pp. 138–164.
11. George Modelski, "Some Continuities in the Structure of World Politics," unpublished paper.
12. *Diplomacy in a Crowded World,* Atlantic-Little, Brown, Boston, 1976, chap. 8.
13. Joseph S. Nye, Jr., "Independence and Interdependence," *Foreign Policy,* no. 22, Spring 1976, p. 145.
14. See Robert Keohane and Joseph S. Nye, Jr., *Power and Independence,* Little, Brown, Boston, 1977, chap. 3.
15. Henry Kissinger, "The Law of the Sea: A Test of International Cooperation," *Department of State Bulletin,* vol. 74, no. 1922, Apr. 26, 1976, pp. 538–539.
16. Richard N. Cooper, "The Future of the Dollar," *Foreign Policy,* no. 11, Summer 1973.
17. "The United States possessed the overwhelming preponderance of capabilities and therefore could have constructed the system unilaterally. Yet the Europeans could have forgone using the system, leaving the United States in possession of a satellite communications system with few if any outlets abroad. The Europeans used this advantage to increase their control over Intelsat. . . . The United States had little choice but to

comply." John G. Ruggie, "International Responses to Technology," *International Organization,* Summer 1975, pp. 562–563.

18. This myth is propounded in Zbigniew Brzezinski, op. cit.

19. Norman Podhoretz, "Making the World Safe for Communism," *Commentary,* April 1976, p. 40.

20. See Richard A. Falk, "Beyond Internationalism," *Foreign Policy,* no. 24, Fall 1976, pp. 65–113.

21. Jimmy Carter's speeches at the Foreign Policy Association luncheon in New York, June 23, 1976, and at Notre Dame University, May 23, 1977.

22. Brzezinski, op. cit. As if West European or American masses in the nineteenth century had been "more inert"!

23. Henry Kissinger, "The Moral Foundations of Foreign Policy," *Department of State Bulletin,* vol. 73, no. 1884, Aug. 4, 1975, pp. 167–168.

24. See Richard H. Ullman, "The 'Foreign World' and Ourselves," *Foreign Policy,* no. 21, Winter 1975–76, p. 120.

25. See Joseph S. Nye, Jr., "Independence and Interdependence," op. cit., pp. 129–161; and Graham Allison and Peter Szanton, *Remaking Foreign Policy,* Basic Books, New York, 1976, chap. 5.

26. For a more elaborate argument in favor of this idea, and suggestions for its realization, see Bayless Manning, "The Congress, the Executive, and Intermestic Affairs: Three Proposals," *Foreign Affairs,* vol. 55, no. 2, January 1977.

27. See I. M. Destler, "National Security Advice to U.S. Presidents: Some Lessons from Thirty Years," *World Politics,* vol. 29, no. 2, January 1977, pp. 143–176. He refers in particular to the Ford-Kissinger request for military aid to Vietnam and Cambodia in January 1975 (p. 173).

28. See Seyom Brown and Larry L. Fabian, "Diplomats at Sea," *Foreign Affairs,* January 1974; and John Temple Swing, "Who Will Own the Oceans," *Foreign Affairs,* April 1976.

29. Andrew M. Scott, "The Global System and the Implications of Interactions," *International Interactions,* vol. 1, 1974, pp. 229–236.

30. George F. Kennan, "The United States and the Soviet Union," *Foreign Affairs,* July 1976.

31. See the report of the Murphy Commission (Commission on the Organization of the Government for the Conduct of Foreign Policy, June 1975) and the seven volumes of appendixes, especially vols. 1 and 2. The innumerable proposals contained therein are not always convincing, but the amount of information provided is considerable.

32. Cf. the study by Edward F. Graziano, in vol. 3 of the appendixes to the Murphy Commission report, p. 18ff.

33. *U.S. Foreign Policy for the 1970s,* vol. 4, 1973, p. 8.

34. "Organizing for Global Environmental and Resource Interdependence," Appendix B to the Murphy Commission report, vol. 1, p. 46ff. On planning, see also vol. 2, Appendix F, p. 209ff.

35. See I. M. Destler, *Presidents, Bureaucrats and Foreign Policy,* Princeton University Press, Princeton, N.J., 1974, especially chap. 9 and epilogue.

36. Report, p. 61, pp. 34ff.

37. The Murphy Commission report, chap. 5, and Bayless Manning, op. cit.

CHAPTER SIX

A Process
of World Order

I shall not try to answer here to my exclusive satisfaction (and even that is in doubt) all the problems that have been so sadistically described in the past five chapters. But I shall try to show broadly what is necessary and possible. I shall begin with some general guidelines and later attempt to apply these to specific problems. My purpose is to suggest a direction and a method.

I have, at the end of Chapter Four, indicated the imperatives of world order within the limits imposed by the conviction that there can be no sudden mutation of world politics, no leap from a world of states to a world government. I have also examined the limits which America's own nature and institutions set to its foreign policy. How can the United States heed those imperatives? What measures do they entail?

SECTION ONE: GUIDELINES

Some of the needed guidelines for U.S. foreign policy refer to America's strategic choices: what kind of an international system do we want to help establish? Some refer to our tactical choices; they concern the methods the U.S. ought to use and the role it ought to play.

241

STRATEGIC GUIDELINES: (1) BUILDING ON EXISTING ELEMENTS OF ORDER

A first strategic directive concerns the nature of the exercise itself: we must protect and strengthen the elements of order that exist already. Let us go back to our earlier comparison between the present world and domestic politics. As we have seen, all the conditions for chaos, all the elements for disaster are present in the international system. However, there are threads of order that can be woven into a common tapestry. First, there are the restraints of nuclear and economic interdependence analyzed in Chapter Three. Second, there are fragile, brittle, almost meaningless, yet not utterly negligible flickerings of "universal consciousness." They do not have the moral content that would allow one to call them *norms* in the sense of the political philosophers of "troubled peace"; and the one thing they share with such norms is the congenital weakness that comes from being left to the mercy of the actors' self-serving and wildly contradictory interpretations. Yet they exist and are the underpinnings of the restraints of interdependence. One is, quite simply, the desire to survive. Nothing new, except that for the first time it is directly connected to the performance of the international system, not merely in the matter of physical protection from violent annihilation, but also in that of starvation, pollution, and an end of vital resources. Another common imperative, only slightly less global, is that of development—the race to welfare, discussed above. Of course, neither this desire nor this race ensure an orderly world. (If it were so, this book and many others would not be necessary.) The will to survive has not abolished the determination to prevail, expand, or free oneself of the chains others have imposed. The desire for development may well, as Robert W. Tucker has reminded us, breed more conflict that consensus, given all the divergences on goals and methods, all the uncertainties about the limits of growth. But our problem is to try to prevent state interactions and interdependence from becoming malignant. The existence of collective forces capable of making such transactions benign allows one to work, and hope, for a solution.

The problem of a world order policy, thus, is double. On the one hand is the imperative against any regression: the restraints must be preserved, the two slim foundations of commonality must be sustained. On the other hand is the need to help the restraints win their race with conflicts, to strengthen these foundations. At present, the elements of moderation are partly mechanical, partly organic. Some result from the nuclear stalemate and the various balances of force, some spring from the nature of economic interdependence. But the latter, if pushed too far, or if it is too uneven in its operation, can easily lead to reactions against it, which could destroy these organic links. It has happened before. Today's restraints correspond to a recognition of common interests, or of necessity: fragile motives for conduct, because calculations of interest can change, and necessity is often resented.

Thus, progress toward world order requires the gradual emergence of a sense of obligation, which would give to agreements on rules of the games greater solidity than is provided by their present foundations, and which would further the creation of new rules and institutions. A sense of common duty often requires a common faith; there is little chance of one emerging out of the present cacophony. But such a sense can develop when the restraints and rules based on necessity and reciprocity have lasted sufficiently long, and when the leaders on whom they apply have established sufficient ties among themselves to be able to curb their respective dogmas and to resist the centrifugal pulls of domestic pressures. In other words, in the absence of a worldwide, single ideology, there is a need for some ideological erosion—not the mere stoppage of ideology by an external barrier, but the dampening of the ideology as a reaction to the effectiveness of that barrier.

And world order requires actual ties—a worldwide application of the "theory of the net" that had proved weak in the realm of U.S.-Soviet relations. The goal would be, not to reproduce the conditions of domestic integration at a higher level, but to translate these conditions: no central power, but effective international institutions; no social or political consensus on a broad range of values, but a dense web of ties signifying the prevalence of mixed interests over adversary relationships and a code of behavior corresponding to a minimum of common values. Because actors tend to behave outside according to their beliefs and in response to internal pushes and pulls, the emergence of such a code requires, not merely the ideological erosion already called for, but the observance of what might be termed minimum standards, or compatible norms, in domestic affairs. A tall order and obviously a goal with two peculiarities—it cannot be reached soon, or ever fully realized.

No Regression Three policy directives can be derived from this definition. The first one is a translation of the imperative of no regression. Top priority must be given to preventing any unraveling of the present incomplete tapestry. In the games of economic interdependence, this entails safeguarding the principles of GATT and the prevention of violent monetary fluctuations (i.e., managed floating) or of new crises with the oil-producing nations—in other words, a series of policies aimed at preventing the break-up of the world economy into separate blocs engaged in the varieties of economic warfare, for prosperity would decline and tensions would increase. It may be true that modern measures of economic warfare, by contrast with old mercantilist policies, often aim only at protecting a state from the effects of other actors' policies, or at safeguarding its internal autonomy, rather than at increasing its relative power at the expense of others. But even at best, as I have stated before, such measures risk boomeranging, or aggravating the plight of others. The importance of trade in the gross national product of states and the flows of money across borders are too high for artificial insulation to work except when it is carefully prepared and internationally coordinated. Moreover, the attempt risks degenerating into a cycle of mutual retaliation, and giving license to states genuinely determined to use their economic power aggressively.

In the strategic-diplomatic realm, protecting one present tapestry of world order means, on the one hand, preserving the central balance of deterrence and regional balances (especially in Europe), and on the other hand, no return to an unregulated strategic arms race between the superpowers, no conventional confrontation between them, and no proliferation of either nuclear or conventional weaponry at a rate, in time and quantity, that could create uncontrollable, large-scale violence. We shall later try to make these broad guidelines more precise; meanwhile, those who find them meaninglessly vague should note that they imply that a SALT agreement that is not perfect—complete, drastic, or symmetrical—is far better than none, and that in the realm of weaponry, the competitive aspects of world policy ought to be clearly subordinated to world order concerns. I am aware of two facts: this would constitute a revolution, and it is difficult to pull off. It means that an abstract consideration should prevail over the most concrete of all criteria: the distinction between friends and adversaries. It means that in the realm of conflict *par excellence* we must seek the cooperation of our rivals, and be ready to oppose our allies and clients when they insist on pursuing policies that run counter to the interests of world order. It could mean that they may, in such cases, turn to our foes and thus worsen our position in the contest, or that they may both feel and be abandoned to the tender mercy of a common enemy and decide to take their own measures against such a peril; these could increase insecurity all around.

The imperative of no regression, however, does not require self-destructive self-abnegation. All it requires is that the world order yardstick be applied first; that the yardstick of "are they for us, are they against us?" not be the decisive one; that the former not be a mere eventual dampener of the latter, but on the contrary that the latter be a (perfectly consistent) safeguard against an excessive, boomeranging enforcement of the former. World order concerns require that alliance relations not be claims for unconditional and total solidarity. But if world order considerations were applied by us as if the contest of the great powers, and the need for balances of force, did not exist, the consequences would be fatal both for world order—since moderation requires balances and restraints—and for domestic support. For the world order yardstick to get priority, does not mean that every request for arms should be ignored. It means that there shall be no automatically favorable response, whenever the claim is presented by a friend. We are only beginning to apply this criterion in the nuclear realm and, more timidly, to the transfer of conventional arms. Neither the goal I have described above, nor the imperative of no regression, mean that world politics will stop being a game of power, played by us with adversaries and often with clients whose overriding concern is the build-up and exploitation of their own power. It simply means that power, already affected by the transformations noted in Chapter Three, shall be used by us to preserve existing restraints from destruction and to place, so to speak, the race of states on safe rails.

Maximum Feasible Understanding   The second and third directives translate the imperative of progress—and are far less "angelic" and more controversial. If universal legitimacy is to be based, at first, on the consolidation and (in the psychological sense) internalization of minimal common needs—survival and development—then those formulating a world order policy must, at first, stress what is known to be, if not generally acceptable (very little is, at the outset), at least non- or minimally objectionable. This means that the cutting edge of one's own ideology, of one's own notion of the ideal social order, ought to be smoothed down. We ought to put forward, not the proposals that will certainly arouse the hostility of all those who do not share America's preference for liberal democratic regimes, or America's belief in the market system, or America's desire to keep the control of, or a veto power over, common institutions, but proposals that simply aim at strengthening the restraints of nuclear interconnection and economic interdependence—without, of course, giving up the possibility of influencing the content of the institutions or rules proposed, once agreement has been reached on the principles.

One will object that stressing the minimum means avoiding the hard and real issues of politics. In reality, it means separating two political processes: agreements on a framework, and arguments on dynamics, control, rewards. To begin with the former is no guarantee of final success, but if the framework is agreed upon, then—as the example of the EEC has shown—there is at least some pressure toward filling in that framework, lest the whole attempt roll backward. Clearly, this suggestion goes against the combative instincts of Americans in foreign policy and risks exposing U.S. diplomats to the wrath of those who want Washington to speak loudly and to reply in kind to the verbal aggressions and extreme demands of opponents. It also goes against an instinct that pervades the American foreign policy elite—the confusion between initiative or leadership and a solo performance. To lead need not mean laying down the law. It ought to mean rallying others to define it in common.

No Preferred Geometry   The third suggestion consists of stating that the choices in policy that were offered some years ago and that still creep into political rhetoric—the Washington-Moscow-Peking triangle versus trilateralism, i.e. the triangle of the non-Communist industrial nations (the United States, Western Europe, and Japan), North versus South—are not alternatives. Equal attention must be given to each of these configurations. Because of their intrinsic importance and interrelatedness, the neglect or demotion of any one of them is bound to have bad effects. We have, in analyzing Kissinger's foreign policy, seen the limits of the priority he had given to the first triangle. The effect of that triangle on other issues was exaggerated. In particular, it failed to cope with the global and regional management of force in a world of multiple arms races; and the application of balance of power methods to the monetary relations with America's allies, once these relations no longer seemed to have to be subordinated to cold war priorities, proved dangerous. However, the downgrading of détente, the new emphasis on the Alliances, either for security reasons, or because of the role of the industrial powers in the world economy, or because of (often exaggerated) common values, does not mean a victory for the trilateral concept. It has just as little to say about the management of force, and especially nuclear proliferation. It also contains an implicit assumption that the U.S.S.R. and China do not create major world order problems because they are absent from the modern arenas of world politics, or that they will change their behavior if confronted with a successful "trilateral" organization of the non-Communist world. This implies that, in the meantime, what happens in the traditional arena can somehow be kept separate: a shaky postulate, unless détente gives way, not to a more realistic attempt to seek agreements with the U.S.S.R. and China, but to frozen hostility, which would not strengthen world order.

In fact, the continuing importance of the strategic-diplomatic chessboard, the worldwide scope of the triangular contest, its implications for the spread of conventional arms or for the control of nuclear proliferation, and the problems which both the abundant resources and the economic deficiencies of Moscow and Peking create for the world economy argue against an excessive swing of the pendulum. Having overrated détente, let us not underrate it now. The triangle dear to Henry Kissinger does not determine the fate of world issues when the relations between its three points are good. But when they are as they were, say, in the 1950s, some of the restraints we need to strengthen are badly strained, and little time, energy, and money are left to cope with all the problems that are not directly related to this contest. A return to the cold war between us and the Soviets would not even have the dubious virtue of stopping the emancipation of states that used to be our clients or dependents. The process has gone too far. We would have both the headaches generated by it, and those created by the new cold war.

Originally, neither the strategic triangle nor the Trilateralists' had much to say about the South. Yesterday's official doctrine had assumed, it seems, that as the competition between the great powers abated, their interest in the Third World as a possible source of "marginal advantages" would diminish and that the capacity of the poorer nations to stir up troubles among the great powers by playing one off against the other would crumble. "Decoupling" between the great powers and the others was seen as a necessary part of the "stable structure." The advocates of a "community of advanced nations" were, at that time, full of pious statements about how "the problem of the less-developed nations is the moral problem of our time." But they made one wonder whether they did not subscribe to Acheson's nasty distinction between moral problems and real ones. For they clearly assumed that the solution of the Third World's problems depended on the advanced nations "generating a major response" in concert: should the rich succeed in defining a common plan, the poor would have to accept their leadership. It was sometimes hinted that such a joint effort would thwart attempts by less-developed nations to exploit their advantages through common fronts (for instance, in oil) and could extend to a joint policing of vital sea lanes. What the rich would offer the poor in exchange was far from clear: increased participation "by all of the advanced countries in institutions designed to improve the lot of the Third World"[1] was a bizarre bait to the less advanced, and arguments about their interest in unimpeded development of their resources by "cosmocorps" may well have appeared as somewhat less than disinterested to them. (Moreover, some of the advanced nations, namely, our allies, did see in our appeal for a common front a clever way for us to gain access to their *chasses gardées* and to cut in on their special deals.)

The need to avoid absurd military entanglements; the fear that bungled interventions in the muddy domestic affairs of Third World countries could all too easily strengthen isolationist drives at home; a hunch that internal turmoil may be better for Third World nations that the social status quo preferred by the West; disillusionment with the effects of foreign aid and the mechanistic theories of "nation-building"; the belief that the network of transnational private organizations was sufficiently strong and indeed (as in the case of oil) more apt to allow for the preservation of mutually beneficial links of capital and trade, even while interstate relations were being decoupled (both from the Third World and from private links): these were some of the causes of the new, temporary wisdom. But it was empirically and normatively unsound. Empirically, it did not take into sufficient account the difference between the strategic-diplomatic chessboard, where decoupling makes sense, and the other arenas. There, although some of the players are private enterprises, all are at least half politicized. The international economy is only partly "private." The companies of the rich deal with the states of the poor, and the former play too important a role in the economic strategies of their parent states, and have too many connections with the political systems of their parent countries, for any decoupling between them and their own governments to be carried very far. Moreover, in these games, power being spread both more widely than in the strategic one, and quite unevenly, some of the less-developed nations that enjoy a monopolistic or oligopolistic position over resources essential to the rich could oblige them to "recouple." This is exactly what they did after 1973.

At that moment, trilateralists as well as officials discovered North-South problems with a vengeance. Both groups improvised policies to cope with these issues—rather similar ones. But they have not gone far in substance or in their suggestions about the necessary institutions of the so-called new economic order. Even if in many respects a concern for efficiency suggests *initiatives* by the advanced nations, *solutions* will almost invariably require the full participation of the less advanced, if only because many of their problems—from population to genocide, from industrialization to pollution—cannot be decoupled from the world of the rich. Sometimes, the Trilateral Commission has suggested what could be called minimal solutions: recommendations that entailed few concessions to the demands of the developing countries and aimed more at "coopting" the more advanced or wealthy among these than at reaching broad agreements. Sometimes, the proposals did not go beyond generalities.

As Richard Ullman has seen,[2] an ambiguity lies in the concept of trilateralism. Is it a concert of non-Communist industrial powers? In this case, its ranks will grow in coming years with new members from outside the present "triangle"—and homogeneity will be lost. Is it a league of democracies? In this case, while it may be useful for consultations, one can hardly expect full policy convergence. Trilateralism is a process with two uses: "to prevent any one of the poles from doing mischief to either of the others" and to consult about problems (such as energy) on which "the trilateral countries share identifiable common interests."[3] But on almost each one of these problems, there are both divergences within the triangle, and some commonality of interest with outsiders. Basically, the concept remains an American device for ensuring smooth U.S. leadership of the industrial "triangle," which may explain why, after the oil crisis, the shaper of the other triangle, Kissinger, borrowed so heavily from what its creators had designed as a counter-Kissinger strategy.

Normatively, everyone recognizes that the goal for world order must be "creating a global community that is stable and progressive." But neither of the two triangles can really mobilize for world order purposes the reservoir of American idealism. It is not only a Machiavellian foreign policy that is "incapable of tapping the moral resources of the American people." A trilateral policy that would appeal only to the skills of the professionals in diplomacy, academia, business, and the media would deepen the gap that, in all the advanced countries, exists between an indifferent or indignant "next generation," and the interconnected managers of what Péguy once called the established disorder.

None of this suggests, of course, that one reject the two North-oriented policies only to follow a predominantly Southern strategy. Those who believe in giving priority, at least for the long run, to the concerns of the less-advanced nations, have often failed to deal seriously with the problems internal to the two Northern triangles, have minimized the huge differences among the less developed, or have tended to see in multilateral undertakings or international organizations a panacea, whereas they are all too often escapes, alibis, or simply forums in which familiar political contests continue. However, the kind of world we should want would do more than bring our adversaries out of their quarantines and allow the advanced nations to pursue harmoniously their restless business. It would also make room for the global planning only a handful of insufficiently political utopians or functionalists have advocated.

We need an integrated and coherent policy, for all three "worlds" constitute parts of the problem of world order. Moreover, none of the three is homogeneous; the Third World is undergoing rapid differentiation; and all the issues are interconnected. A new cold war, or an escalating and universally spread arms race, will leave no resources for North-South relations even if the North resumes its growth. A prolonged economic slump in the trilateral world would have disastrous consequences for the heavily indebted, oil-poor, developing countries. A failure in the Arab-Israeli process of negotiation could lead to a new oil price increase, which would severely tax the "recycling" facilities of the industrial world. And so on. The drama of world order lies in this interconnection, and in the absence of any simplifying formula, any grid, any lever whose manipulation would lift all the troubles. There are different, partial ways for coping with some of them: détente is one, trilateral consultations another, the North-South dialogue a third. But each one is incomplete and imperfect. And any policy that would give priority to one of these ways would soon find that the capacity for mischief of the neglected realms would spill into the other.

STRATEGIC GUIDELINES: (2) PLURALISM

A second strategic guideline can be defined in a single word: pluralism. The best chances for world order lie in the kind of pluralism that makes others share actively in the management, benefits, and burdens of international agreements or regimes and that allows us to accept their greater share precisely because they too will have a stake in preserving that order. Pluralism has three implications. The first is flexibility. In a world in flux, and a world economy whose movements remain hard to predict, one needs structures of order that will not be built in concrete: an international regime, such as that of Bretton Woods, that can be preserved only at costs that become as obnoxious to the chief reserve currency holder as to its creditors, is a bad precedent. One needs international agreements that will be open to revision. Their absence and their excessive rigidity invite unilateral coups to change the rules or to impose new ones. In contemporary international law, attempts at making universal conventions too tight or too precise only provoke epidemics of crippling reservations. Moreover, the more rigid a proposed convention, the more it will seem like a diktat imposed by a preponderant power or group of powers, like a straitjacket aimed at institutionalizing some explicit or implicit discrimination or inequality (a problem of considerable importance in matters of arms and nuclear proliferation). This would only fuel the determination of the second-class citizens to undermine the structure. We must remember that the function of the procedures is double: they should strengthen the restraints on the state system's capacity for violence and chaos, but they should also allow the actors to pursue, with some security, their internal goals and the external policies necessary to the achievement of these goals.

A second implication of pluralism might be called voluntarism. Not all nations are likely to cooperate, however conflictually, in the search for rules and regimes, even if efforts toward world order begin by stressing what is common to all or least objectionable to most. As long as we live in a fragmented milieu, Rousseau's logic of the stag hunt may prevail over that of world order: in an uneven contest for scarce material and psychological goods, each hunter may still be concerned only, or primordially, with having his separate interest prevail over that of his rivals. Sometimes, in the realm of weaponry, a refusal to cooperate may vitiate an effort to restrict races that makes sense only if all the potential suppliers take part; but not always. In the realms of economic interdependence, the absence of some potential actors (such as the U.S.S.R. and China) may persist, and others may be divided by divergences over models of development and different attitudes toward the world economy. Rather than letting discord prevent the establishment of any rules or regimes, one ought to be ready to deal with those who are willing, even if their *substantive* preferences are far from ours. To get the other actors closer to where we would like them to be, traditional diplomacy with its retinue of incentives and disincentives, will remain indispensable. Again, we may borrow from the EEC: it started among those who were willing to accept a certain process; later, attention shifted from the process to substance, and at present, the membership has increased, there is a wide circle of associates and candidates, and the process itself has been modified as a result. Just as Europe *à la carte* is a bit messy, world order *à la carte* may be untidy. But it is our best chance.

A third implication of pluralism is the need for a fallback position. A world order policy must build in the possibility of failure—a lesson from the plight of détente. There is a risk of no conciliation being reached between opposite interests and ideologies in a world without preestablished harmony or usable violence to forge it, or hegemonic opportunities for creating it. We shall need, on each issue, an alternative to success. It should be designed to safeguard U.S. interests, yet allow for ulterior progress, rather than succumbing to the deadly logic of perpetual competition. In other words, even the failure to arrive at explicit rules and formal regimes, as in the case of the oceans, or at arms limitation treaties, should not force one back to the logic of the "state of war." Room should be made for informal understandings or partial agreements that would, to take two examples, save the seabed from becoming a jungle for the technologically advanced, or keep the strategic arms race this side of unilateral or mutual first-strike situations. (For instance, a failure to agree on common limitations or reductions of strategic forces should not lead us to match the Soviets' throw-weight, but rather to reinforce the protection of our land-based missiles against a possible attack.)

A new administration often comes with a bag full of hopes about the breakthroughs its fresh approach will make possible, and when the suspicions, resistance, and intractable interests of other actors puncture the bag, we tend to blame them, rather than our excessive expectations, and to fall back into the traditional routine. This vicious circle must be broken; not by any shrinking of our goals, but by greater skepticism about easy achievements, a more long-range approach, and the preparation of a second-best positions.

STRATEGIC GUIDELINES: (3) NATIONAL SECURITY AS AN ASPECT OF WORLD ORDER

A third strategic imperative follows from the first two. It would be called: turning national security into an aspect of world order policy. More specifically, it deals with the conflict of two logics, that of enmity ("us versus them"), and that of relationships which are only partially adversary and allow for sufficient cooperation to make order possible. The pursuit of the latter logic is plagued by three problems. The first is the absence of any substantive consensus among the actors: in a world where many relations are patterned by the logic of hostility, our very efforts at promoting order are bound to be seen as self-interested by those who do not share our views. The next problem is the risk of turning into partly adversary relationships our ties with friends or clients whose search for conventional or nuclear weapons or whose violations of human rights we dislike, and the risk involved in making concessions to hostile powers (for instance in the Third World) in order to gain partial cooperation. Both risks entail a weakening of our own power position, which is questionable because of the third problem—our relation with the Soviet Union. Clearly, the Soviets, while concerned about the perils of confrontations with us, or about a possible world of many nuclear powers, are worried mainly because their survival, or influence, would be put in question thereby. Their policy may be one of muted hostility toward us—muted by the existence of these threats, by the need to keep watching China's behavior, by the burden of preserving the status quo in Eastern Europe, by the imperative of internal development—but it remains one in which world order is defined as the triumph both of their ideology and state. There is little contradiction between the logic of hostility and the logic of world order in their vision: order will exist when their system has prevailed over ours. There is a contradiction in our case because we aim (or ought to aim) at a lasting, not merely a transitory, coexistence of the two social systems, and at turning hostility into permanent cooperation. (We may, of course, hope that such collaboration would induce extensive change in their system, but this is not our aim, whereas theirs remains the exploitation of cooperative relationships to the advantage of their cause and country.)

How, then, can we overcome the conflict of the two logics? Are we not obliged, in order to survive, to give full priority to the logic of hostility? The answer is no, even if one professes agnosticism about Soviet intentions and looks only at Soviet acts and capabilities. Because our view of world order is different from theirs, our determination to preserve the central strategic balance and to avoid being pushed, in Western Europe, into the dilemma of accepting lightning defeat or else provoking a world holocaust, is precisely compatible with our concern for order—as long as we keep making unilateral and negotiated efforts at preventing a "mad momentum," and at reducing the levels of force. We have the means to thwart any Soviet attempt at strategic superiority, and to prevent the conventional imbalance in Europe from becoming militarily and politically disastrous.

The Soviet's very tendency to play military cards above all in the world game—because of their deficiency in other kinds of cards or reluctance to play them, and their abundance of might—makes it more difficult for them to give up any sizable amount of strength. Their remarkable paranoia about the outside world, fed by sixty years of insulation and the existence of formidable external foes, contributes to this unwillingness. It also explains their reluctance toward multilateral diplomacy, which both requires and promotes mixed relationships rather than "us-versus-them" confrontations (or "we-and-they" collusion). But they are undoubtedly bothered by the costs and the risks of further escalation, and aware of our technological advance. A lack of will on our side to preserve the balance would deprive them of any reason to strike deals. But if this will exists, so do the chances for agreements, if we know how to proceed skillfully.

As for the contest in other parts of the world, it is bound to persist. The Soviet Union cannot let China exploit whatever revolutionary potential exists, and cannot fail to exploit Western weaknesses, lest the West consolidate its power in the contest. But on the one hand the most appropriate way for us to respond is not exclusively or primarily by force, à la Vietnam (or as we tried in Angola). We cannot let our adversary select the battlefields, and we have other means to combat his influence (more on this later). On the other hand, even if our motives differ, our interests converge in a number of instances, such as proliferation and the law of the seas; in other cases, such as arms sales, a partial convergence may occur. Thus, world order considerations can be given their due. A danger for our position in the contest would still arise if their pursuit weakened our main alliances and estranged us from other powers in ways the Soviets could exploit. But most of the states whose policies would collide with ours because of our drive for world order are totally unwilling to be counted on the Soviet side; they are more likely to pursue a nationalist course, and denounce us for colluding with the Soviets. Only if we decide to pursue to the hilt the logic of hostility should we avoid any such risk of entanglement (with, say, Brazil or South Korea), but the costs of this logic would be unbearable, for us and for the world. Thus, we must keep seeking the cooperation of the chief rival, even if this does not put an end to rivalry or solve all problems, and even though we must, in accordance with the principle of voluntarism, proceed without him whenever he refuses. Only such a quest has a chance of affecting his behavior by fracturing his insulation.

An Operational Code: (1) Consistency

How do these general guidelines translate into suggestions for U.S. methods? We shall try to provide the elements of an operational code. A first commandment would be: be consistent. There are three familiar kinds of inconsistencies we should guard against. The first is the failure to think about the impact abroad of measures taken (or of the failure to take certain measures) for domestic reasons. One can think of President Truman's 1945 decision to extend U.S. jurisdiction over the resources of the continental shelf and to establish fishery conservation zones, because of the pressure of fishermen's and oilmen's lobbies. More recently, there was the signal contribution made by changes in U.S. food policy around 1972—the decision to go back to the market mechanism, to let prices fluctuate and food reserves and food aid drop, to use American fertilizers on newly released land to increase home production and exports—to the food crisis that followed. We had no adequate stocks, and fertilizers that could have produced more wealth abroad were not available for export. Of course, farm lobbies everywhere are more influential than Peace Corps volunteers.

But if priority is to be given to world order, not only must a coherent set of external priorities be defined, but the pressures and moods these priorities ignore, reject, or anger must be neutralized. These internal pushes and pulls risk becoming irresistible if they arise, for instance, out of the fear of foreign competition in automobiles, or shoes, or textiles, or television sets, at a time when the domestic market suffers from a recession. Indeed, the recent recession provides a prize example: the domestic measures that provoked it failed to take adequate account of their effects abroad, i.e., of the likely propagation of American economic ills, and therefore of the protectionist epidemic it risked inducing there and here. And these measures themselves were aimed at fighting an inflation that had also spread abroad and undermined the monetary system, because of Washington's failure to take domestic measures to reduce the balance of payments deficit.

What this suggests is that a world order policy must not only prevail, abroad, over the traditional policy of the stag hunt, but also, at home, over the tendency for domestic concerns to become decisive. The barrier between domestic and external affairs has fallen. Our internal energy policy, with its encouragement to the nuclear energy industry, has created powerful domestic obstacles to our foreign antiproliferation policy. Paradoxically, the "primacy of foreign policy," which was almost tautological when the barrier existed, becomes indispensable now that its disappearance creates a real contest between internal and external concerns, whose stake is the substance of foreign policy. But this primacy can be ensured only if we deal effectively with the effects at home of measures taken for foreign policy reasons.

Contradictions and Connections   A second kind of inconsistency consists in forgetting or ignoring both the interconnections and the contradictions between the various games. Any further escalation of the Soviet-American arms race would reduce the resources—material and psychological—available for the world order issues of economic interdependence (and encourage Third World nations to pay even more attention to armaments themselves). Making nuclear energy (or weapons) more easily available to foreign clients because it is profitable to sell enriched uranium and reactors or the most advanced fighter planes, may help one's balance of payments and give one a hope for political leverage; it also contributes to the danger of proliferation and war. To provide conventional arms to potential regional hegemonic powers may diminish their incentives to become nuclear states, but it also contributes to the danger of classical violence, and it may undermine both their economic development (the Prussian model—building a country around an army—is hardly convincing: we are not in the age of Frederick the Great, and can form no instant Prussians) and their internal political stability. To provide weapons (as we do in the Middle East) to all sides of existing or latent conflicts may help preserve a balance that will deter violence, but it could also fuel the flames.

Yet if there exists a contagion of "bad" politics, the contradictions between "good" ones are no less formidable. Each problem, as technocrats like to believe, may have its solution—but these solutions often turn out to be incompatible. A bigger flow of resources to the countries of the Third World may just feed their demand for advanced weapons, conventional or nuclear, and their ability to buy or build them. A stringent nonproliferation policy may make its victims, if they are Third World nations, thoroughly uncooperative on North-South issues, may make us want to avert their anger by deliveries of conventional weapons, or may well make the economic development of such nations more difficult by depriving them of the energy which more dangerous nuclear technologies could produce.

Thus we return to the need for long-range thinking and integration, not only of foreign policy, but of foreign policy with domestic policy. Without such integration, either "bad" policies will be pursued for short-term or narrow reasons, or else "good" ones will be initiated in such a way as to cancel each other out. Instead, an effort must be made to curb the possible evil effects of each, or else to remember that the best is often the enemy of the good, and therefore to establish a clear order of priorities.

Style and Substance   A third inconsistency concerns the style of American policy. In the recent past, as we have seen, it has often been inadequate to our avowed purpose. One does not, as a superpower, pursue "stable structures of peace" in a style that could be called neo-Gaullist or the aggressive defense of self-interest. To be sure, this tone exploited a domestic mood of hostility to outside entanglements. It helped Washington recover some liberty of maneuver—or resort to the same practices as everyone else, especially those who had used them to increase *their* margin of maneuver at Washington's expense. But such tactics, merely irritating when adopted by a lesser power whose capacity to disrupt world order is feeble, does not suit a great power. In the international jungle, the lion, not the rooster, is the pace setter. Others are at least as likely to copy his behavior as to cower when he roars. The adoption of a "world order style," however, is not without problems. At home, it is as risky to ignore the strain of xenophobia, which accounts for Mr. Connally's late appeal, as to let the pool of idealism evaporate. To try to outfox the champions of toughness by wrapping a world order policy in self-righteousness (a temptation that threatens our antiproliferation policy) could backfire abroad, where many remember that America's often hegemonic policies in the containment era had been sold in the loftier wrapping of global idealism.

Thus, a return to an idealistic tone, even on behalf of a true world order policy, could breed sour misunderstandings between our good conscience, and other nations' readiness to suspect in our stance either a clever disguise of crass interests or a way of freezing the distinction between developed countries (entitled to their sophisticated conventional and nuclear weapons) and the developing ones (summoned to restraint on behalf of world order). (The "Gaullist" style has at least the merit of its defects: brutality leaves no dark corners, no ambiguity about motives.) It could also encourage allies and dependents to exploit American meekness-for-world-order, either by playing the familiar blackmail of weakness so often performed in the past by Saigon (or Athens, or Lisbon), or to preserve their special advantages, such as the remnants of Japanese protectionism, or the complexities of EEC's Common Agricultural Policy. Concerns for world order must be spread wide, and even though the U.S. may play a special "shaping role," others may use Washington as a huge Procrustean bed. But, as in many other areas, the role of American leaders will be to explain at home why a world order policy, even if it does not entail the spreading of American features over the world, and even if it means concessions aimed at convincing others that we are not just protecting our power and status, is in America's interest. And it will be their duty, abroad, to convince others that they cannot simultaneously leave all the work to us and resent us for trying to do it. One more paradox emerges: the need to defend a policy of enlightened compromise in terms of (long-range) national advantage, to avoid both arrogance and sanctimoniousness.

AN OPERATIONAL CODE: (2) BARGAINING

A second commandment is: play the politics of bargaining. Here again are three implications.

Negotiation   The first is the need to engage other nations in negotiation, not in a war of principles or a shouting match of mutual recriminations. Much of what they want we dislike, either because it is an ideal we detest, or because it seems to us to be, quite simply, our wealth and power. But to reject their demands outright is the surest way to reinforce their ideological solidarity and to provide our chief rival with fine opportunities at our expense. A declared willingness to deal with our challengers on concrete issues would expose the profound conflicts of interests among them and allow us to exploit our greatest advantage: the need of other nations for America's technological know-how and resources. Even, as we shall see, in the traditional arena, more can be obtained by appropriate forms of bargaining than by mere threats and sanctions. Both in the case of the Conference on the Law of the Seas, and in that of our dealings with OPEC, we have learned that protracted bargaining—overt in one case, covert in the other—brings out the splits between coastal and landlocked states, or between states rich in reserves and poor in population and states poor in reserves and rich in people, or between ideological radicals and moderates. At the General Assembly session of the fall in 1975, Kissinger's multiple proposals on North-South issues produced a remarkably mellow mood and a moderate consensus. His delegation's greater reticence at the UNCTAD meeting in Nairobi in 1976 resulted in greater intransigence and difficulty at reaching a compromise. At the Conference on International Economic Cooperation in Paris, in June 1977, where the new American delegation was a bit more flexible, some agreements were reached.

To pursue such a course, the U.S. would not have to give up building its own coalitions—for instance, of industrial oil-importing nations—for bargaining purposes. And it would still, in each case, have the choice between trying to deal with an issue on its sole merits or within its own arena, and linking it to another set of issues or arenas. This is a bargaining tactic about which it would be foolish to generalize in a world that exhibits both functional fragmentation and countless possibilities of linkage (for example, the structure of military power is not irrelevant to the law of the oceans, even if naval superiority does not produce commensurate rewards; and economic incentives or disincentives are not irrelevant to nuclear proliferation). What the U.S. would have to give up is the high-powered tone and the hard-nosed act. The U.S. would have to learn to react, not as a corporate "free enterprise" society, but as a state skillfully maneuvering with other states; nor should it react as a state whose huge power allows it to crush or ignore others, but as a partner in collective bargaining who aims at entangling his opponents in agreements that it would not pay for them to break.

The Rule of Noncollision   To keep the balance of influence favorable to the U.S. at the end of the bargaining, we would have to learn not to interpret every sign of hostility abroad as an act of aggression, to which we react with sanctions, subversion, or sermons. But we should do better than that. A second implication could be called the rule of noncollision. One bargains *effectively* only with the authentic representatives of other states (or nonstate actors); and one has a chance of bargaining *successfully* only if one does not put oneself, at the outset, in a losing position. Thus, the rule takes two forms, and both go against much of past U.S. foreign policy. On the one hand, noncollision means refraining from interventions in the domestic affairs of others aimed at overthrowing their governments or at thwarting the free exercise of popular suffrage. I am leaving aside (see below) the problem of intervention on behalf of human rights; and I am not excluding the legitimacy of help given to a democratic government, or to a regime that has taken over after a long dictatorship, if it finds itself threatened by subversion.

But intervention aimed at "destabilizing" regimes or at fixing electoral outcomes ought to be avoided for a variety of reasons. Not only are they morally repugnant, but they are usually inadequate at ensuring control of events. One supports the idea of a generals' coup, and it is the colonels who take over, as in Greece in 1967. Or one "wants to give a chance to democratic opposition forces" in Allende's Chile, and one gets Pinochet. Moreover, one's puppets or protégés, once in power, often want to show that they are authentic nationalists. The Greek colonels objected to the U.S. resupply of Israel, in October 1973. The Shah of Iran, restored to power by the CIA in 1953, expressed his gratitude by leading OPEC's oil price increase twenty years later. Even when the client behaves nicely, the result of intervention is usually to make the U.S. the chief villain in the eyes of the domestic opposition and of many other nations—and thus to create opportunities for the U.S.S.R. or Cuba. Also, the necessary promotion of multiple management in international institutions and regimes will remain fragile as long as the voices that speak for the partners in conferences and agencies are not the true spokesmen of authentic national regimes.

In the Third World, no action taken by any such regime can be so seriously destructive of American interests as to justify U.S. interventions unless it deliberately opens up avenues of strategic and political control to our chief rival. Even this is most likely to result from a U.S. policy of support for weak, corrupt, or oppressive regimes. Some governments are more likely than others to provide a favorable milieu for U.S. public interests and private investments. But were this the criterion of U.S. policy, it would commit Washington to permanent entanglement in an unending quest for unachievable control. Moreover, multinationals that find themselves unwanted here or there can always move elsewhere—or home: both the U.S., in need of domestic investments, and host countries, often more likely to benefit from trade than from import substitution, might find some such "disinvestment" from the South advantageous. Here, some decoupling, some relaxation from extremes of interdependence, is necessary. In Western Europe or Japan, a hostile regime might produce disastrous results for the American power position in the East-West contest. (I shall return to this problem.) But even there, little can be said to support American manipulation. Where manipulation can be attempted, as in much of the Third World, the stakes are not vital enough. Where the stakes are higher, our reach is shorter: public directives backfire, covert shenanigans easily get uncovered.

A policy of world order need not have, or spread, illusions about the willingness of present states to reserve their beliefs for the home front and to behave on the world stage according to a different set of principles. They *will* try to act out their beliefs, as we do. As always in political affairs, moral considerations and practical considerations are inseparable. (I do not say, "ethics and expediency," because the decisive practical concerns are those of a long-range strategy of world order.) I have emphasized often enough the collapse of the distinction between domestic affairs and foreign policy. But the *target* of foreign policy, for world order's sake, should be the external behavior of governments. We can try to make it difficult for them to act out their principles, if their acts entail the forcible destruction of a vital military balance, or the unilateral repudiation of accepted rules of economic interdependence. If they act within the shrinking rights of sovereignty, we ought to respect them—for instance, if they ask for the renegotiation of our bases on their soil, or if they nationalize their resources or certain industries. "Friendly" regimes have done this, too. As I indicated above, eventual erosion of ideological hostility can only follow stoppage. Stoppage, not subversion ought to be the goal. For years, we have applied this criterion to our relations with Russia, China, and Cuba, precisely because *we* are stopped from going beyond. Where we have the means of doing so, we should not.

On the other hand, we should, more generally, avoid any direct collision between the U.S. and the rising nationalisms that provide the irresistible dynamics of world politics. Some of these nationalisms we dislike, because, here and there, they have been captured by, or have allied themselves with, communism. But when these are authentic nationalisms, as in Indochina, their coming to power, while no doubt bad for our influence, amounts to neither an extension of Soviet (or Chinese) power, nor to a drastic decline of ours. Should they become expansionist, then the world order criterion would allow, and indeed urge us, to apply the usual methods of deterrence or defense; but not before. Mostly, the nationalisms that are either in power, or struggling to come to power (like the blacks of Southern Africa) are not communist. They will, however, be anti-American if the power and policy of the U.S. stand in their way (as when we divide the governments of an area into moderates and radicals—an artificial and unstable division— and throw our support to the moderates, however flawed), or if the U.S. government chooses to identify the American national interest with private American interests that collide with local nationalisms. Even in an area where the U.S. has a recognized sphere of influence—Latin America—a confrontation between Washington and a Latin American nation—over the Panama Canal, for instance—while ending to our advantage, will produce ripples, such that the nationalist victim will become a model, for instance, in areas where our vulnerability is greater. Such confrontations open the way to Soviet (or Cuban) bridgeheads, as we have seen in Angola—a dangerous development, if one believes that world order requires some dissociation of regional balances from the tensions of the central and some moderating effects of the latter on the former.

Precisely because the Soviet-American contest is here to stay, any collision between Washington and a rising nationalism that gives a chance for Moscow to intervene, restricts thereby the scope for world order politics and the predominance of mixed interests over adversary relations. It is not only the Soviet Union that has to be contained, it is the irreducibly zero-sum game component of world politics. As we have seen before, the multiplicity of nations and their interests provides opportunities for global peace and possible protection from the spillover or escalation of regional violence. These chances must be preserved. Collisions would also disrupt the conditions of mutuality necessary in the arenas of economic interdependence. The unevenness of interdependence between the U.S. and most Third World nations makes these collisions possible. But interdependence exists, and a battle could lead to one of two results: the choice, by the nationalist nation, of a path of self-reliance or of complete nonreliance on the U.S.; or its choice of a policy of antagonistic coalition building aimed at the collective reduction of dependence. Neither would make world order, or bargaining for it, easier.

Groupings and Devolution A third implication of the politics of bargaining is the need to let others form their own coalitions. As we have just seen, our own behavior will determine in part whether these will be hostile or cooperative. Let us call this imperative the encouragement to grouping. Some years ago, I used the word "devolution," to refer to the need to create, enlarge the scope of, and reinforce the authority of international or regional agencies, and to the need for the middle powers to assume more responsibilities. I shall play down the word this time, for a variety of reasons, while repeating the idea.

Institution building is obviously a collective task: the U.S. cannot create them alone—in this realm, collective devolution is called for. Moreover, as we shall see, the establishment of world order, issue by issue, is so formidable an enterprise, that if Washington alone tried to shoulder all the burdens, it would breed not only irresponsibility and resentment abroad, but a violent desire for disengagement—heightened by the continuing belief in America's comparatively greater ability to play solitaire—at home. In many parts of the world, states or groups of states have quite simply acted to increase their power and influence—often, as in the case of India, or OPEC, by means that we disapprove of yet resemble those we have used; sometimes, as in the case of Iran or Brazil, with our help. We have not really "devolved"; they have taken, with our blessing or our mutterings.

In one part of the world, devolution turned out to be meaningless. In a sense, opening American markets to Japanese products, and seeing to it that other countries let Japanese goods and capital in, was a devolution, because it allowed Japan to become a major industrial power. But we have nothing to gain by encouraging Japan to become a major military power. It would upset the international consensus (or balance) in Japan and revive fears of Japanese domination in Asia. South Korea, the Philippines, Taiwan, and Indonesia clearly prefer our presence to Japan's exclusive one. The best way of preventing Japan from seeking to translate economic power into military might, is to organize the world economy so that Japan will have greater economic security: access to the energy and raw materials it needs, outlets for its goods and capital. Nor does it make sense to bolster China's power by providing Peking with weapons it could use in a war against the Soviet Union: the costs, for our relations with Moscow, Tokyo, and New Delhi, as well as the risks of seeing these arms used against Taiwan, far exceed the possible advantages for Chinese-American relations.[4]

Devolution continues to make sense in Western Europe, which we have not encouraged to organize its own system of conventional defense, and which recent American policies have boxed in. We have done so economically, through the creation of agencies such as the IEA, militarily, by equipping NATO with American weapons whenever we could, and politically, by discouraging its diplomatic initiatives, so that the EEC, already troubled by internal discrepancies and by a lack of common will that thirty years of dependence on us have bred, is squeezed between larger bodies in which its identity fades and the temptations of the American-German preferential relationship. (One must note that the trilateral formula also puts the formation of a broader coalition, the trilateral one, ahead of any strengthening of the EEC's limp identity.)[5] By the spring of 1977, the members of the EEC were looking to Washington for initiatives on all their problems—economic recovery, steadier North-South relations, energy and monetary policies, the fate of European armament industries—a sad reflection on the merging of European issues into global ones and the lack of European autonomy (because of insufficient cohesiveness) in facing these. Here, the failure of devolution has been doubly detrimental to world order: politically centrifugal forces are growing stronger, unconstrained by any distinctively European defense system, and the EEC's lack of coherence and substance has prevented it from picking up monetary leadership once America's started slipping—despite the EEC's importance in world trade—or sharing it with the U.S.

Our indifference to devolution, and to the process by which middle powers or key coalitions have emerged, is due to our hold on the dream of primacy. Kissinger's design emphasized the traditional chessboard, on which bipolarity persisted, and tried to exploit America's provision of the "public good" of security to its allies, to regain lost ground in the economic arenas. The trilateral sketch for "common policy planning" greatly favored the one power that has, for thirty years, developed the practices, tools, positions, and lingo of globalism. We have seen what happened to the design. The alternative I suggest is based on the conception of a world of many coalitions with a stable central military balance. It is gloomier about American skills and the enthusiasm of others for playing our game, yet more optimisitc about pluralism and the convergence of essential interests, even (perhaps especially) without American attempts to pull all the strings. The advantages, of course, are exactly the reverse of the flaws of primacy. We would be relieved from playing Atlas, and others would be rescued from the frustrations, humiliations, narrowing of vision, self-doubts, or petulance that dependence breeds. We would become, in effect, a more responsible player by being less intoxicated by world responsibility, and others would become more responsible by having to deal with world (and not just parochial) issues. Above all, the perils of a centralized system in which every local crisis involves the great powers and feeds their contest would be reduced.

The disadvantages have until now, and not surprisingly, appeared to the policy makers far to outweigh the advantages. Dependence is self-fulfilling and self-perpetuating; to let go might create vacuums that rivals would fill, or heady displays of immature independence that could lead to nuclear proliferation or upset the networks of fragile relationships woven over the past twenty-five years. For devolution to be smooth, rather than destabilizing, one may need extraordinary psychological skills and diplomatic subtlety. Moreover, all bureaucracies are better at incremental tinkering with instrumentalities, such as alliances, whose worth has been sanctified by time, than at the kinds of mutation that a world of coalitions and middle powers imply. Some of these would entail material costs as well: a West European military entity would want to buy less of its weaponry in the U.S. Yet, whatever the risks and losses, we cannot stop the process of devolution. It is going on wherever we have had no control. And where we have control, as in Western Europe, our reluctance to encourage a new entity has not prevented its members from competing with us in selling arms abroad or from selling their nuclear technology to third parties, after having received most of their nuclear fuel from us.

The task of tightening the nets and strengthening the restraints of world order requires that the extreme discrepancies of power between actors be reduced. As one wise commentator has put it,[6] there are two difficulties: small countries all too easily become "free riders" who benefit from common rules without contributing to their establishment or to the costs of their maintenance; and excessively mighty and psychologically overburdened big powers wish to remain the "heavy riders" (or raiders). The formation of bargaining coalitions and the rise of middle powers or entities helps restoring some balance, and ought to be encouraged by us—as long as it helps consolidate what I have called "moderation plus"—which means that these powers and entities must be carefully placed, with their cooperation, within the constraints of economic interdependence and the imperatives of limiting violence. In turn, they shall accept such restraints only if we behave in the same way.

Our national style and international experience have not prepared us for a world in which our interest lies in disconnecting dominoes, discriminating among challenges, and allying ourselves with, rather than opposing, defusing rather than defying, foreign nationalisms. Yet we must learn to do so.

An Operational Code: (3) The Art of Politics

This suggests a last tactical guideline: let our policy for world order be political. Let us recognize that we are dealing with a world of states, i.e., interests and dogmas, ambitions and fears made effective and sometimes lethal by state power (however leaky), and legitimacy conferred on states by sovereignty (however fragile). It is, as I have pointed out, at the level of the state that policy is integrated, linkages and trade-offs made permanent. It is the existence of states, the fact that the rights and duties of the individual are controlled by them, that the common good of mankind is defined by them, and that they have at their disposal, however unevenly distributed, formidable weapons of destruction and chaos which makes "moderation plus" both necessary and difficult. What we need to bring about an order that requires their full participation is an awareness of their perspectives, an understanding of their interests, a concern for their future course.

All too often, our approach has been grandly unpolitical. Sometimes, we have looked at their interests only from the viewpoint of our contest with communism or our quest for stability. Now, we seem to be treating the world as a sum of discrete problems, and we seek functional solutions for each of them on its merits, apart from its significance for each state. In both cases, this amounts to our substituting our wisdom for theirs, to our telling them that our higher concern—for the safety of the "free world," for stable structures, or for a better world—gives us a more accurate and sensible view of their true interest than they are able to have. We "know," for instance, that developing countries do not possess the capital skills, resources, and need for nuclear power.[7] We "know" that the satisfaction of many of the Third World countries' economic demands would not improve their condition. We may, of course, be right. But in politics it is consequences that matter. We have to convince them by providing carefully selected incentives and disincentives. A combination of lecturing and strong-arm tactics is likely to lead to conflict, feed local nationalism and self-righteousness, and increase resistances to our "solutions." We have experienced this in our conflict with France under de Gaulle. We may, of course, have to put pressure on countries whose behavior we deem dangerous. But just as we have learned to avoid humiliating foes, we must learn not to antagonize countries whose cooperation we still need on a variety of issues. If we ask them to give up some course of action, we must either reward them in a way that serves their interests or provide them with a substitute compatible with theirs. In no realm is this more important than in that of weapons proliferation, nuclear or conventional. To brandish sermons and threats first, incentives and alternatives later, is a model for serious trouble.

A quest for world order inevitably leads to a preoccupation with the diverse issues which crowd the agendas of states and international agencies, and with multilateral rather than bilateral diplomacy. Yet it also feeds the grand American faith in technical solutions—solutions that result from the mere application of reason and expertise and avoid the passions and prejudices of politics. But reason and expertise prevail only if there is a consensus on the nature of the problem, a deliberate decision (which is political) to treat it as technical, and a possibility of purely technical solutions. This is not what we find in most of the cases we shall have to deal with. It is hard for people used to an engineering approach, and eager for harmony, to accept this fact, and especially to acknowledge that what we deem instrumentally best may be judged politically unacceptable elsewhere. But we will have to, and therefore, while dealing with each problem on its merits, we must also ask what the effect of each proposed solution would be on military, economic, and political relations in each part of the world and on the fortunes of each country.

The strategic and tactical suggestions listed here aim at making possible the understandings, agreements, and regimes that will be proposed below. But above all, their purpose is to contribute to a change of what might be called the mores of the international milieu. In every society, the effectiveness of the laws, indeed their substance, depends on the customs, the internalized rules of behavior of the members. It is a truth that inspired political thinkers from Montesquieu to Rousseau and Tocqueville. It applies to the international society as well. We cannot, by ourselves, shape its mores, even if in our moments of greatest arrogance we see ourselves as the teachers of manners and methods. But we can, by our own behavior, profoundly affect that of others. We look at ourselves as benevolent. Others, even when they seek us out, often fear us as a threat, both because of our dynamism, our impact on their societies, and because of our policies. The guidelines recommended here will not curb the devastating effects which modernization, especially in American garb, can have on a traditional society, but they may make us reconsider policies that contribute to turning a heterogeneous world into a very dangerous place. That countless other actors contribute to it also, nobody denies. But the ability of the main players to influence the tone and quality of the international debate remains considerable.

SECTION TWO: ISSUES

It would take volumes to describe adequately the alternative forms of order conceivable for every issue (many such studies exist or are in progress), and it would exceed by far the author's competence. Moreover, only policy makers are in a position to set a course in specific terms. My objective is to provide general suggestions and criteria with which to judge detailed ones. It is not to propose tactics. Issues, while interconnected, cannot all be pursued at once with comparable vigor, competing initiatives, and equal priority. But pacing and tactical judgment are the statesmen's, not the outsiders', domain. Wise tactics concentrate on issues of greatest long-range importance for world order, that distinguish between cases in which Washington can move alone and cases which first require the cooperation of others, that discern and favor those areas where the chances of early success are highest.

The world into which we are moving presents not only the contradictions and races described abstractly in Chapter Three, but at least three more concrete tensions. One, the rivalry between the two superpowers is likely to persist, and both of them have the means to project it across the globe. While America's economic resources to do so are far greater, the Soviets have the capacity to aid selectively those whom they want to influence. It is unlikely that the rivals will decouple (in recent years Africa has become a new field for their contest), or that China will soon be able and willing to emulate them on a large scale. But at the same time, a multiplicity of "subsystems" will continue, some properly cooperative, such as the EEC; some riddled by conflicts, as in the Middle East; some dominated by one great power, such as the American hemisphere or Eastern Europe; and some influenced by both superpowers. Each of these systems will have its own dynamics, depending on its structure (are its members comparable in power, or highly uneven?), the nature of the regimes, the existence of a major tension in the region, and the relation of the subsystem to the great powers' contest. Thus, changes in that contest cannot, by themselves, move the subsystems in the same direction; but changes in the latter can affect the contest, and the contest is one of the factors that influence the subsystems. None is entirely autonomous, but each one is partially so.

Two, we are witnessing the emergence of a new set of states that are not yet "advanced" but industrializing rapidly: states such as India, Brazil, Mexico, Iran. They contribute to the diversification of the international hierarchy, discussed before. But they are, in two respects, a factor of potential trouble. In one respect, they differ from earlier rising powers (or from the rising middle classes in domestic societies). They are heavily in debt, and they constitute both a strain on the world's monetary institutions and a threat for the advanced nations. If the new "powers" cannot export enough, they risk defaulting, but in order to export, they have to gain access to the markets of the industrial nations and cause dislocations in the latter's production systems. In the second respect, they behave as previous rising states have done: they are eager for military power, often, it seems, at almost any cost. There has been some talk of "co-opting" such states into the triangle of the noncommunist industrial nations through various measures of economic and military accommodation. But this makes little sense. Some do not want to be coopted: they want the rules of the games changed, and therefore have no desire or need to break their alliance with the world's Fourth Estate. Moreover, the latter is not an undifferentiated mass. New middle powers are likely to arise and would have to be "co-opted" in turn. And those who are left behind, whatever their lack of resources, dispose of means of obstruction in many agencies, of disruption in many areas.

Three, every one of the actors of world politics (leaving aside purely "spiritual" actors) participates in the world economy, even if there are considerable differences in degrees of participation. But it is, as we know, a politicized economy. This means, not only that there is a heterogeneity that corresponds, roughly, to the difference between those planned economies that try to limit their dependence on the world market, and those economies that are immersed in it, but also that the key actor on the world market is the state. It is the state that has to mediate between the pressures of the world economy, and the needs of domestic policy; and it is the state that negotiates accommodation with other actors in the world market, be they states, corporations, banks, or international agencies. Hence the original pattern of a world economy that is neither liberal, nor mercantilist, but permanently threatened by the interplay of forces for which borders are no barriers (whether in the form of multinational enterprises, capital movements, or business cycles), with states eager to assert themselves.

THE GAMES OF ECONOMIC INTERDEPENDENCE

This is the field in which the various games of world politics are being played and the tasks of world order must be performed. Let us begin with the games of economic interdependence. There are three main problems here if we decide to take, not a functional look, issue by issue—as does, for instance, the Council on Foreign Relations 1980s Project—but a more political one (world politics being the outcome of actors' policies at least as much as the process by which specific issues are resolved).

East versus West	A first problem concerns East-West relations in these arenas. As we know, neither the U.S.S.R. nor China practices autarky, while trying hard to escape the constraints of interdependence with the capitalist economies. The wealth of both countries in raw materials and sources of energy gives them possibilities of affecting the world economy, and perhaps even disrupting it. Russia and its East European allies have accumulated vast debts and deficits in their trade with the West and have suffered from the effects of Western inflation. The U.S. faces two different questions. One concerns East-West trade. On the one hand, we must give up the dream of inducing fundamental changes in Russia's economic system or foreign policy through trade and technology. On the other hand, some coordination is necessary to avoid the paradox of a growing imbalance in our favor entangling us more than them in a net of soft loans, and the danger that private and state competition among countries of the First World for the Soviet market might actually lead to their being strengthened. Yet trade itself has two advantages over transfers of advanced technology (hardware and personnel). It brings much needed fresh air to the non-Soviet members of the Council for Mutual Economic Assistance (Comecon) and rescues them from total dependence on the priorities of the Soviet economy, although the size of their debts may oblige them to reduce their imports from the West and thus to strengthen their ties with Moscow.[8] Also, as the 1975 grain deal with the U.S. has shown, trade can result in some regulation aimed at reducing fluctuations. This helps introduce a modicum of predictability, in exchange for our providing them with what they need, because their need for such trade is bigger than ours. Similar advantages can be derived from the industrial cooperation that allows outsiders to own, partly at least, the enterprises they have helped establish in the countries of the Soviet sphere. Thus, it is in our interest, in the long run, to expand our imports of manufactured goods and raw materials from Eastern Europe and the U.S.S.R. and to try to reach an agreement with these countries on rules of trade between the market and the planned economies, which would be applied in all the bilateral deals to come.[9]

Beyond East-West relations, would world order be strengthened if the U.S.S.R. and China were entangled in the web of interdependence globally—if they became members of those agencies they have stayed away from, such as the IMF, the World Bank and GATT, and played a more active role in North-South discussions? At this point, they have little to contribute. GATT would have to be drastically rewritten to accommodate the two chief Communist powers. Its experience with those East European countries that have joined it has not been too happy. As for North-South relations, what the South needs to import is not, on the whole, what the U.S.S.R. provides, and neither communist country is likely to open its markets to the products of the South. Soviet contributions in terms of financial aid for development are also limited; their terms are stiff and they often amount to barter deals. If anything, the intensity of the North-South dialogue has been a source of embarrassment for both powers. China, as an anti-imperialist leader, seeks identification with the South, but it also seeks protection from the West and equality with the Soviet part of the East. Russia is eager to exploit Third World resentment of Western capitalism, but as a major industrial power it falls under their accusations, too. Moreover, most of its East European allies, for obvious reasons of deconfinement, are eager to take a more active part in the dialogue.

I have little doubt that in the long run such greater participation is in the interest of world order. Russia's role as a producer and consumer of food, as a producer of oil, natural gas, and raw materials, and as an importer of technology, is considerable. The discrepancy between the constraints that weigh on the U.S.S.R. and that the U.S., due to the difference in the number and types of games they play, hampers the U.S.—which (by contrast with nineteenth century Britain) has been not only the hegemonic economic power but also the main holder of the balance of military power and influence.[10] It also contributes to the heterogeneity of the international system and sharply limits the scope of whatever common rules are adopted.

There is much to be said, however, for trying to bring in the Eastern countries only after a solid network of rules and institutions is established through North-South agreements. Not only is that game already complicated enough, but also more intense East-West interdependence might detract from West-South interdependence. The South and the East are in competition for Western capital and technology, and for Western markets for their labor-intensive industrial products and raw materials. On the other hand, to postpone resolving this competition only strengthens the Soviet grip on Eastern Europe, and there is just as must to be said for trying to get Moscow to participate in a worldwide system of food stockpiles or in a global regulation of trade practices. On balance the long-run advantages of participation exceed the dangers. However, the amount of influence the U.S. could gain if it decided to make Eastern involvement an important objective is limited. (We must recognize that despite the fine speeches about the famout net, we, too, have been highly ambivalent in this respect, and we have no reason to risk disrupting such agencies as the IMF or the World Bank.) Basically, it remains *their* decision, and it will be made largely in their terms, i.e., on an analysis of advantages and disadvantages that remains couched in the classical language of interaction and the logic of separateness.

West versus South   The second problem has almost monopolized attention in the past three years; it is that of Northern—or rather Western—relations with the South. It fragments into many separate issues. But a few general remarks are worth making to apply the earlier guidelines. First, insofar as the imperative of no regression is concerned, one should not interpret any form of national protection as destructive of interdependence.[11] We have indeed, in recent years, witnessed greater controls on capital movements, wider national regulation of the activities of multinationals, restrictions on the admission of foreign workers, and temporary limitations of imports; there is thus some justification for crying wolf (its name in these games being mercantilism). However, we must not confuse these measures with a retreat from the world economy altogether. They do not yet amount to a return to the mercantilist priority of purely national objectives (full employment, encouragement to advanced industries, balance of payments surpluses, etc.) over the objective of global efficiency, nor do they represent the advent of a modern form of mercantilism: a fragmentation of the world economy into separate blocs.[12] These measures often fall instead into one of two categories: Some are temporary reactions to the recent recession or to a specific national economic crisis (such as in Italy or England); others are aimed at decreasing one's vulnerabilities, i.e., at making interdependence less costly to one's economy, yet not aimed at climbing out of interdependence or shifting the costs to others.

Actually, national objectives, whether social and economic, or political (such as increased power), always and everywhere compete with, distort, and compromise global efficiency, because the liberal model has always been a mere ideal. Also, inevitably, the decline in the relative size of the American economy, the loosening produced by the shift from fixed rates to floating ones, which gives nations greater freedom in domestic policy, and the rise of such international cartels as OPEC could not fail to give the appearance of regression. But we must, again, avoid a confusion between the end of the unipolar era of the postwar world economy, between its difficult evolution toward a new, more decentralized order, and an actual lapse into fragmentation, which would breed chaos as surely as, in the strategic-diplomatic realm, it is capable (under certain circumstances) of leading to moderation.

In order to avoid fragmentation, we must aim for cooperative formulas of mutual damage limitation—agreements, not on permanent restraints on competition, but on a spacing of it in time and place (so as to avoid, for instance, that in a given country a number of industries employing many workers find themselves threatened simultaneously). We must also avoid trying to solve the problems of the developing countries' debt through deflationary policies often favored by banks and the IMF. These policies would lead to import restrictions, a reoccurrence of protectionism, a new recession, and serious domestic turbulence.[13]

Next, whatever new order emerges from the multiple negotiations that will take place or are in process (vis-à-vis the oceans, commodities, energy, technology transfers, the code of conduct for multinationals, etc.) will be a precarious compromise between national priorities and the goal of global efficiency. The reason the latter cannot be the sole criterion of conduct has been indicated before: in reality, that abstract ideal takes the concrete form of one power's preponderance and of such instruments as the multinationals, which, however cosmopolitan their operations, however denationalized their criteria for investment, nevertheless have home countries, where decisions are made and to which profits return. Thus, those governments that have sufficient national autonomy and solidity to dare, will increasingly attempt to harness multinationals to their own national objectives in a variety of ways (regulation of their activities, participations, minimum export quotas, tax policies, and the like). With increased power over their national resources and over vast chunks of the neighboring seas, more actors will have to be taken seriously and become involved in the quest for international rules and regimes.

   This does not mean that the politicization of the world economy is necessarily a disaster for efficiency. It has been politicized for a long time, and present international arrangements, especially for commodity trade, are often neither efficient nor equitable. (Before OPEC, so to speak, took over, the multinationals' oligopoly in the realm of oil was somewhat removed from the free market model). As Tom J. Farer has written, "ironically, preservation of the principled foundations of the existing international capitalist system . . . actually requires some practical concessions from the North rather than the South . . . all the South must yield is its rhetoric. . . . It is we who must yield the tangibles,"[14] such as high tariffs and nontariff barriers on imports from the South. One finds in the world economy what one knows from domestic affairs: past a certain degree, inequality hampers efficiency. Efficiency will be preserved only if the world market survives. A sudden lifting of all national controls could easily lead to such extensive dislocations that the market would break up into national or bloc components. A flooding of Europe by Japanese goods or a deluge of manufactured products from the developing nations competing with those of the advanced ones on the territories of the latter and in the Third World, could backfire. Taking into account conflicting national goals is the only way of ensuring, not optimal efficiency, but the greatest amount of practically achievable efficiency.

   Third, a system that will be both more equitable and orderly must follow the imperative of pluralism, in two respects. One is in a multiplicity of negotiations. Obviously, a single, elephantine negotiation covering, say, all commodities or all other aspects of North-South relations would be unmanageable. The experience of the Paris Conference on International Economic Cooperation is conclusive. But there are actual links between the issues; the best way of assuring that each one will be considered on its merits certainly does not consist in resisting the very notion of linkages, which the U.S. itself, in its relations with Western Europe and Japan, had tried so hard to impose. The tactic of resisting an integrated fund for the stabilization of commodity markets, at Nairobi, was the wrong tactic, even if the notion of such a fund is debatable.

Pluralism also means networks of rules, and regimes, that provide states with a choice among strategies. Some may choose voluntary "delinking," i.e., a strategy of individual or regional self-reliance, with priority given to domestic planning and redistribution and attempts at limiting imports. (Few countries meet the conditions that would make such a choice compatible with rapid growth; import substitution strategies and redistribution schemes have rarely succeeded in curbing the growth of imports.) Other countries, interested both in growth and in avoiding dependence on one or a handful of industrial powers, might want to practice what Diaz-Alejandro calls "the politics of selectivity" and to conclude "international arms length transactions." That is, they should be able to establish bonds of trade and financial links that will serve their development; while gaining from trade and from international financial markets advantages in efficiency that import-substitution policies have often sacrificed, they would, through coalitions, be able to fulfill their essential needs without putting themselves at the mercy of an external market or cartel. Many of the developing nations will probably want the common rules to allow for a shift in strategy from the priority of industrialization (often resulting in growth limited to an enclave, with little effect on employment and on poverty, yet much disruption of traditional society) to a "basic needs" strategy, a shift toward self-sufficiency in food, i.e., agriculture, which could better soak up surplus labor. But this shift will appear as an intrusion against the elites and the industrialization of these countries unless they win some of their demands for a new interstate order.

It is therefore in everybody's interest to arrive at a network of global rules—and deep disagreements on the rules do not prevent a very wide recognition of this interest. Both the underdeveloped countries and the advanced ones produce raw materials; both groups have a vital need to have access to these made more secure. Both camps have an interest in preventing wild price fluctuations. Certainly most of the rich and poor nations have no interest in letting middle powers eager for influence or hegemony surround themselves with national or regional barriers. Multinationals, the natural enemies of any regulation of international markets, may end up finding in common rules guaranteeing access to raw materials or setting up ways of resolving conflicts of jurisdiction,[15] safeguards against the rising tide of national controls. But to help reach such agreements and establish genuine international regimes—i.e., rules backed either by institutions or by provisions for the settlement of disputes—the United States will have to effect a triple change of outlook.

The most general is dropping the supercilious paternalism that looks at most of the less-developed countries as irresponsible tribes moved by irrational concerns and led by mischievous elites ready to sacrifice economic benefits to the quest for "status" or prestige. Even if this were true, they would merely be imitating the examples given by Northern elites. When it comes to denouncing the manipulation of economics for political purposes, the U.S. is on shaky grounds. Next, the U.S. must acknowledge both the inevitability and the legitimacy of the demand of underdeveloped countries to reduce their economic dependence and to increase their capacity of autonomous action. We have taken a few steps in this direction: Kissinger's endorsement, at the 1975 General Assembly, of generalized preferences (which will have, domestically, to be accompanied by help to industries that will be hurt by the competition from manufactured products made in the less-advanced countries), his plea for food reserves, and his acceptance of case-by-case negotiations on commodities. The Carter administration has moved farther and accepted the principle of a common fund to back up commodity agreements. But these are timid steps. We have been vague about the stabilization of export earnings and have not gone as far as the EEC in its Lomé agreement with more than forty African, Caribbean, and Pacific states.[16] We reacted at first to the notion of commodity agreements as if these (like the regulation of foreign investment) had not been already envisaged by the postwar International Trade Organization (ITO), and as if they could not strengthen markets by increasing trust and information among buyers and sellers. We have been so outraged by OPEC's methods that we have often failed to see the plight of many non-OPEC developing countries, afflicted by large trade and payments deficits and falling prices for their raw material exports. To them, higher earnings, larger export markets for manufactured products, a higher growth rate requiring foreign capital but not foreign control, and adequate means to feed a rising population are essential—i.e., a better distribution of the benefits from the world economy.

It is in our interest to accept such changes. The poor countries' deficits could have a serious effect on the financial institutions of the advanced nations and on the framework of world trade, and our intransigence would provide many opportunities to hostile states to frustrate our interests or policies—even if a cartel of producers such as OPEC is hard to duplicate for other commodities. To be sure, we are under no obligation to give in to demands that would primarily benefit developed countries (as an increase in some commodity prices would do), or benefit nobody because of inflation (as indexation or commodity agreements sharply raising prices might do) or because they would endanger the developing countries' capacity to obtain more credit (as a general moratorium on their debts might do). But a series of measures—on trade, aid, debts, technology transfers—is needed to promote sustained growth and to accelerate development in the poorer countries. This will require both a continuing flow of investments from the advanced to the developing countries and the possibility for these to draw their own development plans; both a program to steady the income they earn on the world markets, and a considerable strengthening of the World Bank's and the IMF's resources.[17] There is a range of measures that would allow joint gains. The reduction of commodity price fluctuations would protect the world against a factor of recession or inflation. The reduction of obstacles to the import by the advanced countries of competitive manufactured goods from the developing states (along with internal measures of adjustment) or the lifting of obstacles to the processing of raw materials in the country of origin would allow for an expansion of Western exports to these countries now provided with means to buy more goods and services. International antitrust measures, a joint management of the global "commons,"[18] even commodity agreements ensuring a higher income for developing countries in exchange for guarantees of access to supply are realms of mutual benefit.

A change of outlook is needed not only in reply to the question, "who benefits?" but also in reply to the other question of politics, "who commands?" Most American proposals fit the world economy into a structure controlled by the industrial nations: the World Bank and the IMF. The key problem of Third World participation is left hanging. A similar battle, over the powers and composition of the proposed International Authority for the Seabed, has held up agreement on the law of the seas. While it makes little sense to accept formulas of control that would put all power in the hands of those who do not have the financial and technological means to solve even their own problems, it is vain to hope that such formulas will leave control to the advanced countries. We have neither the possibility of, nor an interest in, refusing to share this control. While the Third World needs resources from us, we need theirs, and above all we need regularity and rules. To resist demands for an international regulation of multinationals that would go beyond vague principles, could easily result in a host of national regulations that would tilt the delicate balance between nationalism and interdependence in the direction of the former. Precisely because, as Raymond Vernon noted, the conflicts created by multiple jurisdictions cannot be resolved in the ways that prevail in domestic politics—strikes, law, or courts—we need international principles of and mechanisms for settlements of such disputes.

The longer the paralysis of the Conference of the Law of the Seas, the faster states merely extend unilaterally their jurisdiction, with at least two series of calamitous effects: serious losses for those who are being ejected (for instance, from fishing within the 200-mile economic zone), and a galaxy of causes for conflict (over fishing, pollution, military transit, seabed exploitation, jurisdiction, and so on) without a proper method of settlement.[19] Clearly, the alternative to joint control is not our control, but a free-for-all in which the poorest—here, the landlocked states—lose again,and which the Soviet Union, far less concerned about seabed mining than we are, could exploit. We have even contributed to the free-for-all by dropping, because of domestic pressures, our earlier suggestion for a "trusteeship zone," with collective revenue sharing, beyond a depth of 200 meters.

Moreover, we are unsuccessful when we try to organize fronts of the advanced nations to improve our bargaining position and impose a "harder" line. In the IEA, differences between states doomed to massive imports of energy and states with better prospects of increased domestic production keep holding up agreement on a "floor price" for imported oil. At Nairobi, the advanced nations scattered all over the place. We therefore have an interest in getting nations that have largely been left out of international management to behave, not as free riders, but as partners with a stake in the rules. Financial transfers, access to Western markets, and the Special Drawing Rights (SDR) link (whose importance depends on the fate of the SDR, and which could anyhow be inflationary) may help, but a wider share in the control of institutions would be even more effective. A willingness to share control will help prevent the producers' associations that have already formed and will continue to develop from turning into cartels. The associations are the necessary means to the "politics of selectivity" and to the transformation of present commodity markets into less imperfect ones, less controlled by a handful of multinationals. But cartels would harm the poorest among the Southern countries and increase economic and political rigidities. Similarly, in the matter of oil, only a multilateral settlement instituting a regulated market in which industrialized consumers, producers, and developing countries without oil participate could provide some stability. It would assure the supply of oil, make possible a joint settlement of prices, and entail financial help to the third category of states. Any other settlement would either be less likely to be stable, or unfair to this category. But it is futile to expect such a regime, which could put an end to OPEC's current control of both price and quantities, to be acceptable by the producers as long as the advanced nations have not made some concessions on the control of institutions and on substantive issues other than oil.

The process I suggest is one of compromises aimed at facilitating what has been called a new international division of labor. The economic process is already going on. But because of its inequities and risks of dislocations, it has to be sustained by deals and agencies. Southern guarantees of access, fair pricing practices and fair treatment of foreign capital; Northern measures to dismantle protection against the exports of developing countries, in conjunction with measures of domestic adjustment; Northern financing of buffer stocks and a willingness to increase aid, especially to the poorest *of* the developing countries; joint measures to prevent excessive fluctuations of commodity prices and to orient aid toward projects that could help the poor *in* the developing countries; international bodies with resources derived from the states and from the exploitation of "commons," and capable of providing assistance both for development and against payments disturbances: in other words, not the suppression of the world market, but its management is required.[20] Certainly, in the final analysis, the Third World "countries' economic and social progress depends most fundamentally on their own decisions on mobilization and utilization of domestic resources."[21] But these decisions can be powerfully helped or harmed by the state of the world economy, and as in every political system, the absolute level of income at the bottom (i.e., the absolute poverty of the Fourth World) cannot be changed without outside action: some countries simply have no domestic resources to mobilize. Such action must aim at a delicate balance between the need of each actor to reduce excessive dependence on another actor or group, and the interest most actors have in exploiting interdependence to maximize mutual benefits and minimize mutual losses—a balance that, for instance, the U.S. should seek in its energy policy: it should combine conservation and enough interdependence to moderate (or strain) OPEC.

First World Relations   The third economic game is played in the First World. The main issue here is the future of the world monetary system (which continues to rest on an agreement between the leading industrial nations of the non-Communist world). For the time being, the world is on a dollar exchange standard. But all we have is a pseudo-regime, or a regime that is incomplete and rests more on the inability of the states to agree on a new one, than on a real consensus. There has been an accord on floating rates, but many of the partners see it as a mere *pis-aller,* a stopgap to be dropped as soon as the era of economic turbulence recedes. An agreement was made to abolish the official price of gold, but discord about the future role of gold continues. At present, the common rules on the management of the float define it to be a matter of perpetual manipulation by central banks eager to limit the exchange rate fluctuations that divergent domestic monetary and credit policies and rates of inflation provoke, but that risk disrupting trade and investment. There has been no return to dollar convertibility. "This means that the U.S. can pay its debts with self-created money"[22] as before, a privilege no longer offset, as before 1971, by the need to keep a fixed rate.

Thus there is no adequate control of international liquidity: Its growth, and that of international reserves, are no longer determined by the monetary policy of Washington alone, although it is still largely shaped by U.S. domestic credit policy and by the thoroughly unregulated, rapidly expanding Eurodollar market. And while the floating rates have absorbed the huge economic shocks of 1973–1974, and have been less inflationary that the fixed rate system in its last phase, one must remember that OPEC surpluses have been largely financed by huge credits granted by private banks— hence a colossal growth of national debts—and that floating rates do not have the constraining virtues of fixed rates (for states other than the dominant currency's). They do not oblige a nation whose currency keeps falling to take domestic corrective measures, and they do not aim at preventing excessive differences in prices between countries.

Special functions of the dollar will undoubtedly persist. No other currency can perform all of them, and the time has not come for an international asset to replace it, not merely as a unit of account but as the unit of transactions. It would require a far more centralized world, with nations far more willing to entrust vital powers to a supranational IMF and to give up control of monetary policy as a domestic tool, than is likely in the near future. But a dollar system can be more or less orderly. Fred Bergsten argues convincingly that the U.S. has atavistic foreign policy and economic reasons to want, even more than other countries, "to minimize the external constraints on the pursuit of . . . internal monetary, economic, and hence political objectives,'' and to try to maximize the benefits and minimize the costs of the dollar's international roles, that is, to aim at ''a high degree of exchange rate flexibility in any future monetary system.''[23] But, as he acknowledges, a world order policy would require some restraint: flexibility at full employment would intensify U.S. deficits and world inflation; flexibility at unemployment would intensify U.S. surpluses (through depreciation of the dollar) and world recession.

Thus, world order entails several changes from the present. One, it needs a responsible U.S. monetary policy—not only a reduction of inflation and the avoidance of stop-and-go measures, but also a willingness to limit the creation of money in response to internal demand, and interventions against any drastic depreciations of the dollar, which could be catastrophic for several allies. Two, it needs to move rapidly toward joint rules (with sanctions) to manage floating, and later toward fixed but adjustable rates; this would help restore the possibility of a European ''snake,'' a joint float of, or a tightening of the allowed margins of fluctuation among, West European currencies. It would also allow the currencies of other major economies, such as the Deutschmark and the yen, to play a larger international role.

Third, there will have to be some joint controls of the Eurodollar market, which has been an indispensable source of capital for international trade and for loans and investments both East and South, but also a source of major monetary disturbances, a rapid transmitter of inflationary impulses, and a major contributor to ''cycles of boom and bust.''[24] Fourth, monetary order—as the Europeans have discovered—requires far more coordination of economic policies than the advanced nations have been willing and able to pursue, except, fleetingly and vaguely, during the recent recession. Policy instruments such as interest and exchange rates should be coordinated and national economic objectives should be made compatible, so that simultaneous deflation or export-led growth drives in the leading countries can be avoided. Fifth, in the long run, after the main currencies have been stabilized, Special Drawing Rights, internationally managed, would become the primary source of liquidity growth, and countries would be given the choice between converting their current reserves into SDR, or keeping their reserves but ''agreeing to use them only when necessary to finance a payments deficit.''[25] The objective would be to turn the SDR into the central reserve asset, via a consolidation of the dollar overhang—the mass of dollars held by foreign countries. The dollar would thus cease being the center of the world monetary system—a change that might deprive the

U.S. of benefits (such as the financing by others of payments deficits) that are increasingly resisted by others, and liberate us from the burdens of the overhang.

THE DIPLOMATIC-STRATEGIC CHESSBOARD: THE SOVIET-AMERICAN CONTEST

We now return to the strategic-diplomatic arena. One last time, let us take stock of its importance. It is the realm of violence par excellence: if moderation should disappear from it, the issue of survival, which the relative success of restraints has pushed a bit into the background, would again dominate international affairs. Moreover, the processes of economic interdependence would be affected as well. For despite the fragmentation of the international system into functional slices, despite the relative autonomy of the arenas of interdependence, the possibility for separate hierarchies and different rules to develop there depends on the persistence of moderation in the strategic-diplomatic domain. Indeed, even mere shifts of power, while they are not directly translated into changes in the rules that govern the other arenas, have some effects on these. The decline of American hegemony in the economic realms in recent years has many causes, but the relative decline of U.S. power in the traditional domain, which we have analyzed before, has been one these, even though it has not fundamentally shifted the central balance. What happens on the traditional chessboard of world politics—a metaphor justified, here, by bipolarity—is no longer a cause of all the other processes, but it remains their condition.

On this chessboard we find, also, the most difficult issues. It is the terrain where world order considerations and competitive ones collide most openly, and where indeed the latter (such as containment) can most easily pass for world order concerns, too. Competition is only one form of what I have, earlier, called the rules of interaction. The logic of separateness, which leads to contests between actors, also leads to their determination to put their relative advantage, which is concrete to them, above any common advantage that they deem either fuzzy or a disguise of someone else's gain. At best, it may lead to unilateral, hence revocable, restraints. Yet the logic of world order is one of common restraints. Yet the logic of world order is one of common restraints. Today, on the traditional chessboard, we encounter both types of problems—those of the contest, and those raised by the prevalence of individual calculations. We shall examine these two categories of problems consecutively—and sketchily.

The Balance of Power East-West problems have no end in sight. Insofar as détente is concerned, the disillusioned consensus that appears to have been reached in the United States is wise. We need to keep negotiating arms restraints and to resist efforts at upsetting the regional balances by force. It is fruitless to pursue the debate as to whether the Soviet Union behaves as a traditional great power or as a revolutionary communist state. It acts as a communist great power: its ideology provides it with specific points of attack (and defense), just as American principles do. But its willingness to embrace as allies powers that are anything but communist and to subordinate its communist "brother parties" abroad to its own priorities, shows very classical great power behavior. Are the peculiarities of its arms build-up—the emphasis on megatonnage, the huge tank forces in Eastern Europe, the persistent concern with defense (anti-aircraft and civil)—a product of communist calculation or a legacy of Russian experiences? It is an unexciting subject.

What remains an area of controversy is the extent to which the United States ought to induce Soviet restraint in the diplomatic-strategic domain by tying economic cooperation to such restraint. In my opinion, there are three strong reasons against reviving explicit linkage. First, it is unlikely to work: it is hard to believe that Moscow would give up rich opportunities, say, in Southern Africa, for credits and technology. Second, there is in any case a de facto, implicit linkage. In the absence of restraint, or in the presence of gross Soviet violations of human rights, the climate in American opinion and Congress will not be favorable to any economic deals— and even more suspicious of arms deals. Third, one of the lessons of the Kissinger era ought to be the difficulty of combining, in our relations with Moscow, two different logics: that of bipolar hostility, and that of détente once it goes *beyond* the muting of hostility and becomes a scheme for cooperation. The wall and the web are hard to mix. There is a built-in incompatibility between balance of power dynamics, which requires partial cooperation among the great powers, and the dynamics of two rival camps. As long as the contest continues, we have good reason to doubt that "rewarding" Moscow with economic advantages is in our interest. Cooperation must be sought in the areas that are least likely to arouse domestic controversy and most likely to result in unambiguous benefits to both sides—such as arms control or the quest for common rules in the realms of economic interdependence discussed above. The best way to seek Soviet "moderation" is not to pay for it, but to work simultaneously on old-fashioned containment (as in Europe), on reducing the arms races, and on depriving the Soviets of political opportunities for exploiting weak spots.

Where the superpowers are led to feed a local arms race—as, at present, in Eastern and Southern Africa, and between Iran and Iraq—the very likelihood of a stalemate at best, or a dangerous explosion that the great powers will find difficult to control at worst, should incite them, sooner or later, to try to agree on joint restraints.[26] The same applies to the European theater, where obvious asymmetries in the composition of forces and in the geographical position of the two superpowers vis-a-vis their allies make an agreement difficult, yet where the MBFR negotiation has the merit of getting the two sides to discuss in detail the composition and level of their forces, and where the idea of common ceilings might, in the beginning, be more fruitful than that of reductions. Indeed, parallel, interdependent limitations and reductions undertaken by the two alliances might be the best form of arms control, along with measures against a surprise attack.

In the strategic arms race itself, there is an urgent need to institute qualitative controls before technology completely erodes the distinction between tactical and strategic or even between nuclear and conventional weapons,[27] before the restless search for antisubmarine warfare or satellite killers undermines the principles of deterrence, and before the accuracy of MIRVed and MARVed missiles begins to suggest the possibility of a controlled counterforce or countercity nuclear war. Of limited value for an antiproliferation policy, a comprehensive test ban signed by the two super-powers would be useful. Both sides should agree to stop improving their first-strike capabilities, whether they take the form of throw-weight feats on the Soviet side, or U.S. counterforce targeting with warheads of increasing yield or accuracy. There should be joint limits on the rate of introduction of important new weapons systems and agreements on deployment sched-ules.[28] There is still time to limit the full deployment of cruise missiles, despite the difficulty of enforcing limitations here. (Strategic, long-range cruise missiles launched from the sea or land are redundant, and should be banned, long-range cruise missiles launched by plane ought to be put under a ceiling.) Given the number of nuclear weapons now available—far in excess of enemy targets—qualitative reductions shall have to be negoti-ated (including the elimination, over time, of land-based missiles), espe-cially if qualitative controls have not been established sufficiently to dispel the fear that the other side could destroy that component of the hallowed triad in a first strike or the fear that the other side could choose to wage a limited counterforce nuclear war (two highly destabilizing possibilities).

As the experience of the first half of 1977 has shown, none of this is easy, for technological and diplomatic reasons. The goal of reducing the numbers of inherently destabilizing weapons—the large Soviet ICBMs, our planned MX missile—and that of moving from limitations to actual cuts are excellent. But we shall not reach them if our proposals, as in March 1977, either leave out questionable weapons, such as the new Soviet bomber and our cruise missile, or else offer a menu of reductions that eliminates large numbers of existing Soviet weapons in exchange for a mere renunciation of future weapons on our side. Indeed, stabilization is much more an American than a Soviet concept: the Soviet ideology is one of movement, and only temporary lulls. If there is a rule of thumb, it is that the difficulty of establishing controls is proportional to the connection between the use of arms and possible political results. Only in the strategic realm is there an obvious disconnection. But the more one gets into the fluid realities of third party conflicts that are sufficiently decoupled from the nuclear fuse to allow each outside puppeteer to hope that his puppets will prevail without their strings getting tangled in the nuclear detonator, the more restraints become difficult to achieve. It is no reason for not trying. The American economy remains much more capable than the Soviet one of bearing the burden of a sudden increase in defense expenditures; any such increase—for instance, one that Soviet intransigence in arms control matters would induce—would wipe out any momentary Soviet advantage. This might incite the Soviets to seek joint restraints. So should we.

Indeed, especially in the strategic arms race, the U.S. should give up the game of bargaining chips—deploying weapons it wants to regulate, yet thereby complicating the negotiations and delaying their results. It has "worked" only for the ABM—but even there, for reasons independent of the bargaining chip tactic. The tactic only feeds what is, despite what critics have said, an important component of the arms race (the others being national objectives and bureaucratic politics): the "action-reaction" phenomenon. In the absence of a comprehensive test ban, we should, of course, preserve the capacity, through research and tests, to develop (in the least destabilizing manner) weapons we cannot agree to curtail; but we don't have to deploy them in advance of negotiations or in the hope that their deployment will "force" the other side to make concessions. Moreover, for the control both of regional arms races fed by the superpowers, and of the strategic race, Washington should be willing to resort to unilateral restraints (including restraints on research and development) and ask that they be reciprocated by comparable Soviet ones. Such restraints would be either in preparation for, or in lieu of, formal agreements (which can be delicate to obtain from the other side, for reasons of internal bureaucratic politics or of external embarrassment. No great power wants to appear to gang up with its rival at the expense of its clients.) Nowhere is the Soviet Union so advanced that a temporary restraint on this side might lead to disaster (with the possible exception of the European theater insofar as conventional forces are concerned—but there, the connection to the nuclear detonator remains a formidable deterrent).

The difficulty of reaching restraints is, however, a good reason for recommending two apparently opposite, yet convergent policies. One is, precisely, the preservation of the "coupling" on the European theater. Any decoupling between the strategic nuclear level and the conventional one, justified by excessive rationality—whether it takes the form of massive cuts in U.S. forces, or of the replacement of theater nuclear weapons with nuclear weapons situated outside the European area, or with conventional precision-guided munitions (PGMs)—could actually be destabilizing.[30] So could the neutron bomb, which suggests the possibility of a "controlled" nuclear war in Europe. Rather than making the West Europeans more eager to develop their defenses, such American moves would convince them that Washington intends to protect its national territory from nuclear war, while using Europe as a battlefield. They would then seek accommodation with Moscow. Preserving the coupling of nuclear and conventional forces does not mean that no efforts should be made to reduce the numbers of weapons that have so far been excluded from SALT (and, for the most part, from MFBR) yet could be deemed strategic either by the Soviets or by the West Europeans: Soviet medium-range missiles pointed at Western Europe, cruise missiles capable of reaching the Soviet territory from Europe. Partly because of the cruise missile, partly because of the British and French nuclear deterrents, SALT and the balance of nuclear forces between Western Europe and the U.S.S.R. will not be separable much longer.[31]

The other policy, in "gray" areas where the superpowers compete, such as Africa and the Middle East, would concentrate on trying systematically to find peaceful solutions to the conflicts that underlie the arms race—an attempt that should not be undertaken by the U.S. alone, or only by regional organizations paralyzed by conflicts among their members. One often pays lip service to peaceful change, yet one practices it usually only once war has already broken out. We have begun such an effort in the Arab-Israeli dispute and, with British help, in Rhodesia. Another one is badly needed in the explosive horn of Africa, where old antagonisms between Somalia (Moscow's ex-client) and Ethiopia (which used to be ours, but is becoming Moscow's friend, after the change to a revolutionary military dictatorship) are being heightened by the contest for the control of Djibouti which the French have given up, and by the fight over Ogaden.[32]

The Balance of Influence   The military aspects of the competition are not the only ones. We also have to cope with problems in the balance of influence and, in particular, with the rise in many parts of the world of communist or other left-wing movements supported or encouraged by Moscow. In the previous section, I suggested a guideline of noncollision aimed at avoiding the anti-Americanization of nationalist movements. Yet many of these are or will be anti-American, and their success could result in a considerable loss of American influence: A world of Titos is not a friendly world for the U.S. The old motto of containment is inapplicable to such cases (indeed, in the past, containment often resulted not from Western barriers but from splits within the communist world, as in Yugoslavia, China, and Rumania). The notion of détente provides no real guideline. Paradoxically, détente may be too much for the Soviets insofar as it encourages not only restlessness in Eastern Europe but also the emancipation of West European Communists—their increasing domestic legitimacy, partly a product of détente, also hastens their "nationalization"[33]—whereas détente is not enough for us, since it only provides for some moderation of some interstate relations. The hope that détente would make the U.S.S.R. "more of a state and less of a cause," in Charles Bohlen's phrase, has been disappointed for a number of reasons. First, the rise of communism (as in Italy) is often quite independent of Soviet machinations. Second, whether as a state or as a cause, the U.S.S.R., in its contest with us, can hardly give up the opportunities afforded by its links with foreign communist parties such as in Portugal. To make Soviet abstinence a condition of détente would be to give up détente, especially as a vast area for maneuver exists between the two extremes of total abstinence and the establishment of Soviet bases on "our" side. Last, there is, in fact if not in theory, a contradiction between our rationale for détente and our attempts to stop the spread of Communism to other societies (as in Chile). The two are consistent at the level of balance of power or influence politics; they are not easy to reconcile in public arguments within the U.S. or abroad.

Again, a sound policy requires discrimination. We must combine a variety of criteria: does a given communist breakthrough to power add to Soviet power? Does it affect ours significantly (for instance, through the loss of important bases)? Does it merely reduce our (or increase their) influence? Did it succeed with or without Soviet help, with or without violence? What are the costs of trying to preserve the status quo? Are there serious reasons to cry domino? The application of such criteria suggests that when communists independent of the Red Army are in power, it is in our interest to play the game of diversity and to encourage their pursuit of their national interest as long as it is nonaggressive. When they are in what might be called partial power (as they were in Chile, are inching toward in Italy, and might once be in France), the costs of overt or covert intervention are morally and politically greater than any likely benefits. The best policy is one of prophylactic accommodation, which would aim at disconnecting the issue from the central balance, at trying to minimize the impact on the regional balance of power, and at preserving influence by keeping the maximum of cooperative contacts with the non-Communist part of the forces in power, even if this involves the granting of credits. The catastrophic picture, so vividly and frequently painted by Kissinger, of the destruction of the Western alliance by a communist surge in France or Italy, has no chance of becoming real unless the communists acquire a monopoly of power there—an unlikely prospect. When the communists are in the opposition, we should apply two principles: noncollision (i.e., avoid becoming the main target around which they could rally other nationalists, even if this means giving up nonessential bases) and indirection (i.e., giving priority to the reform of the "threatened" society, if it is one on which we have strong influence, and decoupling altogether if we do not).

Both our competitive interests and the imperatives of world order would be served by such a policy.[34] Its main motto—one I have advocated before—is to trust diversity. Our forces are needed to preserve the central balance and those regional balances that, for reasons both of inherent importance and nuclear linkage, are coupled with it: Japan and Western Europe. But even this essential role, played by our guarantee and by the presence of our forces, should not induce us, in the case of Japan, to restrict the diplomatic initiatives Tokyo might want to pursue, either in Asia or in the economic arenas; nor, in the case of Western Europe, should we refrain from encouraging the gradual formation of a West European Defense Organization, which would coordinate the defense policies of its members and promote joint arms procurement, along lines more fully described elsewhere.[35]

THE DIPLOMATIC-STRATEGIC CHESSBOARD: THE LOGIC OF
SEPARATENESS

Let us turn to the more global problems of order in the strategic-diplomatic realm. I shall examine three different types of issues: human rights, conflicts, and nuclear proliferation.

Human Rights   I have indicated above my reservations about an inclusion of the "quality of political life" among the necessary targets of a world order policy. All other world order issues are characterized by partly adversary, partly cooperative relationships. Even a successful nonproliferation policy, as we shall see, requires the assent of would-be nuclear powers, and can enlist the support of a large majority of states. But the issue of human rights is different in two respects. First, it is an inherently conflictual problem: outsiders are telling a national government to change its domestic behavior even if its external conduct is unassailable and creates no peril for other nations. Secondly, the way in which a regime treats its citizens is directly linked to the regime's philosophy of power and conception of legitimacy, and it is intimately connected with the structure of power. A request to liberalize or to grant "basic human needs" can easily be seen as subversive—as requiring the dismantling of institutions that rest either on the absolute centralization of power or on an inequalitarian model of development. We may protest that we do not *intend* such a revolution; but the recipients of our demands may well believe that it would *result* if they gave us satisfaction, and suspect that we must actually want the likely effects of our acts. I have also stated, however, why concern for human rights seemed legitimate. Not only does this concern appeal to American idealism, but it is also valid in absolute terms—as long as one believes in the values of liberalism—because the difficult quest for the development, not merely of prudential restraints, but of morally acknowledged ones would be considerably helped by the lifting of political standards in most countries, and because of the bond that exists between a regime's behavior at home and its performance on the world stage. A concern for human rights should be one element of a policy for world order, rather than an attempt at enforcing "absolute" values. The problem is a matter of method and degree.

The method would aim at deterring or diverting countries from violations of internationally established standards, rather than at fostering "good" governments—something that is both impossible and an invitation to distortions. Here again, it would be essential to begin with standards that are susceptible of broad endorsement. For it is important to let others know exactly what behavior we would like to see changed: elastic or vague standards encourage excessive hopes among victims, they also feed suspicion and evasiveness among governments. Moreover, few regimes are willing to repudiate such standards openly: the exclusion of torture, summary executions, prolonged arbitrary detention, deliberate starvation, and the like. This does not mean that higher standards are beyond reach: in specific circumstances (to be discussed below) they may well be worth trying for. But if there is a movable ceiling, there ought to be a solid and, if possible, common floor. Indeed, we must try for an international, not an American policy. If it is the latter, not only will others suspect our motives, but it will have a limited effectiveness and sooner or later force us to choose between futile self-righteousness and a return to traditional prudence. Moreover, if we are alone, we can expect, after the first wave of complacent moralism is spent, a domestic reassertion of protest against our assault on right-wing authoritarian regimes that (by contrast with those of the left) do not export revolution or inhibit free enterprise and entertain intimate relations with many Americans.

The method would also consist in looking for effectiveness. On the one hand, we should not be deterred by the fear that a human rights policy could complicate international negotiations on North-South issues, nuclear proliferation, or arms control, or interfere with American security or economic interests. In most cases, we can deal with such risks, either by taking into account legitimate state interests that transcend a particular regime or by using the advantages which America's assets in the realm of advanced technology, management, available capital, and so on, still provide. But our criterion should be the effectiveness of our policy with respect to the rights we seek to promote. If, for the sake of a good conscience, we take spectacular public measures that have no effect on these rights, or even backfire, if for instance we feed a regime's paranoia about subversion and harden its resistance, we have no reason to be proud. Again, discretion (in both meanings of the word) and the use of carrots rather than (or in addition to) sticks are necessary.[36]

Three different directions seem worth exploring. The first, most general—and yet modest—consists in advocating the establishment or the strengthening of a variety of regional and international commissions, under the auspices of the UN and such organizations as the OAS or the OAU, whose role would be to monitor and report on violations of human rights. The records of the UN and the Inter-American Human Rights Commissions are disappointing—not surprisingly, given the lack of any enforcement machinery or powers and their being composed of delegates of the governments, i.e., of the delinquents themselves. The lessons to be learned from this are the need to set up more specialized committees or working parties dealing with specific kinds of violations (torture, the rigging of elections, violations of public liberties, and so on); the need to extend investigation from traditional political and civil liberties to social and economic rights; the need for far greater publicity of the findings of such bodies; the need to have them discussed in the public meetings of the assemblies of the UN and regional agencies, so as to oblige the accused governments to face the charges; the need to resort as broadly as possible to nonofficial members for these bodies; and the need to enlist to the hilt the support of private organizations, such as ad hoc institutions (the Red Cross, Amnesty International) and transnational bodies of scientists, intellectuals, and professionals.

The key to even limited success is the mobilization, in the freer countries, of public pressure around charges that cannot be assailed as politically motivated. The argument about the impermeability of totalitarian regimes to such pressure is excessive. Many governments are repressively authoritarian rather than totalitarian, and somewhat more permeable both because of less than full control and because of their need for outside support (cf. Tito's Yugoslavia). And even totalitarian regimes that want to play an active world role are sometimes susceptible to such pressure. Solzhenitzyn was expelled, not jailed or executed.

The findings of such organizations would provide a legitimate basis for action. The second direction is the treatment of human rights in regimes closely associated with the U.S. through military alliance, or our participation in their creation,[37] and for whose domestic performance we cannot deny a measure of responsibility. Some of the guidelines I have suggested might already contribute to improving a dismal American record that ranges from overt interventions and subversion against left-wing, yet not totalitarian or "communist-controlled" regimes, to support for repressive regimes that were on our side and whose real estate we needed. Watergate and more recent investigations lead one to believe that these acts coincided precisely, in Richard Ullman's words, with the "countless inroads into our constitutional liberties in the name of national security."[38]

I also agree with Ullman that "a central goal of American policy over the coming years should be the breaking" of the "embraces" of repressive foreign regimes and the avoidance of new ones. We are obliged to deal with them in the economic arenas, insofar as they are caught in economic interdependence. But we are not obliged to shower them with favors and to submit to their not-infrequent blackmail, in exchange for their contribution to a favorable balance of power or influence. In many instances, they have nowhere else to go. It may be in their interest to worry us by flirting with Moscow and Peking; it is hardly to their advantage to put themselves at these countries' mercy, or to give up the possibility of American help in case of aggression. As for us, new technologies make it possible in practically every case to dispense with the military bases that usually justify the embrace.

The distribution of American credits, or of credits by institutions largely controlled by the U.S., should be tied to improvements in the treatment of human rights, and not only to orthodox criteria of financial soundness (which make it all too easy to deny such aid to left-wing regimes; witness our policy toward Chile under Allende versus under Pinochet). Congress has begun to take effective steps in this direction (although it left out U.S. behavior in the World Bank). The grant of generalized trade preferences and the abolition of restraints on trade with the developing countries could be tied to progress in the satisfaction of human needs. The sale of police or counterinsurgency equipment to, and the training in the U.S. of the "forces of order" of repressive regimes engaged in the suppression of human rights should be ended.

As for military assistance (including sales of arms), there are cases where, pending agreements on restraints and within limits to be discussed below, the competitive side of world politics might force us to continue to provide it to such regimes. But the very fact that such assistance serves their interest as well as ours, and that we are often the only possible supplier (this side of the common potential adversary) of what they want, should make it possible for us to tie such assistance to the observance of certain minimum standards. This form of "intervention" is hugely different from the traditional open or subversive interference aimed at determining the nature and political orientation of a country's government. The granting of military aid, even in the case of commercial sales, always entails some degree of involvement, if not an outright commitment to another country: many of our weapons come with contractors, advisers, and technicians who train those who might have to use the arms. There is no reason not to request a counterpart that is, at least, not self-serving (unless one believes that self-help should be the only criterion of policy).

In the special case of South Korea, U.S. troops play an important deterrent function; an invasion of South Korea would have profound repercussions not only on our difficult relationship with China, but also on the position and policies of Japan; and any abandonment by us might have a disastrous effect, either in the realm of conventional conflict (i.e., either Seoul or Pyong-Yang might strike first) or in that of nuclear proliferation. Even so, the very need of the Park regime for our physical presence would have allowed us to put pressure on it for its liberalization, and to reverse our past policy that brushed aside the latter because of the intensity of the North Korean threat. A decision to subordinate the continuing presence of American ground forces, and the continuing supply of weapons to modernize Seoul's army, to improvements in human rights, would have been superior to the decision to withdraw the troops unconditionally and to keep supplying South Korea's forces. This is precisely what a priority to world order concerns (without any discarding of competitive ones) entails. In the abstract, there is a real risk of applying to our "clients" standards that have been reached only in a handful of democracies and that would fail to take into account the cultural traditions of the areas. In practice, this danger is probably smaller than the weight of our past laxity.

A third direction is that of American official policies toward human rights violations in countries that are not our allies or close clients, but with which we nevertheless have special relations, such as the countries of the "Soviet bloc," China, or Yugoslavia and Romania, who are linked to us by our interest in preserving their independence. Obviously, the U.S. can do very little to force such countries to change their policies, especially through overt pressure. And such pressure can poison the climate of negotiations on other issues without benefiting dissidents at all. Indeed, as one observer has remarked, even though past détente has not entailed much liberalization, a return to the cold war would doom any chances for it.[39] Any measure (such as the reinforcement of American radio stations aimed at Eastern Europe and Russia) which makes the Soviets suspect a return to the days of "rollback" is a mistake. Our aim ought not to be "destabilization," which would only harden our adversary. And destabilization is far more likely to result from events within his camp.

But Washington has no reason to refrain from expressing occasionally public indignation at infringements of human rights, especially when they also constitute violations of international agreements, as in the case of Helsinki. Neither détente nor the imperatives of balance require the silence that only discourages dissidents and encourages further repression. The "other side" has never refrained from gloating about the evils of the capitalist system.

Moreover, the very fact that all these countries do want at least some things from us—ranging from oblique protection to economic and scientific benefits—gives us the leverage to apply a subtle pressure—not a return to open linkage, for the reasons indicated in Chapter Two, but an explanation that the scope of our contribution is not unrelated to the treatment of dissidents and candidates for emigration, and to intellectual or media access, given the mood of Congress and of American opinion. This is exactly the approach that worked (in, admittedly, more favorable circumstances) before the Jackson amendment. We have no guarantee it will work again, yet we should try, as long as the attempt does not single out communist countries, but is part of a general policy applied to "friends" as well. In the Soviet sphere, we must observe two limits. We should not link human rights and arms restraints, for we have an overriding interest in moving toward the latter. And we must be careful in choosing when to protest: we cannot become so loud and pressing as to become either ineffective—no one paying attention to the routine—or counterproductive—our actions leading only to greater repression. This does not mean that we are, in effect, at the mercy of our adversary's reaction; for, especially if we are consistent in our policy, and given his own concern for a not unfavorable image abroad (particularly among West European Communists), he cannot react with indiscriminate repression.

Conflicts   One particularly atrocious problem of human rights has not been mentioned: genocide, the massacre of whole categories of people by a government. So far, the international milieu has been remarkably indifferent; Biafra, Bangladesh, Burundi, and Uganda received little attention. The chances of either obtaining boycotts and the withdrawal of diplomatic privileges from such regimes, or reaching the desired results through such measures are small.

From the viewpoint of world order, genocide, which usually reflects inexpiable tribal, racial, or ethnic hatreds, as well as another violation of human rights—terrorism—should be examined under the rubric of *conflicts*. It is a rubric as vast as mankind because it also includes civil wars and interstate disputes. It is obviously impossible to equate world order with the elimination of all resorts to force or threats of force. The objectives of order ought to be: the elimination of large-scale interstate violence; or if this proves impossible, its disconnection from risks of escalation (in areas where such disconnection, if announced and assured, would actually increase the chances of war, as in Western Europe, this requires a delicate differentiation between strategy for deterrence and strategy in case deterrence fails); the moderation, as far as possible, of large intrastate violence; and severe international measures against terrorism.

The framework in which these goals should be sought is not a centralized model of world security. This presupposes, in fact, a great powers condominium, but a centralized model would entail excessive costs for them as "tenders" of the system, provoke stiff resistance from other states, and require far more reliance on their joint use of force (for deterrence or enforcement) than they are likely to be able to agree on. Nor is it a model providing for the disengagement of the superpowers, whose role would be limited to their own mutual deterrence and to restraining their proxies. Such disengagement would prove untenable past a certain threshold of localized violence (especially if the nuclear taboo had been violated by a party in an area of importance to a superpower), and it would have to be symmetrical—which is unlikely. One ought to aim at an organized model that would comprise an international regime. It would no doubt be shakier than those built on the restraints of economic interdependence; but it would rest on a principle—the universality of concern (if not involvement)—and it would be provided with an organization whose function and structure could be comparable to those of the OECD (although it could be part of the UN system). Let us call it the International Security Committee. Its role would be to symbolize what Leonard Beaton[40] called the principle of cognizance—the idea that security is both a national and an international function and that arms levels are of international concern. Initially, its role would be one of information: of reporting on troop movements, on arms sales, and on the enforcement of existing agreements; and of analyzing conflicts to put some pressure on states.

Within this framework, there would be a need to distinguish between action to eliminate the causes of conflict, and action to cope with the resort to force. Almost by definition, the former action can never be entirely successful; there are far too many causes, in both meanings of the word, for any effort to dry out all the possible ponds of terrorism. But systematic action on these causes could dry out some and, above all, change the attitudes of governments toward terrorists, who can always count on some passive sympathies among states whose leaders deplore the inertia or the failure of the international milieu on a given festering issue. Obviously, some causes are beyond reach: ethnic or ideological breakdowns in a state, the proliferation of military regimes, or pathological leaders. But many others are susceptible to the "universalization of concern."

Two steps need to be taken. On the one hand, some sources of conflict can be found in conditions of insecurity, related to problems of access (to energy, raw materials, technology, or markets), passage through seas or straits, balances of payments and debts, and so forth These problems should be addressed before they have explored, so to speak, into bilateral interstate conflicts (as, for instance, the Greek-Turkish clash over the continental shelf in the Aegean Sea has threatened to do, or as the dispute between China and Vietnam about the ownership of small South Sea islands could, some day). This can be accomplished by seeing that each of the international regimes that will be negotiated in the "new economic order"—for various commodities, oil, the oceans, the monetary order, new communications systems, etc.—contain provisions about the compulsory settlement of disputes arising out of the application of its rules. Provisions should be drawn to cover the creation of boards of conciliation, mediation, or arbitration; the publication of the reports of these boards; the possibility for a dissatisfied party to appeal to the General Assembly of the institution (if it is an institutionalized regime) or the relevant functional agency of the UN system otherwise; and the enforcement of sanctions against violators within the realm of the regime. Also, the regime should contain provisions for collective action (or authorizing voluntary action) against any state or nonstate actor that resorts to violence (or any state that protects a nonstate actor that uses force) against the regime.

On the other hand, for all the conflicts that have already become interstate disputes or that are of a nature no specific international regime deals with (such as territorial border problems, or political hostilities between regimes, as in the relations between Uganda and Kenya), two directions ought to be followed. One could be called institutional: the systematic resort either to regional organizations, as long as the conflict does not produce a fundamental cleavage among its members or, in that case, to the UN. A major effort should be made to strengthen what could be called the peaceful change arsenal at the disposal of all these agencies. What is required is their permanent engagement in diplomacy, a constant, gentle pressure on states involved in dangerous conflicts. Past failures have, of course, had far deeper reasons than the sporadic quality of these efforts. And more persistent efforts will require the full support of the member states, especially the major powers, on their behalf. One of the reasons for past fiascoes is the simple fact that no state feels it must give in to a pressure exerted *merely* by an international organization. For such an organization to be effective, it ought to be not just the theoretical sum of its parts, but the instrument of action chosen by its more important members. Otherwise, there will only be more Jarring missions.

Moderation will require, as in East-West confrontations, a process of ritualization. The goal should be permanent mediation, rather than the mixture of occasional good offices and belated injunctions against force. One should aim at obligatory settlement: give the agencies, where they do not already have it, the right to evoke a conflict themselves, borrow from the League of Nations a greater variety of diplomatic techniques than have been used in the past thirty years, and provide for compulsory public reporting of findings. The report should include the principles of a proposed solution, clear delimitation of responsibility—which would legitimize international concern—and a listing of possible sanctions against any party that rejects the proposals if these are endorsed by the organization.

The other direction would be more traditional. It should be combined with the institutional effort and should prolong it if that effort failed. The guideline would be: the greater the chances that a conflict cannot be insulated and that the great powers will be dragged into it, the more the U.S. should push toward a settlement, in conjunction with other states (so that we avoid playing Atlas or St. Sebastian). When the chances of a settlement, the probability of a spillover affecting countries other than the parties, as well as the risk of great power involvement in the conflict (or of the U.S.S.R. becoming the main beneficiary of it), are low, it is in the American interest to stay aside (as we should have done in the India-Pakistan clash over Bangladesh). When there is a high risk of involvement or spillover, or a major American loss, or significant Soviet gain of power or influence, we have no alternative to a quest for accommodation: as in the Cyprus case, in the Middle East, in Rhodesia now, as in the case of the Republic of South Africa or in the Horn of Africa soon.

In the Middle East, the history of recent years is clear. First, from 1967 to 1973, the U.S., except for Secretary Rogers' unsupported attempts, tried to avoid any special responsibility and left the field to Ambassador Jarring and to good words about direct negotiations among the parties. The events of 1973 revealed that in that part of the world peace was inseparable from our welfare. The highest priority must be given to an American policy that would, first, sound out the various parties to ascertain their positions and the nature of their disagreements; then try to establish a international conciliation group composed of the U.S., the U.S.S.R., Britain, and France, which would attempt to narrow the gap between the parties, and, when good offices fail, suggest the main principles and outlines of a settlement; and, third, not so much reconvene a Geneva Conference as begin a Geneva-like process. The aim ought to be a settlement along lines I have described elsewhere: essentially, formal Arab recognition of Israel's existence, a return to the 1967 borders (with special provisions for Jerusalem), the demilitarization of the Golan Heights, a solution to the Palestinian problem that will have to result from intra-Arab tests of ambition and force, and a galaxy of outside guarantees, both collective and unilateral (including a curbing of arms sales). At what moment, in what form and forum the Palestinians take part in the process is a matter of tactics (which does not mean at all a secondary matter, since the moment, form, and forum will shape the outcome). Their participation and the establishment of a Palestinian entity (independent or part of a confederation) are the key to a solution.

The United States, as a supplier to arms to both sides and of aid to Egypt as well as to Israel, has at its disposal means of pressure and rewards to move the parties toward a solution. In no area is the connection between domestic politics and foreign policy more obvious: America and Israel, despite the unevenness of their power, have been in a state of mutual deterrence, with Israeli economic and military security partly hostage to our supplies, and American internal concord—in the relation between the White House, Congress, and public opinion—hostage to Israel's ability to mobilize support in the American body politic. Neither side has been willing to carry out its implicit threat, lest the other do the same. And the Arabs have underestimated this link because they have looked only at the respective material capabilities and neglected the crucial question of each side's capacity to mobilize its resources or to prevent the other from marshalling its own. We have two disadvantages: our threat, if carried out, could be lethal, and so we hesitate to do so against a close friend. And Israel's public is less malleable than ours, hence less easy to affect from abroad. This unevenness, which balances that of power, would doom us to drift if the problem was not so important. Our survival is not at stake whereas Israel's may be; and yet, the repercussions of failure—on the Middle East, America's position in the Arab world, U.S.–Soviet relations and Soviet influence, and the world economy—are such that we have no other recourse than convincing Israel to move, using our power to do so, and convincing our own public of the correctness of our policy by stressing the balanced nature of the settlement we seek and the guarantees we are willing to provide to make it work.

In Southern Africa, we must pursue the Rhodesian effort undertaken by Kissinger; we have decided to put firmer pressure on Smith by repudiating the Byrd amendment and applying a strict embargo on sales of chrome. We shall have to keep on the pressure, in cooperation with Britain and with Black Africa's states around Rhodesia. In the case of Praetoria, what is needed now is a combination of disapproval of those South African policies that would deepen the gap between it and Black Africa (such as the setting up of fake black "independent" units), diplomatic pressure toward reform, an embargo on any arms transfers, and the discouragement of new investment. If these measures fail to move the South African regime toward majority rule, we may have to provide diplomatic and financial support to black nationalist groups, directly or through the OAU.

Force This brings us to the measures aimed at coping with the resort to force. The first issue here is precisely that of arms sales, undertaken by many states for political calculation and rivalry, or commercial expansion—and with results that range from the preservation of a regional balance, to the feeding of a military dictatorship, or the fueling of a local conflict. The problem has a quality of hopelessness, not only or even principally because of the inflation of the arms trade in recent years. But it is impossible to distinguish rigorously between offensive and defensive weapons; weapons sold by A to B can be transferred to C; increasingly sophisticated weapons are sent to technologically backward states; the national capacity to create a weapons industry is spreading; and relatively cheap precision-guided weapons have been developed. More suppliers, more self-reliance, a more sophisticated yet less ruinous technology: these are the current prospects.

Considerations on the suppliers' side add to the gloom. Arms transfers can be seen—as in the Nixon doctrine—as an attractive substitute for nuclear proliferation. Yet the supplier thereby buys his relative (and uncertain) disengagement at the cost of inciting local recklessness. Particularly when it is a nuclear guarantee he appears to try to revoke, the transfer of conventional arms can actually feed local eagerness for nuclear weapons, especially because some of the new technologies have dual capabilities.[41]

Three directions can be suggested, not to reverse the irreversible, but to slow down what might become a major incentive to immoderation. The first is informal, area by area understandings with other suppliers and recipients, aimed both at limiting the size of the deluge and at seeing to it that the supplies (which will be piled upon the weaponry produced by the clients themselves, on their own or under license) at least contribute to, or do not upset, the local balance of forces. The refrain remains: it is not easy but it must be tried. These discussions should go beyond a group of suppliers alone (although preliminary discussions among them would be necessary) and include the recipients for two reasons: their growing capacity to produce weapons, and the incentive they would have to manufacture even more, and to exploit rivalries among the suppliers, if they were treated as mere objects or stakes. In these discussions, the U.S. will need to avoid anything resembling, for instance, the idea of a NATO common defense market, which our allies would see as one more American strategy to snuff out their defense industries. But an American decision to buy more NATO weapons from its European allies (thus reversing the trend of recent years) might make it far easier for them to limit their sales abroad.[42] Their defense industries have, in some cases, grown to the point where the means— selling arms to improve the balance of payments—has become an end. Although this cannot be easily or rapidly reversed, it can at least be redirected. The goal—some distance away in most cases—ought to be the creation of regional arms control schemes, with exchanges of inspectors or observers; limits and information on military maneuvers; agreements on ceilings and types of weapons; and the like.

One of the obstacles to such a neat solution is the messiness of regionalism. Regional restraint can be all too easily upset by a neighbor just outside the area (such as Brazil next to the now dying Andean group). Many states (such as Iran and Saudi Arabia) arm against threats arising in several regions. And often the hatreds among neighbors are too strong to allow one to expect agreements on limitations. There remains, however, a second direction: an agreement by the suppliers only, and especially by Washington and Moscow, to limit the sale or coproduction of certain kinds of weapons—for instance, those that could be fitted with nuclear warheads or (like hand-held surface-to-air missiles) could easily fall into the hands of terrorists—and to curtail retransfers.[43] Such agreements are not likely to be easy, unless they are accompanied by substantive moves to deal with the disputes or tensions that feed a local arms race.

A third direction—unilateral action—remains open. Much can be said against unilateral curbs. Other nations—including adversaries—could fill the gap. Why should we forgo the benefits, whether material or political? Indeed, we might have little choice but to respond to a deliberate escalation of arms supplies by the U.S.S.R. Even in some of these instances, however, we might be wiser to let some of our allies become the "countersuppliers." A local balance will thus be restored, without the area becoming a testing ground for the superpowers themselves, a mere stake in their confrontation. Or else it might make more sense to combine our "counter-supplying" with a diplomatic effort toward a settlement, suggested above (as in the Middle East, the effort should serve as a restraint on the drive). Moreover, it is often our supplying that provokes Soviet countersupplying to restive or hostile neighbors of our clients (this is how the Soviet involvement with Egypt began, ca. 1955, and later with India). In many instances the connection to the great powers' contest is pretty distant, as in our arms transfers to Brazil or to Saudi Arabia.

Although the material rewards of arms sales are appreciable, the political advantages are elusive. The amount of "control" one gains by riding a tiger was demonstrated by the Soviet misadventures in Egypt, ours in Turkey, by Soviet difficulties with Syria, ours with Israel. Who becomes whose hostage? With thousands of Americans in Iran, do we gain control over the Shah's ambitions (in the strategic arena at least; we clearly have not insofar as the price of oil is concerned), or does he get the weapons to drag us into his designs, or do we recover the means to stop these only by delivering comparable arms to his potential rivals? Lastly, there is some highly sophisticated technology that only the U.S., or only the superpowers, are able to produce. We have an interest in slowing down its diffusion and are still capable of doing so.

Obviously, a case-by-case analysis is required. But a recognition of political diversity will lead to something better than a case-by-case capitulation only if the same guideline is applied to all: what is the best way to slow down the trend? Only if we apply a general policy of self-restraint shall we have a chance of convincing those arms suppliers who are our friends that we are not moved by commercial jealousy, and thus of having some effect on their policy. Only if our policy is not merely a reaction to Soviet arms exports may we have a chance of engaging Moscow in mutual restraints. In May 1977, the Carter administration announced a series of steps in the right direction; we shall see how (or if) they will be applied.

America's unilateral effort should be able to lean on the International Security Commitee's mission of publicizing and warning. To avoid giving offense to particular clients, we should impose—even before such a body appears—a ceiling on yearly transfers and on the number of American technicians accompanying them, a ban on specific weapons and technologies (dual capable systems, weapons of mass destruction), and a veto on any transfer by a client to a third party.[44] To be sure, frustrated clients would look elsewhere or redouble their own efforts. But our unilateral cuts would be coupled with the collective effort described, and self-help, or the resort to other suppliers, is not yet capable of duplicating the most advanced American weaponry. Here, as in the case of increasing economic competition from developing nations, the domestic losses resulting (in this case, for the defense industry) from a world order policy will have to be minimized by internal measures of adjustment—the conversion of the industries concerned.

Next comes the problem of action in case of a resort to or threat of force. Preventively, one might suggest sending an international peace-keeping force to the territory at the request of a potential victim of attack. This would require a resumption of the abandoned effort of the early 1960s to strengthen the peace-keeping role of the UN. Once force has been used, a world order strategy requires a close coordination between national policy and the action of the international milieu. The latter cannot do much in the case of violent conflicts between one great power and a smaller one. But most conflicts are likely to be between lesser powers (supported or not by major states), or within states. Depending on the case, two strategies are possible.

One is an international or regional finding of aggression. It would legitimize support to the victim, a cut-off of supplies to the aggressor and, later on—when and if world order becomes a priority for its beneficiaries—it could entail the sending of an international force-in-readiness to the side of the victim. The other course, in the absence of such a finding, would be the familiar one of insulation and localization, with calls for cease-fires, and the sending of international or regional observers and peace-keeping forces. The second could also be applied to large-scale civil wars, which always tempt outside meddling and are legitimate subjects of international concern, even if the means of stopping these wars until all passions are spent are, alas, limited.

These various moves would require a reinforcement of the secretariats of the UN and regional organizations, as well as of the UN Military Committee, and a stringent limitation of the conditions in which states could oppose the dispatching or demand the departure of peace-keeping forces (the 1975 Sinai Disengagement Agreement is a useful precedent). They all entail a revival of international organizations at a time when their meetings are often marked by intense demagoguery. But there is a need to distinguish general assemblies and more limited bodies or secretariats. The U.S., precisely to save the useful potential of the UN system, should, as was recently suggested,[45] combine "tough diplomacy" and "practical accommodation" and "boycott UN technical meetings that are being twisted for political purposes," but also press for a collective effort to establish a multinational, permanent peace-keeping force, instead of having to improvise in emergencies. And instead of intervening unilaterally in local or internal conflicts, as we did in Vietnam and Angola, we ought to try to get the broadest possible support from the members of the UN or regional agencies for the action we envisage, as we did in the early 1960s in the Congo disputes.

A final range of measures consists of action against users of force. It remains difficult to treat states as criminals. It may not be impossible, however, to move toward a world in which statesmen guilty of genocide or an internationally recognized aggression would be treated as outlaws. Meanwhile, the notion of piracy should be extended to terrorism, so as to remove the protection that national sovereignty provides terrorists who have taken refuge on foreign soil. Wisdom, here, comes only to the scalded: after the kidnapping of OPEC leaders in Vienna in 1975, Arab statesmen—with the exception of Khadafi—have cooled off considerably toward terrorists. Progress is likely to be slow, but here is a domain where the guideline of voluntarism could be usefully applied. More distant goals could be the establishment of an international police against terrorist activities, and a treaty extending the notion of piracy to the perpetration of specific forms of subversion, with the victim's right to call for an international investigation.

Nuclear Proliferation   There is little hope of extending international criminality to the use of nuclear weapons. Nuclear proliferation is the most disturbing world order issue. Peace has rested for thirty years not only on the maintenance of the central balance, and on the vast distance between the superpowers and the other possessors of nuclear weapons, but also on the slowness of proliferation to other states, those who acquired nuclear weapons—Britain, France, China—being so to speak directly connected to the central balance. The more the bomb spreads, the greater the uncertainty about the link (so far, a deterrent link) to the central balance.[46] Will a superpower be able and willing to allow one of its friends or clients to bear a nuclear attack by a third state? Will it not be tempted either to intervene or to try to deter a local nuclear war by guaranteeing the security of its friend? How will the other superpower then react? If a new nuclear state develops its force in a way that appears threatening to one of the superpowers, will not the latter be tempted to strengthen its force against a possible attack, or to give itself a first-strike capability against the threatening state even at the risk of escalating the arms race with its chief rival and of appearing to seek a first-strike or counterforce potential against it too?[47] The more the bomb spreads, even if the central balance remains stable, the greater also the chances of localized holocausts, for it will be difficult to reproduce the political and technological conditions of the superpowers' mutual deterrence and restraint. There will be cases where a first nuclear strike against a rival, aimed at disarming him if he has nuclear weapons also or at overcoming his advantage in conventional forces, may appear rational.

The study of the problem has gone through phases: considerable worry in the early 1960s (partly an effect of the French bomb), with premature doomsday scenarios; considerable complacency once it became clear that the spread would not, as President Kennedy had once rhetorically suggested, reach Belgium fast; and now, a rude awakening following the Indian explosion. There are good reasons to worry. One, the commercialization of nuclear power—largely under American salesmanship—has increased the number of countries that have a fuel cycle independence, which technically allows them to extract weapons-grade fuel from their civilian programs. This means "both an independence from foreign sources of fuel supply and reactor components and an independent capability to build their own reactors."[48] Even more countries will be there soon. And new technologies for the production of weapons-grade fuel are being developed (breeders, laser enrichment of uranium). Two, several of these countries have been actively selling nuclear technology, either reactors (from which plutonium can be obtained), or uranium enrichment plants and plants for the reprocessing of spent fuel (as in the recent deal between West Germany and Brazil, the first deal that promises to deliver a complete fuel cycle).[49]

Three, the system of international safeguards is imperfect. Thirty-nine states have not signed the Non-Proliferation Treaty, including Argentina and Brazil, India and Pakistan, Israel, South Africa, and North Korea. Thirteen others, including Indonesia and Turkey, have signed but not ratified it.[50] Only signatories of the Non-Proliferation Treaty (NPT) are obliged to accept safeguards on all their civilian facilities; but these safeguards, administered by the International Atomic Energy Agency (IAEA), consist in a deterrent inspection and control of the possibility of diversion, not in the physical protection of specific nuclear materials against diversion or theft. Moreover, inspection procedures are confidential. Even a successful detection is no guarantee of collective action. Nonsignatories are free to build unsafeguarded facilities; the treaties they have signed with suppliers usually apply safeguards only to the facilities and materials they buy; and some agreements (such as the one Canada made with India) do not forbid the use of nuclear material derived from such assistance, for "peaceful" explosions.

Fourth, given all this, to try to reverse the trend by threats is not sufficient. A threat emanating from the U.S. alone ("if you do not accept more effective safeguards, if you do not put your entire nuclear industry under them, if you do not agree to give up any fabrication of plutonium and to return weapons-grade fuel, we will cut off supplies") would be ineffective. Other nations might be only too happy to step into the breach, now that the U.S. has lost its earlier monopoly on enrichment technology. A threat emanating from a suppliers' cartel would be unlikely if peremptory and all-encompassing (i.e., extending to the sale of reactors); insufficiently effective otherwise. A determined state can build a reprocessing plant, or produce sizable amounts of plutonium from power reactors. Nor should one forget that many of the suppliers could themselves become makers of bombs! An embargo would not affect nations that already are "latent proliferators" (such as Israel and Taiwan), and it would probably incite "a counter great-power consortium by aspiring regional status-seekers such as Argentina."[51] It would divide the world into two categories: "tensions between advanced and developing states may occur in the IAEA where they have hitherto been muted."[52] The charge of discrimination would be fed both by the fact that several of the embargoing states persist in reprocessing and by the text of the NPT itself, which entitles nuclear states to facilitate the exchange of peaceful nuclear technology.

Lastly, proliferation is part of the revolt against the established hierarchy of states. This means that while it is, so to speak, encouraged by the superpowers' arms race, it would probably not disappear even if they were more effective in controlling and even in reducing their own nuclear arsenals. It also means that a mere American promise to supply sufficient amounts of enriched uranium for the peaceful energy purposes of other states would probably not deter them from wanting to have their own enrichment or reprocessing facilities: for it is precisely dependence on a single provider that they want to shake off—with the help of states eager to destroy America's past monopoly.[53] To sum up: as Thomas Schelling has put it, "in a terribly important and terribly dangerous sense, they [governments] will practically all have the bomb," i.e., the ability to have it.[54] But a policy of mere technological denial which confuses the capacity to produce bombs and the will to make them risks stimulating the latter.

In these bleak circumstances, one should begin by asking about goals. There are three broad objectives. One is general: the *process* may be inevitable, but its *pace* matters. A world suddenly stacked with nuclear weapons would, first, have no time to adjust to the changes in national outlooks, security conditions, alliances or guarantees, and to the possible conflicts that would result from quick proliferation. The chances that the superpowers might not be able to disentangle themselves would be greater. Moreover, world affairs would be again dominated by the obsession of survival: not only would peace be more troubled, but we would have reached a multiple and universal "state of war." The two other objectives are more specific. One consists in dissuading from nuclear weapons those states whose access to the status of nuclear power would have, through contagion, a profoundly disruptive effect, or would be destructive of world order because of the likelihood that the weapons would be used. Brazil and Iran are in the first group. Pakistan, South Korea, Taiwan, and the Republic of South Africa are in the second. Thus, proliferation is a matter of global process and individual will. The other goal is to deter those states that have nevertheless obtained the bomb (or, like Israel, the capacity to produce it within a short time) from using it.

Can anything be done to slow down proliferation? Ideally, two conditions would have to be met. The measures taken would have to be nondiscriminatory. Any distinction in the treatment of nonnuclear states, based, for instance, on one's suspicion of their intentions, would backfire and incite the victim to look for ways of defying the prohibitions, especially if it is a nation with some industrial capabilities. Also, measures would be most effective if they were adopted jointly by the suppliers. However, this almost guarantees that they will not be the strongest possible measures. The suppliers' conferences that have taken place so far have not agreed on a complete embargo on the sale of enrichment and reprocessing facilities.

The U.S. has observed more stringent controls on its exports than other suppliers (we have not sold such facilities). Late in 1976, President Ford announced even stricter ones. In April 1977, the Carter administration, following the main suggestions of a study group set up by the Ford Foundation, drastically revised America's internal and external nuclear policy. The domestic reprocessing and recycle of plutonium has been indefinitely deferred; the breeder is being redesigned. A plutonium economy is deemed unnecessary for the solution of the world's energy problems. In the future, Washington will require that its clients put all their nuclear materials and equipment under IAEA safeguards, and abstain from retransferring or reprocessing any special nuclear material produced through the use of American equipment. Supplies will be cut off to any nonnuclear state that detonates a nuclear explosive device, violates a safeguard, or terminates IAEA controls.[55] A special ambassador has been appointed to renegotiate our thirty-odd existing agreements to make them meet these requirements. In this realm, a unilateral U.S. policy serves primarily as a goad to others, who cannot use against us the argument that our real goal is keeping the market for ourselves; it is not a useless exercise, as the evolution of France's nuclear export policy in the second half of 1976 and of West Germany's policy in the spring of 1977 have shown. It can also slow down proliferation somewhat. But to go beyond and try to exploit our residual advantage as a major supplier of enriched uranium and the dependence of foreign customers on U.S. licenses or equipment, so as to "punish" those suppliers who export under less-tight restrictions and safeguards, and so as to cut off deliveries to clients who do not accept voluntarily conditions more restrictive than those agreed upon by the suppliers' conference, would probably do more harm than good. It might slow down the process some more—but at the cost of putting the whole issue on top of the world's agenda in the most dangerous, i.e., conflictual way. Indeed, other suppliers and potential recipients would be practically provoked into speeding up an emancipation that is already under way. Here, in order to *overcome* the logic of separateness, we must be very careful not to *provoke* it—which explains why it might be best to move from the suppliers' group to a larger one that would include potential nuclear powers.

The classical distinction is between denials, controls, and disincentives. But a better one is between measures dealing with the technological aspects of proliferation (i.e., the capabilities of states) and the political problems (the will of states). On the side of technology, obviously, collective policies would be best. Lincoln Bloomfield has suggested the internationalization of reprocessing, peaceful nuclear explosions, and the nuclear fuel;[56] Henry Kissinger proposed the establishment of multinational regional facilities for reprocessing and enrichment (an idea endorsed by Jimmy Carter as a candidate, but not since his inauguration). Several authors have advocated a suppliers' cartel to apportion the market for reactors, to provide enrichment and reprocessing services, and embargo the export of such technology.[57] Such a collective embargo is now sought by Washington at the suppliers' conferences. This idea might have been fine some years ago; there are now too many suppliers for easy agreement, and too many clients with facilities of their own. We did not get the Germans to cancel those parts of their deal with Brazil to which we objected. Regional centers seem to be uneconomical for reprocessing and would create formidable problems of political and practical control, both among the suppliers, and on the part of the clients, whose energy policy would thus be entrusted to others. Moreover, it could become a formula for the swift diffusion of technology and might aggravate the risk of theft. These problems would be especially acute in regions torn by violence. The reactors sold by the cartel would still produce plutonium. The regional centers would still provide recipients with plutonium-bearing fuel: they make some sense if one believes a plutonium economy inevitable, little if one thinks one can avoid it. A comprehensive test ban would have an effect on proliferation only if it were signed by all nuclear nations—an unlikely event.[58]

One is thus brought back to actions aimed at tightening and publicizing the safeguards, and at getting clients who have not signed the NPT either to sign it or to accept the same system of safeguards. So far, no country has become a nuclear power by violating them. One should also aim at putting peaceful explosions under international supervision and control, and at removing usable weapons-grade material from nonnuclear states. Two other measures would be even more important. The first one would be to try to get a suppliers' agreement on developing alternative fuel cycles (thorium?) that give states no access to weapons-grade material, and on preventing the export of current enrichment and reprocessing as well as of new technologies, such as fast-breeder reactors and laser isotope separation. The other would be the reduction of international dependence on nuclear energy.[59] We have tried through unilateral measures, but they are not enough. The ideal would be concerted measures aimed at removing government support for nuclear energy (which would increase its costs) or, when it is nationalized, at shifting resources to other sources of energy, especially in the oil-poor developing countries (in this respect, an international regime for oil would be of great help).[60]

But by now many nations, both in the developing world and among the advanced states, are convinced of their need for reprocessing, not merely to achieve independence from suppliers of enriched uranium, but for better waste disposal and for breeders. We see reprocessing as producing large amounts of plutonium which could be diverted into weapons production. They believe, on the contrary, that reprocessing eliminates plutonium if it is recycled immediately. They also believe that our economic calculations about the limited advantages of reprocessing and breeders, and the adequacy of light-water reactors, reflect America's enormous potential in alternate sources of energy, especially coal. They think that they cannot afford to be complacent and to trust our dubious figures.

Thus, we must guard against the technological delusion—the belief that purely technical measures will somehow shrink the size of the problem, or that the problem itself is mainly that of the tempting by-products of civilian nuclear energy, which an expansion of American supplies of enriched uranium would take care of. For here we get caught in a highly political trap. If we use our supplies not only as a carrot but as a stick against states that fail to meet our standards or that commit violations, or if we use them for political purposes, we shall increase the very insecurity that feeds the desire to produce one's own energy (occasional American delays in providing Western Europe with promised deliveries have had that effect). Even if we do not show the stick, the reliance on another state for essential services is precisely what no nation determined and able to acquire autonomy will accept. If it accepts America's economic forecasts, and its main concern is economic security and development, a nation may forgo acquiring or building enrichment or reprocessing facilities and satisfy itself with guaranteed supplies of enriched uranium from abroad. But if independence is its main concern or if it rejects these calculations, such a guarantee will not appear sufficient. Here, as in the matter of arms sales, we are in a kind of twilight zone, where the logic of separateness exploits the rules of interdependence. Interdependence means mutual manipulation, but the end goal, by contrast with the realm of economics, may be the creation of a national arms industry, or of a national military nuclear capability, that will be totally independent.

Since technological measures are not likely to be decisive, one must fall back on political measures. Most of the general collective ones that have been proposed seem of little real value as disincentives.[61] A no-first-use declaration runs into a variety of objections. It could be an incentive to proliferation, if an ally of the U.S. interpreted such a declaration as the removal of a considerable chunk of deterrence; it does not address itself to the problem of states that want to "go nuclear" against a conventional threat; and it is not likely to be trusted. Nuclear-free zones are possible only in areas where there are no states eager to become nuclear or to keep the possibility open. The idea of providing nuclear weapons to nonnuclear victims of nuclear attack (to deter them from seeking safety by becoming nuclear powers themselves) has something grimly humorous about it.[62] It would come too late for the victim; it would lack all credibility as a deterrent against aggression unless a strong bond of alliance (or quasi alliance) already existed between the victim and the protector (in which case it would be redundant); and it would be a perfect formula for escalation if it were carried out.

The conclusion is that political incentives to remaining nonnuclear, or disincentives from crossing the threshold, have to be tailored ad hoc. Here, we move from the general process that has to be slowed down, to the specific objectives outlined above. Consistency, once more, is indispensable. The *general* collective measures which aim above all at slowing down proliferation by making it more difficult, expensive, and risky, should not be so presented as to exacerbate a nation's will to become a nuclear power. The *specific* political measures must aim at affecting this will, and, if this fails, at preventing the crowding of the club from triggering even piecemeal annihilation.

To prevent further proliferation, two kinds of ad hoc policies are needed. The first would be rewards for not going nuclear (for instance, for signing the NPT, and for accepting stringent safeguards). They are neither easy to find, nor universally applicable (would the U.S. want to reward Praetoria?). They would consist, essentially, of encouraging the potential nuclear state to develop other forms of power, as long as these do not weaken international restraints. This implies that the offer of conventional arms as a substitute ought to be resisted: it could give the recipient a yen for the prize weapons; encourage its neighbors to get them first; and in any case either foster a regional hegemony or a regional arms race. Moreover, some of the new conventional technologies are easily adaptable to nuclear weapons. If conventional arms became a regular reward for nuclear abstinence, many states would want to come to the threshold of nuclear power. Rewards, therefore, can best (or only) be found in two realms. One is diplomacy: the recent American-Brazilian agreement on regular consultations might have been an attempt in that direction, although it came at the worst possible moment, given the Brazilian deal with Bonn. The other realm is economic interdependence. Here, case by case, there might be ways of favoring states that refrain from nuclear sin in matters such as trade, aid, loans, technology transfers, etc. But such a policy may clash with the imperative of granting no favors to certain kinds of regimes, indicated in the discussion on human rights. Given the ambivalent effect of rewards for status-seeking tyrants, that imperative should prevail.

This leaves one essentially with the second type of policies, which would be deterrent—I do not say sanctions—against going nuclear. As indicated above in the discussion of technology, individual sanctions are likely to be insufficient, unless most suppliers can be brought to agree. General agreement on a policy of sanctions (such as the end of arms supplies or economic assistance) against any state that, having signed the NPT, violates its provisions is, again, not a likely prospect. But specific agreements might be reached on applying such a policy to states whose accession to the nuclear club would be clearly destabilizing. Until now, the best deterrent has been a security guarantee by a protector. This is likely to remain the case, for instance in Taiwan or South Korea, and it means that the continuing willingness of nuclear powers to give credible (which normally means individual) guarantees to friends and clients, at the risk of being dragged into their quarrels, is directly connected to nonproliferation. "Decoupling" (or disengagement) and nonproliferation are not compatible objectives. And yet this raises difficult problems.

One is that of the credibility of a great power's guarantee, whenever its actual enforcement might lead to further escalation, and given the unwillingness of opinion in the U.S. to intervene abroad automatically. In a sense, the credibility of guarantees depends on the success of nonproliferation: the more the bomb spreads, the greater may be the reluctance of a major power to play all-purpose policeman. The only way of preserving such credibility, so as to slow down proliferation, while avoiding the external disasters and internal backlash in the guarantor's country that would result from the execution of the guarantee, is to pursue a vigorous policy of conflict resolution and arms reduction, along the lines described above. The national decisions to "go nuclear" or not will depend above all on the state of local rivalries and regional fears, as in the relation between India and Pakistan, or in the Middle East, or in Southern Africa.

Another problem is that of the means of pressure a security guarantee gives to the guarantor. It is by no means a simple one. Particularly exposed or industrially weak allies or clients can be blackmailed by a Big Brother who subordinates his guarantees to their nuclear chastity. (We did force Seoul to give up its nuclear deal with Paris.) But in other parts of the world, such an attempt might have exactly the opposite effect and play into the hands of those who question the validity of another power's guarantees in the nuclear age—the old Gaullist argument. Thus, like many other individual deterrents, the effectiveness of this one is strongly tied to its not having to be turned to actual use.

Once a nation has joined the nuclear club, the problem becomes one of learning to live with it in such a way that it is not tempted to use its bombs on a nonnuclear hostile neighbor, or that the latter does not rush into imitation. If the neighbor is already a nuclear power, the problem is to try to create stable mutual deterrence. Clearly, we are now in a realm where rewards would be absurd; (If, in order to establish stable mutual deterrence, the superpowers, separately or jointly, gave assistance to the weaker nuclear power in order to eliminate mutual first-strike incentives, this could easily provoke a contagion of nations eager to cross the threshold in order to receive such assistance.) Only controls and disincentives make sense. Which disincentives? Again, it is a matter of individual cases. In some that depend heavily on American military protection—South Korea, Spain, Iran de facto, Israel almost *de jure*—an American warning that either crossing the threshold or (if it has already been crossed) using nuclear weapons would jeopardize that protection might be effective. In other cases, such as that of Praetoria, American participation in a collective effort at putting some teeth into Security Council Resolution 255 of 1968, which deals in vague terms with a nuclear aggression against a nonnuclear state, might have some use. But guarantees to potential victims are no panacea: collective ones are politically dubious in most instances, individual ones are more credible but constitute a commitment that the guarantor would, in many cases, prefer to avoid. Does either the U.S. or the Soviet Union want to guarantee Pakistan against India, or Argentina against a nuclear Brazil? Do we want to guarantee Syria against Israel?

The most effective disincentive would be a set of carefully prearranged sanctions against the country that first resorts to nuclear weapons against an enemy, unless it is fighting a large-scale attack by a nuclear power. In many instances, cutting that country away from the web of interdependence can be a formidable punishment. The likelihood that one of the superpowers might come to the help of the victim, even if only after the outbreak of the war, and that the attacker might find itself facing a formidable coalition, without any outside military or economic assistance, would also inhibit the use of nuclear weapons.[63] Again, each case would have to be examined in its own terms. But, as long as the pace is manageable, proliferation could be kept on the safe side of disaster.

As for controls, they would be essential between pairs of nuclear countries. Measures against surprise attacks, limitations on deployments of first-strike systems or on systems aimed at protecting one's populace, and quantitative restrictions on delivery vehicles and warheads would aim at preventing the same costly escalation as that of the superpowers, and at trying to imitate the conditions that have kept their arms race stable. Such "regional SALT" agreements—which would remove or reduce the risk of a regional war sucking in outsiders—would be difficult to obtain, unless outsiders, and especially the superpowers, put pressure on the parties.[64]

This half-hearted conclusion is not altogether surprising. The logic of traditional world politics is that of proliferation; it is not in the traditional tools—threats, rewards, deterrents—that a perfect solution lies. And yet a mutation is impossible. And so, the best political chances of slowing down the process and of diverting the candidates lie, on the one hand, in coping with the security reasons states might have for "going nuclear." This means either preserving existing alliances, or making major efforts at resolving substantive disputes. On the other hand, it means meeting a second, and perhaps the main, reason for nuclear fascination—status—by seeing to it that the effective hierarchy of prestige in world affairs does not coincide with that of nuclear weapons. To be sure, we are dealing with a vicious circle. As long as these weapons are not used and violence is restrained, other hierarchies dominate the stage, but should proliferation occur, the restraints might collapse. However, there is still some time. It must be used in such a way that economic power, the goal of many states, becomes dissociated from nuclear power status; i.e., that the example of Bonn and Tokyo, not that of Paris and Delhi, prevail; and that the superpowers begin rolling back the dark shadow of nuclear might on the strategic chessboard (without giving up the benefit of nuclear bipolarity, i.e., the restraints imposed by nuclear interconnection) through a beginning of actual force reductions.[65]

DOMESTIC POLITICS AND WORLD ORDER

Antiproliferation policy is thus inseparable from the rest of world order policy, because the reasons for the spread of nuclear weapons are deeply imbedded in traditional world politics—precisely what a world order policy aims at changing. And it will have no chance of succeeding if it is not ultimately coordinated with, and does not change domestic policy as well. Throughout these chapters, I have mentioned the internal costs of the courses advocated: a loss of jobs resulting from the drop in the sale of arms or reactors abroad or in the production of new weapons systems; a higher price of gasoline or cars if, at last, a new energy policy aimed at diminishing America's vulnerability to OPEC tactics should succeed in getting Americans to consume less; serious foreign competition for old industries in which much capital has been invested and many jobs are held, competition that will sometimes take the form of goods produced abroad by American multinationals; new restrictions clamped on these by foreign governments or by international regulations that try to impose a code of good conduct on them; and so forth. There is another cost: because the only force that can try to make domestic and foreign policy compatible is the government, a nation whose conviction that the management of its economy ought to be as free as possible from state interference is still wide and powerful will actually have to let the state play an even greater role than before in the management of internal economic and social adjustments to the new world.

Is this at all conceivable? Aren't we butting against one more contradiction—between the interconnectedness of the various parts of the program, and the obvious fact that nothing would backfire more than an attempt at moving too fast on too broad a front? Fortunately—or unfortunately—there is no chance that progress abroad will be swift and universal. Thus there will be time, at home, to try to strike the right balance between the need to preserve a safe margin of autonomy—for instance, in monetary and energy policies—because total interdependence means unbearable vulnerability and insecurity, and the need to start giving the interest of the whole (as defined collectively, not by us alone) precedence over the interest of one part. If one believes that only radical social change in America can make this country accept the latter need, we might as well give up. What will have to take place is a gradual adaptation of the social, economic, and political system of the United States to the imperatives of world order. There have been other adaptations to necessity in this century. Still, this will be the most difficult. The penalty for immobility or rigidity is not as evident as a protracted depression, or a victory of totalitarianism. And the effects of growing dependence on goods, trends, events, and policies in the outside world have not yet fully changed an outlook shaped by a long period of insulation, and by a recent period in which we made the moves on which others depended.

Thus, the demands of world order entail a painful process of discovery for many Americans. They will have to realize that others do not share all our values and practices and that the world is not a field in which we can go and apply our preferred policies and techniques with impunity. It is a field where our credit policies can spread, and then bring back magnified inflation or recession; where our investments meet resistance; our sales of weapons or technology breed chaos. At every moment, some will point out that we are being asked to give up tangible rewards and the tested ways of self-reliance, for the uncertain and distant gain of a new order in which we shall not be our own masters. And it will be necessary to prove that the only alternative to trying for that gain is not the cozy past, but an excessive risk of violence and chaos. Not an easy exercise in a nation that is still less affected by external events than many others, and sufficiently confident in its capacity of affecting others to overlook the fact that the way we affect them sometimes boomerangs.

Thus I must end as I began: with the remark that a world order policy is a pattern of education. By trial and error, American leaders must show the people whom they represent why traditional policies must change and obtain enough support to turn these changes into new laws, institutions, and habits. And American intellectuals must keep trying, not to behave as if the world of power were the kingdom of heaven, but to enlighten the public and the leaders about the problems of the present world, about the demands of world order, about the pitfalls of any attempt to meet them, and about the greater peril of politics-as-usual.

NOTES

CHAPTER SIX

1. Zbigniew Brzezinski, "U.S. Foreign Policy: The Search for Focus," *Foreign Affairs,* vol. 51, no. 4, July 1973, pp. 717–726.
2. "Trilateralism: Partnership for What?" *Foreign Affairs,* vol. 55, no. 1, October 1976.
3. Ibid., pp. 12, 13.
4. Cf. A. Doak Barnett, "Military-Security Relations between China and the United States," *Foreign Affairs,* vol. 55, no. 3, April 1977.
5. Cf. Miriam Camps, "First World Relationships: The Role of the OECD," *The Atlantic Papers,* 2/1975, p. 41.
6. Carlos Diaz-Alejandro, "Delinking North and South: Unshackled or Unhinged?" in Albert Fishlow et al., *Rich and Poor Nations in the World Economy,* McGraw-Hill, New York, 1978.
7. Cf. Clarence D. Long, "Nuclear Proliferation: Can Congress Act in Time?" *International Security,* vol. 1, no. 4, Spring 1977.

8. Cf. Richard Portes, "East Europe's Debt to the West," *Foreign Affairs,* vol. 55, no. 4, Summer 1977.

9. On this point, see The Atlantic Council of the United States, East-West Trade, Westview Press, Boulder, Colo., 1977. See also Daniel Yergin, "Politics and Soviet-American 'Trade'," *Foreign Affairs,* vol. 55, no. 3 Spring 1977.

10. Cf. Richard Rosecrance (ed.), *America as an Ordinary Country,* Cornell University Press, Ithaca, N.Y., 1976, p. 228.

11. Gregory Schmid, "Interdependence Has Its Limits," *Foreign Policy,* vol. 21, Winter 1975–76.

12. See Robert Gilpin, *U.S. Power and the Multinational Corporation,* Basic Books, New York, 1975, chap. 9.

13. For contrasting views of the developing countries' debts, see David Beim, "Rescuing the LDCs," and Harold van B. Cleveland and Wilt Bruce Brittain, "Are the LDCs in over Their Heads?" *Foreign Affairs,* vol. 55, no. 4, July 1977.

14. The United States and the Third World: A Basis for Accommodation," *Foreign Affairs,* vol. 54, no. 1, October 1975, p. 94.

15. Cf. Raymond Vernon, "Storm over the Multinationals: Problems and Prospects," *Foreign Affairs,* vol. 55, no. 2, January 1977.

16. On Lomé, see Isebill V. Gruhn, "The Lomé Convention: Inching Toward Interdependence," *International Organization,* vol. 30, no. 2, Spring 1976.

17. See U.N. Department of Economic and Social Affairs, *The Future of the World Economy,* New York, 1976, especially at p. 47ff.

18. See Roger D. Hansen, "Major U.S. Options on North-South Relations," in John W. Sewell et al., *The United States and World Development: Agenda 1977,* Praeger, New York, 1977.

19. See John Temple Swing, "Who Will Own the Oceans," *Foreign Affairs,* vol. 54, no. 3, April 1976; Jack N. Barkenbus, "How to Make Peace on the Seabeds," *Foreign Policy,* vol. 25, Winter 1976–77; Hardy, Hollick, Holst, Johnston, and Oda, "A New Regime for the Oceans," *The Triangle Papers,* vol. 9, 1976; and Jonathan I. Charney, "Law of the Sea: Breaking the Deadlock," *Foreign Affairs,* vol. 55, no. 3, April 1977.

20. Cf. Richard N. Cooper, "A New International Economic Order for Mutual Gain," *Foreign Policy,* no. 26, Spring 1977.

21. Nathaniel J. Leff, "The New Economic Order—Bad Economics, Worse Politics," *Foreign Policy,* vol. 24, Fall 1976, p. 216.

22. Tom de Vries, "Jamaica, or the Non-Reform of the International Monetary System," *Foreign Affairs,* vol. 54, no. 3, April 1976, p. 602. See also Richard N. Cooper, "Five Years since Smithsonian," *The Economist,* Dec. 18, 1976, p. 27ff; and Fred Hirsch, Michael Doyle, and Edward L. Morse, *Alternatives to Monetary Disorder,* McGraw-Hill, New York, 1977.

23. *The Dilemmas of the Dollar,* New York University Press, New York, 1975, pp. 500, 506.

24. De Vries, op. cit., p. 597.

25. *The Dilemmas of the Dollar,* op. cit., p. 536.

26. "The strategic rationale for the administration's new arms sales to Kenya and Zaire is laden with flypaper." Leslie H. Gelb, "Arms Sales," *Foreign Policy,* vol. 25, Winter 1976–77, p. 16.

27. On the cruise missile's ability to do so, see Richard Burt, "The Cruise Missile and Arms Control," *Survival,* January-February 1976; and Alexander R. Vershbow, "The Cruise Missile: End of Arms Control?" *Foreign Affairs,* vol. 55, no. 1, October 1976.

28.   See Paul Doty, Albert Carnesale, and Michael Nacht, "The Race to Control Nuclear Arms," *Foreign Affairs,* vol. 55, no. 1, October 1976, pp. 127–128.

29.   See ibid., p. 128; and Richard L. Garwin, "Effective Military Technology for the 1980s," *International Security,* vol. 1, no. 2, Fall 1976, p. 62ff. See also Michael Mandelbaum, "International Stability and Nuclear Order," in David C. Gompert et al., *Nuclear Weapons and World Politics,* McGraw-Hill, New York, 1977.

30.   Hence certain French suspicions about the PGM. See Marc de Brichambaut, "Les 'Precision guided munitions' et la Defense de l'Europe," *Contrepoint,* no. 20, February 1976. He sees in the PGM "a useful alibi for American disengagement." For a contrary view, see Richard Burt, "Proliferation and the Spread of New Conventional Weapons Technology," *International Security,* vol. 1, no. 3, Winter 1977.

31.   See Richard Burt, "SALT and the Crisis of Superpower Nuclear Duopoly," *Millenium: Journal of International Studies,* vol. 6, no. 1, 1977.

32.   See Tom J. Farer, *Warclouds on the Horn of Africa: A Crisis for Détente,* Carnegie Endowment for International Peace, New York, 1976.

33.   Who would have predicted that the arch-Stalinist Jean Kanapa would write an article for *Foreign Affairs?* See his "A 'New Policy' of the French Communists," *Foreign Affairs,* vol. 55, no. 2, January 1977.

34.   On similar lines, see "The United States and Latin America: Next Steps," a second report by the Commission on U.S.–Latin American relations, Dec. 20, 1976.

35.   Cf. "Uneven Allies," in David S. Landes (ed.), *Western Europe: The Trials of Partnership,* vol. 8 of Critical Choices for Americans, Lexington Books, Lexington, Mass., 1977.

36.   These remarks owe a great deal to the Background Papers prepared for the Survey Discussion Group on Human Rights and U.S. Foreign Policy, Council on Foreign Relations, under the leadership of Tom J. Farer. See also Donald M. Fraser, "Freedom and Foreign Policy," *Foreign Policy,* no. 26, Spring 1977.

37.   I have in mind regimes such as Pinochet's in Chile, or the current military government in Brazil (given our active involvement in the coup that overthrew Goulart in 1964), or the Shah's regime in Iran. There are, alas, many repressive regimes that are not in any way our responsibility—such as Mrs. Gandhi's was in India, or Idi Amin's Uganda. And there is—as usual—a gray zone, as was the case of the Dergue's rule in Ethiopia, where we have no alliance or responsibility for its establishment, but where we provided military aid. In these gray areas, whenever our relationship with the country could easily develop into one of patronage, because of the connection with the great powers' contest (cf. the Ethiopia-Somalia dispute), the same guidelines should apply as in the cases of actual patronage. As for the cases of South Africa and Rhodesia, which have become international disputes and potential sources of violence, see below. For an overview, see Marshall D. Shulman, "On Learning to Live with Authoritarian Regimes," *Foreign Affairs,* vol. 55, no. 2, January 1977.

38.   "The Foreign World and Ourselves," *Foreign Policy,* vol. 21, Winter 1975–76, p. 111. See also Morton H. Halperin et al., *The Lawless State,* Penguin Books, New York, 1976.

39.   See Karl E. Birnbaum, "Human Rights and East-West Relations," *Foreign Affairs,* vol. 55, no. 4, July 1977.

40.   See his last book, *The Reform of Power,* Viking, New York, 1972.

41.   Cf. Richard Burt, "New Weapons Technologies," *Adelphi Papers,* no. 126, London, 1976, p. 29, and his article mentioned in footnote.

42.   Cf. Emma Rothschild, "The Arms Boom and How to Stop It," *New York Review of*

Books, Jan. 20, 1977, p. 24ff. See also Gardiner Tucker, *Towards Rationalizing Allied Weapons Production*, The Atlantic Papers, 1/1976.

43. Cf. David Gompert and Alexander Vershbow, "Controlling Arms Trade: Why, at What Cost, and How?" in Anne Hessing Cahn et al., *Controlling Future Arms Trade*, McGraw-Hill, New York, 1977.

44. See the thoughtful recommendations of the UNA-USA National Policy Panel on Conventional Arms Control, "Controlling the Conventional Arms Race," November 1976.

45. Charles W. Maynes, "A UN Policy for the Next Administration," *Foreign Affairs*, vol. 54, no. 4, July 1976. See also the Atlantic Council of the United States, *The Future of the UN*, Westview Press, Boulder, Colo., 1977.

46. Cf. my essay "Nuclear Proliferation and World Politics," in Alastair Buchan (ed.), *A World of Nuclear Powers*, Prentice-Hall, Englewood Cliffs, N.J., 1966.

47. See David C. Gompert, "On the Choice of a Nuclear Regime," in Gompert et al., *Nuclear Weapons and World Politics*, McGraw-Hill, New York, 1977; and Michael Mandelbaum, op. cit. in footnote 29.

48. Harold A. Feiveson and Theodore B. Taylor, "Alternative Strategies for International Control of Nuclear Power," in Ted Greenwood, Harold A. Feiveson and Theodore B. Taylor, *Nuclear Proliferation*, McGraw-Hill, New York, 1977.

49. See Norman Gall, "Atoms for Brazil, Danger for All," *Foreign Policy*, no. 23, Summer 1976; and William W. Lawrence, "Nuclear Futures for Sale: to Brazil from West Germany, 1975," *International Security*, vol. 1, no. 2, Fall 1976.

50. Nuclear Energy Policy Study Group, *Nuclear Power: Issues and Choices*, Ballinger, Cambridge, Mass., 1977, p. 274.

51. Richard K. Betts, "Paranoids, Pygmies, Pariahs, and Nonproliferation," *Foreign Policy*, no. 26, Spring 1977, p. 173.

52. Nuclear Energy Policy Study Group, op. cit., p. 295.

53. See Hedley Bull, "Arms Control and World Order," *International Security*, vol. 1, no. 1, Summer 1976.

54. "Who Will Have the Bomb," *International Security*, vol. 1, no. 1, Summer 1976.

55. See the complete text in *Department of State Bulletin*, vol. 76, nos. 1975 and 1977, May 2 and 16, 1977.

56. "Nuclear Spread and World Order," *Foreign Affairs*, vol. 53, no. 4, July 1975.

57. For the suggestion of a cartel, see Abraham A. Ribicoff, "A Market-Sharing Approach to the World Nuclear Sales Problem," *Foreign Affairs*, vol. 54, no. 4, July 1976; and Michael Mandelbaum, "A Nuclear Exporters' Cartel," *Bulletin of Atomic Scientists*, January 1977. For a critique, see Betts, op. cit.

58. See Donald Brennan, "A Comprehensive Test Ban: Everbody or Nobody," *International Security*, vol. 1, no. 1, Summer 1976.

59. Cf. Albert Wohlstetter, "Spreading the Bomb Without Quite Breaking the Rules," *Foreign Policy*, vol. 25, Winter 1976–77; and Barry Casper, "Laser Enrichment: A New Path to Proliferation," *Bulletin of Atomic Scientists*, January 1977.

60. Cf. Hearings of the Subcommittee on International Security and Scientific Affairs of the Committee on International Relations, House of Representatives, 94th Congress, 1st Session. "Nuclear Proliferation: Future U.S. Foreign Policy Implications," October-November, 1975, especially Stephen J. Baker's paper, cf., p. 269ff. See also Edward F. Wonder, *Nuclear Fuel and American Foreign Policy*, (Atlantic Council), Westview Press, Boulder, Colo., 1977.

61. The best review of political incentives and disincentives is by Ted Greenwood, "Discouraging Proliferation in the Next Decade and Beyond," in Greenwood, Feiveson, and Taylor, op. cit. See also Ted Greenwood, George W. Rathjens, and Jack Ruina, "Nuclear Power and Weapons Proliferation," *Adelphi Papers,* no. 130, London, Winter 1976.

62. See Alton Frye, "How to Ban the Bomb: Sell It," *The New York Times Magazine,* Jan. 11, 1976.

63. A suggestion made by Andrew Pierre in "Nuclear Proliferation, A Strategy for Control," *Foreign Policy Association Headline Series,* no. 232, October 1976, p. 58.

64. See Jacques Huntzinger, "Regional Recipient Restraints," in Anne Hessing Cahn et al., *Controlling Future Arms Trade,* McGraw-Hill, New York, 1977.

65. I have not dealt with the oft-discussed issue of nuclear terrorism. It is serious, but I agree with Schelling (op. cit., p. 84) that "the organizations most likely to engage in nuclear terrorism will be national governments." For a sober description, see David M. Rosenbaum, "Nuclear Terror," *International Security,* vol. 1, no. 3, Winter 1977.

Conclusion

The sketch of world order suggested in this book will strike some readers as too conservative and others as too radical. It entails national and international practices, rules, and regimes far different from what exists today, yet it accepts the resilience of the states and is based on the conviction that their cooperation must be enlisted. It sees in the interplay of state interests and state-supported ideologies the fabric of world politics. Yet it tries to strengthen and expand the restraints imposed, so far, by nuclear weapons and economic interdependence. It acknowledges the strength of the reactions against or strains on those fragile bonds: the spread of weapons or of nationalist economics. It recognizes that the restraints will have a chance of surviving and growing only if there is, in the system, room for disconnection—for the protection of domestic economies from excessive vulnerability and manipulation, and for the protection of the central strategic balance and the major powers against the perils of universal involvement. But it entails a large amount of collective planning, a growth of joint institutions, a careful distinction between the reduction of vulnerability and the prevalence of mercantilism, and a need for constant vigilance against the escalation of fragmented violence and its effects on the central balance. It does not offer world government, but it proposes steps toward far more ambitious central and regional common policies.

This sketch is not the only conceivable one. Leaving aside utopia, there is one obvious alternative to what might be called creeping globalism—a splintered world, disengaged from the risks of excessive interdependence and nuclear holocaust. The web of economic ties and the global network of nuclear connections breed too much insecurity and exceed the capacity of national structures. Why should order not be sought in a drastic reduction of interdependence, even if it too has costs, and in a strict limitation of foreign entanglements, even by superpowers? Thus, safety would be sought in fragments and compartments, and the tension between domestic imperatives and external constraints would be resolved in favor of the former, whatever the loss of external opportunities. My objection is that this is neither desirable nor likely. It is not desirable because there are too many problems that cannot be resolved except through common action—especially in the realm of economic affairs. It is not likely because, in this realm, the costs and losses would be intolerable to many of the players, both among the developed and among the richer developing countries. In the strategic-diplomatic realm, the capacity and will of the great powers to disconnect is smaller than the determination and ability of many other actors to enlist the support of one or several of the great powers; nor would the fragments remain peaceful by themselves. I do not deny that we may end with a messy mix between this scheme and mine; but I was suggesting what I deemed both desirable and possible, not what I though probable.

Nor is the policy recommended in this book the only conceivable one. There are at least two alternatives—of a much more traditional variety. One would give priority to the competition with our main adversary and assert American interests around the world in terms of the great power contest. The criterion of policy would be the advantage to be derived by Washington or by Moscow if a given move were to be made, a given concession or retreat accepted, a given initiative sprung. Restraints aimed at preventing the contest from blowing up the world would still be sought. But the emphasis would be on the victory of the American national interest, defined in "us versus them" fashion. Such a policy would have the virtue of apparent simplicity: the security dilemma, enlarged to include economic threats, seems to provide an ordering principle, to impose a clarifying grid on the world. As in the past, resistance to the Soviet Union, or to Soviet-supported Communism, would merge with the aggressive protection of American economic interests, political clientelism, and military control. But we would soon discover, not only that the costs and risks exceed the benefits, but also that the supposed criterion provides no guidance, that the grid does not fit.

Another traditional approach—the more likely one, if one had to move back from normative exhortation to empirical prediction—is muddling through: juggling priorities case by case, so that, for instance, human rights would be a top concern in one place, alliance considerations would prevail in another; economic concessions to Third World countries would be made over one issue, but denied over others; a regional hegemony would be encouraged here but blocked there; an arms race pursued in one area but controlled in another, depending on the interplay of external opportunities or obstacles, and of domestic pressures, bureaucratic games and presidential preferences. The very complexity of the present world, which vitiates a policy of pure contest, would serve to justify a policy of piecemeal pragmatism, in which world order worries and competitive necessities would bumpily coexist. Old habits of incrementalism and shortsighted caution would be celebrated as the inspired synthesis between the concern for a livable world and the need to hold one's own in the unending contest. The very pluralism of America's machinery of decision, the porousness of its political system, reinforce the traditional American style in foreign affairs.

But the question is this: can we be as blithely confident of "muddling through" today, as in an earlier period when the rockiness of ad hoc plunges did not disturb the relative stability ensured by the bipolar nuclear stalemate and America's domination of the world economy? The fact is, our postwar statesmen always felt the need for a concept or design to transcend mere pragmatism—and that a policy of expediency would not be adequate to the challenges and perils I have tried to describe in the middle part of this volume. Of the three races that were mentioned earlier, none has, so far, been won by the forces of world order. Domestic priorities, international fragmentation, and generalized insecurity are still battling the external imperatives of "moderation plus," the urgent need to tame technology, the universal aspiration to security. So far, the contest between conflict and restraints has been precariously won by the latter. Yet the danger of unraveling is constant.

Precariousness also characterizes the position of the United States. It has made enormous contributions to the postwar order, and its leaders and national celebrators like to list them. It has also made vast contributions to conflict and disruption, first by ushering in the nuclear era of mankind, later by a series of interventions, overt or covert, that have spread violence and resentment, and also by enthusiastically launching processes of economic growth that could not fail to tear the gossamer net of liberal economic arrangements that we had woven ourselves. Today, Americans find themselves in a double bind. Abroad, America's very power gives us enormous influence, and in no important arena can anything be settled without its participation and commitment. Yet American hegemony is over. Where there used to be the U.S., a far weaker and narrower challenger, and countries that were stakes for their contest, we now find the U.S., a challenger grown militarily bigger, and a bewildering variety of actors that have taken their fate into their own hands, and, silently or rudely, begun to emancipate themselves from our grip—even if they still hold on to us in this or that respect. They use us often as stilts, and we often cling to the illusion that the stilts control the marcher above. To our frustration, we find ourselves challenged directly, not only by communist adversaries, but often by states whose military power and economic means owe a great deal to our contributions. Third World countries have discovered, thanks to OPEC, how to use those of their resources that are indispensable to the industrial world to upset the economic order the latter had established under our leadership. They have hitched their economic grievances to the locomotive of energy, and the Arabs have used their new financial might to extract ideological support against Israel.

Whereas a careful fragmentation of conflicts, a separation of issues, seemed to be one of the requirements for moderation, we appear to have moved back, at least in North-South relations, to the politics of universal linkage that had been the essence of the cold war. And we find ourselves a bit alone in resisting this challenge and in opposing a linkage we ourselves had tried to force on our allies just a few years ago. Today, we cannot lean on partners of equal weight. The other major powers are our rivals. Our allies, for different reasons for which we must share responsibility, have neither the means nor the will to play a world role.

At home, most of our leaders and experts and what is left of our foreign policy elite agree on the main outlines of our action in the world. But the shocks of recent years have ruptured the postwar harmony between the political system and American diplomacy. Such harmony is not preestablished. We owed it to the cold war. We now realize again that success abroad can be undermined by congressional restiveness and economic, ethnic, or ideological groups that have a hold on opinion and on Congress. The strength of solidarity with Israel, the resistance to a costly but necessary energy policy, the pressures of investors in Southern African development, protectionist pulls, pushes from the military and the industrialists interested in arms or in nuclear sales, the cacophony of those who want us to strive for human rights everywhere, those who want to use them as a weapon against our enemies, and those who remain skeptical altogether—what would be wise abroad collides with what appears inevitable within.

Moreover, success abroad requires that opinion and Congress make their peace with some powerful trends in the world: the rise of the left here, anti-imperialist nationalisms there, the drive to replace the law of the market (or of the strongest) with interstate deals in the world economy, the determination of the weak to have their say in the conduct of world bodies—trends that assault deep beliefs and mighty interests in the U.S. Congress and opinion do not willingly accept the idea that America alone can neither "come home" nor draw the lines between which others shall be allowed to cross the streets.

And so we face two sets of troubles. There are those of a nation that still has unique assets, yet confronts a gap between its own bundle of habits, institutions, and beliefs, and a heterogeneous, centrifugal world, whose staggering evolution it neither approves nor fully grasps. A price will have to be paid for having identified stability with status quo, leadership with domination, effectiveness with the "imperial presidency" for so long. And there are all the troubles of a world of unprecedented complexity. As one of the two military superpowers, as the greatest economic power, we have enormous burdens we cannot shed. It is in our interest to see to it that the balances of might and influence and the bonds of solidarity that world order requires be preserved and strengthened. And yet these burdens and this interest far exceed our ability to achieve what is necessary and desirable. Our load is bigger than our reach. We are condemned both to carry the weight and to remain uncertain that we can ensure world order jointly with others whose views often differ immensely from our own.

We are, as the globalists tell us, all in the same boat. But it is not clear that all of us know it; there are many different classes and compartments; we do not agree on where it ought to go and who should steer it; and the maneuvers of many of its passengers seem almost calculated to make it sink. We have to learn that although we are the biggest aboard, with belongings in every cabin, we alone cannot set the course. We have to recognize that joint steering may not succeed in saving the ship, but that there is no alternative; that we have to try for it, even while fighting some of the other passengers whose motives, manners, and destinations we find repugnant; that our force cannot bring others to heel, nor can we heal what ails them with our easy faith in our capacity to rally others around our views; and that we have to argue, resist, maneuver, coax, threaten, and bargain, while keeping our eye on the sea. If we spend all our time fighting, we may soon find some cabins under water, and perhaps the engine room as well. If we know in what direction we want to go, if we have in mind a course that would bring us to port battered perhaps, but together, and if we aim for a port that would be inhospitable only to a handful of irreconcilables, then we shall have at least a chance, if we are skillful, to bring us there—haggling, certainly, but together. If we are uncertain, or if we indulge in familiar hubris, or if we just give up, the best we can hope for is zigzagging through the storms, avoiding shoals or icebergs at the last second, and being tossed around in permanent seasickness. That may well be our fate, anyhow. But it cannot be our goal.

Index
of Persons

Index
of Subjects

ABOUT THE AUTHOR

Stanley Hoffmann, professor of government at Harvard and chairman of Harvard's Center for European Studies, is also a faculty member of Harvard's Center for International Affairs. He is the author of many books, including *Contemporary Theory and International Relations* (1960), *The State of War* (1965), *Gulliver's Troubles: The Setting of American Foreign Policy* (1968), and *Decline or Renewal? France Since the 1930's* (1974). He has also edited or co-edited several books on modern France, and on international law and politics. Prof. Hoffmann holds a doctorate in law from the Université de Paris, where he did research at the Fondation Nationale des Sciences Politiques.